Rural Sociology

Rajendra Kumar Sharma

ATLANTIC

PUBLISHERS & DISTRIBUTORS (P) LTD

ATLANTIC
PUBLISHERS & DISTRIBUTORS (P) LTD
7/22, Ansari Road, Darya Ganj, New Delhi
Tel.: +91-11-4077 5252, 2327 3880
E-mail: orders@atlanticbooks.com
Web: www.atlanticbooks.com

Published by Atlantic Publishers & Distributors (P) Ltd., 2024
Reprint 2011, 2022, 2024

Printed & bound in India by Atlantic Print Services

PREFACE

This book has been written to serve as a textbook for students of M.A. Sociology in Indian Universities in the paper entitled Rural Sociology.

While the matter for the book has been gathered from standard books, Journals and Newspapers, data have been selected from Government Publication 'India' and other such sources. The matter has been presented in an analytical style using central, side and running headings to make the subject easy to understand and remember. The language used is easy and free from technical jargon. In matters of discussion, integral and holistic approach has been adopted to give a balanced view. Selected questions drawn from university papers have been given at the end of each chapter to enable the students to prepare for examination. Thus, an attempt has been made to make this work an ideal textbook on the subject.

Though, India is predominantly still a country of villages, not much progress has been made in the study of Indian villages, their problems and means of amelioration. It is sad that Rural Sociology is not being taught as a compulsory paper in M.A. Sociology in so many universities in India. This is particularly due to aping of the syllabi prescribed at Western Universities. It is now time that Indian sociologists look to indigenous conditions to make the subject useful for Indian society. If the present work could serve to create interest in rural sociology among students and teachers of Sociology the authors efforts will be amply rewarded.

Rajendra K. Sharma

CONTENTS

	Preface	*iii*
1.	Historical Review	1
2.	Introduction to Rural Sociology	10
3.	Relationship with Other Social Sciences	17
4.	Methods of Study	24
5.	The Village Community	35
6.	Rural-urban Contrast	47
7.	Village Life in India and the West	61
8.	Selected Types of Villages	68
9.	Patterns of Change in Rural Society	92
10.	Great Traditions in Rural Culture	106
11.	Rural Festivals and Recreation	116
12.	The Rural Religion	127
13.	The Jajmani System	138
14.	The Rural Caste System	144
15.	Rural Untouchability	159
16.	Casteism	169
17.	Rural Family	175
18.	Rural Marriage	185
19.	Rural Polity	193
20.	Rural Hookah Group, Factions and Leadership	201
21.	Rural Education	211
22.	The Village Panchayat	226
23.	Rural Economy	237

24. Rural Housing 253
25. Rural Welfare and Sarvodaya 257
26. Community Development 268
27. Rural Co-operation 276
28. Rural Reconstruction and Development 284
Bibliography 296

1

HISTORICAL REVIEW

Rural sociology was born due to the need of the study of various conditions and aspects of rural life and its problems before it, several other sciences used to study different aspects of rural problems separately, which did not provide satisfactory solution of the rural problems. Therefore, for a serious study of rural society, a separate social science was born with the name of Rural Sociology. In the words of Charles R. Hoffer, "Like all sciences, Rural Sociology developed in response to a need. It is an elementary fact in the realm of scientific thought that a new science comes into existence whenever phenomena confronting the human mind are not, or cannot be understood satisfactorily by the existing disciplines or sciences."[1]

It may be questioned here that whereas not much attention was given to rural problems for thousands of years why at all it became so much important in 18th century? The reply to this question is that ancient society was not so much dynamic and changing. The elements of dynamism and change have increased the capacity to understand the complex problems of life. It has also led to the realisation of the need to eliminate the impediment in social life. In eighteenth century and even earlier some scientific inventions and discoveries almost revolutionised human thinking and life. The fast process of urbanisation and industrialisation created problems of slums and overcrowding which diverted attention towards the village. The rural people, on the other hand, in contrast to the city life, more and more realised their difficulties and paucities. Gradually, the social scientists discussed the problems of poverty and unemployment, education, health and social disorganisation together with means of welfare and reconstruction. In their book *A Systematic Source Book in Rural Sociology,* Sorokin, Zimmerman and Galpin have described in detail the social change since ancient time to the present day and the problems of rural life. In the history of rural sociology, this book provided the preface to a systematic study of rural life. In due course, a lot of literature was published on the different aspects of rural life.

1. Hoffer, Charles R. : The Development of Rural Sociology, in '*Rural Sociology*' (A Quarterly Journal), Vol. 26, No 1, March 1961.

RURAL SOCIOLOGY AS A SYSTEMATIC SCIENCE

As a systematic science rural sociology is of recent origin. It was born in U.S.A. The American rural society was in a degenerated condition since 1890 to 1920. Its problems were awful. The cultivators had no rights over the land which belonged to the landlords. The life of the cultivators was desolate and disorganised. Therefore many rural people migrated towards the cities. In the words of Sims, "The whole period was one of rural social decay."[2] As the rural youth migrated to the cities, the production of food grains decreased. Therefore, the government had to attend to rural problems and gradually more and more reports were published on different aspects of rural life. Rural sociology was organised for a systematic study of the problems and conditions of rural life in U.S.A. The early works, therefore, include a detailed analysis of different rural problems. These problems were discussed from a humanist viewpoint. The study and remedy of rural problems found a respectable place in national planning. Just as general sociology was born due to the social problems of general life, similarly rural sociology was born due to the problems of rural life. The following stages may be observed in the development of rural sociology in U.S.A.

1. Pre-Parnell Period (Before 1935). In this period not much systematic literature was produced on rural sociology which could have made it a science. All the literature available was uncollected and unsystematic. This was the beginning of rural sociology. First of all some journalists and political leaders in England and America drew public attention towards the conditions and problems of rural life. Several articles and research papers were contributed on the analysis of the problems of rural life. The rural educational and religious institutions were studied in order to understand the problems of rural life. Thus, most of the literature produced in this period, was concerned with the analysis of rural problems, which was acclaimed as the beginning of rural sociology by American scholars.

Gradually, the study of sociology as a new science started in American universities. Its subject matter included rural life and problems. Among the scholars, who particularly attended rural problems, may be mentioned the names of Charles Henderson, K.L. Butterfield, John Morris Gillin, Franklin, H. Giddings and H.C. Tylor. But the most important function of attracting public attention towards rural problems was carried on by Country Life Commission appointed in 1907 by President Roosevelt under the presidentship of Dean Walley. This commission studied rural life and problems by carrying out a survey on the basis of almost half a million questions so that the proper public view might be discovered. Report on the basis of this comprehensive survey was published in 1911. This report was an outline of rural sociology as a new field of study. While it, on the one hand, presented rural problems in a comprehensive form, it also presented useful suggestions for their remedy. The publication of this report accelerated the development of rural sociology. Surveys were carried out and seminars were organised concerning different social problems. A rural life movement was waged to arouse public interest towards the study of rural life.

2. Sims, N.L., *Elements of Rural Sociology*, p. 9.

Till 1908, the literature published as research material and data of social surveys gave birth to rural sociology as a new science. In the year 1917 by the joint efforts of several sociologists a new department entitled rural sociology was opened in American Sociological Institute for the survey and research in rural areas.

By the end of First World War the economic and social welfare of the rural people became an important subject of public discussion. In 1919 the American Agricultural Department opened a new branch known as Bureau of Agricultural Economics to further research activities concerning rural life. Another department known as Farm Life Studies was opened which is now known as Division of Farm Population and Rural Life under the chairmanship of Charles Golpin. This bureau has provided more and more information concerning rural life in collaboration with the agricultural institutions and other government organisations and has thus performed very important service. However, local, state and regional units, particularly the agricultural research centres, could not extend co-operation in this direction. The main reason of this state of affairs was the paucity of finance. In the year 1925 the American Congress passed Parnell Act by which these units were not only given absolute rights for the extension of research work in social and economic field but were also given the facility of using sufficient financial grants for research in the field of social sciences.

2. Parnell Period. The literature concerning rural sociology during this period started with the research activities at Columbia University since 1906 to 1912. During these six years the important works published included *Quaker Hill* by W.H. Wilson, *A Haugier Village* by N.L. Sims, *An American Village* by J.M. Williams. These studies of rural life were based on statistical data and were conducted through the social survey method. In 1915 The Agricultural Research Centre at Wisconsin University carried on research on the basis of which C.J. Galpin wrote *The Social Anatomy of Agricultural Community*, a very important work in rural sociology. Among the textbooks for universities the first book was *Constructive Rural Sociology* by John Morris Gillete, published in 1913. After it in 1917, Paul, L. Vogt published *Introduction to Rural Sociology.* Between 1918 and 1925 several important books besides Galpin's *Rural Life* were published.

3. Pre-war Depression Period. The Parnell Act could not encourage much research work due to lack of sufficient number of properly trained and skilled research workers. Therefore, whatever research and survey work was carried out for the utilisation of grants at the agricultural research centres and whatever literature was published were of a very low level. This considerably retarded the growth of rural sociology. In order to clear up this impediment, The Social Science Congress of U.S.A. started a scheme by which selection of able persons, provision of scholarship for studies in advanced institutes and participation in the research activities of agricultural institutes of different states was carried on. This started development of rural sociology. In Agricultural Research Institute the research work on rural problems carried out by so many sociologists resulted in valuable contribution to rural sociology.

The year 1936 saw the publication of *Rural Sociology*, a quarterly magazine in U.S.A. This journal fulfilled the need of a forum for publication of research papers concerning rural life. Gradually, it achieved an important place among the social science journals. In 1937 an organisation with the name Rural Sociological Society was established. In 1930 Sorokin, Zimmerman and C.J Galpin published their eminent work *A Systematic Source Book in Rural Sociology* which was considered a landmark in rural sociological literature.

4. War Period. The widespread conflict, upheaval and confusion led to realisation of the need of able rural sociologists. The American government established government departments in which scholars of rural sociology were appointed for the study of rural problems and conditions not only in U.S.A. but also in other countries. Many of them were sent to other countries as advisors. Some of them conducted research concerning agriculture while others started teaching rural sociology in universities. Thus, the American rural sociologists started attempts to evolve this branch of knowledge through research and publication in different countries. However, not many books were published during this period. Mostly, studies were published in the form of research papers from time to time. Of the few important publications in this period, may be mentioned: *Studies in Rural Social Organisation* by Charles Loomis, and *Brazil: People and Institutions* by Smith.

5. Post-war Period. This period may be called the period of eminence for rural sociology. During this period rural sociology was popularised by widespread research and publication of literature. The scope of rural sociology during this period, was not confined to rural problems only but included the areas of rural social life; rural social institutions, rural social change, rural community, rural education, rural-urban contrast and rural health. Several notable text-books were published during this period. Of these the notable was *Rural Sociology* (1948) by Nelson and *A Study of Rural Society* (1952) by Kolb Bruner. *Rural Sociology* by Loomis and Beagle presented the subject through a factual interpretation and novel method. Along with publications, the study of rural sociology was prescribed in colleges and universities. In some institutions new subjects concerning rural life such as rural education was prescribed. Thus, at present rural sociology is a growing branch of sociology in U.S.A. due to the collaboration of thousands of research workers and research scholars in so many colleges, universities, research institutes and government departments.

RURAL SOCIOLOGY IN INDIA

The real India lives in villages. Traditionalism, simplicity, poverty, illness, illiteracy, backwardness and other problems of Indian villages attracted the attention of sensitive Western scholars during British rule in India and some literature was published on this subject. However, research in the direction of rural sociology started only after the country achieved independence. Rural reconstruction and welfare were given a prominent place in the five year plans resulting into the growth of community projects, co-operative movements and village panchayats. The Indian Constitution has declared the aim of secular welfare state which will safeguard the fundamental rights of citizens. This requires the elimination of the problems of unemployment, illiteracy, poverty and illness etc. To achieve this purpose these problems were intensively studied in the rural context.

NEED OF RURAL SOCIOLOGY IN INDIA

It goes without saying that in a nation consisting of 77% rural population, the study of rural sociology is very important. In different parts of the country, however, villages exhibit local differences which should be studied in detail. The five year plans, the fast development in education and means of transport and communication together with contact with the urban societies have resulted in fast and extensive changes in rural society. This change has resulted in disorganisation as well as progress. The guidance of the rural sociologists is needed to give direction to the social change, and to establish the plans of reconstruction and welfare on sound footing.

The problems of poverty, unemployment and illiteracy, the biggest problems in India, are primarily rural problems. These problems cannot be tackled unless studies and surveys about them are conducted in the villages. Such surveys have resulted in the formulation of so many plans of rural economic development in five year plans. The efforts to advance agriculture, animal husbandry, cottage industries and others in the rural areas require the help of rural sociologists for introducing new tools and new techniques. Therefore, today the study of rural sociology is an important branch of syllabi of the teaching of sociology in the colleges and universities in India. Besides these academicians, thousands of government officers in different departments are working upon different aspects of rural sociology. Details concerning the development of rural sociology in India may be acquired by a survey of the studies concerning rural society in India. This leads us to the discussion on history of the study of rural community.

HISTORY OF RURAL STUDIES IN INDIA

Description of Villages in the Vedic Literature

The importance of villages is in no way a novel feature of India. From the pre-historic period the village has been an important unit of the Indian social and economic organisation. The oldest books in India are the Vedas. And even among them, Rig Veda is considered to be the most ancient. And this too has not been devoid of a mention of villages. According to Rig Veda, society is divided into many dynamic, hierarchical groups. Of these the smallest unit is the family. Many such families constitute one village. One *vish* is composed of many villages. Many such *vishes* taken together constitute one *jana* and many *jana* together make one nation. In this way, according to Rig Veda, the village is the unit of social and political organisation of India. In the ancient literature, the word village was interpreted as a group of families living at one place. The leader of the village was known as *Gramini.* In this way, Rig Veda has mentioned the village as a unit but has not described its internal organisation.

Description of Village in the Mahabharat

Literature succeeding Rig Veda is more profuse in its description of the village. Mahabharat, whose period is estimated at between 2 B.C. and 2 A.D. has mentioned many types of groups. According to Mahabharat, forts were constructed for the defence of the local groups. The population surrounding the forts was called the village. Towns were bigger than villages but smaller than cities. The Mahabharat does not confine its description to the organisation of the village but also includes the description of inter-village organisation. According to Mahabharat the village is the rudimentary unit of administration. Its leader was called *Gramini.* The duty of a *Gramini* was to arrange for the defence of the village within a radius of two miles. A group of many villages was governed by their leader. As a general rule, such a group contained ten villages whose leader was called *Dash Gramini.* The ten villages in this group had intimate mutual relationship with each other. Over two *Dash Graminis,* or in other words, over two groups of ten villages each there was one *Vinshatik* leader. Accordingly, the *Vinshatik* had twenty villages under his governorship. The group of villages is not limited to so small a number but goes on to a hundred or even a thousand villages. The leader of a group of hundred villages was called a *Shat Gramini* while the administrator of a thousand villages was called an *Adhipati.*

Description of Village in Manusmriti

Besides Mahabharat, many other books of ancient literature have mentioned the village but none of them has much wealth of detail. Mahabharat was succeeded, in its description of village, by Manusmriti. Manu has clarified the distinction between a village, a town and a city. These are placed in an increasing order of population. According to Manusmriti, the village is the smallest unit of administration. The village had its own officials and its individual organisation. In Manusmriti, as in Mahabharat, the leader of the village has been the *Gramini.* A majority of the problems arising in the village were solved by the villagers themselves. For example, things and places of public utility like wells, tanks, meadows, parks etc., were looked after by the people of the village. Besides this, various problems relating to the different aspects of family, caste and society were taken up and solved by the villagers in their different villages. According to Manusmriti there was an authoritative person named *Sahastresh* over one thousand villages. The *Sahastresh* governed the *Shatesh* who held a charge of a hundred villages. In this descending order the *Shatesh* was followed by the *Vinshi* who was incharge of twenty villages. Next came the Dashi who was responsible for ten villages. And finally, there was the leader of each village who was called a *Gramini.*

In this way, the villages in India have been continually developing over a very long period extending back into hundreds of years. Fundamentally, the village is still the unit of the country in spite of the innumerable changes which it has undergone since the days of Mahabharat and Manusmriti.

Today, no less than at that time, there is a leader of the village who is responsible for the entire village in all matters. Even today many villages combine together to form groups in which many different mutual relations are possible. Hundreds of villages even today combine to constitute one cultural area which lends its individual cultural characteristics to each of these villages. But notwithstanding this fact it has to be remembered that no village in India today is completely self-dependent and independent. From every viewpoint, be it social, economic or political, the village of today is dependent to a large extent upon people not belonging to the village. The village of today is no longer a member of just a single rural community but member of a caste, a religion and a nation as well. Hence, while he has some responsibilities with regard to the village, many social, religious and political reasons compel him to think in terms of other people who are not members of his community. India is a democracy in which there are many states which, though united under a central government, are independent in many respects. Every state is further sub-divided into districts and each district into tehsils. In each tehsil there are several villages. In this way, from the administrative viewpoint the public representatives or the leaders, depend upon the officials of the tehsils. Different villages are governed by different men because they belong to different tehsils. But nonetheless, the general laws of the state have to be obeyed by everyone. Besides this, in a big village or in a number of small villages grouped together there is a panchayat which serves to solve many of their social, economic and political problems. It is obvious that the modern Indian government wants to make the villages in the country self-dependent and independent units. The future of the country depends upon the villages. The more these villages are prosperous and organised, the more will the country be organised and prosperous. All the intelligent people in the country are aware of this fact. This has encouraged the study of the villages and movements have been organised for improvement in the villages and these movements have been helped by the government.

Contemporary Studies of Rural Community in India

In the modern era, the study of rural communities has become indispensable in the field of sociology and anthropology. Among these studies, one of the oldest is the study of a Mexican village by Robert Fedfield. Besides Robert Fedfield, John Gillin and Ralph Beals have presented some of the most mature studies of rural communities. These studies of rural communities have been carried out on a large scale in America.

The study of sociology in India is not very old but even then there has been quite a detailed study of the different aspects of rural communities. Since the country became independent, the Indian government have paid special attention to the progress and improvement of the village, thus the studies of rural communities were assisted by the government. Similarly, studies were further encouraged by the Point Four Programme and America's Ford Foundation. Under the direction of professor D.N. Majumdar the study of Mohana village in Lucknow district was carried out by the economic assistance rendered by the Ford Foundation. Later, some assistance was forthcoming from the Planning Commission. The results of this study were published in 1958 in a book by Dr. Majumdar entitled '*Caste and Communication in an Indian Village*'. This assistance by the Planning Commission was not a novel enterprise since similar research had been financed by it even before and after this particular instance, Dr. D. G. Karve, who was at that time the chairman of the Programme Evaluation Organisation of the Planning Commission, invited Oscar Lewis who studied Rampura, a village near Delhi. The results of this study were published in 1958 in a book entitled, '*Village Life in Northern India*', published by the Illinois University. Before the publication of either of these two books, Dr. A.R. Desai, in 1935, in his book, '*Introduction to Rural Sociology in India*', shed some light on the study of rural community and made an impassioned appeal for research in this direction. In 1955 when this book was no longer available, Dr. Desai, published another book, '*Rural Sociology in India*', in which the latest studies of rural community in India were assimilated.

Besides Dr. Majumdar and Dr. Desai, the name of Dr. S. C. Dubey deserves mention among other scholars who have studied the rural community in India. The study of Shamirpet village in Hyderabad, made by Dr. Dubey, was published in 1955 under the title '*Indian Villages*'. This book occupies an important place in literature relating to rural community in India. In 1958, another book, '*India's Changing Villages*', was published by Dr. Dubey. In 1956, the Journal of Asian Studies published a research paper, 'Cultural Factor in Rural Community Development' which was written by Dr. Dubey. Besides Dr. Dubey, Prof. M. N. Srinivas also did important work in the field of rural sociology in India. In 1961, he edited a book, '*India's Villages*' which was a collection of studies of various villages in the different states of India. The year 1962 saw the publication of his book, '*Religion and Society Among the Coorgs of South India*'.

The books mentioned above do not constitute the entire body of literature on this subject, besides which a number of other works have been published on the study of rural community in India. It is neither feasible nor indispensable to make a detailed description of these books and research articles. Accordingly, a list of such articles and their corresponding dates has been compiled. The following list will serve as a brief outline of the studies of the different aspects of the rural community in India.

1953 A.R. Beals — "Change in the Leadership of a Mysore Village."
(Economic Weekly)

1955 A.R. Beals — "Interplay Among Factors of Change in a Mysore Village."
(Village India)

1955 A S. Dhillon — "Leadership and Groups in a South Indian Village" — Govt. of India.

1954 Edvin Eames — "Some Aspects of Urban Migration from a Village in North Central India."
(Eastern Anthropologist)

1955 Edvin Eames — "Population and Economic Structure of an Indian Rural Community."

(Eastern Anthropologist)

1955 E.K. Gough — "The Social Structure of a Tanjore Village."

(Village India)

1951 Hazari — "An Indian Out Caste."

1952 N.G.D. Joarder — "Village Administration in India."

1955 Majumdar and others — "Inter-caste Relations in Cohana Kalian, a Village Near Lucknow."

(Eastern Anthropologist)

1955 Mckim Marriott — "Western Medicine in a Village of North India."

(Health, Culture and Community)

1952 E.J. Miller — "Village Structure in North Kerala."

(Economic Weekly)

1951 Shridhar Misra — "Caste Survey in a Model Village with Stereotyped Discriminations."

1950 M.E. Opler — "Village life in North India."

1948 M E. Opler — "The Division of Labour in an Indian Village."

(A Reader in General Anthropology)

1955 N.S. Reddy — "Functional Relations of Lohars in a North Indian Village."

(Eastern Anthropologist)

1955 M.N. Srinivas — "The Social System of a Mysore Village."

(Village India)

1955 K.S. Mathur — "Some Aspects of Social Organisation in a Malwa Village."

(Journal of Research, Agra University)

1950 K.S. Mathur — "Occupational Structure of a Malwa Village."

(Eastern Anthropologist)

1956 A.C. Mayar — "Development Projects in an Indian Village."

1952 M. Smith — "The Misal: A Structural Village Group of India and Pakistan."

(American Anthropologist)

1955 T. Shea — "Economic Study of a Malabar Village."

(Economic Weekly)

1956 R.D. Singh — "The Unity of an Indian Village."

(Journal of Asian Studies)

QUESTIONS FOR EXERCISE

1. Review the history of rural community in India. List the studies made in this direction.

2. What are the factors leading to the growth of rural community? Mention the ecological factors influencing village community.

2

INTRODUCTION TO RURAL SOCIOLOGY

Rural Sociology, as is clear by the nomenclature, is the sociology of rural society. In other words, it is the branch of sociology which studies the rural society. Rural society is generally an agrarian society. Therefore, rural sociology is the study of agrarian society. Rural society has also been called peasant society in a certain sense. Thus, rural sociology includes the study of peasant society. The modes of community life have led the sociologists to classify it into rural and urban community life. Of these, rural sociology is concerned with rural community life. The social structure, social processes, social dynamics and social control in rural society is in contrast to urban society. Therefore, an independent branch of sociology has been developed for the study of rural society. Thus, rural sociology is a special sociology. Sociology is the scientific study of social relationships. It is a systematic study. Society is the web of social relationships. Rural sociology is, thus, the study of the web of rural social relationships.

Rural society is found in the villages. Therefore, rural sociology is the study of villages. It is concerned with village ecology, village life and social relationships in the village. It includes the study of social organisation, structure, functions and processes in the village. In fact, it is a systematic study of every aspect of village life. It is a sociological analysis of rural community, rural social change, rural social problems, community development projects and rural welfare. Its subject matter includes rural morphology, rural social structure, rural social institutions, rural problems and disorganisation and rural reconstruction. Just as general sociology is concerned with the scientific study of general human society, similarly rural sociology is concerned with the study of rural society. It is based upon ruralism. Ruralism is at the heart of rural sociology. Thus, rural sociology studies all the aspects and elements of ruralism.

DEFINITION OF RURAL SOCIOLOGY

The above discussion of the meaning of rural sociology will be further clarified by a perusal of some of the more important definitions of rural sociology advanced by eminent Western and Indian rural sociologists. These are as follows:

1. *T.L. Smith.* "Such sociological facts and principles as are derived from the study of rural social relationships may be referred to as rural sociology."[1]
2. *F.S. Chapin.* "The sociology of rural life is a study of rural population, rural social organisation, and the rural social processes operative in rural society."[2]
3. *D. Sanderson.* "Rural sociology is the sociology of life in the rural environment."[3]
4. *A.R. Desai.* "...the basic task of rural sociology, is to discover the laws of development of rural society."[4]
5. *A.R. Desai.* "...the prime objective of rural sociology should be to make a scientific, systematic and comprehensive study of the rural social organisation, of its structure, functions, and objective tendencies of development and on the basis of such study to discover the laws of its development."[5]
6. *House.* "In its beginning rural sociology, like much of the rest of what passed for sociology in the United States of America consisted largely of ethical evaluation and practical proposals the improvement of rural life."[6]
7. *Dwight-Sanderson.* "...the ultimate justification of all study of rural sociology as a science is in its use in programmes of rural social organisation or the betterment of rural life."[7]

Of the above mentioned definitions, the definition offered by A.R. Desai is the most comprehensive. It includes the theoretical as well as applied aspect of rural sociology. It points out the aim of scientific rural sociology. It gives a proper perspective towards rural social life. Rural sociology clarifies the laws of rural social life and points out the necessary conditions of progress in it. Keeping this is view, A.R. Desai has written, "Rural Sociology is the science of rural society. The laws of the structure and development of rural society in general can aid us in discovering the special laws governing a particular rural society. Rural sociology... is the science of the laws of the development of rural society."[8] Thus, rural sociology is the mirror of rural social life. It provides a complete and detailed media for the knowledge of different aspects of rural life, its problems, its culture, its religion, its economic and political life.

NATURE OF RURAL SOCIOLOGY

As is clear by the definitions given above, rural sociology has a scientific nature. Its utility, however, lies in the utilisation of its principles for rural reform and development. In other words, the facts and principles discovered by rural sociology should be utilized in planning rural reconstruction. Thus, rural sociology is both a science as well as an art. It involves the co-operation of so many social and physical

1. Smith, T.L.: *The Sociology of Rural Life*, pp. 9-10.
2. Chapin, F. Stuart: *Social Structure in Rural Society*, p. 7.
3. Sanderson, D.: *Rural Sociology and Social Organisation*, p. 10.
4. Desai, A.R.: *An Introduction to Rural Sociology in India*, p. 10.
5. *Ibid.*
6. House: *Development of Sociology*, p. 341.
7. Sanderson, Dwight: *Rural Sociology and Social Organisation*, p. 1.
8. Desai, A.R.: *Rural Society in India*, p. 106.

sciences such as economics, psychology, botany, zoology, etc. Research into the causes of any social condition requires the probing into not only the social causes but also economic, geographical and cultural causes. It may be questioned here whether rural sociology is a synthetic structure of findings of different social sciences about rural society or it is an independent science. Of these the latter view is more popular. If the former view is accepted, rural sociology becomes not a science but an art or technology. It becomes a mere applied science. On the other hand, if it discovers laws of rural social life, it is an independent science in spite of taking help from so many other sciences. Even if it helps in social reform and development, it is not by actually doing it but by providing theoretical basis for it. Science is the theoretical study of a problem while its application is an art or technology. In a certain sense, rural sociology may be called an art or technology. In the words of Sanderson, "The art of dealing with problems of rural life is necessarily a technology involving the application of many sciences and disciplines just as the technology of bridge building involves not only mechanics, but metallurgy, geology, meteorology and other disciplines, for the determination of the method of constructing a particular bridge."[9] Every problem in a village requires the collaboration of more than one science. In the ultimate analysis, rural sociology is first a science and then an art.

SCOPE OF RURAL SOCIOLOGY

Rural sociology is comparatively a new branch of sociology. It is a science with its own characteristic standpoint and methods. Therefore, its scope should be clarified to distinguish it from other social sciences. In the words of N.L. Sims, "The field of rural sociology is the study of association among people living by or immediately dependent upon agriculture. Open country and village groupings and groups behaviour are its concern."[10] According to Lowry Nelson, "The subject matter of rural sociology is the description and analysis of progress of various groups as they exist in the rural environment."[11] Thus, the scope of rural sociology includes the study of all the social groups in the village. In the words of Burtrand and associates, "In its broadest definition rural sociology is the study of human relationship in rural environment."[12] Thus, the scope of rural sociology includes all the social relationships in rural environment.

An analysis of the scope of rural sociology leads to the study of the following:

1. Rural problems. The subject matter of rural sociology includes the problems of rural life, such as social, economic, political and cultural problems. These problems are studied in isolation as well as in relation to each other. In the former sense each problem is analysed separately and effort is made to arrive at some conclusion for its remedy. From the second viewpoint all the rural problems are taken as different aspects of one single problem. Sometimes this viewpoint leads to confusion since

9. Sanderson, D.: *Rural Sociology and Social Organisation*, p. 11.
10. Sims, N.L.: *Elements of Rural Sociology*, p. 13.
11. Nelson Lowry: *Rural Sociology*, p. 13.
12. Burtrand and Associates: *Rural Sociology*, p. 8.

the problems get entangled into each other. Therefore, in the integral standpoint towards rural social problems, it is necessary to remember similarities as well as distinctions. Some problems cannot be solved unless studied separately such as the rural problems of poverty, illiteracy, disease, low standard of life, inadequate housing, lack of recreation, traditionalism, religious superstitions etc.

2. Rural social life. Smith has rightly called rural sociology as the sociology of rural life. It aims at the study of rural social life. Rural social life includes rural people, rural population, rural environment, rural standard of living, rural vocations and rural economic conditions. Thus, the study of rural social life involves the observation of different social forms in rural environment.

3. Rural social organisation. The most important function of rural sociology is to provide knowledge concerning rural family organisation. Rural social organisation includes rural family, rural marriage, rural social stratification, rural education, rural administrative system, rural religious and cultural institutions and rural division of labour etc. Thus, rural sociology studies both enacted and developed rural social organisations.

4. Rural institutions. Rural sociology includes the study of rural institutions. Institutions are procedures of activities which are developed to fulfil a certain aim. Such institutions may be economic, political, social, religious or cultural. Rural sociology studies all these types of institutions in the context of rural society.

5. Rural community. In the words of Sanderson, "A rural community consists of the social interaction of the people and their institutions in the local area in which they live in dispersed farm-steads and in a hamlet or village which forms the centre of their common activities."[13] Thus, rural community includes all the general activities of rural people. Rural sociology studies the characteristics, forms and activities of rural community.

6. Rural social structure. Social structure is the most important basis of social life. Therefore, rural social structure is the most important element in the scope of rural sociology. Thus, the rural sociologists concentrate on the analysis and the study of rural social structure.

7. Rural urban contrast. As has been already pointed out, the village and city present two contrasting modes of community life. Rural sociology studies this rural urban contrast. In other words, it studies the fundamental distinctions between rural and urban culture and also their relationship. Thus, it is also a comparative study. Rural society and social institutions can be more easily understood in contrast to urban society and social institutions.

8. Rural planning and reconstruction. Rural planning and reconstruction is particularly important in such societies as the Indian society which is mostly constituted by villages. In contrast to urban planning and reconstruction, rural planning and reconstruction has its own principles and applications. These form important subject matter of rural sociology. To quote A.R. Desai, "Rural sociology will help the rural worker to make a correct diagnosis of its ills and will further

13. Sanderson, D.: *The Rural Community*, p. 481.

enable him to evolve a correct prescription or programme to overcome these ills. If the diagnosis of the ills is erroneous or imperfect the prescription itself will be unscientific and therefore futile."[14]

AIMS OF RURAL SOCIOLOGY

1. Scientific study. Ever since the attention of social scientists was attracted towards rural social problems, it was realised that a scientific study of their nature and remedies is necessary. This was a significant reason for the birth of rural sociology. Thus, rural sociology aims at the study of laws and principles of rural social life which may be utilised for solving rural social problems and realising the ideal of rural reconstruction and development. A. R. Desai has rightly pointed out, "That the prime objective of rural sociology should make a scientific, systematic and comprehensive study of the rural social organisation, of its structure, function and objective tendencies of development, and on the basis of such a study, to discover the laws of its development, since every science, social or natural has for its aim the discovery of the hitherto hidden laws of development of domain of nature or society, the basic task of rural sociology, they unanimously declare, is to discover the laws of development of rural society."[15]

2. Reform and reconstruction. The rural sociologist is interested in rural reform and reconstruction not only as a social scientist but also as a social being, as a citizen. Therefore, rural sociology cannot be isolated from the practical aim of rural social welfare and reconstruction. However, as the nature of a science is generally theoretical, it should be remembered that the primary aim of the rural sociologist is the discovery of the laws and principles of rural social life. As a social scientist he is concerned with the discovery of principles and laws concerning rural society while as a useful member of society, he may be equally interested in the application of his knowledge for rural social amelioration. Thus, while rural sociology aims at the theoretical study of rural social life, it also aims at eliminating rural social evils and establishing a new progressive society in the villages. Today, due to the influence of industrial revolution and fast urbanisation, the rural life is lagging behind the general social life in progressive countries. The rural sociologists aim at eliminating this cultural lag and providing theoretical basis for bringing the rural society in level with the general society in a country.

IMPORTANCE OF RURAL SOCIOLOGY

The above discussion concerning the aims of rural sociology also clarifies its importance in modern societies. It may be remembered that it is particularly important in those societies which are primarily rural such as Indian society. Historically speaking, rural sociology was born due to the need of intensive study of different aspects of rural social life so that it might be properly developed. Therefore, the importance of rural sociology lies in rural reconstruction, rural welfare and the solution of rural problems. In most of the countries today,

14. Desai, A.R.: *Rural Sociology in India*, p. 10.
15. *Ibid.*

urbanisation and industrialisation are fast increasing and influencing the rural social structure, traditions, mores and social institutions. This has created a dangerous situation for maintaining characteristics of rural life. The importance of rural sociology in this situation, has considerably increased. Therefore, its study is being encouraged by public as well as private agencies and universities and research institutions everywhere. This is particularly true about developing nations such as India and other nations in Asia and Africa.

Importance of Rural Sociology in India

India is a country of villages. Eighty per cent of the Indian population still lives in the villages. Even the urban population is constituted by the people migrating from the villages to the towns. By and by many villages grew into towns. The villages are the wellspring of Indian culture. India's economy is fundamentally agricultural and not industrial. A major portion of the citizens of the Indian Republic are residents of villages. Thus, it is impossible to achieve a national awakening without redeeming the rural population from its obscurity. In this way, from every point of view, economic, cultural or political, the future of India very much depends upon villages.

It is necessary to understand and to act according to the laws prevailing in the village in order to achieve progress of the villages. Only then can the improvement and development be permanent. Only then will the rural population be able to treat the development plans as their own and offer their co-operation. This necessitates a special study of the rural society. In order to effect a desirable change in the rural institutions and communities, the laws of their development and change should be discovered because any change introduced against their laws will be an imposition which will not be able to attain permanency. Without understanding the special features, qualities and defects of the rural religion and culture, the village level workers will not be successful in effecting rural reconstruction.

Thus, rural sociology is of no little importance in India. In the theoretical background of the plans for the country's progress, the study of rural society is essential. Such a study will reveal the laws which govern the development, change and control etc. of society, and these laws will have to be kept in view if the plans for the villages are to achieve any measure of success. Today the Indian government is desirous of developing villages in all their various aspects. The government officials who are engaged in this work must be equipped with a knowledge of rural sociology in order to ensure success.

QUESTIONS FOR EXERCISE

1. What do you understand by rural sociology? How does it help in bettering the condition of rural society?
2. What is rural sociology? Indicate its place in the general scheme of sociology studies.

3. The sociology of rural life is a study of rural population, rural social organisation and the processes operating in the rural society. Explain.
4. Explain the scope of rural sociology.
5. What is rural sociology? Describe its scope.
6. Discuss the scope and need for rural sociology in India.
7. Discuss the salient features of rural sociology and its importance in the Indian context.

3

RELATIONSHIP WITH OTHER SOCIAL SCIENCES

Scope of social sciences has been helping since long in increasing and improving gradually the range and the depth of human understanding into the workings of Nature and man This has, in turn, led to gradual unraveling and unfolding of the secrets of physical nature and social organisation, thereby organising into a system of our knowledge of man and Nature. Thus, we are now able to study and investigate systematically and scientifically various aspects of society and Nature. Now the whole gamut of human knowledge is divided into three branches: (1) Humanities; (2) Social Sciences; and (3) Natural Sciences. In Humanities are included art, literature and philosophy etc. In Natural sciences are included physical, biological and environmental sciences. In the Social sciences we study man in relation to other individuals and human associations. In the Social sciences are included subjects like Sociology, Civics, Politics, Social Psychology, Anthropology, Economics, History etc.

Of course, the various disciplines covered by the generic name social sciences all deal, in a systematic manner employing scientific methods and techniques with various aspects of society; nonetheless, the difference in their nomenclature — Economics, Anthropology, Political Science, Psychology and Sociology — clearly indicates the difference in their subject-matters. Though there is a certain amount of overlapping in the subject-matter between various social sciences, there is distinct and well-defined uniqueness about each of them. The uniqueness and specialty of each social science notwithstanding, there is also an underlying thread of unity among the various social sciences. The thread running through all social sciences is the fact that the ultimate subject of study for all of them is man. Man's actions are manifold and so are his associations. In order to comprehend man and society we have to pool the knowledge furnished by the various specialized branches of the social sciences. Therefore, though separate and unique, the various disciplines included in Social Science cooperate and draw upon the materials of each other. Being a branch of Social Science, Rural Sociology, too, can draw upon the material furnished by other Social Sciences and also use freely their methods and techniques in its investigation of the various aspects and facets of rural life and society. Elaborating the fundamental unity of all social sciences, Lowry Nelson writes: "Yet in spite of the division and sub-division of social science there is a fundamental unity of purpose and a growing unity in method and point of view... Rural Sociology, as the scientific study of rural society, should certainly avail itself the approaches, methods and techniques of all other sciences, in so far as they may be useful in understanding and describing that society."[1]

In this branch of social science we study specifically the problems and complexities of rural life and society in order to develop well-ordered and organized knowledge of rural life. By a systematic study and analysis we gain insight into the causes and background of the problems of rural society. Thus, not only our knowledge of these problems becomes firm and clear but we also achieve a means, an organon or an instrument to facilitate the solution of the problems and determine and direct to some extent the process of change. The discipline of Rural Sociology is comparatively new and, in this context, it is well to remember that any subject before branching off and emerging as a new full-fledged discipline is part of some other discipline. Thus, the subject matter of sociology once formed a part of Philosophy, Ethics and Political Economy and Rural Sociology was part of Sociology. Therefore, the subject-matter of Rural Sociology is closely linked with other branches of Sociology and there is mutual sharing between them of methods and techniques of social sciences.

RURAL SOCIOLOGY AND GENERAL SOCIOLOGY

Rural Sociology is a branch of sociology. Its specialized task is to make an intensive as well as extensive survey and investigation of rural society, the peculiar problems which are due exclusively to certain typical characteristics of the rural society Though rural and urban societies are merely two aspects of general society distinguished by certain geographic, economic and social organisational factors, the range and scope of rural and urban problems is both vast and complex. It is not possible for general sociology to do justice to the finer aspects of rural organisation. Moreover, it is not possible to reduce the problems of rural or urban society to those of society in general. Accordingly, rural and urban societies could not be fully explored and studied by general sociology. As a consequence there arose two distinct and specialised disciplines known as rural sociology and urban sociology. The business of rural sociology was to study the village life and that of urban sociology to study the life of urban societies. To illustrate how the two disciplines differ and how the peculiar problems of these can be at most peripherally touched by general sociology we may cite the problems of slums and Hookah Club. The problem of slum is peculiar to cities and will be studied adequately by urban sociologist alone whereas Hookah Club exists only in a village and has no role to play in city life. Both urban and rural sociology share a common approach and follow similar methods but there is a vast difference in the two with regard to the subject matter. Both sociology and rural as well as urban sociologies study social events, actions and organisation. But whereas sociology is indifferent to the geographic and environmental factors and tries to grasp the most general

1. Nelson, L., *Rural Sociology*, p. 4.

laws of social action and organisation, the rural and urban sociologies study the same in their environment, that is, whether a problem or event occurs in rural or urban context. Moreover, while the scope of rural sociology is confined to village life, the scope of sociology includes both rural and urban life and also extends far beyond. Thus, while rural sociology is a specialised discipline, sociology, on the other hand, is a generic discipline. To sum up: rural, urban and general sociologies all are similar in regard to approach, viewpoint and methodology but differ from each other with regard to nature and context of social problems.

RURAL SOCIOLOGY AND URBAN SOCIOLOGY

From the point of view of economics and topography the society is divided into two groups of communities engaged either in agriculture or industry primarily and showing relative difference in the density of population. As can be easily seen, the two groups are rural and urban and that the rural group is less dense and engaged primarily in agriculture as profession whereas the urban group is more dense and engaged primarily in the industry. However, the study of one group involves necessary reference to the other group. Therefore, if we are studying Rural Sociology, we can do so accurately, scientifically and usefully only if we mark off the scopes and ambits of rural and urban sociologies precisely and unambiguously. As a matter of fact, the relation of rural and urban sociologies is akin to the relation between figure and ground, it is not possible to have one without the other. If rural sociology forms the subject of study and is in the fore-ground, urban sociology will form the background and *vice-versa*. The two fields of study complement each other and none of them, therefore, can be studied in isolation.

Accordingly, we can study rural sociology effectively only by drawing upon and seeking the close co-operation of urban sociology. The subject-matter of both rural and urban sociology is inter-linked and inter-dependent. In the simple language this means that life in the villages and cities can be fully analysed and understood by mutual consideration, that is the distinguishing characteristics of rural life can only be brought into relief by comparing and contrasting those with the chief characteristics of the urban life. The villages and cities affect each other economically as well as socially. It is not possible to understand either of the two exclusively and in isolation. Therefore, there is no exaggeration if we say that the studies of rural and urban sociologies are possible only if both are there. A society cannot be considered from the urban or rural point of view unless both rural and urban communities exist.

RURAL SOCIOLOGY AND SOCIAL ANTHROPOLOGY

The rural sociology and social anthropology are so close to each other that it is indeed impossible to draw any dividing line between them, their subject-matters are inter-linked and overlapping. The science of anthropology studies the primitive man and his activities. The ancient societies, untouched by the influence of modern science and technology, form the subject-matter of anthropology. The social anthropology describes the structure of primitive societies and behaviour of man under these structural influences. The rural sociology, on the other hand, discusses the behaviour of man under village society and rural environments. Thus, the scope and limit of social anthropology is confined to primitive man's behaviour in primitive societies and that of rural sociology to man's behaviour in village organisation. Barring the difference in scope there is no difference in the methodology and the approach of the two disciplines. As a matter of fact, the only difference between social anthropology and rural sociology is nominal, that is, in name only. It is not possible to demarcate and differentiate adequately between a primitive and a village society. The socio-economic conditions and the environment of the two are very similar, and, therefore, it is rather arbitrary to treat social anthropology and rural sociology as two separate and distinct disciplines. The organisation of both village and primitive societies is rural but the only differentiating characteristic between the two is that whereas primitive groups inhabit areas which are widely separated and too distant to affect and influence each other, the modern villages are closely situated and are also near cities and, therefore, there is much mutual impact between modern villages and urban societies. As primitive societies, as a rule, are situated in remote forest areas or uneasily accessible mountain resorts, they are free from urban contact and impact. Therefore, there is little change in them over thousands of years and this non-changing character provides justification for our referring to them as 'primitive'.

From the above discussion it is clear that rural sociology and social anthropology are not only closely inter-linked but are extremely proximate disciplines. Both study the rural society under natural circumstances and conditions. Both subjects pay special attention to structural and functional aspects of village organisation, family organisation, class and caste-structure, folk art, dance and literature, folk culture and customs and traditions. But whereas rural sociology studies the above mentioned themes and topics in the context of modern villages and rural organisation, the social anthropology studies them in the context of primitive societies which inhabit generally remote and inaccessible forest areas of mountainous tracts. There may have been some change in the structural organisation of the modern villages and also some transformation in the attitudes of the villages; but, on the whole, the change is marginal and the rural and primitive societies are similar in all essential respects. That is why Kluckhohn says, "The sociological attitude has tended towards the practical and the present, the anthropological towards pure understanding and the past."[2] Thus, it is clear that rural sociology and social anthropology have the same subject-matter though the attitude of the former is present-oriented and that of the latter future-oriented.

RURAL SOCIOLOGY AND ECONOMICS

The science of economics deals with those human activities the purpose of which is to harness natural resources and distribute them to satisfy human needs and wants. In order to meet and satisfy human demands there is production and distribution of goods which are ultimately consumed and this produces satisfaction of needs,

2. Kluckhohn, *Mirror for Man*, p. 269.

wants and desires. There are circumstances in which the demand increases while in different set of circumstances it goes down. It is the business of economics to study the mechanisms of demand and supply, to study if there obtains between them an inverse relation or there are some other factors which influence the relation of supply and demand. It also studies how far demand can be controlled by social and political factors. And how can there be equitable distribution of wealth? Is it possible to remove disparities in incomes? And what are the economic and social consequences of economic disparities? Should industrialisation be widespread and cover every corner of a country? Or, is it more desirable to localise it at few selected centres? These are the topics which come under economic studies. Rural economics has grown into a full-fledged subject. The rural economics is, as a matter of fact, Agricultural Economics. The study of economics of villages can suggest ways and means to improve the agricultural produce by the use of new techniques and better seeds; but no economic programme can be implemented without understanding and overcoming the resistance of tradition and patently conservative rural psychology. Therefore, the success of any economic programme presupposes a penetration into the psychological attitudes of the villagers and for this rural sociology comes to the aid of economics.

On the other hand, the economic activities affect deeply the social life in villages. The nature and distribution of land holdings, the system of agriculture, the problem of indebtedness of small farmers and land labour, inadequate means of livelihood of a majority of villagers, particularly landless labour are some economic factors which deeply influence the rural society, its orthodoxy, traditionalism and opposition to any social change. Without an adequate study and understanding of these economic factors it is not possible to understand the rural society, particularly to devise ways and means to manoeuvre change in its structure. With regard to the nature and subject-matter, and rural sociology and economics are deeply interlinked, interwoven and involved. Indeed, rural sociology investigates the economic life and structure of rural society from a social and human viewpoint while economics studies the rural society and its structure and function from the financial and economic viewpoint.

RURAL SOCIOLOGY AND HISTORY

Both rural sociology and history are included in social sciences. In history we study the social structure and organisation as it evolves during the course of time. Therefore, from history we learn the history of village societies as they were under tyranny, monarchy, feudal lordship, democracy etc., but the history studies important and crucial aspects. For a detailed study of rural organisation we need separate independent discipline of rural sociology. Thus, whereas history gives us a general but evolutionary account of village life, we need rural sociology in order to understand village life both extensively and intensively. History is a study of rise and fall of states, nations and empires and the mutual relations between nations such as commercial and trade links, diplomatic and cultural exchange and, above all the affairs of war and peace. Rural sociology, on the contrary, has no direct interest in peace and war, except insofar as these affects social stability; but it does study the social and economic structure of rural society as also interpersonal relationship the society which are indeed the causative factors of peace and war. Thus, it is not rural sociology alone which needs the help of history in order to obtain a historical and evolutionary perspective upon rural problems, the social science of history, too, needs the knowledge of information of rural sociology in order to appreciate and know the real causes of war and peace; indeed, of any historic change. Both history and rural sociology are involved in the study of social events. The former studies them as a chain, one leading to the other, the latter studies in depth the structure and background of social events insofar as they occur in a given rural society.

RURAL SOCIOLOGY AND ARCHAEOLOGY

In archaeology we study the ancient and prehistoric civilisations. By extensive excavations at a number of sites we have been able to learn about the life and culture of many unknown civilisations. By archaeological excavation we learn about the structure and organisation of villages in the prehistoric times. Such knowledge is obviously very useful in understanding the origin of villages. The archaeological studies investigate the art and culture, language, dress, the ideas, religion and social organisation in the pre-historic times. Almost all ancient civilisations have their roots in villages. The village type socio-economic organisation of human race is apparently more ancient than the urban organisation. In villages we find a more fundamental and basic type of organisation and therefore, a true or pure form of culture is to be better found in villages than in cities. In ancient India, too, we discover a rural type of civilisation. Thus, we find that, on the whole, the science of archaeology is basically concerned with the rural life. From this viewpoint there is a deep relation between Archaeology and Rural Sociology.

Though there is a certain amount of similarity with regard to subject- matter between Archaeology and Rural Sociology, there is a fundamental difference between the two as regards the approach or viewpoint. While rural sociology is primarily interested in the villages of today, archaeology is primarily interested in the villages of pre-historic times.

RURAL SOCIOLOGY AND POLITICAL SCIENCE

Rural sociology and political science are very closely related. According to Weinberg and Shabat, "Political science is the study of the way in which a society organizes and operates a state."[3] Thus, defined and understood political science is a part or branch of sociology. As rural health, education, religion, economic structure and organisation, social structure and organisation, family system etc. are the elements of rural sociology, in the same way, political institutions, associations and organisations are the elements which constitute the fabric of political science.

3. Weinberg and Shabat, *Society and Man*, p. 13.

Whereas, political science studies the institutions like Panchayats, various subsidiaries of Panchayat associations, District Board, Notified Area Committee etc., from the political angle, the rural sociology considers them as constituent elements of rural society and studies them from the social angle. The viewpoint of political science towards certain institutions responsible for rural administration and justice is narrow and limited to strictly political implications of such institutions, the viewpoint and approach of rural sociology towards these institutions is broad; it considers them as features of the broad canvas of rural life and institutions in general. As a matter of fact, it is not quite possible to study and understand the rural political institutions in isolation from social institutions. Therefore, knowledge of rural sociology is essential to political science for understanding the rural government and administration. Thus, we find that political science and sociology are closely interlinked disciplines.

The above close similarities between rural sociology and political science notwithstanding, there is an important difference between the two. This is that whereas rural sociology studies political, social, religious and cultural institutions, Political Science studies only the political institutions, The former studies all types and varieties of social relations and institutions in villages while the latter studies the political relations and institutions in society only. Thus, we can say that political science relies heavily on sociology, in general, and rural sociology, in particular, while making study of political institutions in the context of rural society.

QUESTIONS FOR EXERCISE

1. What is the place of Rural Sociology among other social sciences?
2. Write short note on Rural Sociology and Sociology.
3. Distinguish between Rural Sociology and Sociology.
4. Discuss the relation of Rural Sociology and Social Anthropology.
5. Discuss the relation between Rural Sociology and Economics.
6. Write short note on Rural Sociology and History.
7. Distinguish between Rural Sociology and Archaeology.
8. Distinguish between Rural Sociology and Political Science.

4

METHODS OF STUDY

Rural sociology is a branch of sociology, and, therefore, the study of rural community makes an unrestricted use of all the methods of social research.

All these methods are scientific and all the common characteristics of any scientific method are to be found in them. Hence, it would be quite in keeping with the context to describe the major steps and common characteristics of the scientific method before we proceed with an individual study of each of these methods. In this context, an exposition of the difficulties of the scientific studies of rural community will also be advantageous because all these difficulties are applicable to each and Everyone of these methods.

DIFFICULTIES IN THE SCIENTIFIC STUDY OF RURAL SOCIETY

Now the question which arises here is as to whether rural sociology is a subject which has all the above mentioned qualities and admits of the use of the scientific methods. Some of the major difficulties in this context are:

1. Possibility of subjective ideas and prejudices. Rural society is a network of social relations. These relations make their impressions upon the person who is studying them. Consequently, the possibility of prejudice and the thoughts and experience of the observer becoming manifest upon the study cannot be ignored. Thus, the objectivity necessary for scientific study cannot be overemphasised.

2. Difficulties in maintaining scientific objectivity. In this way the following difficulties arise in the achievement of scientific objectivity in the study of rural society:

(i) From his very childhood an observer is obsessed with certain prejudices and bias which it is very difficult to eliminate.

(ii) If forceful diminution, of these prejudices is attempted, there is a great likelihood of contrary prejudices being acquired.

(iii) In the study of rural society, values too are an important consideration but these values can neither be controlled nor studied objectively.

(iv) There are many different communities in rural societies whose culture, customs, conventions and geographical conditions do not, in the least, concur.

Hence, it is difficult to be objective in their study and there is no small possibility of prejudice. A man's impressions of his own society act as an obstacle in studying some other society.

3. Complexity of rural society. A third difficulty in the study of the rural society is its complexity. Rural society is a network of innumerable social relations and these social relations have a multitude of factors. It is due to this complexity that it becomes difficult to expose all the factors involved in any aspect of the study of rural society.

4. Changeability of rural society. Rural society is very much susceptible to change and this is another drawback in studying it scientifically. Society is a network of relations among human beings. Man is a conscious and dynamic being who makes use of his reason. He can, with consummate ease, mark his behaviour, thoughts and opinions. At the same time, these do not remain static but change constantly. This continuous change aggravates the difficultly in studying social relations. And secondly, even if they have been successfully studied, this success may be obstructed by this changeability of the relations.

5. Dearth of universality. There are many rural societies which differ from each other in respect of their cultures, customs, conventions, physical environments and other relevant aspects. And even within one rural society the customs, standards of living, ideas and values of the different classes of people are different. And even the individuals within a single class differ from each other in many respects. In this way, rural society is a subject in which each unit does not resemble any other. Thus, its study is not conducive to the formulation of any universal laws. Consequently, the scientific method cannot be of much use here.

6. Difficulty in the control of the units of rural society. The scientific method is applied only to those subjects which allow control over their units. In the study of rural society, its units — individuals and groups — cannot be controlled and it is not possible to locate a particular person in a circumstance and control him because it is in no way essential that ail people be identically affected by the situation or that the individual be at all influenced. Therefore, rural society cannot be scientifically studied.

7. Hindrance by vested interests. The scientific study of rural society is rendered even more utopian by the vested interests which make any progress impossible. No society, group or community can hear without objection the criticism of its shortcomings, because, in it, are latent the individual, social or class-related interests.

8. Study of Values. The scientific method cannot study values due to which it cannot be applied to the study of rural society which possesses so many values. While, on the one hand, it necessarily neglects the axiological aspects of society, it, on the other hand, hinders the study of facts because social facts are not utterly removed from the impact of these values.

9. Other difficulties. Besides the special difficulties which arise in the application of the scientific method to the study of rural society which we have mentioned above, it is further beset with all those difficulties which are inherent in any subject which does not have the necessary characteristic qualifications for scientific study. Values and facts are found mixed in rural society. Therefore, it is by no means easy to discover any cause-effect relation among them by using the scientific method. The fact that rural society is sub-divided into almost innumerable communities makes it difficult to formulate any universal law based upon the study of rural society. These laws are further related to the conscious and changeable man, a fact, which debars these laws from being examined for their validity and neither can they, for the same reason, be considered useful for prediction. Some people assert that the scientific method cannot be used in the study of society because it is not possible to establish laboratories and use the apparatus.

METHODS IN RURAL SOCIOLOGY

In spite of the difficulties in the scientific study of rural society that we have seen above, rural sociology, which studies it, is believed to be a science which makes use of the statistical and social survey methods and also of the other scientific methods. Though it is true that scientific method cannot be applied to the study of the rural society as it can be to the natural sciences, there is no reason why the study of the rural society should not be done according to a method recognised by science if such a method can, with facility, be used in social sciences like psychology, social psychology, economics, political science, etc. If seriously thought over, it will be quite evident that the above difficulties which confound the study of the rural society, also arise in the study of all psychological and economic activities. But, nevertheless, psychology and economics respectively use the scientific method. All that can be said with regard to these difficulties is that the scientific study of the rural society is far more difficult, less factual, less realistic, less definite and less objective than is the case with the study of physical objects. But, in the future, some progress can be made in this direction, though undoubtedly it will entail a certain amount of effort, with the result that the subject can become more conducive to rural scientific study.

We are now in a position to acquaint the reader briefly with the different methods which are applied to the study of the rural society. The major methods of investigation used by rural sociology are the following:

1. Questionnaire
2. Schedule
3. Interview
4. Participant observation
5. Social survey
6. Social research
7. Statistical methods.

1. Questionnaire. In social research the questionnaire is used comprehensively. In the questionnaire method, as is evident from the name, a list of such questions is compiled, which throw light upon the different aspects of the problem. Usually the questions are accompanied by 'yes' and 'no' as their answers and the informant have to reject the wrong answer. The questionnaire method has several difficulties. Often, people prevaricate in answering the questions. Sometimes the questions are so framed that they are interpreted differently by the observer and the informant. Quite often the questions are answered without grasping their full significance. Notwithstanding these difficulties, the questionnaire method is, by far, the most popular method in rural social research.

2. Schedule. The schedule method resembles the questionnaire to some extent, inasmuch as it, too, requires a list of questions, the answers to which supply the data. But these questions are taken by the observer to the informant and filled by the observer himself. Usually, this method is made use of only in a limited sphere. The data compiled by this method is more valid, but compared to the questionnaire method, it involves more time, energy and money. This method achieves greater minuteness in detail.

3. Interview. In the interview method, evidently enough, the observer faces the informant and questions him across the table, noting down the information which the questions elicit. This certainly does elicit much useful information but it simultaneously becomes plagued by the effect that much information which the informant can offer indirectly cannot be expected in a direct interview. Actually, much of the success of the interviewer depends upon his individual ability. If the informant shows hesitation because the information is being transcribed, a tape recorder may be used.

4. Participant Observation. As is evident by the name, in the participant observation method, the observer participates with the people whom he is observing. This gives him the opportunity to come into direct contact with the people who are to provide him with his information and obtain much useful information. This provides much detailed information along with the facility of its execution. But this method involves extensive use of time, money and energy. Yet, in spite of these defects, it assists in a profound study of rural and primitive groups, because other methods like the questionnaire method do not prove efficacious about them. This method finds an uninhibited use in many anthropological studies.

SOCIAL SURVEY

The word survey is derived from two words sur or sor which means over and the word *veeir or veoir* which means to see. In this way, the word survey means to oversee or to look over. According to the Webster Collegiate Dictionary, the word survey connotes, "A critical inspection, often official, to provide exact information, often a study of an area with respect to a certain condition or its prevalence as a survey of school."

Social survey is intended to be the study of the social aspect of a community's composition and activities. It aims at the collection of quantitative facts. It makes a concrete study of society, especially the social problems inherent in the society.

It presents programmes for improvement and development It is conducted within fixed geographical limit; it is related to problems of social importance and assists in formulating constrictive programmes.

Objectives and Subject-matter of Social Survey

The following are the major objectives which social survey strives to achieve:

1. Collection of data related to the social aspect of community. Social survey studies individuals as members of society and in this way studies social circumstances and problems.

2. Study of social problems, labour class and its problems. In social survey, social problems and in particular, problems of the labour class like illiteracy, poverty, insanitation, unemployment, drinking, crime, juvenile delinquency, prostitution, labour problems etc., are studied.

3. Practical and utilitarian viewpoint. Studies of social survey are made from a practical and utilitarian viewpoint in order that suggestions for constructive programmes in solving different problems may be offered.

In this way, the subject-matter of social survey includes — (1) Demographic characteristics, (2) Social Environment, (3) Activities of the members of the community, (4) Opinions and attitudes.

The following are the important kinds of social survey:

1. General or specialized surveys. Originally, social survey was taken to be of two kinds — general and specialized. In the general survey the whole community is made the subject of study like a country, state, town or village. In the specialized or topical survey the study is confined to some special aspect only *e.g.*, unemployment, health, cleanliness, labour welfare, child welfare, etc.

2. Direct or indirect surveys. Direct survey is one in which the facts can be quantitatively interpreted while, on the other hand, no such quantitative interpretation is possible in the case of an indirect survey, *e.g.*, the survey of population is direct, while on the other hand, the surveys of the state of health or the level of nutrition are indirect. Different problems of social sciences are studied by both kinds of survey.

3. Census survey or sample survey. In the census survey the different parts of the entire area are individually studied and the figures are then compiled into one. On the other hand, in the sample survey, instead of the whole area being studied, a part which represents the entire area is taken. Now, this representative part is studied. The Indian government has conducted many such sample surveys. Compared to the census survey, the sample survey is far less expensive and it is, therefore, very popular in the study of rural sociology which makes much use of it.

4. Primary or secondary surveys. In the primary survey, the survey work is started right from the beginning. In this, the surveyor himself collects facts concurring with his objectives and hence the primary surveys are more reliable and purer. But, if some data have already been collected in the study of any subject, a new start has not to be made. The survey conducted under these circumstances is called a secondary survey. It is obvious that when the situation is favourable to a secondary survey there is much saving of time and money.

5. Initial or repetitive surveys. If the survey conducted in the area is the first of its kind, it is called an initial survey while if some survey has been done in the past then the present survey is termed a repetitive survey. An initial survey involves comparatively greater effort and exertion and comparable data are not available. In repetitive survey the information obtained is more reliable and can be compared.

6. Official, semi-official or private surveys. As the names indicate, official survey is the survey sponsored by the government, semi-official survey is the survey conducted by universities, district boards, municipalities and other similar semi-official institutions, and private survey is a survey attempted by an individual. Among these, official survey has the greatest probability of success because it is not hampered by a dearth of finances or trained personnel. Semiofficial survey is not only less economic but also more difficult. In the private survey, the problem of expenditure, time and trained personnel is even more acute. But, in spite of the fundamental difficulties, some semi-official and private surveys have yielded better results than some government surveys.

7. Widespread or limited surveys. Surveys are given these names according to their extension or coverage. A survey covering a greater area is called widespread survey while a more delimited or less extensive survey is known as a limited survey. A limited survey is comparatively more reliable and less liable to mistakes but it carries with it the probability of some of the facts being omitted. On the other hand, a widespread survey includes many aspects of the subject under study and presents a more complete picture. But, due to its extension, it becomes less reliable because the probability of irregularities is increased.

8. Public or confidential surveys. It is evident from the very name that public surveys are those in which the processes and results of study are not concealed while the confidential surveys are those in which the processes and results are not revealed to people. Whether the survey is going to be public or confidential depends upon its nature and aim.

9. Postal or personal surveys. Postal survey, as the term itself implies, is a method in which the surveyor obtains the answers by sending the questionnaire by post. If the survey is to be a personal one, then the surveyor has to move about in the area to be surveyed and collect information. Postal survey certainly does economise upon effort and money but the information which it can obtain is very limited and lacks reliability. Although personal survey demands more time, energy and money the information obtained is correspondingly more comprehensive and more reliable.

10. Regular or *ad-hoc* surveys. Regular surveys are conducted after the lapse of a fixed period of time, as for example, the surveys conducted by the State Bank of India. The organisation made for an *ad-hoc* survey is temporary and is dissolved after the survey has been completed. An *ad-hoc* survey, in comparison with a regular survey, supplies less extensive and less comparative information but it, at the same time, involves the expenditure of less time, money and energy.

In the book *Social Survey in Town and Country Areas*, Herman N. Morse has accepted the following steps in the scientific method of social survey:

1. Definition of the purpose or object.
2. Definition of the problem to be studied.
3. The analysis of this problem in a schedule.
4. The delimitation of the area or scope.
5. Examination of all documentary sources.
6. Field work.
7. Arrangement, tabulation and statistical analysis of the data.
8. The interpretation of the results.
9. Deduction.
10. Graphic expression.

Social surveys are carried on by official or non-official bodies with a set purpose or object, for example, to explore particular facts regarding a particular problem. This problem should also be well defined and precise. Clarity of the problem is the *sine qua non* of all scientific research. Now each problem involves several important aspects which should be minutely studied. Hence, after defining the problem, it should be analysed in a schedule. Then, the researcher should delimit the area of scope or survey. Without this delimitation, survey would be neither possible nor useful. For example, there can be no general survey of the working conditions of the labourers. Only the working conditions of the labourers at a particular factory or city may be studied. Now actual survey starts. This is a two-fold job, first, examination of documentary sources and second, field work. Examination of documentary sources is table work and if done properly, it will save much labour besides clarifying the actual lines of field work. The field work involves on the spot enquiries from the persons concerned. For this, the surveyor should visit the area of survey and gather necessary information in the preplanned schedule. After the gathering of the data through the above mentioned steps, facts are systematically arranged, tabulated and analysed. These results are now to be interpreted. This requires a statistically keen understanding of the problem and an objective approach. In fact, interpretation of the results is the most important step in a survey. This interpretation helps in the deduction of useful principles. Finally, the results are graphically expressed so that the whole thing may be understood at a glance.

As is evident from the meaning and purpose of social survey, this method has certain limitations. It studies only one part of the society. In it the study of the working of the lower classes is made something of a specialty. Obviously enough, in social survey, there is no endeavour to obtain detailed information about the middle and the upper class people.

But to be limited is no defect in any scientific method. The scientific method invariably studies only a delimited subject, a fact which constitutes its limitation, but it is, at the same time, the secret of its success and validity. It is for this reason that the survey method yields organised, systematic and scientific information about the problem, on the basis of which, programmes for social development and social reconstruction can be formed. It also protects the society from becoming disintegrated. Information regarding different aspects of social institutions and society is supplied by the use of the survey method.

SOCIAL RESEARCH

Another important method of rural study is social research. Social research is the discovery of new truths about society. It is a systematic method of discovering new facts or verifying old facts, their sequences, inter-relationship, causal explanations and natural laws. In this way, social research or investigation discovers new facts about social activities, social circumstances, social assumptions, social groups, social values or social institutions etc. and investigates the old facts on these subjects. It locates inter-relationship or causal relations among social incidents. It locates those natural laws which stimulate different phenomena in social life.

In this way the objective of social research is to formulate general laws by collection, analysis, interpretation and generalisation of facts, having studied social incidents and activities, and to predict on the basis of these general laws as well as to indicate future changes and reactions. The aim of social research is obviously and purely theoretical and scientific, lacking any direct relation with human welfare.

Social research is, by nature, scientific. Its aim is to gather fresh knowledge and to verify the knowledge which has been obtained. It is not connected with practical and immediate social planning or social engineering nor with ameliorative and therapeutic measures. It is not concerned with administrative changes and refinements of administrative procedure as with social reforms.

There are the following four steps in the method of social research:

1. Forming a hypothesis.
2. Observation and collection of data.
3. Classification and organisation of collected data.
4. Generalisation.
5. Verification of general laws and examination of their truth.

Social research starts with the formulation of a most probable hypothesis regarding a particular problem. For example, in order to investigate the relation of broken family with crimes, one may form a hypothesis that broken family is a cause of crime. The result of the research will either prove or disprove this hypothesis. The next step in social research will be the observation of several broken families and collecting data about criminal tendencies in them or observing criminals and finding out as to how many of them come from a broken family. This requires an alert, keen and objective approach in the researcher.

After observation and collection of the data it is classified and organised in that the implicit pattern may become sufficiently explicit. In the above mentioned example, the researcher will classify the families of the criminals under observation. Now, one may generalise broad principles on the basis of particular cases. By seeing that most of the criminals come from broken families or that the members of broken families generally exhibit criminal tendencies one may conclude that the broken families tend to breed crime. This proves the initial hypothesis. But before it is accepted as a scientific principle in sociology, it should be verified by many sociologists in different concrete situations.

Essential qualities of a social research worker

Compared to other fields of research, social research demands better social qualities in its research worker. He should be equipped with an appropriate knowledge of the subject; have experience of conducting research; possess knowledge of past research and historical facts corresponding to the present one and the ability to profit by the experiences of others. He should have knowledge of the necessary machines and be able to handle them. He should also be capable of choosing tools appropriate to the time, place and subject. But besides these qualities, which are characteristic of scientific research worker, the social research worker must also supplement them with some special qualities because while other scientists conduct their research in the laboratory, the social research worker has the society as his laboratory where he has to cooperate with individuals, depend on their co-operation. Hence, he must be possessed of an attractive, adaptable and cheerful disposition. He should be a master of etiquette, and be a skilled, intelligent, impartial, alert, active, balanced, good conversationalist, forbearing and constructively imaginative.

The community vs. regional approaches

The community and regional approaches are the two important approaches to the study of rural social life. The relative importance of these approaches depends upon the nature of rural habitats in a particular area.

The community approach

The community approach takes the village as a unit of study. It studies the various aspects of a single village both in its historical and contemporary context. To give an example of a village community study, one may investigate the study of Shamirpet by S.C. Dube. Shamirpet is a village in a Telugu speaking area. Dube's is a comprehensive study of the different aspects of village life, *i.e.*, historical, geographical and political setting and the social, economic and ritual structure. At the outset he stresses upon the nature of Indian culture as being ancient and rich. This large village, with its population of the various Hindu castes and considerable Muslims, has a complex form of integration. Indian village is always a unit in a wider social system and a part of an organized political society. Villages are governed by traditions both local and regional. The dress, speech, manner as well as lay-out of the village and the construction of houses follow the prescribed pattern of culture area. In the opinion of S.C. Dube a village hardly represents a culture area.

However, the three common characteristics of an Indian village which emerge out of several studies are:

(1) As a territorial as well as social, economic and ritual unit the village is a distinct entity.

(2) The village has composite population of various castes and religions.

(3) The members of the local group are bound together by ties of mutual obligations.

Regional approach

On the other hand, the regional approach takes into consideration a large territorial or geographical unit. The prominence of the region in the study of rural population arose on account of the desire of rural sociologists to view larger areas than the communities for their study on the basis of elemental factor of space. A region is a geographic area or unit with certain limits and bounds. It consists of several villages. The concept of a region plays an important role in geographical studies as it is a spatial unit. Thus, we have geographical cultural regions depending on the criteria of delineation.

From the sociological point of view Dr. Barnard defined a region as "an area" within which historical and environmental factors have combined to create a consciousness of individuality. This definition clearly indicates the three aspects of a region:

(1) The region exhibits homogeneity in more than one aspect.

(2) In a region people are aware of their uniqueness.

(3) A region is necessarily an area with a core.

Comparison

Thus, the regional and the community approaches both have their own merits and demerits. The community approach gives us a detailed and exhaustive picture of village life in a particular village. It allows us to discover varieties and diversities in village cultures of a given area. Thus, it allows us to conduct several small scale studies of several villages say in a region or in different regions which we may compare to arrive at broad uniformities. It gives us a broad glimpse of the mosaic of village social life. It allows us to pin-point the position of a village in a region as also in relation to its historical and contemporary context. It is the best suited method of study for isolated villages which have no contact with each other and also to know the inherent complexities of a particular village when we want its reconstruction or wish to introduce changes in its set-up.

However, the village community approach is time consuming and expensive. It does not further supply us with laws of rural development but its particularities.

It does not at once give us a wide picture of life in a region as it is based upon the study of the aspects of a particular village. Further, the villages studied are not always representative of the total culture of a region.

The superiority of village community approach over the regional approach lies in the fact, that it is a total study of all aspects of village life. On the other hand, the regional approach is mainly confined to a study of geographical divisions and is best suited for countries like U.S.A. where broad areas exhibit cultural uniformities. This can be further clarified by looking into the characteristics of a single region in U.S.A. such as the cotton belt. The cotton belt is a hot weather region situated in the South-Eastern part of U.S.A. It is said that almost all the economic and social activities of the rural people in the south are attuned to the rhythm of cotton production, certain times are busy and certain times are slack. Churches, recreation groups and other organisations plan their activities according to the processes of cotton cultivation. Rural schools may not open until cotton is harvested. The traditional southern hospitality may have been the by-product of the periods when there were little pressure of work and people could visit one another at length. The cotton belt has a sharply defined class system with the plantation owner operating at the top of the social pyramid and the mass of tenants, sharecroppers, and labourers, at the other rungs. Many sociologists have associated the rate of illiteracy and generally low level of living in the region to its class structure. The Negro has been associated with the cotton culture and has influenced many phases of life in the south despite his general lack of education and economic position. His contributions are notable in the field of art, literature, music and humour. Most cotton is grown with one horse implements and hand labour. The cotton belt has resisted change and long remained a male economy. For last 3 to 4 decades mechanization has entered into this area.

Thus, the regional approach gives us the best ecological study of life in a broad territory and serves the purpose of rural sociology in establishing broad laws of development. But, it cannot account for minute cultural diversities wherever they exist.

QUESTIONS FOR EXERCISE

1. Discuss the methods employed in the study of rural India. What defects do you find in them?

2. What method or methods will you use to study the social structure of village community in India? Give reasons.

3. Discuss two important methods of rural social research and show how far they differ from urban study methods?

4. Discuss the relative merits and demerits of the community and regional approach in the study of rural life.

5. What is the community approach to the study of rural sociology? How does it differ from other approaches?

5

THE VILLAGE COMMUNITY

When man was ignorant of the art of agriculture, he was compelled to wander in search of food and he could not settle down at any one place. Even today the nomadic tribes do not lead a settled life. Gradually, as man acquired skill and knowledge. In agriculture, he became proficient in procuring all his needs from the same tract of land, which eliminated the necessity of ceaseless wandering. Secondly, fertile land was not available everywhere with the result that people settled permanently when they came across some fertile area and became engaged in farming. In this way, when some families lived as neighbours in the same area, shared in each other's joys and sorrows and joined hands in the struggle against the physical elements, a community feeling originated in them and this marked the foundation of village communities. It was natural that an economic organisation would have developed where the people lived together in the rural community. Some laws about social relations, conduct and mode of living came into being which, after being habitually obeyed by the people became traditional dogmas. A village community can, therefore, be defined as a group of persons permanently residing in a definite geographical area and whose members have developed community consciousness and cultural, social and economic relations which distinguish them from other communities.

THE GROWTH OF VILLAGE COMMUNITY

The growth of village community is not caused by any one factor. Various factors like topographic, economic and social, have been active participants in this growth. A brief survey of the important factors in the growth of village community will explain the growth of village communities.

1. Topographical Factors

Topographical factors in the growth of village community include all those geographical factors which cause different families to migrate and settle in some particular locality. The more important of this kind of factors are land, water and climate.

(1) Land. The most important topographical factor with respect to permanent village community is land. In this both the fertility and the layout of land are important. It is difficult to carry on agriculture on land which is rocky and uneven. If the land is completely infertile and sandy then the village cannot easily develop there. In the desert of Sahara and Arabia vegetation and habitation are equally scarce. On the other hand, one can observe villages at every two or three miles in the plains of the Ganges and Jamuna. The obvious reason for this difference is the plain surface and the fertility of the land in these plains. The village communities settled on fertile land are more developed because they are more prosperous. Hence, the village communities in Punjab are more developed than those in some other parts of India. The villages show signs of prosperity by their larger size. The smaller rural communities in the mountainous terrain are not so well off in respect of the economic conditions. The layout of the land is such that, apart from the exigency of obtaining food grains, even, suitable area for residential building is at a premium. It is much easier to construct houses in the plains than in a mountainous terrain. It is equally difficult to live in houses in the deserts where there are frequent sandstorms.

(2) Water. The facility of water has to do with the growth of a village community at any particular locale. It is almost inconceivable that villages can come up where water is not available. Besides water required for the daily recurring needs of men, like drinking, bathing, washing etc., the villages must use it for irrigating the farms. As the rivers are a perennial source of water the village communities which exist on riverbanks are particularly prosperous and well-developed. In India the villages along the banks of the Ganges are in a much better condition than those which are seeking out a miserable existence in the deserts and hills. If water is scarce, not much use can be made of even the most fertile and cultivable land. In the desert, where water is not easily available the villages are scattered far and wide. In the Oasis where water can be found some palm trees and grass grow and the villages crop up. Greatest cultures of the world have grown and developed along the banks of the mightiest rivers. But those rivers which are apt to flood their banks are not likely to encourage the settlement of any permanent village community anywhere within their vicinity. The banks of some rivers are a quagmire for miles around in which dense forests grow up. In Africa such areas are not at all conducive to the growth of a village community and most of the population is found in a barbaric state. There can be no vegetation in the absence of water and even animal husbandry is not possible in such areas. Even areas rich in minerals are no attraction for the people to form a community and settle permanently if there is no water.

(3) Climate. The climate of a place is also an important factor in the growth of village communities. A temperate climate is the most favourable to the health of man as well as to agriculture. Thus, the village communities of these areas are the most prosperous, cultured and developed. Man cannot lead a natural and proper life in areas of extreme climate. Hence, village communities inhabiting the Equator and the Polar region are bound to exhibit extremely undeveloped and barbaric conditions. In warm climate, people become supine and lazy. In

India this is another operative factor which has been the cause of the low living standard in the village communities. The village communities of Europe are in a far better condition than their counterparts in India. The progress which science has made has, to a great extent, counteracted the effect of climate upon urban life. In London, people can move about in their homes in single shirt even in extremely cold weather because the houses can be kept warm through scientific devices. But the villages of Europe are, even in this era, exposed to the vagaries of the climate against which man cannot rebel nor do anything. In this way, the growth of village communities is everywhere profoundly influenced by the climate.

2. Economic Factors

The state of development of agriculture, economy and cottage industries is very much important among the economic factors which offer positive assistance in the growth of village communities.

(i) Condition of Agriculture. Even today the mainstay of the village communities is agriculture and thus their growth depends upon the state of agriculture. The phrase 'state of agriculture' means the state of production by farming. If farming yields a fair amount of produce then the village communities will be prosperous and they will have more time to engage in cultural activities. If, on the other hand, the members of a village community have to exert themselves to the point of exhaustion in order to get just enough to keep body and soul together, their social condition degenerates along with their economic condition. In those countries of the scientific world where agricultural production has increased due to inventions and favourable natural conditions the village communities are in an advanced stage of development. The village communities of the United States of America are exemplary in this respect. In India, the village communities in states like Punjab are more developed due to greater production in agriculture than in any other part of the country. On the other hand, the village communities in hilly or infertile areas are in a very poor, disintegrated and at times precarious condition.

(ii) Rural Economy. Besides agricultural production, the village economy is another important economic factor in the growth of village communities. If greater production is to be achieved in agriculture then animals of good breed and proper implements like good ploughs, good seeds and good manure will have to be acquired by the farmer, for which he needs money. Secondly, besides greater agricultural production, there is also the need for adequate consumption. It is necessary that the farmers should have the facility of being able to raise loans in times of need. If the creditor is allowed to keep the farmer always under his thumb and there are no proper facilities for marketing, the farmer will always remain in poverty, however much he may produce. For this reason it is necessary that in order to set the rural economy on right lines there should be co-operative societies for capital good, seeds, ploughs, implements and manures and sale of the agricultural produce in markets. In India institutions like co-operative banks, co-operative seed stores, co-operative ware-houses and community projects have led to an improvement in the condition of the agriculturists. In a village community, a prosperous and organised economy is essential for the growth and development of other occupations and cottage industries. Moreover, there should be proper arrangements for the purchase of raw materials and machines for the cottage industries and for selling the products of the industries.

(iii) Cottage industries. Cottage industries are a very important economic factor in the growth of the village community. In the village the cottage industries are connected with the manufacture of hand-spun cloth, ropes, baskets, toys, gur and molasses etc. While on the one hand, these cottage industries provide a means of livelihood to landless people, they also offer means of utilisation of the farmers and female labour in productive activities. In India the farmer is completely unoccupied for a very long period in the year. Besides this, the old and disabled people should also be able to utilise their time in some profitable occupations. They can quite easily spin cotton. This will not only improve their financial condition but will also lead to proper utilisation of their time.

3. Social Factors

Social factors in the growth of village community include peace, security, co-operation, intelligence and labour etc.

(i) Peace. For a permanent and healthy development of the village community it is essential that there should be external and internal peace. In countries where there exists an atmosphere of perpetual unrest and dark clouds of war are always hovering on the horizon; the development of village communities is hampered.

(ii) Security. Peace is based on security, the permanent growth of village communities being impossible in the absence of the latter. Security includes various kinds like security from disease, security of business, security of agriculture, security of property and security in the other activities of life. There cannot be any permanent development in areas where there is unceasing strife, looting and murder because the destructive forces will obviate all constructive plans. Actually, permanent village communities grow only in places which are not, in any way, ruinous to life and property. Agriculturists and villagers also need security from such natural catastrophes like famine, epidemics, excessive rains, floods etc. In this regard the government shoulders a very heavy responsibility.

(iii) Co-operation. Community development is difficult to achieve when there is no co-operation. There are many activities in a village which depend upon the collective co-operation of the whole community and cannot be entrusted to the responsibility of anyone individual. Such activities are public health, security, peace and proper use of public property as well as other allied activities. In these the people of the village co-operate and bring about a communal development of the people and no matter how favourable the geographic conditions, it is difficult to achieve permanent development of the rural communities without a proper co-operation of the whole community.

(iv) Intelligence and labour. The biggest single social factor responsible for the growth of a permanent village community is the labour of the people. Ultimately, the development of the village communities depends upon the intelligence and the labour of the villagers. Lacking this they cannot face natural exigencies of life and problems concerning agriculture etc. They cannot increase agricultural output nor profit by the scientific discoveries nor understand the theories of social welfare. The credit for the improved conditions of village communities must go to their efforts and intelligence. It is due to these two factors that the village of the Western countries are prosperous and happy and it is the absence of these two factors which has left the Indian villages in their backward state.

A permanent rural community can develop only when all these topographical, economic and social factors are found to coexist and are readily available. Each of these three factors makes important contribution to this end.

4. Ecological factors

Ecology has a significant effect upon the life of man. Steiner writes that the importance of ecology is evident in the organisation and development of communities. The social order of any community is affected by the structure of the land surface, means of transportation, kinds of industries and the entire economic order. These factors also determine the limit of its development. The way of living of different people differs from village to village according to the variation in ecological factors.

The following are the more important ecological elements influencing village community:

(i) Population. The life in a village is considerably influenced by its population. When population increases, the villages are denoted by the term town while a further increase leads to the same unit being called a city because the increase in population also means the construction or establishment of markets, increase in the number of shops, where new commodities are available, the opening of schools and colleges, increase in the number of those belonging to the middle class, and the arrangement of police and other security measures. All these are nothing but the external characteristics of a town. Even the types of the different elements of the population influence the life of the people. The cultural and social life of a village which is inhabited by the people of the Hindu, Muslim and Christian communities differs from the social and cultural life of a village in which the people belong to the same community. In India the difference in the social life in villages inhabited by Hindus and those inhabited by Muslims can be observed. The life in the tribal villages is of an entirely different type. The mutual relation between different groups of the population also influences the life of the villages. In a village the general social relations are also considerably influenced by the relations of the landlords and agriculturists, Hindus and Muslims, the rich and the poor.

(ii) Occupation. The occupation of the village people also affects the rural life of the village. The social and economic life in a village where persons are predominantly agriculturists differs from the social and economic life of a village inhabited by weavers. Some difference between their economic activities and mobility is obvious.

(iii) Distance from the town. The village community is also influenced considerably by the factor of its distance from the town. The villages which are at a great distance from the town are unable to obtain such commodities from the town as cosmetics, new clothes, fashionable objects etc. The social life of such people is based on ancient dogmas. Their economic life is more static. Their social life is more organised and they attach much importance to religion in India. There is a marked difference between the life of the people who live in dense forests and high mountains, and that of people living within a stone's throw of big cities like Calcutta and Bombay on the plains. The towns exert a lot of influence upon the villages which form their hinterland because the business of the village depends upon the town and the villagers come into closer contact with the town people. In such villages the social, economic and moral life of the people is influenced to a great extent by the towns. Many of the people living in villages near such industrial cities as Calcutta, Bombay, Kanpur etc., migrate to these cities and enlist as labourers and are, in the process, compelled to leave their families in the village. In the materialistic and ambivalent atmosphere of the cities they suffer much moral degeneration and its effect is communicated by them to other persons in the villages. On the other hand, their economic condition improves because they can get work in the town and it is through them that many occupations come into being. Milk, vegetables, fruits, ghee, food grains etc., are transported from the village and sold at a good price in the towns. People living in a village in the vicinity of a town are more intelligent, clever, business-minded, prosperous and progressive. Their social life is more disintegrated. Egoistic, rationalistic, materialistic and such other tendencies, as are abundant in the town, grow in them.

(iv) Social Organisation. The fourth important factor which influences the village community is social organisation. In Indian villages where social organisation is based upon the caste system are easily distinguishable from the villages inhabited by tribes whose social organisation is based on the joint family system. In organised villages the occupation, social status, economic condition and standard of living are determined by the caste. Often the untouchables live segregated from the village, their entry into the village is controlled by numerous taboos and social restrictions. Dormitories are a special feature of the tribal villages based on joint family system. In these people there is more intense community feeling. The head of the biggest joint family is the ruler of the village.

(v) Geographical location. Besides the above mentioned elements, the geographical location of a village also affects its life to a considerable extent. In the villages situated in forests, mountains, plains, deserts, or in the polar regions there is apparently a marked difference in respect of their social, economic, cultural and political life, and in such other aspects as dietary habits, occupations, clothing, living etc. Among them the villages in the plains are more prosperous and organised, whereas the life of the people living in the mountains is generally rigorous, poor and superstitious.

In fact, the ecological elements are not identical in all villages. Thus, the above mentioned ecological elements affecting village community present only the general laws which are modified by particular conditions.

SOCIOLOGICAL IMPORTANCE OF VILLAGES IN INDIA

From the viewpoint of sociology the village and the town differ in respect of their importance. In our society the major features of the importance of the village from the sociological point of view are given below:

1. A village is a unit of society. In India there are more than half a million villages. According to Max Weber, the German scholar, "India has always been a country of villages." 77 per cent of the Indian population lives in villages. India is predominantly an agricultural country. Thus, in every respect the future of India depends upon the villages.

2. Intensity of primary and familial relations. The relations between the primary groups and families in the villages are intimate. The family fulfils the needs of its members in all aspects of their life and exercises control over them. It is through the family that the new members are initially introduced to the customs, conventions and culture of the society. In this way the village people hold family as an institution having revered status and the result is that individuality does not develop properly in the members of a family. Due to limited contact with the external world, their viewpoint is narrow and they are aggressively opposed to violent change. In the village the relations among the people are direct and intimate so that often the entire village is organised like a family.

3. Simple and economical life. The life of the villagers is simple and economical. They have very limited needs. The spirit of ambition and competition is generally absent and they are not constantly devoured by a consuming desire for progress as is the case with their urban counterparts.

4. Preservers of the ancient culture of the community. From the sociological viewpoint also the villages are important because they preserve the ancient culture of society. India is an agricultural country. The life of the villagers depends considerably upon natural forces due to their occupation, which is agriculture, and thus they worship natural forces like the sun, rain etc. They are sometimes observed resorting to magic in order to gain the assistance of these forces. The villages in India still exhibit faith in the doctrine of *karma*, a fundamental principle in Indian culture, and lead a simple and natural life dominated by sacrifice, theistic tendency and the importance of religion in every aspect of life.

5. Ideal democracy. In ancient times the Indian village was an ideal democracy. Life in each village is self-dependent. Most of the people are agriculturists, and besides agriculture the farmer is quite capable of handling the work generally done by a carpenter, blacksmith, mason, veterinary surgeon, wood-cutter and sometimes even a weaver, in some developed villages these occupations are carried on by different people but whatever the conditions, all the needs of the villages, are generally fulfilled in the village itself. In the village even today the sense of neighbourhood is not ignored and is given considerable importance. The community of ideals and customs and social forbearance is even today an important feature of the village. In its long history, the Indian society retained its strength and organisation as long as the villages were well-knit and well-organised. From the medieval ages till now the condition of the village has continuously deteriorated. But now, after the country has become independent, the work of social reconstruction is being implemented with the village as the unit and the basis. Thus, from the sociological point of view, the villages are more important than the towns.

In this way, the importance attributed to the villages is far greater than the importance which may be attributed to the towns of India. It is for this reason that thinkers like Mahatma Gandhi accorded a central place to rural reconstruction in the overall plan for the reconstruction of the entire country. The Ram Rajya of Mahatma Gandhi is based on the uplift of the village. The Indian Government have also accepted the importance of the development of rural industries and rural reconstruction. Social and economic reconstruction of India's rural communities is being implemented through the establishment of co-operative societies and community development plans. India is democracy, hence the future of the country depends upon the villages because the major portion of the population lives in the villages and the country cannot hope to achieve any progress without removing the social and economic backwardness of the villages. Social and economic reconstruction of the country can be achieved only by a social and economic reconstruction of the villages.

CHARACTERISTICS OF VILLAGE COMMUNITY

A major characteristic of an Indian village is the small number of its people, another characteristic is the intimate relation of its people with nature. Although, it is incorrect to assert that agriculture is the sole occupation of the villages, it is the major occupation in villages everywhere. In the words of T.L. Smith, "Agriculture and the collecting enterprises are the bases of the rural economy, farmer and countryman are almost synonymous terms."[1] Besides these characteristics, the people of the village also exhibit a homogeneity of population due to which they do not frequently come into conflict with each other and maintain mutual intimacy and harmony. Based on these characteristics of villages, the features peculiar to rural life are as follows:

1. Village is a community. The villagers satisfy all their needs in the village. They have a sense of unity and a feeling of amiability towards each other. In this way, the village is a community because its people have community consciousness.

2. Village is a primary institution. The development of the villages is influenced considerably by the life of the village. In this way village is a primary institution.

1. Smith, T. L., *The Sociology of Rural Life*, Harper and Bros. (New York, 1947), p. 16.

3. Faith in religion. Faith in religion and duties is found in the life of the villagers. The major occupation of the countryman is agriculture in pursuing which man has to struggle constantly with Nature. Very often Nature lays waste the result of very hard labour on his part and the farmer cannot comprehend its mystery. Hence, he acquires an attitude of fear and awe towards natural forces, starts worshipping them and even tries to gain command over them by magic. In this way faith in religion and sometimes even in magic is found in the life of the villagers.

4. Neighbourhood is very important in village life. Not many people live in village and thus they assist each other as and when any occasion arises in their struggle of life. They are generally in need of one another's assistance. Secondly, there is not enough of individuality and speed in the life of the village to disable one from paying attention to another. Hence, neighbourhood is of great importance in a village and neighboured have intimate relation with each other.

5. Joint families. Another characteristic of the life of the village is the joint family system. In the village the family has strict control over the individual. Generally, the father is the head and representative of the family and is also invested with the duty of maintaining discipline among the members. His orders are obeyed by all the members of family. In marriage, festivals, business etc., it is he who manages the affairs of the family. All the members of the family share the burden of the family occupation. The men plough the field, the women harvest the crops and the children graze the cattle. In this way, working together, the villagers maintain a sense of co-operation among themselves. Much attention is directed towards the preservation of the family honour and utmost care is taken to observe and maintain the traditions of the family.

6. Group feeling. In the life of the villagers group feeling occupies an important place. They respect the judgment of their superiors and obey the orders of their elders and the Panchayat. Society, caste and panchayat have control over the individual. People are afraid of being publicly criticised or condemned.

7. The villagers lead a simple and plain life. Hence, phenomena like theft, misconduct, chicanery etc., are not found to occur very often in the villages. The villagers have limited means and they do not license ostentation. In the villages people who go about in a manner calculated to attract attention are not looked upon with respect. Even in the materialistic age of today the generally accepted ideal in the village is a simple life and high thinking. In the village every individual endeavours to attain and observe the ideals of his family and caste. The villagers are a simple and plain people. They are incapable of making a false pretence at cultured behaviour and gaudiness, nor are they capable of boasting. They have sympathy for man and want to meet each other on a natural and human footing. Their life is tranquil, peaceful and plain. Mental conflicts and complexities are almost absent. They spend a natural life in the lap of nature. In their life there is a determined pattern and method for everything so that they are spared of the labour of continually pondering over them. Certain norms governing marriage and business etc., are irrevocably fixed. Hence, there is no occasion for mental conflict. Trade in the village is not carried out on a large scale and consequently there is not much specialisation of occupations. The small needs of life are fulfilled by the farmers themselves. Class conflict is generally lacking. Rich and poor, small and big, high and low, all live in an atmosphere of natural co-operation and accept the discipline of the village. The level of morality in villages is high. Any girl in the village is generally treated as a daughter by most of the male members of the village, by the very virtue of her being a member of the village.

In this way, life in the village is more natural and orderly. There are not many occasions for conflict between father and son, master and servant, creditor and debtor, husband and wife, mother-in-law and daughter-in law etc. In spite of the fact that the income of the villagers is rather low, their life continues in a vein of satisfaction because of its very simplicity.

CHANGE IN VILLAGE LIFE

But the elements of village life which have been delineated above, can be found to exist only in those villages which have remained unaffected by the influence of the towns. Otherwise, as a general rule, these elements are vanishing from the village life. The community consciousness in village life is steadily decreasing. The control of the caste panchayats is almost non-existent. The villagers who work in the towns as labourers, acquire such habits as drinking, prostitution, telling lies, unnecessary show and needless boasting, and when these villagers return to their native village they spread extreme immorality. The village youths studying in the towns also become addicted to irresponsible and sedentary habits and when they exhibit the same habits in their villages the other simple-minded adolescents are also corrupted. The village belle living in the town is even more adept at the use of cosmetics and on her return to the village they too spread this habit among her sisters in the village. Now-a-days the villagers are using aids to beauty in a larger measure than before and the level of health in the villages is fast deteriorating because milk and its bye- products from the villages are sold in the towns and secondly, the money thus earned is being wasted on useless things. Though, education is spreading in the villages, it has led to turning their back to the old ideal of simple living and high thinking. Even though they may appear plain in their dress and way of living due to poverty and simple due to insensitivity, they do not have the least scruples in adulterating the commodities which they sell.

The convention of hospitality is no longer observed. Sex relations are marked by a lade of responsibility. The joint family is fast disintegrating. The number of thefts, abortions, murders, assaults, litigation etc. are also increasing. The old customs are being violated. The bonds of caste and society have been disregarded. Individualism, materialism and rationalism are increasing. Hence, the only elements which now characterise life are agriculture which is the major occupation of the villagers, small population, lack of transport facilities, lack of scientific comforts, mud houses, unmetalled roads and natural environment etc.

Actually, the villagers everywhere are at present passing through a transitional period. The old relations, bonds and ties have fallen into disfavour and they cannot be reinstated in their original form. Even now the villages can be given an equally simple if not simpler, plainer and higher quality of life by improving the conditions in the village, through the establishment of panchayats, spread of education, economic reform in agriculture etc. Rural reconstruction through scientific methods is very essential for this. In all the agricultural countries in the world, this matter has received considerable attention and much progress has been made in Russia and China. It is a matter of great satisfaction that the Indian government is not oblivious of this. Crores of rupees are being spent on new plans of rural reconstruction directed towards the improvement of life in villages. As a result of these endeavours the village will once again become as well organised and integrated as before.

QUESTIONS FOR EXERCISE

1. Define village community. Mention the regional, economic and social factors which contribute to the growth of permanent village community.
2. Explain the concept of a village. Explain various views about little community.
3. State the ecological factors which influence the life of persons in your town or village.
4. Point out the sociological importance of the village.
5. Describe the main features of rural society.
6. Analyse the structure of rural community organisation.

Table 1: *Distribution of Villages in India According to Population*

State / Union Territory	Less than 1,000	1,000 to 1,999	2,000 to 4,999	5,000 to 9,999	More than 10,000	Total
1	2	3	4	5	6	7
Andhra Pradesh	14,085	6,464	5,609	1,058	163	27,379
Bihar	49,617	10,841	5,842	1,054	192	67,546
Gujarat	9,814	5,108	2,725	418	49	18,114
Haryana	3,275	1,883	1,346	221	20	6,745
Himachal Pradesh	16,348	364	93	3	—	16,807
J & K	5,017	1,046	393	20	1	6,477
Karnataka	18,631	5,239	2,722	401	35	27,028
Kerala	7	13	72	222	905	1,219
M.P.	61,029	8,118	2,046	155	4	71,352
Maharashtra	26,101	8,954	3,604	579	16	39,354
Manipur	1,758	174	90	12	1	2,035
Meghalaya	4,793	85	24	—	—	4,902
Nagaland	921	143	47	1	—	1,112
Orissa	40,710	4,561	1,234	47	1	46,553
Punjab	8,146	2,819	1,256	120	1	12,342
Rajasthan	26,823	5,468	2,335	321	21	34,968
Sikkim	372	60	8	—	—	440
Tamil Nadu	5,698	4,570	4,381	1,000	182	15,831
Tripura	265	253	274	56	8	856
U.P.	83,235	20,380	8,148	751	52	112,566
West Bengal	25,319	7,538	4,383	702	82	38,024
Andaman & Nicobar	460	23	8	—	—	491
Arunachal Pradesh	3,176	63	16	2	—	3,257
Chandigarh	12	5	7	—	—	24
Dadra & Nagar Haveli	33	27	7	3	—	70
Delhi	54	74	71	15	—	214
Goa, Daman & Diu	185	102	90	34	—	412
Lakshadweep	1	1	4	1	—	7
Mizoram	629	62	30	—	—	—
Pondicherry	209	48	28	6	—	291
India	4,06,723	94,486	46,892	7,202	1,834	557,137

6

RURAL-URBAN CONTRAST

Difficulties in Comparison

It is very difficult to compare rural and urban society, and this has prompted Gist and Halbert to write, "Thus, the familiar dichotomy between 'Rural and Urban' is more of a theoretical concept than a division based upon the facts of community life."[1] Generally, these difficulties are the following:

1. There is no universal definition of village and town. The major difficulty which confronts any comparison between the societies of village and town is that there is no universal definition which can clearly distinguish between a town and a village. One cannot say just where a village ends and a town begins. If a castle is constructed twenty miles away from Bombay, it could not be called in town. If the atmosphere of a village is created in the middle of a town, the town will not be called or thereby become a village. Even the criteria for designating the names of village or town in any country are different in different contexts. Before a place can be called a town it must possess a population of 2000 in France, 2500 in America, 5000 in India and in Japan. Secondly, any place is considered to be town not only on the basis of its population. There are many other factors but there is no universally recognised definition of village and town. In the words of Bergel, "Everybody seems to know what a city is but not one has given a satisfactory definition."[2]

2. There is a difference of degrees between village and town. Actually, the difference between town and village is merely one of degree, as a result of which it is very difficult to make a clear distinction between the two. Every village possesses some elements of the town while every town exhibits certain features characteristic of the village. MacIver and Page are quite right when they say, "But between the two there is no sharp demarcation to tell where the city ends and country begins."[3]

3. The environments of the city and village are different. The environments of the village and the town are not the same. And, in the same town, a variety of environments can be seen. Thus, how is one to compare villages and towns? Which

---

1. Gist and Halbert, *Urban Society* (1954), p. 3.
2. Bergel, *Urban Sociology,* McGraw Hill Series (1955), p. 5.
3. McIver and Page. *Society,* p. 311.

of the mutually conflicting or contradicting environments is to be considered characteristic of a town and which not, and which of them is to be compared with the environment of the village?

4. Both village and town change. Yet another obstacle in the comparison of village and town is the fact that both keep on changing. Each influences the other. Industrialisation has brought a complete change in the form of the village, and this change is continuing. Amidst this change it is difficult to decide how long it should be considered a village and when should it be allowed to pass into the category of towns. With the advent of new factors like electricity and education, to mention only two, the distinction between village and town is being steadily diminished. In respect of most of the characteristics of population, like birth-rate and family-size, both resemble each other.

DIFFERENCE BETWEEN RURAL AND URBAN SOCIETY

But, in spite of the existence of these difficulties, sociologists have shown distinction between village and town societies. The chief among them are the following.

1. Difference in Social Organisation

The biggest distinction between rural and urban society is that of social organisation. These exhibit differences in the following respects:

(i) *Family.* The families in the villages and towns exhibit the following differences: (a) In the villages the families are comparatively stronger than the families in the towns, where greater importance is attached to the individual than to the family, (b) In the villages the system of joint family is to be found in greater number than in the towns, (c) In the villages there is greater control, intimacy and organisation than in the families in towns, (d) In the towns, as compared with villages the functions of the family are more steadily decreasing.

(ii) *Marriage.* In respect of marriage there are the following differences in the societies of villages and towns: (a) In the towns there is a preponderance of love marriages in comparison with the villages, (b) In towns, as compared to the villages, one finds a greater number of divorces, (c) In the towns rather than the village, greater freedom is allowed in the selection of life partner.

(iii) *Condition of women.* Generally, the women in the villages are not much, if at all educated, and their social status also is low.

(iv) *Neighbourhood.* In the villages the neighbourhood has a greater importance than it has in the towns. In the towns sometimes people do not even know their neighbours.

(v) '*We are feeling*'. In the rural community the 'we-feeling' is found to be far stronger than in the urban community. The influence of the community on the individual in the village is greater than in the towns.

(vi) *Inequality of classes.* The inequality of classes is much more demarcated in the towns than in the villages and there are correspondingly more conflicts in the towns. In the words of Bogardus, "Class extremes characterize the city."[4]

2. Differences in social restrictions

A great difference is evident between the social control characteristic of the rural and urban societies. About the social control in the village, Biesanz and Biesanz write, "In the rural community custom is the king, the folkways and mores control most of behaviour."[5] On the other hand, the society does not exercise much control over the individuals in the urban society. In the crowds and the high velocity of life in the towns no one has time to look to another. In the words of Kingsley Davis, "He can escape the oppressive control of any primary group when he wishes, simply by disappearing into the sea of strangers."[6] But the control of police, law, court etc., is greater in the towns than in the villages.

3. Differences in social relationships.

The following distinctions between the rural and urban population in respect of their social relations are evident:

(i) In comparison with the social relations found in the cities those in the villages are more personal. In the words of Gist and Halbert, "The cities encourages impersonal rather than personal relationship."[7]

(ii) In the villages the relation of the individual is usually with primary groups, family, near relations etc. In the towns their relations tend more towards secondary groups.

4. Differences in social interactions. The social interactions peculiar to the rural and urban societies exhibits the following distinctions:

(i) In comparison with town the social relations in the villages are far smaller in number and those that do exist are personal. On the other hand, the social relations in the town are numerous, of which most are indirect and impersonal.

(ii) In the towns but not in the villages to quite the same extent, division of labour and specialisation are found to exist. In this way the scope for social co-operation is far greater in the towns than in the villages.

(iii) The activity of competition has a far greater velocity in the towns than in the villages.

(iv) The conflict in the villages is usually direct while the conflict is comparatively indirect in the urban context.

(v) When compared to villages there is greater toleration in the towns and consequently a larger degree of accommodation.

---

4. Bogardus, *Sociology,* p. 144.
5. Biesanz and Biesanz. *Modern Society,* p. 144.
6. Davis, K., *Human Society,* p. 331.
7. Gist and Halbert, *Urban Society,* p. 263.

(vi) The process of assimilation takes place rather slowly in the villages as a result of a near absence of cultural difference. In the towns people of different cultures live side by side and thus the process of assimilation operates much faster.

5. Differences in social viewpoint. The following differences are found in the social viewpoints in rural and urban society:

(i) According to Newmeyer, "Rural culture tends to be conservative."[8] In the words of Ross, "The city is cosmopolitan whereas the country is nationalistic and patriotic."[9] In this way the village is more progressive than the town.

(ii) In the towns, more than the villages, people take interest and active part in politics.

(iii) In the villages greater importance is attached to religion and rituals than in the towns. Whereas the religion of the rural people is based upon faith, the religion in the city is relatively more based upon reason.

(iv) The villagers are more fatalistic than the urban people because the lives of the villagers are affected, to a very large extent, by natural forces while the urban people are equipped with scientific knowledge and techniques in handling natural calamities and catastrophes.

(v) There is more artificiality in the urban people than in the villagers. Bogardus has correctly written, "Rural people are frank, open and genuine; they scorn the artificiality of many phases of city life."[10]

6. Differences in social mobility and stability. There is greater social disorganisation in the towns than in the villages. To quote Sorokin and Zimmerman, "The rural community is similar to calm water in a pail and the urban community to boiling water in kettle. Stability is the typical trait for the one, mobility is typical for the other."[11] In this way, cities possess greater mobility than the villages.

7. Differences in economic life. There is great difference between the economic lives of the villages and towns. In this respect the major differences are the following:

(i) "Two fundamentally different modes of getting a living set the rural and urban worlds apart." In the villages the major occupation is agriculture while in the towns the major occupations are of an industrial nature.

(ii) Standard of living in the villages is lower than that of the towns because the means of earning money are limited in the villages. Besides making more money, the urban people are more prodigal than the villagers. In the words of Ross, "Country life, then suggests 'save'! city life suggests 'Speed!"[12] At the same time the villagers do not get much opportunity to spend whereas the man in the city is at his wits' end as to the means of making enough money to enable him to buy the commodities displayed for consumption.

---

8. Newmeyer, *Social Problems and the Changing Society*, D. Van Nostrand Co., Inc. New York, p. 63.
9. Ross, *Principles of Sociology*, p. 77.
10. Bogardus, *Sociology*, p. 77.
11. Sorokin and Zimmerman, *Principles of Rural Urban Sociology*, Henry Holt and Co. (New York, 1929), p. 44.
12. Ross, *Principles of Sociology*, p. 76.

8. Difference in cultural life. The cultural lives of the city and the country exhibit the following distinctions:

(i) Culture is more static in the villages than in the towns.

(ii) In the village the basis of culture is caste and purity. In the towns it has a secular basis.

(iii) Traditions have a very important place in rural culture, while urban culture does not attach much importance to them.

URBAN INFLUENCE ON RURAL SOCIETIES

The foregoing distinction between the urban and rural societies is apparent only in those rural societies which are far removed from the cities and which have remained immune from the influence of the latter. In India the influence of urban life can be clearly seen in rural societies in the vicinity of large cities like Calcutta, Bombay, Delhi etc. This influence is evident in such identical aspects like social structure, family organisation, food habits, standard of living, dress habits, cosmetics, religion, rituals, beliefs etc. A description of this influence will show those peculiarities of rural life which are in the process of transition:

1. Change in social life. The greatest influence of the city upon the social life of the villages has been upon the caste system. The relation between caste and profession is no longer necessary because the people are adopting new professions according to interest and profit, in place of the professions determined by the caste. Members of all castes have taken to shopkeeping. The work of a milkman is no longer confined to those who are traditionally connected with it. The business of food grains is now carried on by members of many castes, besides the one caste which had been set aside for this purpose. Members of the highest caste are seen working in many kinds of professions. The ancient mode of thinking in terms of untouchability does not prevail any longer. Intercaste marriage is still the exception rather than the rule but the restrictions placed upon the various castes regarding the normal exchange of social contact have now been lifted. This is true at least about the Brahmin, Kashatriya and Vaishya castes. The social laws about untouchability have lost a good deal of their former sting due to buses, railways and other modern means of transportation. The untouchables are demanding all kinds of rights which have been legally given to them, though even then villagers are as yet not prepared to give them equal rights in all respects.

2. Decrease in the influence of panchayats. Another effect of the city upon the social life of the village is evident in the way in which it has influenced the control of the panchayats in the village. The influence of the panchayats of the castes is gradually being lost because the punishment imposed by it is no longer considered obligatory while there is no fear of social extermination. Nevertheless the thoughts and conduct of the people in the village are still controlled to a certain degree by the family and the society. The form of the village panchayat has also undergone change because as a result of the influence of the city they are being disregarded.

3. Change in the family organisation. The city has influenced the organisation of the family in the rural community to a very large extent. In former times the families in the villages were well organised. The order of the elders was treated as a divine mandate. The elders arranged marriages. The family exercised significant control upon the conduct of the younger people. Whatever be the context, the honour of the family was invariably the first consideration. Generally, the system of joint family prevailed in which near relatives from the paternal side lived in co-operation. Now, this tradition of the joint family in slowly disappearing from the villages. The families are growing smaller and showing distinct signs of disintegration. The younger generation, when they return from the cities, treat their elders as conservative and do not tolerate their control. Not only in respect of marriage but even when it comes to thought and conduct, they consider the control of the elders as improper and despotic. The facilities and the comforts of the city like electricity, cinema, radio, newspapers parks, clubs, hotels, libraries, post offices, colleges, etc. are not available in the villages, due to which the educated youngmen of the villages develop a hatred and scorn for the life of the village and deem it better to become clerks in the city than to engage in agriculture in the villages. This is leading towards a complete disintegration of the erstwhile organisation of the family. Any young lady who has spent a few months in the city becomes proficient in the use of cosmetics and considers herself superior to her sisters in the village. Consequently, the other young ladies of the village also take to initiating the superficial airs of this model. Their conduct takes on a colourful and irresponsible attitude, and they desire greater freedom in their daily routine. When the villagers return from the city they describe the incidents which they had witnessed in the city, thus creating a craving for similar ways in the minds of the uninitiated boys of the village. Due to the influence of the city the power of the rural families has been destroyed, the organisation has broken down, the standard of morality has fallen, expensive habits have been acquired. Life has become more artificial and selfish. Individualistic, materialistic and atheistic tendencies are gaining ground.

4. Difference in means of transport and occupations. As a result of the influence of the city the means of transportation in village have undergone a radical change. Formerly, the people did not hesitate in walking twenty miles but now they spend hours waiting for a bus but they will not prefer to walk. The cycle is becoming extremely popular. The landlords and rich businessmen have started using cars. The roads are now repaired. People have also accepted rail travel. Along with the change in the means of transportation newer occupations have found their ways into the village life. Wheat grinding machine and the like are, more or less, a familiar sight in the villages. With the introduction of new agricultural implements the facilities for repairing them have also become available in the village. The blacksmiths, hair-dressers, gold smiths, carpenters etc., of the village have adopted modern tools in their work in preference to the old ones. The use of new implements in agriculture is becoming popular.

5. Change in modes of recreation and other facilities. Due to the influence of the city the means of recreation in the villages are on the increase. Radios and gramophones are becoming popular. Younger people can be seen playing football and volleyball. Cards, chess and other such games are also popular. Besides the means of recreation, the other facilities of life are also increasing in the villages due to the influence of the city. One often finds a doctor in a big village, and one is not surprised at the presence of electricity either. Schools are being opened in the villages and arrangements made for bringing such modern innovations as the open air theatres. Newspapers have access to villages which are near the towns, the people of such villages being in the habit of visiting the city whenever they have need for seeing a cinema or doing any shopping.

6. Change in the mode of living. The city has great influence upon the living, dress and food habits etc., of the rural people. The young men in the villages have started using collared shirts, bush shirts, coat and pantaloon, shoes, etc. The ladies wear coloured saries and blouses with deep plunging necklines. The children are also outfitted with urban types of dress. Utensils made of glass, aluminium and china clay are also being used in the village. The city has made popular the use of tea, betel, tobacco, vegetable ghee, cigarette, etc. Wrist watches, sun-glasses, fountain pen, torches and safety razors are being commonly used in the villages.

On the other hand, rural districts are essentially homogeneous. There is not much of social differentiation.

7. Social stratification. The principles of class and caste operate differently in rural societies from the way they operate in the urban world. There are four major differences between the pyramids of rural and urban area:

(1) The rural society is not classless, nevertheless the number of social classes is less in rural society than in urban society.

(2) The extremes of social pyramid are not so far apart in rural societies as in urban.

(3) It is not only that the range of social classes is less in rural society but that rural classes tend to be intermediate or "middle" classes. The city is, on the other hand, not only the home of the millionaire but also that of pauper.

(4) The caste principles in city are not so rigid as in the rural society, Movement from one class to another is easier in the urban context than in rural societies.

8. Social mobility. Sorokin and Zimmerman said, "The rural community is similar to calm water in a pail and the urban community to boiling water in a kettle." In rural areas the members are more strongly attached to their social status which is ascribed. In the urban area they are shifted from one status to another more often and more easily. This applies to social mobility, physical mobility and also occupational mobility.

9. Social interaction. The rural system of social interaction differs from that of the urban system. There are qualitative and quantitative differences in the social contacts of rural and urban people. The number of contacts in the country is much greater than in the city.

Sorokin and Zimmerman point out the important qualitative differences between rural and urban system as follows:

(i) The area of contact of the rurality is narrower and more limited than that of urban persons, (ii) The totality of contacts by the rural person consists more largely of personal and primary face-to-face contacts than those of the city dweller. They are more enduring.

10. Social solidarity. There is basic difference in the social solidarity and cohesion of rural and urban societies. The rural society has a unity based on similarities and informal and non-contractual relationships. Urban solidarity is based on differences and dissimilarities which arise out of division of labour and specialisation and formal contractual relations.

THE ROLE OF MIGRATION

Rural and urban societies form two ends of a continuum and they exist side-by-side and interact with one another in several ways.

Rural urban migration is a main form of rural-urban contact which is promoted by the development of transportation and means of communication.

There has been a great amount of migration of rural people to urban areas. The cause of migration mainly lies in rural unemployment. These rural migrants become exposed to city life in all its varied aspects. These rural migrants communicate their new experience to their rural relatives and friends and thus act as agents of contact between the rural and urban culture and social life. Rural-urban migration has three types of impact as regards urban influence over the rural society.

(1) There are villages in which sizeable number of people have sought employment in far-off cities. They live there leaving the members of their family in villages. In Madhopur it was noted that 75% of the total migrants send money regularly. Further, 83% visit the village from 4-5 times a year to once in two years. Some migrants have invested the money they have earned in the city in building houses or buying land in the villages. In such villages urban employment often becomes a symbol of higher social prestige.

(2) Most of urban impact relates to the villages near industrial cities like Bhilai. When an industrial town comes up amidst several villages, some villages are totally uprooted. The people who migrate to other villages create housing and adjustment problems. Thus, in the villages near an industrial town there is the problem of immigrants to the village.

(3) When a metropolis expands, it intrudes into some of the nearby villages.

Rural-urban migration, if it increases the number of contacts between the two habitats, provides a channel for constant cultural contact and cultural exchange. Temporary commuting by the vendors of the village or city people who live in rural suburbs keeps up the tempo of contact of the two habitats. Rural migration helps the urban areas with its necessary manual labour and the rural habitat gains in income. As the rural migrants travel small distances and keep up contact with their rural families they constantly travel between the two habitats.

Rural migrants spread the novel ideas of urban production process like the use of machinery and the novelties of urban social world like the various fashions in dresses etc. Rural migrants, by their glamorous description, create in the minds of the people who remain behind, a craze for urban ways of life. Thus, more and more people visit the city and bring back with them features of city life into the rural habitat. The migrants come into contact with diversified ideas about all aspects of life and become keen to adopt suitable ones to their native habitats so as to improve its conditions. Thus, they learn and begin to use hybrid seeds, pump sets to draw water, electric lights, radios etc., which bring the rural area a step nearer to an urban. Further, migrants set in motion a process of continuous and constant migration. Migrants also act as agents of trade and transit for many rural products like fresh vegetables, fruits etc.

Thus, although transport provides the necessary channels of contact it is rural-urban migration which establishes and maintains constant contact between the two forms of habitats.

ROLE OF TRANSPORT AND COMMUNICATION

Rural and urban habitats form the two halves of a continuum. While rural societies represent the natural aspects and its influence upon human life, the urban aggregates depict man's works of ingenuity and intelligence. Hence, the relationship between them is in the essential sphere of life.

Transport and communication means form the main artery which establishes essential social relations between the two forms of habitats. While it brings about changes in the structure of rural society as isolated and self-sufficient units, it supplies to the urban area all its essentials of existence. It may not be difficult for an Indian to understand the implications of the introduction of a bus service to a village not more than 5 miles away from a town or city. Before the introduction of transportation and communication the town was totally ignorant of the existence of village so near it and *vice versa*. This influence is as follows:

1. The basic factor affected by means of transportation is that of surplus agricultural produce and urban market. As the urban area is usually incapable of producing its agricultural requirements, it depends upon, the village for its essential supplies of perishable products like fruits and vegetables etc. Thus, urban areas provide gainful markets to the surplus village produce. Many a time it acts as an inducement for commercial enterprise and introduction of cash crops. Thus, the people of villages around Mandya in Mysore took to sugarcane production on a large scale due to efficient roads and means of transport. It also gives additional occupation and provides more opportunities for employment in the fields of dairying, production of fruits and vegetables etc.
2. In the second instance, transportation supplies the much needed labour force to the urban needs while it reduces rural unemployment to some extent.
3. The introduction of transportation creates the necessary relation between a village and the national government.

4. In the social sphere, it breaks up the essential framework of the rural social structure since youths essentially go out to urban areas in search of education and employment. It breaks up many of the essential prejudices of rural society. For example, people of all castes, even untouchables, must sit beside each other during travel by bus. It introduces new attractions to the rural people and breaks up the simplicity of rural social life. Rural people are attached to urban cinemas, hotels and other novelties and gradually a visit to a city becomes an essential point of pride in the rural society. The hitherto accepted norms and ways of life appear obsolete to an urban influenced rurality. In short, the impact of urbanisation upon rural life takes place. The novelties of urban social life say drinking coffee, wearing fashionable dresses, etc., enter into the rural social life. The generation gap in the rural society, which has remained hitherto unnoticed, becomes a principal cause for tension, clashes etc.

Folkways and mores lose their hold upon an urbanised rurality. Transportation introduces an element of rush into the placidity of rural society. Transport and communication increase the number of contacts between a village and a town and introduces the urban element of rush and time consciousness in the urban connected rurality life such as that of the vegetable seller and milk vendor etc. Urban contact increases the villager's knowledge about improvement of agriculture, animal husbandry etc. Contacts with a rural area also help in the shifting of ancillary industries to such areas.

Thus, while in developing countries transportation is a must and an essential part of any habitat since they depend upon technology and large scale production in every sphere of life, in traditional societies transportation forms a basic agent of rural-urban contact which introduces gradual changes in the social structure of economic framework. Rural urban contacts increase the monetisation of rural economy and society and open up additional avenues of money supply into the rural society. Transportation breaks up the inhibitions and rigidity of rural life and make it flexible and somewhat secular.

In short, transportation and communication results in successful rural-urban contacts. It reduces the hold of religion and folk beliefs upon rural people and introduces at least some aspects of the scientific attitude into the rural mentality.

RURAL-URBAN MIGRATION IN INDIA

Most of the studies of migration in India have revealed that the migration from rural to urban areas is very small in comparison to migration from one rural area to another. Migration by marriage is generally from one rural area to another. It is only in the search of occupation that migrants go to urban areas from the village. The speed however, is very slow. According to the Census of 1971 among the migrants in India 70.66% were from one rural area to another. The rural-urban migration was 14.88%, the urban-rural migration was barely 4.88%. In the study of rural-urban migration, four aspects have to be particularly studied. These are: 1. Rural to rural migration or rural turnover; 2. Rural to urban migration or push-pull activity; 3. Urban to urban migration or urban turnover; and 4. Urban to rural migration or reverse push back. According to the estimate by Zachariah, the rural-urban migration in India during the period 1951-1961 was 5.2 million. This is 8.4% of the 1951 urban population. According to a recent report India continues to be predominantly rural although its urban population increased by more than 49 million during the 1971-81 decade. The rural-urban distribution of the population obtained from the quick tabulation of provisional totals of the 1981 Census shows that 76.27 per cent of the population is rural.

The Census Commissioner recently released figures putting the urban population in 1981 at 15,61,88,507. The balance of the total population 65,81,40,676 is considered rural. These figures exclude Assam where the Census has not so far been held and Jammu and Kashmir where the Census was taken two months after the February-March enumeration in the rest of the nation.

The 1981 urban population of 23.73 per cent compared to 22.22 in 1971, 18.26 in 1961, and 17.62 in 1951 when the first post-independence Census was taken. The urban population was a mere 10,40 per cent in 1911. Dadra and Nagar Haveli as well as Lakshadweep entered the stream of urbanisation for the first time during the 1971-81 decade. Maharashtra is the most urbanised State with 35.05 per cent of its population in urban areas. Tamil Nadu, Gujarat, Karnataka, Punjab and West Bengal follow in descending order. These States have a higher urban population than the national average of 23.73 per cent. At the other end, Himachal Pradesh, Dadra and Nagar Haveli and Arunachal Pradesh have more than 90 per cent of their population in rural areas.

Kerala, Meghalaya, Uttar Pradesh, Sikkim, Nagaland, Bihar, Orissa and Tripura have more than 80 per cent rural population, Nagpur, Lucknow and Jaipur crossed the one million marks at the 1981 Census. They joined the group of Calcutta, Greater Bombay, Delhi, Madras, Hyderabad, Ahmedabad, Bangalore, Kanpur and Pune as big cities or urban agglomerations. Together the 12 cities and urban agglomerations account for 44.56 per cent of the urban population.

Trichur in Kerala has the highest literacy rate of 81.09 per cent. Sambhal in Uttar Pradesh is the least literate city (24.84 per cent).

According to the 1971 Census, of the 548 million population in 1971, 376 million remained at their place of birth, 310 million in the rural areas, and 66 million in the urban areas. Among the remaining 172 million persons, 108 million were enumerated within the district of enumeration and another 36 million within the State. Only 19 million persons were enumerated in a State outside their place of birth and 0.9 million persons born in countries other than India. Most of the 19 million persons who migrated outside the State of their birth moved short distances and to border districts.

QUESTIONS FOR EXERCISE

1. Distinguish between rural and urban communities.
2. Distinguish the rural and urban patterns of life.
3. Write short note on Rural-Urban migration in India.

Table 2: *Comparison of Rural-Urban Literacy Role in India*

	State/Union Territory	Urban	Individual	Males	Females
	1	2	3	4	5
1.	Andhra Pradesh	Total	44.09	55.13	32.72
		Rural	35.74	47.28	23.92
		Urban	66.35	75.87	56.41
2.	Arunachal Pradesh	Total	41.59	51.45	29.69
		Rural	37.82	47.00	25.31
		Urban	71.59	77.99	62.23
3.	Assam	Total	52.89	61.87	43.03
		Rural	49.32	58.66	39.11
		Urban	79.39	84.37	13.32
4.	Bihar	Total	38.48	52.49	22.89
		Rural	33.83	48.31	17.95
		Urban	67.39	77.72	55.94
5.	Goa	Total	75.57	83.64	73.38
		Rural	72.31	81.71	82.87
		Urban	80.10	86.33	73.38
6.	Gujarat	Total	61.29	73.13	48.64
		Rural	53.09	66.84	38.65
		Urban	76.54	84.56	67.70
7.	Haryana	Total	55.85	69.10	40.47
		Rural	49.85	64.78	32.51
		Urban	73.66	81.96	64.06
8.	Himachal Pradesh	Total	63.86	75.36	64.06
		Rural	61.86	73.89	49.79
		Urban	84.17	88.97	78.32
9.	Karnataka	Total	56.04	67.26	44.34
		Rural	47.69	60.30	34.76
		Urban	74.20	82.04	65.74
10.	Kerala	Total	89.81	93.62	86.17
		Rural	88.92	92.91	85.12
		Urban	92.25	95.58	89.06
11.	Madhya Pradesh	Total	44.20	58.42	28.85
		Rural	35.87	51.04	19.73
		Urban	70.81	81.32	58.32
12.	Maharashtra	Total	64.87	76.56	52.32
		Rural	55.52	69.74	40.96
		Urban	79.20	86.41	70.87
13.	Manipur	Total	59.89	71.63	47.60
		Rural	55.79	67.64	43.26
		Urban	70.53	82.11	58.67

1	2	3	4	5
14. Meghalaya	Total	49.10	53.12	44.85
	Rural	41.05	44.83	37.12
	Urban	81.74	85.72	77.32
15. Mizoram	Total	82.27	85.61	78.60
	Rural	72.47	77.36	67.03
	Urban	93.45	95.15	91.61
16. Nagaland	Total	61.65	67.62	54.75
	Rural	57.23	63.42	50.36
	Urban	83.10	85.94	79.10
17. Orissa	Total	49.09	63.09	34.68
	Rural	45.46	60.00	30.79
	Urban	71.99	81.21	61.18
18. Punjab	Total	58.51	65.66	50.41
	Rural	52.77	60.71	43.85
	Urban	72.08	77.26	66.12
19. Rajasthan	Total	38.55	54.99	20.44
	Rural	30.37	47.64	11.59
	Urban	65.33	78.50	50.24
20. Sikkim	Total	56.94	65.74	46.69
	Rural	54.38	63.49	43.98
	Urban	80.89	85.19	74.94
21. Tamil Nadu	Total	62.66	73.75	51.33
	Rural	54.59	67.18	41.84
	Urban	77.99	86.06	69.61
22. Tripura	Total	60.44	70.58	49.65
	Rural	56.08	67.07	44.33
	Urban	83.09	89.00	76.93
23. Uttar Pradesh	Total	4L60	55.73	25.31
	Rural	36.66	52.05	19.02
	Urban	61.00	69.98	50.38
24. West Bengal	Total	57.70	67.81	46.56
	Rural	50.50	62.05	38.12
	Urban	75.27	81.19	68.25
Union Territories				
1. Andaman and Nicobar Islands	Total	73.02	78.99	65.46
	Rural	69.73	75.99	61.99
	Urban	81.69	86.59	75.08
2. Chandigarh	Total	77.81	82.04	72.64
	Rural	59.12	65.67	47.83
	Urban	79.87	84.09	74.57

	1	2	3	4	5
3.	Dadra and Nagar Haveli	Total	40.71	53.56	26.98
		Rural	37.00	50.04	23.30
		Urban	78.44	86.35	68.42
4.	Daman and Diu	Total	71.20	82.66	59.40
		Rural	61.55	75.23	46.70
		Urban	81.61	91.14	72.35
5,	Delhi	Total	75.29	82.01	66.99
		Rural	66.90	78.46	52.15
		Urban	76.18	82.39	68.54
6.	Lakshadweep	Total	81.78	90.18	72.89
		Rural	78.89	88.66	68.72
		Urban	83.99	91.31	76.11
7.	Pondicherry	Total	74.74	83.68	65.63
		Rural	65.36	76.44	53.96
		Urban	79.88	87.70	71.98

7

VILLAGE LIFE IN INDIA AND THE WEST

The difference in the cultures of East and West is reflected in the villages of East and West. Though the rural societies both in East and West are predominantly agrarian, we find considerable differences in the Indian villages and the Western villages. Besides the geographic factor, which has paramount importance in determining the nature and structure of a village, the social structure, economic conditions, political situation and a number of other factors determine the nature and character of a village. A comparative study of the Indian and the Western villages will reveal the differences between the two. Such a study will also reveal the elements, conditions or factors which affect the Rural Dynamics, that is, we shall know the correlation of causes and effects: what conditions produce what effect. In his famous book, *Village Life in Northern India*, Professor Lewis has made a comparative study of an Indian village Rampur, near Delhi, with a Mexican village Tepoztlan. Lewis has found that the differences between the two are more vital than similarities. A review of Lewis' findings will make abundantly clear the difference between Indian and Western villages. Tepoztlan is situated 60 miles South of Mexico City, the capital of Mexico. The population of this village is 3500 and it was established about 2,000 years ago. Rampur is 15 miles from Delhi and has a population of 1100. The people of this village subscribe to be Hindu faith, whereas people of Tepoztlan are catholic Christians.

While the villagers of Rampur speak Hindi, those of Tepoztlan speak two languages. About half Tepoztlans are bilinguists. About 750 years ago, a Jat king had conquered Rampur and since then it is a jat dominated village. The majority of the Rampur population belong to jat community. Hindi spoken in Rampur is influenced by the Punjabi language. A few persons in Rampur can speak English.

Both Rampur and Tepoztlan are peasant societies as majority of the population of both villages is engaged in the profession of agriculture. Both villages are connected with the state through the district and are subject to the law of the land. That is both villages have civilised society and not a primitive society. Both, again, are connected with the neighbouring villages and influenced by them, yet both have certain distinctive elements of their respective cultures. In both villages, primitive agricultural implements are used, that is, sophisticated modern implements are not common in these villages. The main implements used in agriculture are the plough and oxen. Both villages are primarily agriculturists and live on farm produce and daily products. In both villages the rates of illiteracy and infant mortality are very high and the standard of living is very low. In both villages the goods are exchanged and the medium of exchange is currency notes and coins. In both villages a mixed feeling of well and ill-disposition towards the government is found, this is so because both villages have had a long spell of foreign domination and rule. The chief points of difference between the two villages, symbolic of East and West are the following:

(1) Structural Differences. There is difference in the structure and layout of Rampur and Tepoztlan. Rampur is not built to any plan. The Tepoztlan, on the other hand, like most Western villages is built to a plan. Its layout is orderly and its streets meet each other at right angles. The streets are broad and well laid. Tepoztlan has one central church. It has its own market, official buildings and a public park. Rampur, contrariwise to Tepoztlan, is ill-laid out and housing is disorderly. The streets are narrow and some of them are blind alleys. The houses in Rampur are huddled together and ventilation in these is poor. The houses in Rampur are not sufficiently commodious and, consequently there is not enough space to live in. On the other hand, the houses in Tepoztlan are airy and commodious. Whereas, in Rampur, men and beasts usually sleep under the same roof, in Tepoztlan we find a small garden in front of each house where cattle are lodged. There is no housing problem in Tepoztlan. It is possible to find few vacant houses. Like all villages in West, we find that the quarters for male and female are not separate but mixed, in Rampur these are separate.

(2) Difference in Agriculture. As described earlier, agriculture is the main profession in the two villages. In Rampur, agriculture is more intensive than in Tepoztlan. About 90% of area of Rampur is used for agriculture. On the contrary, only 15% of the area of Tepoztlan is used for agriculture. Whereas in Rampur a number of crops are taken per year, in Tepoztlan only one crop is taken in a year. Due to good irrigation facilities in Rampur about 115th of the total area yields two crops per year; but on account of poor irrigation facilities in Tepoztlan, only one crop in a year is possible. The difference in the irrigation facilities between Rampur and Tepoztlan cannot be generalized. As a matter of fact, the actual affairs with regard to Eastern and Western villages, are quite opposed to one obtaining in Rampur versus Tepoztlan pair. The irrigation facilities in the West are, on the whole, much better than in India; Tepoztlan is an exception to the general rule. The farmer in West, on the whole, takes a higher yield and employs sophisticated agricultural implements.

(3) Difference in Land. The topographical differences between Tepoztlan and Rampur are fairly representative of differences between Western and Eastern villages in respect of land. Whereas nearby Tepoztlan there are green pastures and forests, there is neither green pasture nor any jungle near Rampur. This is why in Rampur and other Indian villages there is acute shortage of firewood and, therefore, cow dung is used for fuel purposes instead of manure. On the other hand, there is plenty of firewood available in Tepoztlan and the entire cow dung is used as manure.

(4) Private and Public Land. In both Rampur and Tepoztlan we find both kinds of land — private and public. But whereas in Tepoztlan every individual has equal right over the public land and can use it freely without any let or hindrance, in Rampur, on the contrary, certain castes are debarred from the use of public land. While 80% of the total land in Tepoztlan is public, only 7% of the land in Rampur is public and this includes village tank, roads and barren land. Compared to India we find a far greater proportion of land in the West as public. This in due to greater area of the land and improved public utilities like roads and sanitation. There are no uneconomic holdings in the West. Compared to about 80% of Indian population engaged in agriculture, only 15% of the Western population is engaged in agriculture. Naturally, therefore, each agriculturist in the West has large holdings. In both villages, there are disputes over public land, though the causes in two cases are quite different. In India the quarrels over public land are due to the fact that some families try to snatch or usurp the public land, while in Tepoztlan the cause of the quarrel usually is the contending claims over public land by some families.

In Tepoztlan, the area of land per head is 75 acres, whereas in Rampur it is hardly 1-5 acres. As a rule, the land area per head is far greater in Western villages than in the Indian villages. Besides more land, the Western farmer enjoys the facilities of green pastures and forests. As a consequence, he is much more well off than his Indian counterpart. But as far as the individual and private ownership of the land is concerned, a higher percentage of land is under private ownership in India than in West.

While 36% of the families in Tepoztlan have private ownership of the land, 52% of the Rampur families possess their own land. The socio-economic conditions of those who do not own land is much better in West than in India. In the West, landless villager can freely use public land and pastures, while in India such a person has no option but to become a landless labourer. Though the land holdings in Tepoztlan are small, this is not the case with other villages in the West. The similarity in regard to landholdings in Tepoztlan and Rampur is typical and cannot, therefore, justify a general conclusion. What can be said at best is that in certain villages in West the conditions are rather like those obtaining in India.

(5) Profession. About 90% of Tepoztlan families are engaged in agriculture. The percentage of those engaged in agriculture in Rampur is 53%. Like other Indian villages, in Rampur there are washermen, barbers, potters etc. In Western villages, however, there are not so many professions. The number of landless labourers is very high in India but very low in West.

(6) Animal Husbandry. In India as well as in West, cattle are brad and reared. But whereas in West cattle breeding is mainly done for the purposes of food, that is, obtaining meat, in India, on account of religious beliefs, animals are not primarily bred for feeding. In fact, meat is sparingly consumed in India. Though there is ample pasture ground in Tepoztlan the number of animals being bred is relatively less. In India, on the other hand, the number of livestock is relatively very high but their condition is very poor. In India milch animals yield about 1/4th of milk produced by their Western counterparts. The reason for the great number of livestock in India is that animals are used for ploughing the field, whereas in West agriculture is mechanised and, therefore, the primary use of animals is for milk and meat.

(7) Social Structure. The social structure is based on culture. With changes in the culture, the social structure also undergoes the corresponding changes. As there is fundamental difference between the Western and the Indian cultures, the social structures of the Western and Indian villages are fundamentally different. For example, in Indian villages, blood relationship plays very crucial role. Not only is family based on blood relationship, but a number of families in a village are closely linked by blood relationship. On the other hand, Western social structure is based on class rather than blood relationship. Therefore, Indian village society is based on caste structure and caste is determined by birth, in Western villages we find either no social class stratification or the classes based on professions. We find much less economic and social differences among various classes in the Western villages than in Indian villages though we find in Indian village a sense of fraternity not to be found in West. The evil of untouchability is peculiar to India and is not found in West where equality of men is emphasised.

(8) Social Stratification. As there is no caste system in Western villages, the relationship amongst villagers is democratic and the sense of community is very high. But in spite of the democratic character and high community sense found in Western villages, the relations among individuals are becoming increasingly impersonal, whereas in spite of the casteism of Indian villages the relations among villagers are still personal and intimate in India. However, there is no gainsaying the fact that casteism and presence of communities pulling in opposite directions is inimical to social structure. The fact that Western society is democratic and free from casteism does not mean that there are no classes in Western society and that it is wholly classless. In fact, classes are formed on regional, religious and cultural bases; but the peculiar features of casteism like restrictions on marriage, sharing of food and mixing up on festivals etc. are to be found in Indian society only and not in the Western Society.

(9) Social Dynamics. In both Rampur and Tepoztlan are found a number of groups. But whereas groups in Tepoztlan are not well-organised, these are very well-organized in Rampur. In India, the groups are formed to protect and preserve social and economic interests and due to contrary interests of groups there is tension among these. On the other hand, groups in West are formed mostly on political basis and conflicts among them are politically motivated.

(10) Family structural differences. In West we find small family units of husband, wife and their small children. There is no joint family system in West and as and when a son marries he sets up a separate family. On the other hand, we find joint families in India. In India a family does not consist of husband and wife but includes parents and brothers of the husband and may sometimes include uncles even. In Indian villages the larger a family the better is its prestige. The chief of large family finds it easy to become leader in the village. The relations of a family are spread over far-flung villages as the practice of exogamic marriages prevails in India.

(11) Communal feeling and village organisation. As we have said earlier, a high sense of community or strong communal feelings are found in Western villages. On account of this the residents of a village in West are dedicated to communal welfare and think in terms of and act in ways beneficial to their village as a whole. On the other hand, it is the caste that predominates the rural life in India, in elections to panchayats and assemblies, an appeal to caste interests is made and usually the pattern of voting is determined by the caste structure of the village. From the legal and constitutional point of view, villages are regarded as corporate bodies both in West and in India and are, therefore, legal persons so that a village can be plaintiff or defendant in court cases. Both in India and West villagers face external dangers as one man. This disposition of villagers can be utilised for effective community development. If villagers as a whole are given common aim and ideal, they can be made to work hard for its realisation. Thus, villages provide great potential for useful development.

(12) Political conditions and leadership. The villages in West are much better organised politically than the Indian villages. However, in so far as local self-government is concerned, Indian villages are not far behind their Western counterparts. Panchayats in India are well-developed institutions. Moreover, they have a basis in Indian history and are wholly indigenous in character. If these are given full freedom to function and develop and government assist them properly there is no reason for their lagging behind in any respect in matters of political organisation and self-government. However, the state of affairs at the moment is not very encouraging. Indeed, whereas the village leaders in West represent whole of the village, this is not the case in India. In India each leader represents his own group and for any scheme concerning whole of the village it becomes necessary to achieve a consensus among the leaders of different groups. Though on account of this, the work of community development becomes difficult, but a redeeming feature of the situation is that various groups are closely knit in coherent units so that once a consensus among various groups is obtained there is no further hindrance or hurdle in the way of development. As a matter of fact, the community sense and feeling, though covering the whole village, are not very intense in Tepoztlan whereas these are very intense in Rampur though confined to groups and extending to the whole village. In India, on account of exogamy, there is friendship among various villages because there are marital bonds between most of them. As endogenous marriage is practised in Western villages, bonds between various villages are not very strong.

(13) Inter-village relations. Though, both in India and the West, villages are part of district and state, the Western villages are more independent and self-sufficient than Indian villages and the relationship of villages with district and state is federal in character in West. In India villages are parts of districts and state and much more dependent than their Western counterparts, in as much as exogamy is practised in India, we find close bonds are relations among different villages. In West, marriages take place within the village and therefore, there is no possibility of marital bonds between different villages.

(14) The personality of village. It is a common place fact, that Indian villages are poor and much more squalid are unhygienic than their Western counterparts. But due to strong impress of culture on their character, they appear to be generous, hospitable, contented and happy. The children in an Indian village are filthier and more starved than their Western counterparts but they appear to be more contented and satisfied than their Western counterparts. Womenfolk of Indian villages are neither depressed nor underdogs: they, in fact, are hardworking and quite assertive. In work efficiency and capacity they are second to none. As regards health and disease, conditions are worse in India than in the West. Infant mortality is high in India and average age is also low. In spite of this there is no expression of despondency on the faces of Indian villagers. Indian villages are deeply influenced by the Indian culture and on account of this, display greater conviviality than the villages of the West. The rate of literacy is much low in India. Gregariousness is natural to an Indian villager: he cannot survive in isolation. Everywhere we find crowding of children, women or men. Indian women use more ornaments than their Western counterparts though their economic condition is not as good as that of their Western sisters. A comparative study of villages of India and West shows up relative cultural differences; other differences are due to economic factors. With an improvement in economic condition Indian villages will not lag behind Western villages in any respect.

CONCLUSION

Comparative data from these two villages demonstrate the wide range of culture that can exist in peasant societies. When he left India in 1952, Lewis expected to find many similarities between Indian and Mexican peasant communities. Despite of his earlier critique of the folk-society concept, he did find similarities, but on the whole he was more impressed by the differences. The similarities were greatest in material culture, level of technology and economics, and the differences were greatest in social organisation, value systems and personality. In terms of raising the standard of living the problems seemed much the same, for the bulk of the population in both villages was poor, illiterate, landless, and lived so close to die survival margin that it could not afford to experiment with new things and ideas. However, the poverty of the Indian people seemed so much greater and the agrarian problems so overwhelming and complex as to defy any easy solution even on the theoretical level.

Summing up his study Oscar Lewis writes, "In making comparisons between Mexico and India, we must remember that they are in different stages of evolution in terms of nationhood. Mexico has had its political independence for almost 150 years and has lived through the great revolution of 1910-20, while India has only recently gained its freedom and has not had the equivalent of the Mexican agrarian revolution. These broad differences are reflected in many ways in our two villages.

One of the most striking findings in our study of Rampur, especially when compared with the report of Beals (1953) on a South Indian village is the remarkable stability of local village life and institutions, despite the proximity of Rampur to Delhi and the many urban influences on which it has been subject, such as Arya Samaj, the Congress and other political movements, and increased opportunities for education and jobs. The stability is particularly evident in the agricultural economy. The Jats still love the land; in the last fifty years there have been only two families who sold their land and left the village. The land-tenure system continues as of old, with the Jats still in control. The caste system still remains strong and dominates the thinking of the villagers despite the many reformist movements and the coming of independence. But the jajmani system has weakened, and this has increased inter-caste tensions, particularly in Jatavs.

Rampur and Tepoztlan face many common problems. In both villages population has increased rapidly in the last thirty years, means of communication have been improved, there is greater dependence upon a cash economy, education is increasingly valued, and general aspiration level of people is going up. There have been no comparable changes in agricultural production.

We have seen that both villages are meaningful units for comparative study. However, our analysis has shown the complexities involved in evaluating the extent to which each village is a community. From some points of view it would seem that Tepoztlan is more of an organized and centralized village community, that is, in terms of the internal settlement organisation, village government with elected and paid village officials, the religious organisation with a central church, the village market and plaza, and the absence of multiple inter-village networks based on kinship. From the point of view of ecology Rampur is a more clearly defined and self-contained community than Tepoztlan."[1]

QUESTION FOR EXERCISE

1. Analyse the difference between the rural communities of India and the West.

1. Lewis, Oscar, *Village Life in Northern India*, University of Illinois Press U.S.A., 1958, pp. 322-323.

8

SELECTED TYPES OF VILLAGES

Dr. S.C. Dube has, in his book, given a descriptive study of the village of Shamirpet in the State of Andhra. It is an outcome of the Social Service Extension Project sponsored by the Department of Sociology and Anthropology. His aim, in this book, has been to give a clear and intimate picture of some aspects of life in an Indian village.

I. THE SETTING

Shamirpet is a village situated at a distance of about twenty-five miles from the twin cities of Hyderabad and Secundrabad, on the road that links the capital city of Hyderabad with Karimnagar. According to Dr. Dube, "No village in India can be singled out as being typical of the country as a whole, but Shamirpet possesses most of the characteristics which are common to the rural communities in middle and peninsular India."[1]

1. The people. According to the census of 1951, the total population of Shamirpet, which included the two neighbouring hamlets of Baduguda and Upparpalli, was 2,494, with a total of 508 houses, this includes two sections — Hindus and Muslims. The Hindus include 1,434 Clean Castes and 680 Untouchables or Scheduled Caste persons. The Muslims are 340 in number. The predominant language in Shamirpet is Telugu. The Muslims speak Urdu. Thus, the two major divisions in the population of the village may be distinguished on the grounds of religion and language. The Hindus can be classed under three broad divisions: 1. Cultivators; which include the Reddi, the Muttarasi, and their sub-divisions. 2. Occupational castes, with traditional crafts and professions regarded as clean and respectable. These include the Brahmin (priest), the Komti (traders), the Kummari (potters) and the Golls (shepherds) and the five sections of the Panch Brahma group of artisan castes, such as the Wadla (carpenters), the Kammari (blacksmiths), the Ausula (goldsmiths), the Kase (workers in bell-metal) and the Kanchari (sculptors). 3. Depressed classes, subsist by humble and lowly callings. These include the Mala and the Madiga of which the Malas are considered as superior. In point of dress the Hindus and Muslims differ widely. The women are extremely fond of ornaments.

---

1. Dube, S.C., *Indian Village*, Routledge and Kegan Paul Ltd., London 1975, p. 18,

2. The village. Shamirpet cannot claim to be a village of any great age. The village itself is not built according to a definite plan. There is a school, a dispensary, a post office and a police station in the village.

3. The houses. The dwellings in Shamirpet can be classified into three main groups: the Bhawanti, the Penkutillu and the Gudse. The Bhawanti is a large house with stone walls and tiled roofs, its own compound and having five to six rooms. The Penkutillu is smaller and less ostentatious and is built by average cultivators with small holdings, who are neither rich nor poor. The Gudse are the commonest type of dwellings found in Telangana and are indeed the most numerous in Shamirpet. It is a hut, small and circular, made from sheets of weed-matting, about 20 ft. in diameter and only six feet high.

4. The neighbourhood of Shamirpet. The surrounding of Shamirpet is quite densely populated. Three miles to the North is another village Aliyabad. People living in different villages have very few occasions on which to meet each other as a whole.

II. SOCIAL STRUCTURE

1. Caste in the village community. The Hindus and the Muslims constitute two distinct sections in the population of Shamirpet. All The Muslims belong to the Sunni Division. The Hindu social system presents a division of society into castes. Of these the Brahmins, the Kshatriyas and the Vaishyas constitute the first three caste groups. The fourth group is composed of numerous occupational castes who are relatively clean and are not classed as untouchables. Finally, in the Fifth major group we can place all the untouchable castes. Besides, there is the Panch Brahma group which comprises of five divisions: The Wadla, the Kammari, the Ausula, the Kase and the Kanchari. Of these, only the first three sections are found in Shamirpet. Among Hindus the Brahmins hold the highest place. The Komtis rank next to the Brahmins. The Reddi sections of the Kapu group, the Kummari and the Golla castes are of equal caste status. All the castes are endogamous. Each caste has a traditional occupation sanctioned by religion. Most of the castes are sub-divided into endogamous divisions which for all practical purposes are themselves independent castes. Each independent endogamous division is divided into exogamous gotram; these in turn may be further sub-divided into numerous vansham. The main function of these divisions is the regulation of marital unions.

2. Internal organisation: Authority and machinery of Justice. In the internal organisation of Shamirpet two different units can be clearly delineated. The socio-religious organisation of the village with independent set of office-bearers and functionaries are quite distinct from the administrative organisation of government and semi-government officials. The Deshmukh is the hereditary headman of the village. The panchayat or village council consists of the headmen of all the major communities living within the village and in addition several other rich and influential persons. The panchayat performs several important functions such as hearing and deciding minor disputers, fixing the details of ceremonies, reporting epidemics and fixing communal contributions etc. The Deshmukh is the head of the government village officials. The patwari occupies a pivotal position. The sub-inspector of police with head constables, masters and constables under him enjoys wide powers. Besides, there are fourteen classes of village menials:

(i) Kawalkar, (ii) Talari, (iii) Majkuri, (iv) Neerudi, (v) Begari (vi) Yetti, Wadla, (viii) Kammari, (ix) Kummari, (x) Sakali, (xi) Mangali, (xii) Ausula, (xiii) Dappu, (xiv) Kummu. These perform routine duties in the everyday life in the village. The division of work among them is based upon traditional occupations. The payment is nominal.

3. Inter-caste and inter-village organisation. The village is the smallest but most significant territorial unit. Persons belonging to different castes are united by common values and obligations. The caste social organisation cuts across the narrow boundaries of the village and extends to a wider area. Two types of inter-village organisations deserve to be noted. They are councils of the different castes and inter-village councils. While all villages and nearly all castes have their own panchayats, inter-village panchayats are formed time to time when they are demanded by a special situation.

III. ECONOMIC STRUCTURE

1. Caste in village Economy. The economic system of rural India is founded mainly on the functional specialisation and inter-dependence among castes. According to Dr. Dube, a closer scrutiny of the economic system and its consequent bond of mutual obligation and expectation reveals four major types of economic dealings and obligations within the caste network into which the community is organised. These are (i) Obligations to render to the agriculturists occupational services having a direct bearing on their agricultural activities, (ii) Obligations to render some occupational services, to the agriculturists as well as to many non-agriculturists, having a bearing on their socio-religious life, (iii) Obligations to render some occupational services to other occupational services in return for their traditional services, (iv) Occupational services rendered with an expectation of cash payment in return for the work."[2]

The main economic functions and activities of the major caste groups in the village are traditionally specified. The Brahmin is the local priest as well as an astrologer. The Komtis are traders. The Kummari are the potters. The Golla are shepherds. The Sale are the weavers. The Gaondla sell fermented palm juice at their shops. The Panch Brahma Group perform various functions such as the Wadla are carpenters, the Kammari are blacksmiths and some others are goldsmiths, workers in bell metal and carvers of images. The Sakali and the Mangali are the barber and washermen respectively. There is only one family of Katike Hindu butchers in the village. The solitary family of the Darzi (tailor) with an old sewing machine is obviously a new addition. The Erkalas earn their livelihood through a variety of means such as hunting, begging, singing, fortune telling, basket making

2. *Ibid.*, p. 56.

and rearing pigs. The Madigas are affiliated to the households of the substantial agriculturists in the village. They perform all types of jobs.

2. Agriculture. The settled area of Shamirpet, including the two neighbouring hamlets, is spread over an area of 58 acres. Out of this Shamirpet proper occupies 31.4 acres. The total land area of the village according to government records is 5,777 acres. Out of these 2,012 acres are uncultivable; 1,628 acres being covered with rocks and shrubs. In all 3,765 acres are under cultivation in the village: 3,339.5 acres are classed as 'dry land', for this area is irrigated entirely by the rains; and 425.6 acres are classed as 'wet land' as extra irrigation is available. An analysis of the pattern of land-ownership in the village reveals the following: (i) A fourth of the land is owned by 1 family having 800 acres, (ii) One-fourth of the land is owned by 8 families having 100 acres each, (iii) One-fourth of the land is owned by 20 families having 40 acres each, (iv) One-fourth of the land is owned by 160 families having 5 acres each. The headman of the village is biggest single land owner. 40% of the land is held by the Reddis; the rest being shared by other castes specially the Brahmins, the Komtis, the toddy-tappers and the shepherds, as well as the Muslims. Seceding member of a family gets a share of the family's ancestral land. The land belongs to family, and normally the head of the family exercises control over it. Analysis of the family budgets of the agriculturists in the village revealed that 10% of them were surplus, 24% were balanced and the rest were deficit budgets. Agricultural wages differ from Rs. 28 to Rs. 120 per year which may be paid in cash or kind.

3. The Agricultural Year. The agriculturists in Shamirpet follow the local almanac. They go to the Brahmin to fix an auspicious day for planting vegetables and creepers in their backyards. Kharif crops such as maize and millet are sown in the second half of June. The harvesting of the Kharif crops has to be completed by October. The Rabi crops, *i.e.*, gram, castor, chillies, mustard, tobacco, til (sesame), or oil seeds are sown in winter. They take three to four months to ripen. After the harvesting of these crops the annual cycle of agricultural activities comes very near to completion.

4. Cattle and domestic animals. Agriculture in the village still largely follows the age-old pattern of bullock-drawn wooden ploughs which are being used in the fields. The shepherds keep large herds of goats and sheep. Cows and she-buffaloes are kept for milk by the agriculturists. Pigs are kept only by the Erkalas. Some people may also keep a few goats. Poultry is kept by all sections of the village population except the Brahmins and the Komatis.

5. Other economic pursuits. Hunting is done regularly by a very limited number of people. Similarly, fishing is done by very few people, mostly by some young Muslim men. Children and women engage in collecting fruits, honey, medicinal herbs, roots, tubers and barks. Only a limited quantity of fuel is collected from the surrounding forests. Different kinds of coloured earths are collected for domestic purposes.

6. Non-agricultural occupations. These include the potter, the carpenter, the blacksmith, the barter, the washerman, and the menial servant, the Madiga.

The economy of the village is only partially self-sufficient. The traders, both Komtis and Muslims, buy their goods wholesale from the city and retail them in their shops in the village. People frequently visit the valley bazars also.

IV. RITUAL STRUCTURE

1. The character of religion. The rural religion includes folklore and myths, religious teachings of saint-poets, and contacts with persons having knowledge of scriptures and popular religious books, animism, polytheism and even monotheism also, beliefs in spirits, ghosts, demons, witches and magic. In the words of Dr. S.C. Dube, "The complex of all these diverse factors constitutes the picture of the supernatural world as it is understood by the people in the countryside."[3] Shamirpet is predominantly a Hindu village. The Muslims are Sunni. The members of both these religions carry out their religious and ritual practices. Besides, several cultist rituals and worships of purely local nature are shared by both the communities. The distinctions between the religious practices of the Hindus and the Muslims are obvious and clear.

2. Beliefs in gods and deities. The Muslims believe in one God and follow the way of life laid down for them by the Prophet. The Hindu concept of Trinity, comprising three manifestations of divinity — Brahma, the creator; Vishnu, the sustainer; and Shiva, the destroyer has an all-India spirit. The people of Shamirpet worship all the major gods of the Hindu pantheon. The Godavari is worshipped by the Hindus. The local gods and goddesses include: 1. Pochamma — goddess of smallpox, 2. Mutyalamma — goddess of chickenpox, 3. Balamma — goddess of fertility whose wrath causes sterility in women, 4. Mahakalamma — goddess of cholera, 5. Durgamma — goddess presiding over the destinies and welfare of the village, 6. Maisamma — goddess protecting the village boundaries. All the characteristics of Hinduism having all-India spread are in evidence in the religion of the people of Shamirpet.

3. The religious year. Three major types of religious ceremonies and festivals are observed in the community: family ceremonies, village ceremonies, and caste ceremonies. The Muslim section of the village population has its own family festivals and some communal ceremonies. They participate with their Hindu neighbours in the observance of common village ritual. The Hindu festivals include Ugadi (Telugu New Year's Day), Ram Navami (Birthday of Rama), Toli Ekadashi, Nagula panchami, Rakhi Purnima, Krishna Asthami, Chauthi, Peitramasa, Dusshera, Deepawali, Til Sankranti, Shivaratri, Holi etc. Some other important festivals accepted by the higher castes include Neela Gauri, Narsimha Jayanti, Shravana Somwar, Ananta Chaturdashi, Kartika Purnima, Basanta Panchami and Ratha Saptami. Ceremonies organised by the village as a whole are: the Pochamma festival, Batkamma festival and the Maisamma festival. The

---

3. *Ibid.*, p. 88.

Muslims observe seven important festivals. They are Moharram, Meelad Sharif, Gairwin Sharif, Shabe Miraj, Shabe Barat, Ramzan and Id-ul-Zuha. These festivals follow the Muslim calendar, and unlike the Hindu festivals, always occur in the same season but, their specific time varies from year to year. Besides the three village festivals pointed out earlier there is the fair of Jalal Miyan attended by everyone in the village.

4. Ritual of the life cycle. The basic pattern of ceremonies connected with the life cycle is the same in all sections of the Hindus in the village community; but in the minor details of the ritual there is considerable difference in the practices of different castes. The practices of the Muslims and the Hindus concerning birth, pre-puberty rites, marriage, death etc., differ considerably, and are governed by their respective religions.

5. Religion in disease and difficulty. Most of the common diseases are interpreted as a 'fault in the physical system', and are treated with herbal medicines or modern drugs obtained from the dispensary. But persistent headaches, intermittent fevers, continued stomach disorders, rickets and other wasting diseases among children, menstrual troubles, repeated abortions, etc., are attributed to supernatural forces. The major factors that cause difficulties, distresses and deaths are (i) The wrath of ancestor-spirits, (ii) Unfavourable stars, (iii) Ghosts and spirits, (iv) The wrath of gods, (v) Black magic and witchcraft.

V. THE WEB OF FAMILY TIES

1. The structure of the family. The patrilineal and patrilocal elementary or joint family is the normal type of family unit met within this part of rural India. The joint family is approved by social tradition. The ideal joint family includes paternal grandparents, parent's brothers and their wives, nephews, nieces, sons and their wives, grand-children, unmarried sisters and unmarried daughters. The family term used in the community denotes: (i) the elementary family or the 'houses', (ii) the extended family unit, or (iii) a still larger group comprising the near kin on the paternal side.

There is great variation in the family ideals and ethics of the different social levels. The population of the village may be broadly classified into three levels — (i) Upper Level: comprising the twice born castes of Brahmins and Komtis; rich Redis and Muslims and others who have had urban contacts or education in the city, (ii) Intermediate Level: all ordinary agriculturists; clean occupational castes and Muslim tradesmen constitute this group, which is by far the largest in the village, (iii) Lower Level: all the poorer sections of the population, such as the untouchable Malas and Madigas, and semi-tribal Vaddars and Erkalas, as well as poor Muslims, can be placed in this category. There is unanimity in all three levels that the structure of the family is founded on its recognition of the four basic principles. These are: (i) Respect for age. (ii) Respect for position in the scale of kinship, (iii) Superiority of the male, (iv) Necessity of keeping certain family matters confined to the responsible members of the family, or at the most, within the family.

2. Inter-personal relations within the family. The husband is an authoritarian figure whose will should always dominate the domestic scene. Both husband and wife watch each other's activities closely. In a joint family the daughter-in-law does not have any independence unless she becomes the mother of two or three children. The wife does not dominate the domestic scene, but if she is tactful she can manipulate things in such a way that her husband will rarely go against her wishes. In general, the attitude of the children towards their parents is one of respect and obedience. The nature of the parent-child relationship changes with the age and status of the children. Traditional opinion regards a son as an asset; a daughter, a liability. As a rule infant are treated with affection. After five or six years of age the parents start disciplining the child. Tradition lays down fairly strict norms regarding the treatment of aged, dependent parents. The daughter-in-law gets a cordial reception at first and more strict watch later on. The mother-in-law-daughter-in-law relationship is not very cordial. The daughter-in-law must maintain sufficient distance from her husband's father and his elder brothers. Social ideals demand that there should be solidarity between siblings especially between brothers. The older siblings can claim some 'authority' over the younger ones. Affinal relatives do not maintain close contacts. Outside the family circle the relations between a person and his or her mother's brother are of special significance. Among Muslims, besides cross-cousin marriage, marriage between parallel cousins is permitted and indeed encouraged.

VI. THE LEVELS OF LIVING

1. Status differentiation in the community. According to Dr. S. C. Dube, "Six major factors contribute towards status differentiation in the village community of Shamirpet. They are: (i) Religion and caste, (ii) Landownership, (iii) Wealth, (iv) Position in government service and village organisation, (v) Age, (vi) Distinctive personality traits."[4]

2. Standard of living: Four levels. In Shamirpet, four levels denoting different standards of living are vaguely recognised by the villagers. They are: (i) Rich, (ii) well-to-do, (iii) Average, (iv) poor. Their average in local population is Rich 4%, well-to-do 22%, average 34% and poor 40%.

3. Work Division of Labour. Division of labour in the community is governed by a variety of factors. Important among them are caste, sex, age and social status.

4. Diet. The standard of living of a family is judged very often from the quality and quantity of its food, those who can afford eat three times, others eat only twice daily. According to the seasons, there are variations in the type of food and also in the time when the principal meals are eaten.

VII. LIVING TOGETHER

1. Inter-personal Relations. The people of Shamirpet, exercise considerable reserve in their initial dealings with outsiders. It is not uncommon for people to analyse and describe the personality traits of other inhabitants of the village as

4. *Ibid.*, p. 61.

well as of outsiders coming into the settlement. Subjects coming under the critical eye of society are: (i) breaches of traditional norms, (ii) display and exhibitionism, (iii) sexuality, (iv) efforts to rise in the power hierarchy, (v) conspicuous success, and (vi) originality and 'too many new ideas'. Anger is freely expressed. Concepts of 'manliness' and 'defending the honour', play a significant part in governing inter-personal relations within the community. Inter-caste attitudes find expression in several stereotypes which are a part of the thought patterns of the people and find expression both in jest and banter as well as in quarrels and outbursts of anger. Adverse comments are frequently heard from the educated and uneducated people against each other. The uneducated specially have some stereotypes regarding the educated, and the later often express derogatory opinions about the illiterate members of the community. The general pattern of comment regarding urban and urbanised people is the same as that of the comment of the uneducated about the educated. The people with urban contacts, regard the village folk as rustic and crude, and consider themselves more forward and civilised. They are gradually coming to the fore in village leadership.

2. Childhood, youth and old age. Apart from the family and the caste, people spend most of their time in their respective age-groups, and through this process of growing up together, common play and participation in youth activity, the people tend to have a common value-orientation and certain common basic attitudes towards life. For the first two or three months of a child's life the mother remains almost in sole charge of it. After this stage of early infancy, during the pre-walking stage the pattern of treatment accorded to the child is somewhat different. With some modifications this continues even during the early childhood, up to the age of about three. After five the children form their respective age-groups. Most children's games involve competition in the use of skills and stamina. Adolescence brings about a significant change in the life of both boys and girls. By this age girls are expected to become proficient in all the major domestic tasks. After marriage the young men and women have to give considerable attention to their economic pursuits and crafts, and as such they have relatively little time left for group activity. Middle-aged people have their own groups. These are informal conversational gatherings; but their membership and attendance is nearly fixed. Groups of men and women meet separately.

3. Co-operation and conflict. Within the village community there is an appreciable degree of inter-caste and inter-family co-operation. Emergency aid is rushed to friend and foe alike. In inter-village quarrels as well as on all such occasions that demand vindicating the honour of the village, the residents of the settlement often act with spirited union. Shamirpet, however like any other village, has its due quota of conflicts, factions' rivalrics, court cases and fighting. Living together is very much governed by rules governing caste behaviour.

VIII. THE CHANGING SCENE

In the pre and early Jagir period in Shamirpet, the contacts between the village people and State administration were on a very limited scale, and were confined mostly to payment of land revenue and settlement of land disputes. In the second half of the Jagir period these administrative contacts increased very considerably. The State administration initiated some of its welfare and nation building activities in the countryside. In the dress and ornaments of the village people there has been very noticeable change. To the list of articles of daily requirement there have been several significant additions. In the food habits of the people there has not been much change. Side by side with the traditional recreations of gossip, loafing and playing indigenous games, several new varieties of entertainments are now available to the village people. Changes in tools and technical processes are also important. Communications too have now improved. The opening of small dispensary in the village, and the availability of excellent facilities of modern medical treatment in the city have considerably changed the attitude of the people towards them and their treatment. The social structure of the community is basically the same, although with every administrative or political change in the village there were several organisational changes. In the organisation of the family the changed conditions and changing attitudes of the people have brought about some significant variations. The caste system in the community presents only slight variations in some directions. Traditionally, the membership of the village council is hereditary and should be inherited by the eldest male child on the death of the father. At present government officials residing within the village discretely pull the strings and exert pressure on the council to secure favourable judgments in certain cases in which for some reason they happen to be interested. In place of their traditional occupation people have started accepting other vocations. The Police Action undertaken by the Indian Union in 1948 changed the fortune and status of the State of Hyderabad. The first definite change is that Muslims who occupied a privileged position during the former regime now no longer do so. The second noticeable change is that under the administration, forced labour and forced extraction of hospitality by government officials have been prohibited. Thirdly, the abolition of feudal estates has been a big step in the direction of land reform. Fourthly, the government has intensified its welfare and nation-building activities. Finally, there has been considerable activity in the rural areas by the political parties, culminating in the first general election of December 1951. The reason for change must be sought in a multiplicity of factors. So far State compulsion has been instrumental in bringing about little social and cultural change in the village community. The factors of utility, convenience and availability have played a more important role in bringing several new elements into the life of the community. Adoption of several new tools and instruments for occupational works, as well as of several other items of Western technology, such as buses, railways, razors and electric torches, introduced in the comparatively recent times is due to their efficiency and utility. Influence of the city has brought about adjustment and modification in several spheres, but the need of balancing different extremes in the organisation of the community has so far prevented any drastic structural change in village communities. Viewing the country broadly we find three major trends: (i) the regional culture, founded on the traditions, customs and life-ways of the culture-area; (ii) the national culture, comprising some all-India traits inspired by the national renaissance, cemented by the struggle for self-government as well as by social and economic reform, and sustained by the will to find a rightful place in the community of nations; the elements in this category being partly revivalists and partly conscious innovations; and (iii) adoption of traits and elements from Western technology and culture. Traditional social institutions and culture, traditions and life-ways are idealized: they originated long, long ago when man first appeared on the earth and the salvation of people lies in their faithful observance of these divinely ordained ways. The focus is local and regional, confined to family, kin, caste and some neighbouring village. The fundamental drive in the thought and activities of the group seems to be towards the goal of the adjustment of the individual to the universe. In interpersonal as well as inter and intra-group relations, the people tend to view everything as hierarchically structured. The fundamental concepts of the rights and equality of men mean little to these people, whose visions are thus bounded by their own observation of the world.

KISHANGARHI OF U.P.

A view of an Uttar Pradesh village may be obtained by Mckim Marriott's[5] study of Kishangarhi village. This study was conducted in 1951-52. Marriott stayed in this village situated in the Agra Division of Northern Ganga-Jamuna plain for 14 months. The study was financed by U.S. government. Its findings were published in *The Economic Weekly* of 23rd August, 1952. The following is a brief outline of this study.

Social Structure

The social structure of most of the villages in Uttar Pradesh is based upon caste system. In each village members of different castes may be found which have jajmani relationships among them. In jajmani system, members of a caste serve members of a superior caste and in exchange receive some money and goods. Different castes have jajmani relationships with specific castes. According to Marriott, Kishangarhi has 24 local caste groups which are well organised and are living in the village for the last so many years. Each caste group, on an average, consists of 35 members distributed in five and a half families. The total population of the village is 850 which is more than the average population of a village in Uttar Pradesh. The Brahmin group is the biggest among caste groups. They include 43 families who are generally farmers. The next following Brahmins, are Chamars, Jats, Kumhars and Muslim fakirs. Each of these groups consists of 10 families. But there are some smaller caste groups in the village. Some caste groups consist of only one family. Each caste group includes members of several generations and several lineages. Each lineage is named after its chief member and its characteristics are specified according to its ritual duties. These lineages have been constantly

5. Mckim Marriot, *The Economic Weekly*, 23 August, 1952.

increasing since due to marital relationships about 25 new families have come to live in Kishangarhi. Each family is very much devoted to its lineage. As the village includes 26 lineages, it makes the social organisation considerably loose since each lineage claims devotion only towards itself.

The lineage organisation is, however, gradually being weakened. The members do not co-operate as actively as they were doing some 80 years earlier. Formerly, the agricultural families used to cultivate land belonging to their lineages, collectively carried on in the name of one or two persons. Such cultivation was sometimes carried on by even 6 and 7 families jointly. They used to distribute investments and profits among themselves according to ability and need and also maintain a common store of grains for festivals and special occasions. Though outside the joint family, the co-operation among the members of the lineages is not very strong yet, more importance in exchange is attributed to the members of the lineage as compared to the outsiders. In the times of need one could get help from members of his own group. But now joint cultivation has become difficult. Co-operation among members of different lineages has considerably decreased. On the occasion of implementation of Zamindari Abolition Act, the joint cultivation was shown in the name of all the male members of the group. On every occasion many farmer families think it better to give names of all the male members of the family. Even the names of minor boys are given as private partners. Thus, the co-operation and consideration for general welfare in the family is gradually decreasing.

Artisans and the landless labourers even now manage their fields jointly. But like the other castes, the discipline of their own caste associations is gradually weakening. The main cause of this change is the widening gap between the status of different members of the same caste. Another reason of this disorganisation of the caste associations is the outside village contact of the members and the conflicts within the castes. Yet another important reason is the disappearance of those cultural elements which were formerly considered to be characteristic of the caste group. For example, the religions peculiar to lower caste are gradually disappearing and giving place to Brahmanic ritualism.

The lineage group of the Jat landlords in Kishangarhi has some influential organisation even outside the village. Their ancestors were the conquerors of Kishangarhi and their realm was sometimes extending to hundreds of villages of Agra Division. Therefore their relationships are wider than other people. But due to so many economic changes in the last generation this local landlord group is also disintegrating. The landlord group, however, has become even more powerful since some of its members have attained government posts and it is difficult to find so many rich and educated persons in any other group.

Marriage

Almost all the families of Kishangarhi are connected to people outside the village through marriage. Kishangarhi observes village exogamy since the boys and girls within the village are considered as brothers and sisters descending from the same ancestors. Not only within the village but even in half a dozen villages around Kishangarhi this concept of blood relationship is extended and no marriages within these villages are possible. There has been only one marriage within these villages extending in the area of two kilometers in last three generations. According to Marriott, the average distance of a village from Kishangarhi for the purpose of marriage is almost 12 miles. The members of the village have migrated everywhere and there is marital relationship with almost three hundred villages. Of these, almost half the marriages have taken place in 80 villages. Each village connected through marriages believes in the myth of blood relationship.

Marriage in Kishangarhi is patrilocal and mostly travels in one direction. In other words, the villages from which brides come are regarded as lower and therefore daughters are not offered to them and they are expected to observe all sorts of rules of regard. The village in which a daughter is offered is considered high and respected and therefore more and more girls are offered in the same village. No one likes to offer his sister in marriage in a village from which he gets his bride. According to Marriott, the feeling behind this system is that one's daughter or sister requires constant help after being married in another group. Presents are regularly offered to the family of the bridegroom in order to ensure good and liberal behaviour. It is clear that these custom influences economy. Not only the marriage ceremonies involve high expenses but for years together the parents have to spend for the girls which is sometimes a formidable economic pressure. According to Marriott, of the milch animals in Kishangarhi about one-fourth have been presented by relatives in marriage. Of the total amount of debt, about one-fourth covers the demands of marriages. Marriott has rightly pointed out that this organisation of the marital system considerably lessens the economic capacity of the village.

Caste System

The different castes achieve different status of regard in society in Kishangarhi. The status of the various castes, in social stratification may be observed from the following table:

Number	Caste	Status in Social Stratification
1.	Brahmin	Highest
2.	Jat, Bania, Kayasth, Carpenter, Jogi, Mali, Kachi	High Castes
3.	Gadaria, Dhimer, Nau Kumhar, Darji, Koli, Khatik	Low Castes
.4.	Faqir, Manihar, Rangrej, Teli,	Mulsim Castes
5.	Bhangi, Kanjar	Lowest Castes

The status of different castes in social stratification determines the customs concerning eating and drinking, social contacts, welcome and community smoking, etc. In the same caste group also different individuals occupy different status which are not definite. The power and property in the village is mostly equally divided in caste groups though sometimes status based upon castes is different from the status based upon wealth, post and property. For example, though in the social system the Jats belong to a caste lower than the Brahmins in the economic and political affairs they dominated the Brahmins as landlords about fifty years earlier. After Zamindari abolition this status has deteriorated. For example, formerly on the occasion of Dussehera there used to be a regular darbar at the house of the landlord. This has ceased to be held. On the other hand, the lower castes are also trying to rise in social stratification. Customs connected with inter-caste behaviour are also gradually changing. The respect of the caste has changed along with change in political power and wealth. However, as a general rule customs concerning food and drink and services have not changed very much.

Personal regard

Besides castes, individuals in Kishangarhi are also seen attempting to achieve social regard. In this achievement the importance of the caste is 45% while that of the property and political power and political contact is 55%. Thus, as compared to caste, the economic and political changes very much influence the regard given to an individual. Therefore, personal regard is not necessarily linked to the regard of the caste. For example, the Brahmin caste is the highest in the village and the Chamar caste is the lowest but some wealthy and politically powerful Chamars receive more social regard than the Brahmins.

Pointing out changes in the social system of Kishangarhi village, Marriott has written that these days there is a keen competition between castes for status and between individuals for social regard. This competition has increased after the Zamindari abolition. The Panchayat system has increased this competition since almost all the members of the village take part in the elections of village Panchayat and Panchayati Adalat. The Brahmin cultivators are trying to dominate due to increase in their economic power on land. However, it is difficult for them to create a strong social organisation though their population is one-fourth of the village and they are owners of half of the land in the village since they cannot be unanimous about their leader. They fail to understand as to how one individual can be representative of the whole caste. In them everyone speaks for himself or at the most for his relatives, or he does not speak nor does he cooperate with others. Among the eight other castes, the wealthy artisans and the farmers are trying to achieve higher status and to make their economic status stable. In this they are getting the help of political and religious movements to raise the caste status even outside the village. However, most of the members of a caste cannot even cooperate to come together since like the Brahmins, they have also their internal differences. The Jajmani custom in the village is gradually disappearing. Some old villagers are seen pointing out that the old behaviour of regard has ceased to exist leading to social disintegration. They do not differentiate between the caste system and social system and therefore consider the disintegration of caste system as the disintegration of social system.

Inter-group Relationships

In Kishangarhi, members of different groups rarely meet except on some public festivals. Most of the groups come in contact due to certain festivals. These festivals, therefore, provide an occasion for inter-group relationship. However, generally, there is lack of such contacts. The social groups of men and women are also separate. Due to this division of groups on the basis of sex, sometimes husband and wife may develop social relationships which are contradictory to each other and against the patterns established by castes. The children have an important role in the contact between different caste groups, since in spite of what the elders say, the children do not make caste distinctions in play groups. The greatest impediment in the inter-group relationships is the prevalent idea in Kishangarhi that strong contact outside one's own caste or group diminish his caste loyalty. Therefore, no one thinks it correct to have contact with other caste groups openly. Even those who do so, try to keep their relationships secret. Those who do so openly are considered fools or nuisance. However, one may observe inter-caste and inter-group relationships which have led to the disintegration of caste groups. And yet due to social opposition such contacts are not sufficient and wherever found are generally based upon friendship or factionalism.

Festivals and Ceremonies

The public ceremonies provide an occasion for the inter-caste contact. In the ceremonies of marriage, members of other castes also participate. In the marriage ceremonies, one to four dozen women without any formal invitation gather in the house of the bride and the bridegroom and sing for ten nights preceding marriage. Only males participate in the procession and feasts of marriage and that too only on formal and proper invitation. In the procedure of invitation, the foremost right goes to nearest relative, after which representatives of other lineage within the caste group have their place. Then, some such members of other castes are invited to help in the conducting of ceremonies. Some people outside the village may be also invited but such invitations must observe consistency. For example, it is not possible that other caste or family member may be invited preceding one's own caste and one's own family member. Any violation of the procedure and order of invitation creates a lot of annoyance which is revenged on the occasion of similar ceremonies in future. This strict observance concerning formal invitations is not considered important on other occasions. However, as a general rule, birth celebrations and death celebrations are generally preceded by the same order of invitation.

Besides the family ceremonies Hindu festivals provide important occasions for inter-caste contact. Generally, these festivals are celebrated by the entire village. Of these, Deepawali and Holi are the most important. Besides these, there are dozens of other festivals in which women and children participate. These festivals are celebrated in every home and children and women of all the castes participate in them. During the festival of Holi all sorts of restrictions upon contacts are ignored and everyone behaves as he likes. Besides the festivals, some sport competitions or occasions for singing are important for inter-caste relationships. Similarly, the annual fairs and the annual worships of deities provide an occasion for participation to males and females of all the castes.

Village Factions

In spite of so many occasions for the mixing of different castes, Kishangarhi village never had any inter-caste organisation. No associations were ever formed which may cover the entire village or which may concentrate on problems of the total village. Though in the leadership of the landlord some sort of discipline was observed in the village, the entire village was never organised. People from outside the caste seldom participate in the caste associations. This factionalism is so dominant in the village that in the past elections different candidates generally represented different caste groups and most of the votes were given on caste basis. This factionalism is the biggest social problem in the village. It has made village panchayats and panchayati adalat centres of intrigues. The village panchayat includes members of several castes. These members, however, seldom cooperate. The most active group is the local Brahmin association which is the most numerous and wealthy in the village. The old landlords are busy in intrigues outside the village panchayat. The village Panchayats have failed to achieve their aim. They could not recover even half of the revenue claimed by them. In the last three years a very small part of the fines imposed by them has been recovered. The plans of village development could not work. Only one person could be punished and he belonged to the Brahmin caste. Only in two cases the lower caste persons were punished. In almost, all cases dissent of opinion had to be recorded and generally the help of police, landlord or the court was sought. This failure of the Panchayati Adalat exhibits social integration in the village.

Panchayati *Adalat*

However, though the panchayat could not decide most of the cases, a new case was filed, almost every month. Thus, 50 cases were filed, of which 25 were sent to rural court of Braj Garhi. Most of these were concerned with insult, threats or disputes of plots. Generally, the witnesses presented many new evidence which complicated even the smallest complaints. Often several cases continue side by side till one of the parties wins the case. The opposite party files several new cases on the very next day. On an average, a çase in village Adalat continues for two months and the villager devotes at least one day in a month for litigation.

The rural court of Braj Garhi decides the cases concerning Kishangarhi and some other four villages within its area. The representatives to it are elected by the same procedure as adopted in rural panchayats. Hands are raised to vote on some names decided earlier. Almost all the 25 members of village Adalat are landlords. However, since there is no organisation of landlords, they are generally fighting among themselves. Therefore, instead of providing justice they are generally busy settling matters among themselves. They take no interest in settling the disputes but rather encourage litigation, Generally, cases rejected by them are taken to higher courts. Most of their decisions are taken for appeals. However, these former landlords go on dominating the village *Adalat* since they are helped by their higher contacts. The Tehsildar and the Sub-Divisional officers these days hear so many cases that they cannot easily decide themselves. Formerly, such cases were decided by some influential members of the village. But this inner conflict in the village is sometimes advantageous to the administration. In fact, generally the administrators try to fulfil their ends by creating conflict among various factions. During the past years in the three big criminal cases the police acquired necessary information by fanning factional rivalries. For the recovery of revenue concerning Zamindari abolition also such conflicts were encouraged. Again, the politicians win votes by fanning factional rivalries. Factions, however, are the biggest hurdles in the development of the village. In India, the development of villages requires co-operation by rising above caste distinctions and considerations of personal regard. Internal conflicts are the biggest impediments in the success of cooperative movement and community development projects. They are sources of so much waste of energies of rural people. The caste systems have disintegrated, the jajmani system has broken down and the lineage groups have fallen apart. Though these are signs of change, these have created social disintegration. These, however, cannot be revived. The society cannot return to old organised caste system. The old foundations will have to be dismantled in order to establish new structure. This requires a new social organisation, in place of the old one. The constituents of this new social organisation, however, will not be different since not revolution but development is the need for social reconstruction in India.

The five hundred forty-seven acre area connected with Kishangarhi is plain and fertile. However, there is lack of means of irrigation since the fifty wells used for irrigation are mostly 30 feet deep. This, sometimes requires seven or eight persons together with bulls to take out water from these wells. However, the other functions in cultivation do not require more than three persons at a time in a field. The village grows sufficient fodder for 400 cattle and more than enough grains and also some oil seeds for sale. Most of the members of lower caste are caught in debt trap. Most of the persons borrow to purchase grains and work in exchange. After zamindari abolition the labourers do not work for the whole year, they are generally changed every year. Besides farmers, Kishangarhi includes men from other professions such as priests, carpenters, barber, potter, tailor, weaver, cobbler, washerman, hunter, singer, accountant etc. These professionals have their clients even from outside the village. Thus, the socio-economic structure of Kishangarhi is sufficiently complex.

THE KERALA VILLAGE[6]

Kerala villages are very much different from the villages of northern India. In them the houses are not built close to one another but scattered in the fields. Thus,

6. Eric J. Milier, *The Economic Weekly,* Vol. IV, No. 6, 9, Feb., pp. 159-60.

they continue for miles and it is difficult to distinguish one village from another. Another significant characteristic of Kerala villages is the rigid caste system. Though caste system is also found in north India but the social gap between the higher and lower castes observed in south Indian society cannot be seen in the north. The Kerala farmer plants palm trees and the banana trees around his house. The houses of the lower castes are also scattered. Due to the houses being scattered low caste group are found to be living together.

Social Organisation

Of the traditional four Varnas of Hindu society, the Kshatriyas are almost non-existent in Kerala. The Vaishyas are also few in number. Thus, the population mostly includes Shudras or the untouchables. In the society the Namboodiri Brahmins occupy the highest place. They constitute patrimonial group. Most of them are rich landlords. The leaders of some other castes also have equal economic and political status but they occupy a lower social status. They form matrilineal group. Many of them claim to be Kshatriyas. They generally quarrel about the question of higher and lower castes. They are generally exogamous. They give their daughters in marriage to Namboodiri's while they get wives from the Nayyars. Nayyar is a big matrilineal group which constitutes the middle class and the backbone of Kerala society. Traditionally, they are soldiers and some of them occupy government posts but primarily, they are soldiers. Some of the Nayyar's constitute the lower castes of temple servants. Among the Nayyar's the lowest sub-castes are constituted by washermen and barbers. All these castes are known as Hindus. The Shudras have a common culture. They have the custom of polygamy. In Kerala, even males from the lower castes and subcastes sometimes take their wives from the lower castes. Due to endogamy, this custom is gradually disappearing. Due to the relationship of Nayyars with Namboodiri's the different castes among Hindus exhibit some sort of organisation. Among the Hindus about 1/4th are Nayyars. Other Hindu castes constitute about 10% and the rest 2/3rd are untouchables. Of these also there are two groups. In the higher group there are labourers and small farmers who are known by different names at different places. In this group are also included the carpenter, the iron smith and the washerman among the untouchables are included Chamars, Artisans, Singers, Nut, Beggars and most of landless labourers.

According to Miller, the relation of caste system with the land of the village is particularly related to the cultivation of paddy. In north Malabar, generally, the most important family of the village possesses maximum amount of land. The landlords are mostly Namboodiri. The main family of the village keeps some land for itself while the rest is distributed to others for cultivation. Thus, most of the land is cultivated by others while the Namboodiri and the Mukhiya castes are the owners of the land. The higher Nayyar sub-castes are either farmers or Khanamday meaning non-cultivating owners who are permanently engaged in farming. Among the higher untouchable castes most of the persons are landless labourers while among the lower untouchable castes most of the people are serfs who change the masters with the change of land? Thus, relationship with land also shows social status in Kerala villages. In the village at some time or the other every family comes in contact with every other family but besides this some occupations and rules of behaviour, are connected with every caste which determine its social status. These days there is often conflict on the question of higher and lower among different castes.

Formerly, in the village different castes were inter-dependent. Each one was fulfilling everyone's needs. Thus, the villages were self-dependent. The local members of every caste were closely connected. Due to the custom of Kulin marriage, endogamy was observed. Each caste had its own organisation under its elders which used to settle the cases of dispute. The local temple was generally looked after by members of Namboodiri family, but the political power and economic control was generally in the hands of Nayyar caste. The chief Nayyar family also provided the head of the village and generally this headship was hereditary. Though, most of the castes had some power over the lower castes but the responsibility of maintaining the local law and order was entrusted to the Nayyar castes.

Several villages together constituted small estates. These estates together were ruled by bigger rulers. In the religious field the superiority of Namboodiri Brahmins balanced the superiority of the Nayyars, in the political field. Most of the conflicts were not between different castes but between the territorial units such as villages, estates and the kingdom. The relationships among different castes were not contraries but complementarities. Their rights and duties were determined by traditions. The judicial power was vested with the head of the village who was also the chief trustee of the villages falling within his jurisdiction. The village was known as desha while the head was known as *deshvari.* He was not the ruler but the first among the powerful Nayyars. Though, he managed the village temple but he did so not as an individual but as the chief of the association of Nayyars. Thus, the Nayyar associations were very powerful and in the matters of justice the head had to abide with their decision.

Each caste in the village had its own internal organisation which solved the internal matters. This organisation was not strong among lower castes of agricultural serfs since most of them were attached to different landlords. Like the other Indian villages one finds a dominant caste in the social stratification in Kerala village. The disputes of lower castes were generally decided by members of the higher caste. The Tiya caste is the highest and, therefore, has the responsibility of maintaining peace among lower castes. On the occasions of marriage etc., the leader of the Tiya caste is present. He or his representative also accompanies the marriage procession of the lower castes. If he fails to solve some disputes, then some Nayyar or Deshvari solves it. Whenever, someone is excommunicated from the village, it requires the sanction from Deshvari who also sees to it that the punishment is executed. According to Miller, there is a correlation between the social status of different castes and their distance from untouchable castes.

The more a caste is lower the more distance its member has to observe from the members of higher caste. Any violation of this rule makes the individual of the higher caste contaminated. Thus, the members of the Tiya caste have to keep a distance of 24 feet from the members of the Nayyar castes. For the serfs this distance is 64 feet.

In the caste system in India almost everywhere a member of a higher caste can exploit and misbehave with a member of lower caste. Kerala village is no exception to this rule. There also the member of the higher caste generally exploits the members of the lower castes. As the caste system is backed by religious sanction, the members of the lower castes do not oppose this tyranny. Even if he feels it bad his opposition is not to the caste but to some particular person. Generally, misbehaviour with a member of higher caste is considered to be very bad. For example, if a male from a lower caste commits adultery with a woman of higher caste it is considered an unpardonable crime, equally condemned by members of both the castes.

Generally, both are turned out of the village. If their family members do not excommunicate them, they are also excommunicated along with the culprits. Thus, like other Indian villages in the villages of Kerala also, the caste organisation is sufficiently strong as a means of social control.

Temple festivals

Like the villages in other parts of India, the Kerala village also shows inter-caste relationships. The village temple plays an important role in increasing inter-caste contact. In the festivals of temple, members of all the castes come together. Formerly, the untouchable castes were not allowed to enter the temple, but since 1947-48 they have started entering the temples. They can now enter every part of the country. Thus, all the castes are equal so far as entry to the temple is concerned. However, the castes are not equal in celebrating temple festivals. Different castes observe different distances from the temple on the occasion of festival and the lowest castes keep the maximum distance. Thus, the temple festival shows different status of different castes in social stratification.

Economically, different castes are inter-dependent. Several families of the lower castes are tied with high caste families in servant-master relationship. Castes involved in similar occupations also come together. Members of different castes from the villages go to the nearby city and engage in the same occupation which provides them an occasion for meeting together. However, even now in the village members of different castes consider it better to take up the caste occupations.

Since, many villagers have migrated to the city and also due to inter-village migration, the social organisation of the village has become loose and yet some families in the village form a nucleus as centre of the village as was in the past. These families were living in the village from the very beginning. Even otherwise, as compared to the villages of the other parts of India, the Kerala villages are less self-dependent and less organised since the residences in the village are not concentrated but scattered in the fields. Whereas in the same village one finds a unity in the sequence of different castes, the caste relationships also extend in the area outside the village. Thus, one finds both vertical and horizontal order among castes.

Jajmani System

Like other Indian villages, the Kerala villages also have Jajmani system. In the villages of Cochin, the women of Velum caste wash the clothes of members of Iraven caste. In Velum families, some families serve Raos while the others serve only the Nayyar. Thus, the Velum caste has been divided into sub-castes. Among these sub-castes every family serves some definite persons. But the services of all the castes are not confined to the members of the village. Some persons serve even outside the village. For example, the astrologer family serves several villages as it does not get sufficient work in a single village. Similarly, families weaving baskets also serve several villages. Again, the barbers serve several villages. Thus, members of the lower castes are related to members of the higher castes due to some services. According to Miller, when two Nayyars meet in Cochin, they do not ask as to from which villages the other has come but enquire as to whose Nayyar they are. This shows that each Nayyar family is tied to a particular Namboodiri family. Thus, like other villages in India Kerala village also has Jajmani custom.

Modern Changes

Ever since British Rule started in Malabar, the South Indian villages have been constantly changing in political, social and economic areas. The British granted pensions to the families of former rulers and created new departments after abolishing the boundaries of former kingdoms. Thus, the political authority of the old landlords was abolished and their power was limited to economic and social status. The old states in Kerala were known as *Nad*. For administration the Malabar district was sub-divided into *Talluk, Firaka, Ansham and Desham*. The village chief was known as *Adhigari*. The accountant of the village was called *Memon*. Both these worked for *Ansham* who was equivalent to the old *Desham*. There is no officer corresponding to modern *Desham*. The Britishers carried on similar administrative divisions in Cochin as well. Thus, Desham was no more a village but a part of it. Several *Deshams* together constituted a village whose chief was formerly known as *Deshvari* and now *Paravadayam*. Like other villages in India one finds village Panchayats in Kerala villages as well.

The village chief *Adhigari* was formerly elected from *Deshvari* family. But when the British employed them in smaller jobs their prestige diminished. Since then *Adhigari* was not the chief of *Deshvari* family but one of its members. The head of the *Deshvari* family was even more respected than *Adhigari*. Cases which could not be settled by the Adhigari were brought before the *Deshvari* family.

On *Desham*, a part of the village, some powerful Nayyar joint family ruled. The oldest member of such a family was called *Yajmanan*. The Yajmanan enjoyed social rights. He could punish any member of his area for any unsocial act.

Today, the rights of Yajmanan have become limited. However, they are even now powerful due to economic status. They also have much say in administration. They have also been given some power by the state but most of their power is derived from the status of landlord. Most of the members of the lower castes go to the higher castes, particularly to the Yajmanan for settling their disputes. The Yajmanan even settles the disputes among the Hindus and Muslims. As has been already pointed out, disputes which could not be settled by Adhigari were placed before the Yajmanan. Though, the Yajmanan is not himself Adhigari, he is an adult of the Adhigari family. The Yajmanan realises his responsibility in settling the disputes of his domain. Generally, he tries to bring opposite parties to some sort of compromise. Besides the cases concerning property, he also deals with cases of physical violence. Sometimes he imposes fines and keeps with him the money realised. He does not allow the majority of the cases to go to the courts since both the parties are generally under him and he can even restrain them by force. Since, the domains of different Yajmanans have not been clearly demarcated, sometimes their followers fight and the disputes are taken to the courts. The Yajmanan is the trustee of the temples of his area and has the right over the temple income. Besides, he enjoys special prerogatives.

According to Miller, one does not find the same unity and organisation in Kerala village as seen in a north Indian village. Sometimes even neighbourers are not intimate since they belong to different Deshams. But whenever neighbourhood relationships prevail, the Desham bond is weakened. Since, most of the members of different castes are connected with other members of their castes outside the village, one hardly finds any economic unity in the village. If there is some powerful Deshvari family, it maintains organisation and develops community life. According to Miller, whatever would have been the condition in 19th century at present one does not find well-coordinated and independent rural communities in Kerala villages.

PUNJAB VILLAGES

Rural Structure

In contrast to Kerala village, the Punjab village has residences at one place so that the village appears an organised unit. The walls of the houses are interconnected, forming lanes which lead to one another. The wider lanes serve the purpose of roads. Generally, there is only one road to enter the village which leads to an open area where there are shops and the meeting places of the villagers. Tanks are found sometimes within the village and sometimes on its border. Besides the tanks one finds wells in the village. The fields are all around the village. After the fields one finds sandy land. The areas which are more fertile have villages connected with one another. Some villages have a boundary wall around them.

On page 33 of the Gazetteer of Lahore District of 1916 it has been pointed that the village structure can be seen in the form of Pattis. Ordinarily, Sikh village is divided into four Pattis by the main roads. Thus, all the villages, including those belonging to Jats, Hindus and Muslims are divided into Pattis. But sometimes due to increase of population in the village or due to some other reason a resident of a Patti may live in another Patti. Thus, the membership of a Patti is definite and its boundaries are limited. However, it is not necessary that the members of a Patti may always be found within their own limits. Each Patti has its own shops, public ground and religious place. Each Patti shows a widespread community consciousness. It is said that even the dogs recognise the limits of their Patti and do not allow dogs from any other Patti to enter their boundary. Thus, not only the Punjab village is an organised unit, but even its sub-divisions are organised.

Group Exogamy

Generally, the residents of a village are considered to be descending from common ancestors. Thus, even members of a Patti consider them connected to some common ancestors. It is believed that the four Patties of a village were initially established by four brothers and the present population has descended from them. The name of this ancestor is carried on by the residents of the Patti. Thus, though not related by head, they consider themselves related and therefore do not many among themselves. Thus, in the Punjab village one finds exogamy not only in the village but even in the Pattis of the village.

Ethnic Group

According to Smith, in Punjab there are more ethnic groups than caste groups. These ethnic groups do not have peculiar beliefs or customs but some of their characteristics are peculiar to themselves. Near Amritsar and Lahore one finds Jats and Rajputs who may be Hindu, Muslim or Sikh. Among Sikhs the Jats are maximum in number. Similarly, the Muslims include the maximum of Rajputs. While Jats are known for dairy farming, the Rajputs are cultivators. Both have proved to be good soldiers. Some other occupations are also carried on by them. One does not find much segregation among members of different religious groups in Punjab village. Thus, one finds Jats at one place whether they may be Hindus, Sikhs or Muslims. The domestic animals are sometimes kept within the house and sometimes outside. Thus, one finds similarity in ways of living among members of an ethnic group, whatever may be their religion.

Caste System

According to Smith, one does not find castes based upon occupations in Punjab. In Sikh religion, members of all the castes are treated as equal. Similarly, the Muslims also do not admit caste distinctions. However, caste can be seen in the social life of Punjab not only among the Hindus but also among the Sikhs and the Muslims. Sometimes a Muslim cobbler and a Sikh cobbler are considered to be members of same occupational caste though belonging to different religious groups. Again, caste groups are found not only among the Hindus but also among the Sikhs and Muslims.

Division of Labour

Like the villages of the other parts of India, the castes in Punjab are also interconnected, since members of different castes have abilities for different occupations. For example, in the village a woman purchases wool from a Muslim, gets it cleaned by a Sikh and coloured by a Muslim. Finally, some Muslim or Sikh weaver weaves it and in the end a Hindu tailor makes clothes out of it. Thus, even the manufacture of a jacket involves the contribution of so many castes and religions. The division of the country adversely affected the rural economy in Punjab since most of the professional persons left the village. But then, refugees from other villages gradually learned these vocations.

Village Exogamy

The Punjab village is exogamous. Even those villages which have a population of 3000 or more do not observe endogamy. Thus, the marital relationships extend far and wide. Daughters are not given to the village from where brides are taken. The villages to which daughters are offered in marriage enjoy higher status. For example, if a male of a village A marries a female of the village B, the village A will have a higher status and the village B a lower status and in future the girls will always go from B village to A village and never *vice-versa.* The villages providing brides to B village will also be considered lower than A village. Thus, the connections of a village due to marital relationship extend far and wide. These traditions are observed for centuries and some villages have been permanently labelled as higher and the other lower. For example, most of the Sikh girls are married from south to north. The north Punjab village is, therefore considered to be higher. It is believed that the nearer a village is to Amritsar, the higher it is. According to tradition, each village has some definite villages to offer daughters in marriage and to select brides. The Punjab villages not only observe village exogamy but also Gotra exogamy. As the inhabitants of a Patti are known as belonging to the same Gotra, they do not marry among themselves. The whole village is named after the religion of majority of the members such as Sikh village. Again, villages are labelled after the majority of the ethnic group such as Jat villages, Rajput villages etc. Thus, neither any village has only one religious group nor is it inhabited by a single ethnic group. Generally, each village includes members of different religions, ethnic groups and Gotras. But the village exogamy and Gotra exogamy is also based on certain other considerations. One such consideration is the distance between villages. It is considered necessary that the boy and girl should not see each other before marriage. Therefore, marriages are prohibited within such areas where meeting may be possible. Thus, no one marries in village within a radius of 4 miles. Marriages are contracted generally in the villages which have a distance of 8, 12 or 16 miles.

Family

The family in the Punjab village is mostly patrilocal and after marriage the wife resides in the house of the husband. Most of the families are joint. As the number of the members of the joint family constantly increases, the burden upon them also increases. In order to solve the problem of this burden, the younger sons are sent to seek jobs outside the village. Their wives and children are left in the joint family and they regularly send money to meet their expenses. Thus, the income and expenditure of the family is generally joint. Those who are employed outside continue to have their status in the family and return to their villages after retirement. Thus, each Punjab village has a quota of former soldiers etc.

The Village Panchayat

Like other villages of the country the Punjab villages also have panchayats. Besides the village panchayats one finds panchayats among pattis. A patti Panchayat solves internal matters of the patti. Cases concerning inter-patti relationships are brought before the village panchayat. Each patti has a team of players. Generally, competitions are organised for sports and games between different patties and the winner team goes to compete with other villages. Though, each patti has its own organisation, all the patties act united in the question of the village. All the castes and religions are organised in questions concerning the villages boundary, the irrigation water, the insult to women and the disputes with other villages. Thus, one finds communal organisation in the Punjab villages but mostly for political purposes. The Punjabis are very clever in political matters. This cleverness is explicit in the communal organisations such as Akali Dal. These communal organisations are active even in elections to village panchayats. Though, the old caste system is breaking, the communal organisations are becoming even more strong. According to Smith, though a Punjab village may appear as an organised unit in some particular cases, on other occasions it does not act as a self-dependent community. For example, in the economic field, marital relationships, religious and political organisations the connections of the members of a village extend far and wide. The units in these areas are naturally wider than those of a village.

QUESTIONS FOR EXERCISE

1. Give sociological analysis of any one village of India.
2. Compare and contrast Kerala village and Punjab village.
3. Write a note on social organisation in a village of Uttar Pradesh.

9

PATTERNS OF CHANGE IN RURAL SOCIETY

Purpose of Study

Pointing out the purpose of his study of the dynamics of Rural Bengal Society with the above mentioned title, R.K. Mukherjee writes in the preface of his book, *The Dynamics of Rural Society*, "The objective behind the present study is to examine the dynamics of a rural society and to show that the dynamics of a society cannot be revealed without an analysis of its economic structure."[1] Further explaining the hypothesis of his study he says, "This hypothesis will be tested in two stages. Firstly, only the economic sphere of a society will be taken into consideration, and it will be shown how without an analysis of the economic structure it is not possible to have a true understanding of the character of its economy, which undoubtedly plays a basic role in the social development of any people. Secondly, in the social-ideological sphere of a society it will be shown what an important effect the economic structure has on the social organisation of the people. In this way, the present study will endeavour to prove that even while accepting a schematic formulation of human society as obeying these sets of laws, *viz.*, economic, social and ideological, an examination of the economic structure of a society is basic to its proper understanding."[2] He selected rural Bengal in British period of India's History for two reasons. Firstly, rural Bengal represented an egalitarian society, that is, as composed of a mass of undifferentiated or little differentiated people. Secondly, the social organisation of rural Bengal was regarded as basically governed by the institution of caste system.

I. PEASANT SOCIETY AND ECONOMIC STRUCTURE

1. An Egalitarian Society. Indian village has been called an egalitarian society due to its almost complete dependence on agricultural production, the primitive state of her productive forces in agriculture and the poorly developed techniques, of production. R.K. Mukherjee, however, calls this an illusion. As he points out

1. Mukherjee, R.K. *The Dynamics of a Rural Society,* Akademic Verlage, Berlin, 1957.
2. *Ibid.*, Preface, p. X.

in rural Bengal there was an appreciable range of incomes in different classes of society received from different sources. Therefore, the *rural society is neither static nor egalitarian.*

As Mukherjee shows from the data concerning per capita income, the number of households and percentage of total households in rural Bengal, the households did not form a compact group of similar economic position, of which income is evidently the simplest measure. Although the incomes ranged over a somewhat wide dimension, the overwhelming majority of the people was restricted within a small range. This made the distribution asymmetrical and peaked with a heavy density in a narrow sector. In the words of R. K. Mukherjee, "The important conclusion which emerges from the above is that inequality in income distribution leading to sharp differentiation within a society is possible even when the average income of the people is very low and the total range narrow." Thus, Mukherjee shows the presence of well-defined income hierarchy in rural Bengal. The inequality in income distribution and the presence of an income hierarchy naturally suggests a concentration of income in a sector of society. According to Mukherjee, "the criterion to determine the economic structure should be such that it will not merely segregate the people into abstract statistical categories of various "elements" of a society; it must express the social significance of the economic hierarchy." Thus, the criterion must be traditionally recognised in the society.

2. Economic criterion. According to Mukherjee, "In India a person living in a rural area is usually described as (a) inhabiting a particular territory or village, or (b) belonging to a particular caste or community, or (c) living by a particular family or household occupation." The household incomes of the Bengal villagers differ considerably. The villages have been classified under the criteria of village, caste and religious groups, and household occupation. All these have been examined by Mukherjee before arriving at his own economic criterion. The religious classification of Bengal villagers can broadly be done as Hindu, Muslim and others. Their household occupations may be defined as those from which each of the households derived most of its income. On this basis the people of rural Bengal could be classified under nine occupational groups: Landholders, Supervisory farmers, Cultivators, Sharecroppers, Agricultural Labourers, Artisans, Traders, Service holders and others including ill-defined lowly occupations. According to Mukherjee, household occupations can better segregate the rural population than the religious groups. Out of the above-mentioned nine occupational groups, Mukherjee distinguishes the following three classes: (I) Landholders and Supervisory farmers, (II) Cultivators, artisans and traders, (III) Sharecroppers, agricultural labourers, service-holders, and others. Of these while the class 1st comprises only 4% of the total households, it has an income of nearly 1½ times more than the overall average. The class IInd comprises nearly half of the total households and has an income of a little more than the general average. The class IIIrd comprises more than the half of the total households but has an income of less than the general average. According to this analysis, the economic structure of rural Bengal is represented by the above three classes, defined in relation to her socio-economic units.

3. Classes and production-relations. According to Mukherjee, "The operation of an economy is the total manifestation of the inter-relationship of the people in regard to the production of wealth in society. Consequently, the composition of the economic structure should be the total representation of the different types of production-relations, which the people have entered into in course of their economic activities."[3] An examination of the specific roles of the three classes shows the production-relations of the agrarian economy of Bengal. The class 1st is composed of the landed gentry, *viz.* the landholders and supervisory farmers who did not actively participate in agriculture but enriched themselves from the concentration of land. The class IIrd is composed mainly of self-sufficient and self-cultivating peasants with proprietary rights on land, as well as traders and the artisans. The class IIIrd is mainly composed of sharecroppers and agricultural labourers with very little or no land of their own, as well as the non-agricultural occupational groups. According to Mukherjee, "The operation of the economy of rural Bengal in the British period of her history is thus seen to have been dependent on two sets of production-relations in society; one between the classes I and III owner and not-owner of the means of production (land) and as user-supplier of labour, respectively and the other of the Class II as owner of the means of population and user of own labour."[4]

4. Class II and the production-relation in pre-British days. In pre-British days there was community system in the village characterised by self- sufficient and autonomous village units, communally held land so that each household lived on subsistence production on the land allotted to it. In those days, "agriculture was the main occupation of the villages but each of them had usually its own compliment of weavers, potters, carpenters, oil pressers and goldsmiths."[5] The communities were autonomous. Their jurisdiction extended over houses, streets, bazars, burning grounds, temples, wells, tanks, waste lands, forests and cultivable lands. The village council looked after village defence, settled village disputes, organised works of public utility, acted as a trustee of minors and collected the government revenues and paid them into the central treasury. The central state governments could reach the people and discharge their function mainly through village councils. Kings could impose taxes but these could be realised only if the village councils agreed to collect them. An individual's hold on land in ancient India was more in terms of possession than of ownership. The land was used for subsistence production instead of as a property for profit making. The disposal of any land within a village was impossible without the prior permission and direct supervision of the village council. Whether or not land alienation and transfer took place, the land was only for possession and use by the rural household for subsistence production. In broad sense, the possession was in common in self-sufficient and autonomous village communities. In this system it was not difficult

3. *Ibid.*, p. 12.
4. *Ibid.*, p. 14.
5. R.C. Majumdar and A.S. Alteker, *The Vakataka-Gupta Age*, p. 266.

for a person to become a self-possessing and self-working peasant. Secondly, there was no extensive house or external market for the agricultural produce. This situation remained the same in Muslim period. Thus, throughout the pre-British period, land grants meant predominantly the confirming of right to land revenue. They did not lead to the establishment of private property right in land and to the growth of landlordism. The class second of the economic structure was predominant. It governed the only form of production-relation in society. It was only after the British established the concept of private property, creative landlords, disintegrated village community system and made the crops a commodity that this system was disturbed.

5. Emergence of the classes I and III. The production-relation in rural Bengal underwent transformation in the British period resulting in the emergence of class I and III due to introduction of private property right over land and the other reasons mentioned above. During the British period the production relations were dependent upon the permanent Zamindari Settlement introduced by the East India Company in 1793.

6. Function of the economic structure. The above analysis only explains how the class I and III emerged in rural society, it does not discuss why they emerged. Under British rule the character of rural trend changed, firstly, due to the policies of British merchant capital and secondly, due to industrial capital. Production was henceforth geared to the demands of the market. From about the middle of the nineteenth century railways and steamer·ways were introduced in India with the primary object of bringing the raw materials for the British industrialists from the remotest comers of the country to the ports for export to England and with the aim of circulating British manufactures into even the smallest village. And with this development more and more the crops began to possess a monetary value and were ultimately turned into commodities. Thus, the land owning became more and more interesting in directly securing crops from the land instead of settling peasants on it. The disintegrated peasantry, in the absence of the relationship between a supervisory famer and an agricultural labourer, adopted the landholder-cum-sharecropper relationship. This, on the one hand, secured their employment throughout the year and on the other hand, maintained their status of a grihastha or husbandman. Thus, he no more belonged to the class of agricultural labourers. Why Study Economic Structure? The economic structure expresses the economic forces working within the agrarian economy. The essential character of the rural economy in Bengal under British rule was that of a disintegrating system. This retrogressive character of the rural economy could be understood only by an objective analysis of the economic structure of the society. In the words of R.K. Mukherjee, "One may, therefore, conclude, that this truth could be unravelled only by a study of the economic structure of the society which showed that the agrarian crisis was due to the colonial system imposed on the country and the rule of the parasitic landowning class as an appendage to that system, whereby their profit-motive could find ample satisfaction while preserving the peasant cultivation without any capital outlay in order to improve the state of the productive forces..." Herein lies the importance of studying the economic structure of a "peasant society".[6]

II. SOCIAL ORGANISATION AND ECONOMIC STRUCTURE

1. Caste system and social organisation. About the role of caste in India, diametrically opposite opinions have been given. The question that requires to be examined is: did the rural life in British India sustain caste or did it slowly lead to its liquidation? Mukherjee answers this question by an analysis of caste and economic structure in rural Bengal.

2. Caste and economic structure in pre-British days. The main attributes of a caste are: (i) common hereditary occupation, (ii) endogamy, and (iii) commensurability. The unique characteristic of the Indian caste system is that within the four-fold Varna Dharma there are hierarchies of jatis which are usually occupational groups, further distinguished by sub-caste rules. Increasing social division of labour in the Aryan society led to further differentiation within Varna structure and thus created several jatis. This jati division was, however, not limited only to the Aryans but extended to the entire Indian society. Thus, the caste system is a typical Indian Institution not belonging to any particular religious group. It is due to caste system that the village units did not burst because of contradictory aspirations of the people in social and material life. In the words of R. K. Mukherjee, "In this way, the caste system supplied the social foundation to the village community system in India by providing the society with an unalterable division of labour: so that this system remained as the most important economic institution of Indian society until its basis to be altered from about the fourteenth century with the rise of new forces in Indian society and until it was finally destroyed in the early years of British rule."[7] The caste system thus supplied the social force to economic stability. It was itself established by Hindu philosophy and religion, particularly the doctrine of Karma, the theory of reincarnation. In the words of Mukherjee, "The doctrine of Karma and the theory of reincarnation taught the people that their position in society was the consequence of their work in the previous birth and that their obedience to the ethics of the society would improve or deteriorate their caste position in the next life or might even lead to their deliverance from any future worldly existence."[8] Thus, the caste system played a significant role in Indian social organisation so long as the village community system dominated Indian life. Simultaneously, it transformed a self-developing society into a never changing one. The economic basis of society which led to the flowering of the caste system and its stabilisation in society was supplied by the jati division of society and the establishment of village communities on the basis of stable relation between different groups. Thus, while the Varna Dharma represented the class-relations in conformity with social demands of its time, the jati Dharma built the economic structure of Indian society. The Bhakti Movement failed to abolish the caste system, which even more straightened as India became a British colony.

6. Mukherjee, R.K., *The Dynamics of Rural Society*, p. 58.
7. *Ibid.*, p. 71.
8. *Ibid.*

3. Caste hierarchy and economic structure in Bengal under British rule. The policy pursued by East India Company during its rule resulted into retrogression of Indian society. The policy of the British was to drive a wedge between the Hindus and the Muslims, the two largest communities in India. The renewed role of Brahmanism revived caste system and established its grip on the ideological life of the Indian people, particularly the Hindus. The establishment of definite forms of land tenures all over India with the common characteristic of introducing the concept of private property in land and with the special characteristic of creating landlords out of the previous revenue farms in the areas brought under the permanent Zamindari settlement of land in Bengal, further increased orthodoxy and established caste system. The caste hierarchy within the Hindu community and the upper castes and lower castes and the scheduled castes reflects the first, second and third classes of pre-British structure as explained earlier. Caste was established not only among Hindus but also among Moslems. In Moslem community, the Sayyed Moslems consider themselves as true Moslem and regard the Moslems belonging to functional castes as socially inferior. Corresponding to the upper, lower and scheduled Hindu castes, one finds Sayyed Moslems, Moslem functional caste and Scheduled Tribes in Moslems.

4. Caste system among the Hindus and the social order. Thus, the caste system was re-established with renewed vigour with the consistent support to Brahmanism from the ruler. It gained stability by establishing its structure within the newly evolved economic structure. As Brahmanism prevailed, the so-called Scheduled Castes and Tribes tried to rise in the social ladder by acculturation. In the words of Mukherjee, "Thus, it is seen that not only the loss of its previous economic basis did not destroy the caste system, but even the distinction by wealth in an economy of commodity production, which under normal circumstances should have cut across social distinctions based on birth qualification, led on the contrary to further intensification of the institution within the society."[9] The reasons for this were that the crops had become commodities, the relation of worker and landlord changed and the upper caste Hindus dominated social life.

5. Moslem community and the social order. According to R.K. Mukherjee, like the ideological domination over the other members of the Hindu community by the upper Caste Hindus, the persistence and elaboration of the functional castes among the Moslems, although Islam does not encourage any caste barrier, and the introduction of the dowry system in marriage among the wealthier Sayyed Moslems in place of their traditional practice of ensuring the security of the bride through a mehar, nam or bride-price, are two typical examples of acculturation into the Moslem community from the "upper Caste Hindus".[10] Moslems have been conventionally divided into two classes: Ashraf or noble, including all undoubted descendants of foreigners and converts from the higher Hindu castes, and Ajlaf, or common people, including most of the Sikhs and the various functional groups. These functional groups have panchayats who manage their affairs, and

---

9. *Ibid.*, p. 119.
10. *Ibid.*, p. 121.

who, in many parts, exercise almost as rigorous a control as the managing body of a Hindu caste. Amongst the social offences of which they take cognizance are the eating of forbidden food, adultery, divorcing a wife without due cause, making a false accusation against a caste-fellow, and marrying person not belonging to the group. Inter-marriage between Ashraf and Ajlaf is prohibited, and it is seldom that a man of the higher class will give his daughter to one of the lower. It is not so objectionable for an Ashraf man to take a wife from amongst the Ajlaf, but he is looked down upon he if does so, unless he has already one wife of his own class. Amongst the cultivating Shaikhs, the restrictions on marriage are slight. In the words of R. K. Mukherjee, "To sum up, it may he said that, though caste is unknown to the Muhammadan religion, it exists in full force amongst many of the Muhammadans of Upper India, and in all parts of the country amongst the functional groups that form the lower strata of the community. The other Indian Muhammadans, though they do not recognise caste, have, nevertheless, been so far influenced by the example of their Hindu neighbours that they have become far more particular about their matrimonial alliance than are their coreligionists elsewhere."[11]

6. Destructive role of the social order. According to O'Malley "In the past it (caste system) has helped to save Hindu society from disintegration and Hindu culture from destruction. Through successive conquests and revolutions it has been a stable force, and its stabilizing influence is not without political importance at the present time, when the communist movement is said to be a menace to India. A system which is permeated by religion is utterly opposed to the Bolshevist doctrine of a war upon religion. The idea of a class war is alien to a people who believe that the social hierarchy is divinely ordained and that equality is not only contrary to experience but is impossible because each man's state of life is predetermined by his actions in past lives. Many thoughtful Indians are, therefore, strongly in favour of the caste system on the ground that it is a bulwark of society against revolutionary assault." Agreeing with O'Malley, R.K. Mukherjee concludes his discussion by saying, "There cannot be any doubt, therefore, that, in order to examine the dynamics of a society, and for a 'peasant' society also, it is indispensable to study its economic structure and that this is necessary even for a proper understanding of its social institutions."

CHANGING SCENES IN OUR VILLAGES

Some or the other change is invariably taking place in the human community everywhere. Change is the law of nature. Change is demanded by life. Wherever there is life there is change. Death is only another name for complete immobility. Thus, change in the human community is natural. The communities of the villages are less dynamic than the urban communities, but this should not be taken to mean that the farmers have absolutely no mobility. The village communities, too, are changeable even though the rate of change within them is very slow. This fact can be verified by looking at the history of rural community in any area of India.

11. *Ibid.*, p. 128.

Importance of the Study of this Change

A study of the factors and patterns of change in the rural community will provide an insight is to the development of welfare work in the rural sphere because development is nothing more than change in any desired direction. In order to affect social, economic, political and any other kind of development in the villages, it is necessary to change them. With respect to the way in which this change can be brought about, it is necessary to know the effect of some particular factors upon the rural community, as well as the direction of and the reason for this change.

Factors of Change

Even though it is very difficult to analyse all the direct and indirect causes of change in a community, rural or otherwise, it nevertheless, is possible to recognise the major factors in change in the rural sphere which may be placed in the following classes:

1. Natural factors
2. Technological factors
3. Social factors
4. Economic factors
5. Cultural factors
6. Political factors.

It would be advantageous to make a brief study of factors which cause the change in rural life.

1. Natural Factors. The natural factors of change in the rural community include all those natural elements which are found in the place in which that specific rural community exists. For example, these villages which have sprung up close to the rivers and the villages prospering in the mountains show apparently the effects, respectively of the rivers and the mountains. The social, economic, cultural and religious life of the rural community settled in the bamboo forest exhibits the effects of the bamboos. In places frequented by seismographic disturbances, the houses are constructed of wood. The vegetation and the animals peculiar to any place are most frequently consumed and employed in their native land. In the same way, the cottage industries which develop in any place bear a direct co-relation to the minerals found in that area. In this way rivers, seas, floods, storms, rain, hail-storms, earthquakes, mountains, vegetation and animals etc. are the natural factors which influence the rural community. Whenever any one of these changes, the life of the rural community also changes at the same time. The geographists have written numerous books on the subject of the effects of geographical environment upon human life. The natural factors shape the geographic environment. Their effects are universally known. If the Ganges River alters its course miles away from the one which it was previously pursuing then not only the economic life but also other aspects of the rural community situated upon the old banks of the river will be changed.

2. Technological Factors. The natural environment alone does not transform human communities, because man constructs a fair portion of his environment for himself, and this also has widespread effects upon his life. Man creates a novel environment with the assistance of the technical factors and adapts natural environment to himself. These technological factors include all the inventions. Wherever electrical power has been made available to the villages, it has completely transformed the rural community. According to Prof. Ogburn the invention of the radio alone has resulted in nearly 150 major changes in social life. Machines have not been used as much in the Indian villages as they are in the villages of the West. But even then the work of grinding wheat and refining cotton has lost its flavour for the rural families since the machines for such purpose were installed in their village. This has influenced the life and the conditions of the women. With the invention of steam and electrical power all the aspects of human life have undergone some or the other change.

3. Social Factors. The social factors have comprehensive effect upon the social life of the rural community. For example, the existence or the non-existence of Sati custom, child marriage, negation of widow remarriage have some effect upon the life of the rural community, its effect being particularly evident in the condition of the female population. The major social factors which influence the life of the Indian rural community are caste system, joint family, Jajmani custom, various laws of marriage as well as social and religious customs and traditions etc. Any change in any one of these factors results in a change in the rural community. For example, when the caste panchayats grow weak or lose power completely the inter-caste relations in the villages undergo continuous change. In the same way changes can also be seen in the mutual relations between different castes due to the Jajmani relations having been broken off.

4. Economic Factors. The economic factors include those which are related to agriculture, business and industries. As a result of the pressure upon land having increased in the villages, many people have migrated to the towns in search of employment. Living in the towns the moral life and values of a rural youth undergo a change which have their influence upon the moral life and values of the other people in the village when he returns to the village. Wherever factories or mines have been established in the villages, the relations between men and women have been influenced by their working together. Poverty is an economic factor and its widespread effects upon the life of the community are only too well-known.

Cultural factors include beliefs, assumptions, values etc. Changes in them have repercussions in the entire social life. In India, wherever the Hindu, Muslim and Christian culture have had an opportunity to meet, the cultural life of the rural community evinces clearly the influence of this. As a result of the influence of Western culture the institution of youth dormitory is vanishing from many tribal villages. In rural girls and boys, who are influenced by Western culture, the tendencies of individualism, materialism and irresponsibility intrude and these exert important influence upon rural institutions like family, marriage, caste system etc.

6. Political Factors. The rural communities are also influenced by the political factors. For example, distinct differences may be seen between the rural communities under Hindu, Muslim and British governments. After the country achieved independence much awakening has been in evidence in the villages. Besides the government, political partyism also influences the villages. India is a democracy in which the public elects the representatives who run the administrative machinery. This is awakening political consciousness among the villagers.

METHODS OF RURAL CHANGE

Alongside the study of the foregoing factors which bring about change in the rural community it is also necessary to know the factors by means of which social organisations or political parties create change in the rural community. The description of these will also make evident as to which method should be employed in bringing about the desired change in the rural community in developing the rural welfare work. Sims and other prominent sociologists have enumerated the following among these kinds of methods:

1. The method of reasoning. Some people have confidence in reasoning with the village people in an effort to bring about some change in the rural community. This method does have some benefit but its major defect is that the people who make use of it do not themselves do anything actively and thus their word does not carry enough weight.

2. Demonstrative method. Thus, more importance is attached to the demonstrative method than to the method of reasoning, for it sets examples to the villagers. For example, advocacy about the utility of any agricultural implement cannot be as beneficial as making use of it in some farms. As a result of viewing its functions the farmers will themselves take interest in it and adopt it.

3. Compulsory method. As is obvious from its name this method resorts to enforcing the change compulsorily upon the rural population. In other words, the population is obliged to accept the desired change, and it is obvious that only the government can employ this method. The states have made quite extensive use of it. For example, many states in India have forced the villagers to behave gently towards untouchability making it to be a crime. The advantage of this method is that the changes are affected quickly but it suffers from the *drawback that it cannot create internal change. Internal change can he brought* about only by the reasoning and demonstrative method.

4. Social pressure method. Social organisations and institutions make most use of the method of social pressure in controlling or transforming the conduct of the individuals. As is obvious from its name, this method obliges the individual by exerting social pressure upon him. For example, the caste panchayat of the villages obliges the members of the caste to accept their decision by threatening social excommunication or extradition. This method certainly does prove quite effective due to men's sociability but it too suffers from an inability to achieve internal transformation. The first two methods are more appropriate for an internal change.

5. Contact method. It is a common fact that changes in men occur through contact. A person adopts many mannerisms from the people with whom he comes into contact and among whom he moves. In much the same way major changes can be seen in the rural communities which have come into contact with urban communities. Change in the mode of living, dress, customs and values is seen when the tribal villagers come into contact with Hindu and Christian culture, when the uncivilised people come into contact with the civilised people and when the villagers come into contact with Western culture.

6. Educational method. Education is an extremely important factor in the development of the personality of the individual. It is very essential to pay attention to the proper education of the child, besides watching his inherited tendencies, according to the aim for which the child or the parent is striving for. The same fact is, more or less, true with regard to communities as well. In India efforts are being made to introduce change in the villages through basic education and social education etc., and much success is also apparently being achieved. In order to create communal and political consciousness in the villagers it is necessary to impart proper education.

There are limitations to each of these methods for creating change in the rural communities and thus any method alone cannot serve the purpose. For this reason need is often felt for using more than one method. In order to achieve the desired changes in the direction of rural development reasoning needs to be supplemented by demonstration. Where some people are not prepared to take the trouble of understanding it, it is proper to introduce the compulsory and social pressure methods. In every change, education complementary to it should be imparted. In this way the desired changes in the rural community can be attained only by understanding all these methods and making use of them according to need and occasion.

SPHERES OF RURAL CHANGE

1. Change in the caste system. During the British rule the caste system suffered a severe shock in the village. Due to the British economic policy and new laws different castes abandoned their traditional occupations and adopted other professions. Many Brahmins and Kshatriyas started farming. The members of the untouchable castes became agricultural labourers. The control of caste panchayat weakened. It is seen in the villages now-a-days that the status of an individual in the villages is determined not only by his caste but also by his personality, financial condition and activities as well. Although, the Brahmin is addressed respectfully, the wealthy untouchable is not the recipient of any less respect even though he belongs to a lower caste. And at some place it may even be that he may be respected even more than the poor Brahmin. Being assisted by government laws the lower castes no longer look upon themselves as inferior and in south India at some places the untouchables consider themselves defiled if they touch a Brahmin. If any Brahmin happens to come into their sector he is assaulted with brooms and in extreme cases strict measures are taken to purify the place which he has defiled by his touch.

In this way in the present age the members of each caste are engaged in strengthening their own organisations. Some castes have formed their own improvement organisations, by holding meetings, for the protection of their interest. But even then the power of the caste panchayat, exercised in the form of control over the individual's behaviour, food habits, ways of living etc., have gradually disappeared. Even in such villages where the laws regarding touchability in the caste are necessarily observed, freedom is given towards violating them in the towns. Although, marriages are still contracted within the same castes even then there is no obstacle to behaviour, eating, conversing etc. between different castes. But although in this way the caste system appears to be growing weak on the one hand, it seems to be gaining in strength upon the other. Casteism is increasing due to vested interest. In recent times, it is seen that most of the people vote for the members of their own caste. Most of the political parties' issue tickets only to those members whose caste is in majority in that electorate. The same had been the case in the previous election and most elected persons had even tried to gain advantage for their own castes. In this way due to political and other interests casteism is increasing. Most administrative authorities in government and non-government factories, offices, colleges and other works think it necessary to employ only the members of their own caste.

2. Change in the jajmani system. In this way, in regard to the caste system both weakening and strengthening tendencies are in evidence but the jajmani system is undoubtedly crumbling. Jajmani system was based upon the exploitation of the Kameen by the Jajman. As a result of the declaration equating all the citizens of free India and the efforts of the government to improve the backward classes, the backward classes have now gained a certain degree of self-respect and their jajmani relations with other castes are in the process of being broken off. Secondly, the circulation of money in place of services in the villages has also had a degenerating effect upon the jajmani system. Thirdly, the jajmani relations are also dying out because the caste panchayats have lost their power and the occupations are no longer based on caste. Mobility is also increasing in the rural areas due to an increase in the facilities of transport. All these causes have together worked towards the detriment of the jajmani system, but this does not mean that the jajmani system has been completely eliminated from the villages. Remnants of the jajmani system have been found in all the recent studies of the rural communities although signs of their growing disability are also evident in most studies.

3. Change in the family. Although the joint families are still viewed with respect they are no longer the units of rural community, having been replaced by single families. Groups based upon similar interests are becoming stronger in place of the groups constituted from ancestry. With the increase of individualism the families are becoming smaller and smaller and the control exercised by the family over the individual member is also decreasing. But the ancestral group has not yet lost its power over the family completely. In the villages, as is wont to be in the towns, many of the activities of the family are being taken over by other agencies. For example, in the villages where a grinding machine has been installed, the wheat is ground in the mill instead of at home. The women are progressively being more educated and being given many social, economic and political rights with the result that they are conscious of their position.

4. Health and Medical Facilities. With the progress of sanitation and an increase in the number of doctors in the villages the general standard of health has improved in a few villages. Although medical facilities have definitely increased, this progress has been counteracted by an increase in the number of diseases. Not much enlightenment has spread among the village-folk in spite of the propagation of family planning and birth control by the government. The state of health of the women will definitely improve when the simple means to birth control heralded by proper education become available. Due to the food problem existing in the country the poor people of the villages cannot get adequate and nutritious food and thus their health has not moved up to the mark. As a result of the arrangements made by the government for vaccination and distribution of patent medicines some control over smallpox, malaria etc., has been achieved. The health of the female members can be said to have improved with the end of the purdah system and the improvement in the condition of houses. But, on the other hand, the increasing use of tea, tobacco, vegetable oil etc., is undermining the health of the villagers.

5. Education. Literacy is increasing among all the members of the villages. Basic education and social education are increasing, many of the states are making efforts to provide free and compulsory education to all the children in the villages. Many of the young men of the villages are going to the towns to receive higher education. In the bigger villages high schools and even intermediate colleges can be seen. In the rural area many rural institutes, agricultural colleges and degree colleges have been established.

6. Change in the economic field. The standard of living is rising in the villages, creating a demand for new things, for which new shops are being opened. The educated young men from the villages prefer service. The use of new tools is increasing in agriculture. The production has increased as a result of the new tools, new seeds and modern methods of farming. The condition of minor professions has improved with the opening of co-operative societies. The condition of finance and capital has been improved with the opening of cooperative credit societies, grain banks and co-operative banks, and the indebtedness has decreased. The cottage industries have been encouraged by government aid. The per capita income has increased but so have the prices of the commodities. The condition of the farmers and people engaged in minor occupations has improved with the removal of intermediaries.

7. Changes in the political field. With the establishment of panchayats in the villages political consciousness has increased. In some villages even newspapers are available which, along with the radio, help to increase the political knowledge of the villagers. But some political parties have also created disunity and factionalism within the villages. The villagers are not as afraid of the government officials as they used to be before independence. Even though there are panchayats, litigation has increased in the villages. The community feeling has decreased even though national consciousness has been aroused. Selfishness and individualism have increased along with co-operation.

From the foregoing glimpse of the changing scenes in our villages, it is evident that the Indian villages are changeable. In the words of Dr. Altekar, "Our history shows that the observations made by early writers like Metcalfe and Maine about Indian village communities being unchanging have to be accepted with great reservations: (a) The differences between the Western and Northern communities that were pointed out in The last section were all due to the fact that the communities in the North had changed owing to the factors that were not operating in Western India, (b) Since the days of Elphinstone and Metcalfe, we have actually noticed before our very eyes how most of the village institutions that excited their admiration have gone into oblivion. So the myth of those communities remaining unchanged must be given up. (c) Nor can it be maintained that leaving apart from consideration the changes introduced by the Muslim and British influences, there were no changes taking place in the Hindu period. For, we have seen how the influence of the Vedic Sabha dwindled down in the Brahminic age, how under the Maurya Imperialism, the jurisdiction of the local council and panchayat was considerably curtailed, how flekhakar' or the accountant did not exist in earlier times but came into existence subsequently, how the regular council of elders was not in existence down to the Vallbhi period and so on. To conclude, history shows us that both internal and external forces have been working out changes in our village communities, the Mohammadan influence was not powerful enough, so the institution continued to exist but their growth was arrested and efficiency weakened. The British influence, dominant and all-sided, has all but killed most of the village institutions. The headman has lost his importance, the accountant has ceased to be hereditary, the village council no longer exists, the panchayat is never heard of. The village fund has also vanished. Village life to a great extent remains the same, people still till their land and sow their crops in the old manner, but even here changes are coming and coming fast enough. The theory, therefore, that the Indian village communities do not change is completely disproved by the teachings of history."[12]

QUESTIONS FOR EXERCISE

1. Analyse the distinct features of rural stratification and social mobility.
2. Bring out the role of transport and communication means in rural-urban relation.
3. Explain with example the changes that have taken place in the Indian rural family.

12. Alteker, A.S., *A History of Village Communities in Western India*, pp. 128-29.

10

GREAT TRADITIONS IN RURAL CULTURE

The social life in every country is grounded in its concept of ultimate reality in the world and man, it is the philosophical basis of social life. This is particularly true of the communities which have a long tradition of social institutions. Such is the case with Indian society. Ever since the time of ancient Vedas, Indians have developed a systematic *Weltanschauung* which, in spite of all diversities, has an inherent unity in it. This may be understood by a perusal of the common characteristics of Indian philosophical systems. Again, charges levelled against Indian philosophy and the refutation of them will help the reader to assess the soundness of the philosophical basis of Indian social life. Here we will discuss the chief elements of Indian social philosophy, *viz.* the Varna System, Ashrama System, *Purusharthas* or *Trivarga*, concept of Rinas, Doctrine of Karma and the Sanskaras.

THE VARNA SYSTEM

The idea of *varna* is started in the Purusa Sukta of *Rigveda*. In it was laid down that the whole cosmos is the Purusa, of which the Brahmin represented the mouth, the Kshatriya his arms, Vaishya his thighs and the Shudra his feet.[1] Again, in *Rigveda* one finds mention of the four *varnas* when it is said, "One to high sway, one to exalted glory, one to pursue his gain and one to his labour — all to regard their different vocations, all moving creatures hath the Dawn awakened".[2] The above mentioned suktas also point out the duties of the four varnas. In *Mahabharata*, the sage Bhrigu explains the theory of the origin of the varnas to Bhardwaj.[3] In *Manusmriti* it is held that the four varnas proceeded from the limbs of the creator.[4] Manu maintains that Brahmin, Kshatriya, Vaishya and Shudra are the only varnas existing.

In *Nirukta*, Shri Yaskacharya evolved the word "*Varna*' from the root 'Vri' giving the meaning of choice or *varana*. In this way, *varna* is that which a person chooses according to his nature and his function. *Varna* has been used for 'colour' as well. Originality, the word "varna' was applied to white complexioned Aryans

1. *Rig.*, X, 90, 12.
2. *Ibid.*, 1, 113, 16.
3. *Mbh*, Santi, 188, 1-17.
4. *Manu*, 1, 31.

and black-complexioned slaves or servants. At a later stage the word came to be used for the four social classes *i.e.*, brahmin, Kshatriya, Vaishya and Shudra.

The aim of the four *varna* system propounded in India was division of labour, similar to the division of labour propounded by Plato and Wells. The theory of division of labour is one of the fundamental theories of social organisation. It maintains that for an orderly progress of work in society it is necessary that it be divided into classes, according to natural tendencies. Dr. Bhagwan Das has rightly divided the traditional Indian social system in the following classes: (1) teacher class, (2) governing class, (3) business class, (4) physical labourer class. These are respectively the Brahmins, the Kshatriyas, the Vaishyas and the Shudras. Thus, the responsibility of the Brahmins was to see the proper execution of academic work like study and teaching, and the religious activities. The government of the state, defence and administration were left to the Kshatriyas while the Vaishyas carried on the agriculture, dairy-farming and business. The Shudras served the other *varnas.* As has been said earlier, this class division is not peculiar to India, it has been the common feature of all the organised societies of the world.

While speaking on the subject, Sri Krishna said of the *varna* system in the Gita that I am the one who has created the four *varnas* according to nature and function. In this way in the *varna* system, the division of labour has been affected on the basis of inherent qualities and mental tendencies. Indians have accepted four tendencies among human beings, satvika, *satvika-rajasika, rajasika-tamasika, and tamasika.* The division of the varna system has been made on the basis of these tendencies. The Brahmins were of the rajasika nature, Kshatriyas of the *satvika-rajasika.* Vaishya of the *rajasika-tamasika*, and. Shudra of the tamasika. Thus, originally, in the varna system greater preference was given to the nature and tendency than to birth. It is said in the *Atharvaveda* that I do not take a man to be a slave or Arya from his birth. I evaluate him from his qualities. In the Hindu Dharmashastras, it is said that everyone is a Shudra at birth, becoming a Dwija only after *sanskara* like *upanayana*, etc. Being fundamentally based upon quality and tendency does not mean that the theory of *varna* system utterly disregarded the influence in heredity. Actually, this theory makes heredity a part of environment. Generally, the children are expected to adopt the same *varna* as is of their parents. The question of qualities and tendencies arises only when some departure from heredity class in the present tendencies is exhibited.

Developed Social Order

The *varna* system is a developed social system. Social stratification is found in all societies but it is difficult to find one as systematic as the Indian varna system. The object of this system is to put the different powers of man to proper and productive uses in order to maintain the solid, organised and balanced state of society. The Indian scholars, like Plato of Greece, gave the highest, position in society to Brahmins, experts in the field of thought and spirit. The second place was given to the protectors, the Kshatriyas and third to the producers, the Vaishyas with the servants of the society in the fourth place. People unable to perform any expert activities were included in the Shudra class. In the *varna* system the higher classes got special rights and prerogatives but special responsibility corresponding to their authority was also attached to it. This is clear from the provisions for punishments made by the penal authorities. According to Manu the retribution made for theft should be of the value of eight times in case of Shudra, 16 times if the person is a Vaishya, 32 times if a Kshatriya and 64 or 100 times if a Brahmin.[5]

Another major advantage of the *varna* system was the decentralisation of power. Concentration of all the powers of society in the hands of one class may lead to exploitation and despotism. In the *varna* system the power of knowledge, power of arms, power of wealth and power of labour, were evenly distributed among the Brahmins, the Kshatriyas, the Vaishyas and the Shudras respectively. In this way, society was made safe from the evil results of centralisation. The rewards of their work differed. The Brahmins were rewarded in the form of respect, the Kshatriyas in the form of authority, the Vaishyas in form of wealth and the Shudras in rest etc. Thus, by keeping respect, authority and wealth distinct, the society was saved from the present day defects of centralisation or localisation of power.

In this way the *varna* system shows a fine synthesis of the fundamentals of social organisation, division of labour, decentralisation and the correct position of the different values. This idea was not rigid and being based on inherent qualities and tendencies, it was, at the same time, quite psychological too. But, at a later stage, it became a rigid system and lost its good qualities.

Distinctions between *Varna* and Caste

Pointing out the distinction between the *varna* and the caste Vavalkar maintained, "Here, it would be advantageous for us to firmly fix in our mind that the '*varna theory*' of society is not to be confused with the *jati* system which we meet with today in the Hindu society, and which is usually described by the term the caste system.'[6] According to N. K. Datta, the word caste was first used in India by the Portuguese to denote the several *jatis* which they found existing here and which continue to exist even today.[7] E. Senart maintained that *varna* and *jati* are distinct and essentially independent and that the two institutions may have been fused only later on.[8] Iranian and vedic scholars like Geldner and Oldenberg and the Indologists like Barth and Jolly agree with this view.[9]

The present caste system in India differs from ancient *varna* system in the following distinctions:

1. Literal distinction. Caste and *varna* are completely different from each other. The difference in their literal meaning shows this. '*Jati*' is evolved from a Sanskrit root "*Jaha*" meaning 'to be born'. Thus, caste means birth. On the other hand,

5. *Manu*, VIII, 336.
6. Valvalkar, P.H., *Hindu Social Institutions*, pp. 296-97.
7. Datta, N.K., *The Origin and Growth of Caste in India*, p. 1.
8. Senart, E., *Caste in India*, 153.
9. Mason-Oursel, *Ancient India and India Civilisation*, p. 83.

varña means to select or choose. In this way, caste is determined at birth whereas *varna* is acquired by a person according to his nature.

2. Caste is based upon birth, varna is based upon action. Thus, caste is based upon birth while varna is based upon action. In the caste system an uneducated Brahmin is respected while an educated Shudra is looked down upon. In the varna system more emphasis is laid on action than on birth. A Brahmin is respected under the varna system, only if he has acquired knowledge and imparts it to others. The idea of varna mainly lays emphasis on the ethical and intellectual capabilities of man. In the caste system special importance is given to birth-rights and respect enjoyed on that account.

3. Varna system is flexible and caste a rigid one. The *varna* system was a flexible and changing system. There were many examples of change in *varna* and 'inter-*varna* marriage, during and even after the Vedic period. The Kshatriya Vishvamitra became a Brahmin on the basis of his penance. Parasurama was Brahmin by birth and Kshatriya by action. The same thing happened to Indra. In the *Mahabharata* there is a mention of Devapi, Sindhudip and Vitahavya becoming Brahmins, and there are similar instances in the *Bhagwat Purana*. In the Padma Purana we have a mention of low born Vyas and Vaishya Vashishtha becoming Brahmins. There are numerous examples of inter-varna marriages in the Mahabharata. Kshatriya King Yayati married the Brahmin Devayani while Dushyant married Shakuntala. Although Shantanu was a Kshatriya, he married low born Satyavati. Caste system forbids marriage among different castes, each caste considering marriage right if these are in the same caste itself.

4. Difference in numbers. There is a vast difference in the number of varnas and castes. Varnas are four. In the tenth Mandal of the *Rigveda* it is said that the Brahmin does the work of the mouth in giving knowledge, the Ksthatriya is comparable to the arms because he defends society, the Vaishya works like the legs in the production and distribution of wealth while the Shudra serves the society like the feet. Thus, there were four *varnas*. On the other hand, Rose has put the number of castes at 400, on the authority of census reports.

Thus, although the caste system originated from the *varna* system, it is different from it. It lost the advantages of the *varna* system and became detrimental to the society. Shri Jawahar Lal Nehru had said correctly that though there was cultural and social development due to the caste system, it made victory easy for the foreigners.

THE ASHRAM SYSTEM

Writing in *Encyclopaedia of Religion and Ethics*, the German scholar, Paul Deussen, gives two meanings to the word *ashram*: (1) That place where people labour or make effort. (2) To labour or make effort. The word ashram comes from the Sanskrit root giving the meaning of 'making an effort' — ashram. In this way *ashram* literally means a step in the journey of life. According to Hindu ethics, the final aim of life is liberation. And every ashram is a step in the long journey to that aim. "The whole of the life of a human individual is, for the Hindu", says P. H. Valvalkar, "a kind of schooling and self-discipline."[10] In the Shanti Parva of *Mahabharata*, Saint Vedavyasa has described *ashram* as a four rung ladder which takes one in the direction of Brahma. Vedavyas says, *Chatushpadi hi nishreni brahman yesha Pratishthitha, etamaruhya nishreni brahmaloke mahiyate.*[11] In this way in each ashram the person prepares himself for every succeeding ashram state. Literally an ashram is a halting or resting place. The ashram system is a means of systematic development for the better life. Dr. P. M. Modi has tried to prove that in the beginning there were only three Ashramas and that Vanprastha and Sanyasa were considered as one *ashram.*[12] He has cited instances in his favour from *Chandogya Upanishad* and *Manusmriti.*[13] It is in *Jabala Upanishad* that one finds the mention of four ashrams for the first time. Hindu Dharmshastras maintain that each individual should normally pass these four stages of life.[14] The four ashrams are as follows:

1. Brahmacharya Ashram. Taking man's average life to be 100 years, the span of each ashram is believed to be 25 years. The first of the four is the Brahmacharya Ashram. Brahmacharya Ashram starts with the Upanayana ceremony.[15] Brahmacharya means the leading of the life according to Brahma. In this Ashram the student or Brahmachari used to spend 25 years with his teacher studying the Vedas and leading a life of self-control. The education and control of the Brahmacharya prepared a person for future life.

2. Grihastha Ashram. After spending 25 years as a Brahmachari and finishing his education, a man married and entered the Grihastha Ashram. According to the *Gautama Dharmasutra*, the Grihastha Ashram is the foundation of all the ashrams. Manu maintains that just as all beings subsist on air, so do all beings take life from the Grihastha Ashram.[16] This *ashram* feeds all the other Ashrams. According to Manu, the three ashrams attain fulfilment through the Grihastha ashram and live on Its help, just as all the big and small rivers become fulfilled upon reaching the ocean.[17] The main duties of the Grihastha Ashram are the following — reproduction, production of wealth, feeding the family and giving education, help or rendering service to other members of society, etc. In this ashram the person learns the lesson of selflessness, sacrifice, pity and sympathy, besides fulfilling his own needs and satisfying his desires.

3. Vanaprastha Ashram. The third is the Vanaprastha Ashram. Manu says that when a person finds his hair grey and his son has a son, he should hand over

10. Valvalkar, P.H., *Hindu Social Institutions,* p. 65.
11. *Mahabharata,* Santi Parva, 242-15.
12. Modi, P.M. Art on "Development of the System of Ashrams" in *Proceedings of Seventh All India Oriental Conference,* Baroda, December, 1933.
13. *Chandogya Up.* II, 23, *Manu,* II, 230.
14. *Manu,* VI, 88, *Gautama.* III, *Apa.,* II, 21-2.
15. *Grih Sutra,* II.
16. *Manu,* VI, 87.
17. *Ibid.,* VI, 90.

every piece of work to his son and leave for the jungle in order to pray to God and practise Yoga.[18] In the Vanaprastha Ashram, the person busied himself in the search for liberating having given up all his worries of the world.

4. Sanyasa Ashram. After 25 years of conditioning in the Vanaprastha ashram one entered the last the Sanyasa Ashram. Entering this *ashram* one had to take a vow that, "I have completely, from this day, bidden farewell to all desires and anxieties regarding son, wealth and the world. All living beings may be made fearless by me." In this way, having completely given up ail such selfish desires, a *sanyasi* roamed about in the world with a desire to teach the people in order to emancipate mankind. This is the supreme duty of a *sanyasi*.

The ashram system is indicative of an integral approach to human life. By it a complete development of human power, physical, mental and spiritual, takes place and their proper satisfaction leads to an integral development of man. It maintains the balance of social and individual development. It is the most unique system in human social history and has eternal value.

PURUSHARTHAS AND TRIVARGA

The idea of Purusharthas is a fundamental principle of Indian social ethics. According to it, the aim of every person in the world is to attain the four *purusharthas* — Dharma, Artha, Kama and Moksha. Kama or sex is a natural tendency in every person. Artha or wealth is the means of fulfilment of sex and other needs and the life system of society. Dharma implies the laws or principles on which society is based. According to the Vaisesika philosophy, Dharma is that which leads to improvement in this world and to liberation in the next. Dharma, Artha and Kama relate to objects of this world. These are, in brief, called the Trivarga. Duty, wealth or sex indicate respectively ethical ideals, physical means and physical, mental and vital desires of man. It is man's duty to fulfil all the three. Beside trivargas, liberation is just as important in human life. At one time the Hindus interpreted *trivarga* as a means to liberation though generally all the four *Purusharthas* have been stressed. Vatsyayana has written, "A man in hundred years of age should gain knowledge in childhood, sex satisfaction in youth and attend to duty and liberation in old age."[19] Manu stated clearly: "Some people attribute more importance to duty, some to wealth and some to sex."[20] Manu had gone to the extent of saying that one should try for liberation only after he has passed through the three Ashrams to fulfil duty, attain wealth and enjoy sex, and has rid himself of the three debts to God, ancestors and teachers, because a person not doing so will find himself in trouble. In this way, it is clear that with regard to the aim of life, Indian social ethics emphasises an integral approach.

In Man's history there are many instances of the balance between the society and the individual being lost due to laying of excessive emphasis upon one aspect of life. Buddhists, Christians, among them St. Paul and Tartulian and priests of the

18. *Ibid.*, VI, 2.
19. Vatsyayana, *Kamasutra*, II.
20. Manu, *Dharamshastra*, III.

middle ages in Europe laid excessive emphasis on abstention with the result that there was a strong reaction in the direction of immorality. Varna Margi Buddhists took women and wine to be an important part of the means. Immorality was conspicuous by its absence in groups like Choli Marga. In Europe in the middle ages, the monasteries had become centres of corruption. This reaction was manifested in other directions in the form of cruelty and violence. Indian seers were acquainted with these psychological possibilities. They, thus emphasised all the four purusharthas equally. This kept the organisation of society and the individual integrated and balanced.

THE CONCEPT OF RINAS

The Indian social thinkers paid particular attention to the idea of Rinas or debts along with the four ashrams and purusharthas. Four types of debts have been enumerated in the *Sharpath Brahmana*: (1) to gods, (2) to seers, (3) to ancestors, and (4) to fellow beings. Ordinarily, Indian thinkers have accepted three types of debts: (1) Paternal debt, (2) Debt towards teachers, and (3) Debt towards gods. Debt to parents is the highest because they look after a person in his infancy, suffering much pain themselves in the process. According to the Indian commentators, the way of repaying parental debts is to have children oneself and look after them in the same way. Besides the parents, the seers and teachers impart knowledge to a person and make him capable of doing all work efficiently in the world. As for the repayment of this debt the means are to study the Vedas and to obey the laws of the Brahmacharya Ashram. The debt to gods is paid off by performing different yajnas. A person owns these debts the moment he is born and he cannot hope for liberation unless he clears the debts. The idea of debts conveys the lesson of unselfish fulfilment of duty and responsibility to man.

THE DOCTRINE OF KARMA

The doctrine of *karma* is the ethical background of Indian social organisation. There are three major elements in the doctrine of *karma*. (1) Every human activity entail results which may take any of the following forms — physical, mental or ethical. It effects the person's nature, character and tendencies. Man reaps the harvest of past life in the form of sanskaras. (2) Karma necessitates another life because man cannot reap the reward of his actions in one life. (3) The diversities, *i.e.*, poor or rich, happy or sorrowful, intelligent or foolish etc., are all results of the actions of previous births. (4) The doctrine of *karma* makes indispensable a belief in the immorality of the self. To reap the reward of actions of this life the *jiva* should be reborn just as the *karmas* of this life prove the previous existence of *jiva.*

The doctrine of *karma* prevents people from bad actions, it does not encourage fatalism. A.K. Keith holds that it encourages fatalism and hinders moral progress, and this criticism is valid for the present distorted form of the doctrine. But in its pure philosophical form it preaches *purushartha* instead of fatalism and morality in place of immorality. According to this doctrine, although man's present state is due to past actions, his future still depends on him. Every person can improve his future by good actions. Actually, the doctrine is based on real facts and its message to the people is to improve their lives by making use of natural laws.

THE SANSKARAS

Sanskara means to purify. According to Manu, sanskaras purify the body.[21] Starting with Garbhadhana they end with Antyeshti. Every *sanskara* starts with a yajna. Opinions differ in regard to their number. Whereas *Gautam Dharmasutra* details some 48 *sanskaras*, most sutras put their number at 40. Some of the more important *sanskaras* are — Garbhadhana, Punsavana, Jatakarma, Namakarana, Upanayana, Samavartana, Vivaha and Antyeshti.

1. Garbhadhana. *Garbhadhana* is the first *sanskara* of human life. After marriage, the couple make sacrifices to the fire and promising to lead a life of love they pray to Vishnu, Sinivali, Ashwinau, Agni, Indra and other gods, to grant to them the most powerful and innocent children to enable them to follow *dharma*. The first *sanskara* performed with this pure feeling is *garbhadhana*, it being done for the being to come into the womb of woman.

2. Punsavana. The *punsavana sanskara* is performed in the third month of the wife's pregnancy. In this the prayer is directed to God who protects pregnancy. The aim is the desire for a powerful son and the safety and health of the embryo.

3. Jatakarma. The *jatakarma sanskara* is performed when the child is born. In this the father touching the child whispers some mantras into his ears expressing the desire that he be intelligent and live to a ripe old age. Following it, OM is inscribed on the child's tongue with a pen of gold. The aim is to create an atmosphere for the complete development of the child's powers right from birth and to remind the parents of their responsibility in his character formation.

4. Namakarana. Ten or twelve days after the child's birth the *namakarana sanskara* is performed. Following it are performed the *niskramana* in the fourth month and *annaprashana* in the sixth, *churakarma* in the third year, and the *karnavedhan sanskara* in the fifth year. On the subject of *namakarana*, Manu opines that the names given should be according to the *varna* and ideals.

5. Upanayana. The *upanayana sanskara* takes place in the eighth year. Of the two parts of the word, the former 'up' means near while the child was taken to the teacher. In India in the past the child used to live with the teacher to study after *upanayana*. The aim of the *sanskara* is to establish as close a relation between the teacher and the taught as possible. He is given the sacred thread to wear and told the laws of Brahmacharya.

6. Samavartana. After the person has finished his studies, observing all the laws of Brahmachaiya, he comes home and it is the occasion for the *samavartana sanskara*. At this stage he is shaved for the first time and given cosmetics to use. He is now considered as one possessing the right to spend a domestic life.

7. Vivaha. *Vivaha* or marriage is an indication of the person's having entered domestic life. According to Valvalkar, "From the social side *Vivaha* may be said

21. *Ibid.*, II.

to be a recognition and acceptance by the bride and the groom of the *acharas* and *dharmas*, the practices and the ideals, that prevail in and rule the community to which they belong."[22] In the marriage *sanskara* many rituals like *madhuparka, shitarohana*, etc., are observed, to impress the importance of holy wedlock.

After Grihastha Ashram at fifty, the person entered the Vanaprastha and the Sanyasa Ashram at 75.

8. Antyeshti. The *antyeshti sanskara* is performed at the person's death. In this sanskara the tradition is to burn the body on a wooden pyre. Mantras are chanted as ghee is sprinkled on the fire. Normally, it is the eldest son on the occasion who performs the last rites.

The above mentioned *sanskaras* have a great importance from the viewpoint of social ethics. The whole system of *sanskara* points out that some new responsibilities are being put on man for social and individual good and it is his major duty to respect them. Marriage and other *sanskaras* are not only for individual good, but they also represent one's responsibility to society. Thus, the balance and harmony of the individual and society is maintained and both progresses simultaneously.

In this way, the Hindu ethics maintains a balance between the individual and the social good, good of this life and the next, means and end, rights and duties. In an integral approach to life all these combine naturally and exist as mutual complements.

INTEGRAL STANDPOINT IN INDIAN CULTURE

In the evolution of a world culture each country has given particular contribution through its culture, this leads us to the conclusion that no culture should be called higher or lower and each adds to the richness of the human culture as a whole. Thus, each culture must grow independently and fully so that it may contribute its share to the world of human culture. This again, is the principle of the fulfilment of 'Swadharma'. Thus, the Indian culture will contribute to the world culture only that which has been characteristic to it. Secondly, in the realm of thought only that idea can be effective which along with being universal, fulfils the local needs as well. Hence, in India only that ideology can act as a guide which is in tune with the Indian culture and national consciousness provided that it should not be contradictory to world consciousness but complementary to it.

Integral approach has been characteristic to Indian culture. Indian philosophy has emphasised one ultimate element underlying the multiplicity of the phenomenal world. Leaving aside exceptional philosophies as that of Charvaka, from the philosophers of the ancient Vedas down to the contemporary Indian thinkers including Rabindranath Tagore, Sri Aurobindo, Swamy Vivekanand, Mahatma Gandhi and others, one finds an integral approach in philosophy. While some philosophers have negated multiplicity from unity, most of the Indian thinkers have considered multiplicity as increasing the richness of unity. Not only in the philosophical fields, but in economic, social, political and all other

22. Valvalkar, P.H. *Hindu Social Institutions.* London, p. 98.

fields of life, the Indian approach is integral. Hence, Integral Humanism is more suitable to the genius of this country.

In social life the Indians have everywhere advocated a multisided integral progress as the ideal. Since ancient times the Indian ideal of four Pursuharthas *i.e.*, Dhamia, Artha, Kama and Moksha, has presented an integral view of life. Some maintain that the ideals of renunciation and liberation in Indian thinking exhibit other-worldliness and escapism. Admitted that in some philosophical schools the ideal of liberation has been presented in a way which has no consistency with the terrestrial aim of life, it is however, necessary to go deeper into the meanings of these values before arriving at any final conclusion. In spite of Buddha's ideal of Nirvan, his characteristic sympathy for human beings makes it difficult to admit that his philosophy should be called other-worldly. In Hindu social philosophy the concept of Varna again, shows the same integral approach. While Samkara has emphasised the value of liberation in human life, the sage Vatsyayana has laid emphasis upon the ideal of Kama in his famous treatise *Kamasutra.* In the history of man, wherever any culture too much emphasised some one particular aspect of human personality or life and left the other aspects unfulfilled, it led to cultural degeneration and the birth of opposite reactions. The conflict observed everywhere among man and man, man and society, nation and nation, and even the conflict within the individual himself only exhibits Nature's attempt everywhere to achieve harmony, synthesis, balance and integrality. This tendency is found not only in human society but even in the animal and plant life. In man it becomes more conscious. This is proved by the fact that man cannot rest peacefully unless he solves his problems and removes his tensions. The integral philosophy of life shows the limitations of every need and value, gives it a sufficient place, leaves none since the warp and woof of human life has been knitted by all these and however one may wish he cannot remove any element of human personality and life though by suppressing it, one may make his life one-sided, frustrated and full of tensions. In his effort to achieve spiritual values if a man rejects the physical or the mental values, it is an effort which is bound to fail since in the ladder of evolution the higher is only that which is reached after passing through the lower. The creative sources of human life are available not only on the spiritual level but on the biological and mental levels as well. Thus, the integral standpoint gives importance to all these aspects.

QUESTION FOR EXERCISE

1. Explain the Great Traditions in Indian Rural Culture.

11

RURAL FESTIVALS AND RECREATION

The present chapter is devoted to only two important aspects of rural cultural life *i.e.*, village festivals and sanskaras. Festivals and celebrations have a great importance in Indian rural life, and, particularly, in the Hindu community. It is rare unlucky month in which the village people do not celebrate some festival or the other. Studies concerning these festivals have been made in various parts of India. In 1918, Mukerjee made a special study of the festivals of Bengal and Uttar Pradesh. In 1919. Gupta based an exposition concerning Indian festivals on his study of Bombay, Bengal and Madhya Pradesh. Stevenson, in 1920, based his description on a study of Kathiyavara and Gujarat. It was Maharashtra which became the object of study in 1921 when Underhill undertook this task. Briggs in 1920 and Fuchs in 1951 made a study of individual tribal festivals. In 1958 Oscar Lewis presented a description of the festivals performed by the rural community in Rampur village, which he was studying. In the same year D.N. Majumdar studied the festivals of the community of Mohana village, in the course of a study. In this way, the Indian rural festivals have been studied from various aspects, all of which differ from each other in one way or another. The difference in rural festivals corresponds to the variations in caste, community, area of residence, culture, etc. And yet there are some festivals which are celebrated in almost all villages in India. Different festivals are celebrated in different months. This is explained in the following table:

Months	*Festivals*
1. Magh (January-February)	1. Sakat
	2. Makar Sankranti
	3. Bansant Panchami
2. Phalgun (February-March)	1. Shivratri
	2. Holi
3. Chaita (March-April)	1. Worship of Jagannath
	2. Ram Navami
4. Baishakh (April-May)	1. Worship of Jagannath
5. Jaith (May-June)	1. Dushehra of Jaith

6. Assar (June-July)	1. Assari
7. Saavan (July-August)	1. Raksha Bandhan
	2. Nag Panchami
	3. Teej
8. Bhaadon (August-September)	1. Janmasthami
9. Kwaar (September-October)	1. Vijay Dashami
	2. Kartika Poornima
10. Kartik (October-November)	1. Karva Chauth
	2. Kartika Poornima
	3. Dipavali
	4. Bhaiya Dooj

All the villages in India do not celebrate these festivals in their entirety, but, nevertheless most of them are celebrated by the Indian villager. A brief description of these festivals now follows.

1. Sakat. Sakat is a festival celebrated to guard against catastrophes. On this occasion, the mothers of male children pray to Sakat Maharani to defend their children from evil. On the day on which this occasion occurs fried food is prepared. In the evening the Sakat Maharani is worshipped, following which the females take milk and fruits, but no grains.

2. Makar Sankranti. This particular festival is celebrated every year on the 14th of January. On this particular morning everyone rises and bathes early in the Ganges wherever possible. The food in the morning consists of rice and pulse, the fried food being taken with the evening meal. Presents of rice pudding, ghee, salt, etc., are made to the Brahmin. Among lower castes, the members of the head's family and his relatives gather together and jointly partake of rice pudding known as khichari.

3. Basant Panchami. On Panchami in the month of Magh, Basant Panchami is celebrated, it being the fifth or Panchami of Basant. On this day, prayers are addressed to the family god or to Shiva or to one of the other deities. In most villages there is no convention of donning yellow garb on this day, but this practice can be seen in some villages which are near towns, since this convention is the result of the influence of town.

4. Holi. It is the biggest festival of the Hindus, falling on the day of the full moon in Phalgun. The day following is called Dhulaindi. Long before the actual day young boys roam about the village and collect firewood which they pile on the place reserved for the lighting of the bonfire on the occasion. The female population make hats corresponding to round objects like sun, moon, etc., a week in advance. In the centre of every bat there is a hole, many of them being threaded together on to thin strings to make garlands. The time for lighting the holi is determined by the village priest. At the same time he discovers some letters, the people whose names begin with these letters being forbidden to take part in the proceedings. The time of lighting the fire is broadcast to the entire village. On this day, the houses in the villages are given a proper wash and brush up. They need it. The walls are whitewashed and the floor cow dunged. Most of the persons buy a new outfit of clothes and shoes. At the appointed time, the entire village collects at the place. They take with them plants of barley. When the fire is to be lit, a particular person makes three rounds of the pile and then sets it alight. At the same time the assemblage roars in unison 'Holi Hai'. The entire congregation then takes five or seven rounds of the fire and at every round people throw grains of barley at fire of Holi, at the end of which five or seven garlands of bats are added to the blaze. On this occasion many people sing a folk song called Phag. Those who have been forbidden to take part in the activity or proceedings stand at a distance and look on. At some places after the communal circling of the fire the younger people touch the feet of their elders and utter 'Rama Rama'. At other places the same words are intoned whenever someone meets another member of the family.

The day following Holi is called Dhulaindi and is a day of even more vigorous enjoyment and pleasure. On this day the villagers give their animals a bath and make an imprint of their hand on the animal's back. After the sun has come out, colour is thrown at each other. At present in most villages this part of the festival is restricted to the adolescents, but in other villages age is not considered any disqualification, and everyone takes part in it heartily. Often the fun makers fall into a group which tours the village, one of them distinguishing himself by acting the part of a clown. It is not uncommon for these people to be intoxicated. This group visits every place in the village, the people making an infernal din all the while. This occasion carries with it a licence, accepted by convention, for all sorts of uncouth remarks, no one taking umbrage when made the butt of joke. Uncouth remarks are passed without any consideration of propriety. Some people dance along with the group, accompanied by others singing phag or other songs. The children use syringes of the most unclinical size and shape, to project coloured water over a fair distance upon the merry makers. The grown up people keep to drier modes of disfiguration. Some inconsiderate barbarians sling mud and not of the proverbial variety, either besides coal tar and such things, but such practice is generally looked down upon and considered bad. It is thought good to let bygones be bygones and to be friendly once again on this occasion. The colour throwing is generally stopped at noon. The people put on their new garments in the evening and visit one another at this time to convey their good wishes. Generally, people belonging to the lower castes visit their social superiors, there being some more group singing in the same vein at this time as well. Most of the people visit members of their own caste. Meeting each other, they embrace joyfully. But on meeting a member of a higher caste a verbal greeting is considered adequate. On this day, all activities are restricted to those appropriate for the occasion, no other work being done.

5. Shivaratri. The festival of Shivaratri is celebrated in Phalgun. As is obvious from its name, this day is reserved for the worship of Shiva during which flowers of dhatura and other material are put on the idol of Shiva. After the prayer sweets are distributed in the Shiva temples. Some people fast on the day of Shivaratri, but even upon breaking the fast, they still abstain from grains. The women worship Shiva within the confines of the house. On this day, too, some people bathe in the Ganges and collective singing of devotional songs is carried on.

6. Worship of Jagannath. Although the idol of Jagannathji is established in the famous Jagannath temple in Puri, yet the worship of Jagannath is carried on in Chait or Baisakh in most Indian villages. It is believed that the worship of Jagannath may lead to prosperity. People from every comer of the country make devotional journeys to Puri, and on returning from this pilgrimage they take back with them pictures of Jagannath. After this pilgrimage the people do not have to make annual offerings to the dead ancestors, since it is believed that with the blessings of Jagannath, the desires of the ancestors will be satiated. On this day, too, the house is given a thorough cleaning and scrubbing. Fried food is taken in the morning. The worship of Jagannath consists in the recital of his story and the offering of prayers to his picture. As a general rule, only the married women worship Jagannath, fast on the particular day restricts their diet to mere cold drinks. It is believed that the worship of Jagannath is conducive to the welfare of the members of the family.

7. Dushehra of Jaith. As is obvious from the name given to this festival, it falls in the month of Jaith. On this day some people fast and offer water in the temple of Mahadeva, while the members of lower castes do the same at the supposed residence of the local deity.

8. Asaari. The festival of Asaari falls in the month of Asaar. On this day the higher castes choose their diet from amongst fried food and fruits while the lower or inferior castes eat vegetables and roots etc. It is mainly a women's festival. Hence, the women pray to the goddess. The newly wed women accompany their husbands when the latter visit the temple. Men and women draw lines of cow dung on the walls of their houses, believing thereby to have gained immunity from an invasion by the snake. The children get their heads shaved while the adult women take this opportunely to visit their parent's residences. It is believed that, as a result of worship, the goddess fulfils the desires of women concerning their sons and husbands.

9. Raksha Bandhan. The festival is one of major importance among the Hindus. On this day, sisters tie colourful Raakhis on the right wrists of their brothers and give them sweets, and the brothers return the sentiment by the giving of some present or money to their sisters. The Raakhi is the symbol of the protection which a brother offers to his sister. In the village it is not only a sister who ties a Raakhi on the wrist of the brother but even members of the lower castes do the same to the people of higher castes. The Brahmins of the village also tie Raakhis to the people of other castes, getting money or food in return. If a long distance separates the sister from her brother, Raakhi is sent to him by post or by any other means at hand. The brother also conveys his feelings and concrete token as best as he can. On this day the girls are seen almost bursting with enthusiasm. They paint their palms with vermilion and sing traditional songs on the swings.

10. Naag Panchami. On the occasion of Naag Panchami, the snake god is worshipped. This day falls on the fifth (panchami) of Saavan. On this day the people wash themselves and carrying milk, rice pudding, etc. make a beeline for whatever place they consider to be a possible snake hole. There they pray, and leaving their rice, etc. they return. After the prayer is over they themselves take food. In fact, it is not the worship of the snake god which is the most important, the pride of place, in this respect, goes to the wrestling competitions which are organised. The wrestling matches are held within the village and sometimes people from other villages are also invited. No distinction of caste is allowed in wrestling. If age and weight coincide, the contestants are allowed to wrestle. Men of all ages, varying from children to senile folk, take part. Any person desirous of wrestling steps into the ring and challenges the congregation. Whoever accepts the challenge walks in the ring and weight and age permitting, the two get on with it. The wrestlers are also given prizes by the spectators. Often the oldest and most prominent members of the community perform the function of judges. All the time the wrestling is going on a menial play on the drum to the tune of 'pick him up and sling him,' or some similar tune. Besides the wrestling, people make most of occasion and thrash old dolls after the wrestling is over. On this day, one girl from every family goes to the predetermined spot, taking a doll along with her. All the dolls are collected at one place and are thrashed by boys of every caste. The girls also distribute fried nuts to the boys. The married girls go to their parents on this particular day and if they cannot come, their parents send them money and clothes in the form of presents. On this occasion, the swing is in great demand and so are the songs appropriate to the occasion and its spirit. On this day most people take fried food. The festival of Naag Panchami is of great importance for village life.

11. Janam Ashtami. The festival of Janam Ashtami is celebrated to commemorate the birth of the revered God Sri Krishna. It is a matter of belief that Lord Krishna was born on the day of Ashtami in the month of Bhaadon. On this day, men and women keep a fast lasting till midnight, when they celebrate the birth of Lord Krishna. After offering their prayers and receiving Lord's blessings and sweets the people break their fast. On this day some people construct monumental scenes in their homes depicting events related to Lord Krishna's life. But more often a Ramdol is constructed in the house of a prominent and influential person of the village, and an idol of the Lord is placed in the Ramdol. People of every caste collect in front of this Ramdol and sing devotional songs. The entire village makes contributions towards the expense incurred in the construction of the Ramdol and in the sweets distributed. This singing continues till midnight, when the priest prays to God. In exchange for his troubles he is presented with some money. After the prayer, sweets are distributed. The Ramdol stays with the important person for three days after which the barber takes the round of the village, accompanied by the priest. Everyone makes some cash present. Of the entire amount collected, the priest takes three-fourths while the barber gets the remaining one-fourth. In some places the custom is to deposit the Ramdol at some particular spot, after it has been taken round the village, and to enact scene from Lord Krishna's life.

12. Teej. Teej is primarily a festival for the women-folk. Both married and unmarried girls wear colourful clothes, sing what is known as the Kajri, and pray. Worship of Mahadeva on the occasion of Teej is considered to be a good omen for married life. Only fried food is taken. The girls take their food after they have prayed.

13. Vijaya Dashami. Vijaya Dashami or Dushehra, no less than Holi and Divali, is an important festival for the Hindus. It is celebrated in remembrance of the occasion when Rama triumphed over Ravana. Durga is also worshipped on this day. Durga is worshipped with a lot of pomp and splendour in the villages of Bengal. Ten days before the occasion of Vijaya Dashmi, Ram Lila is started in the bigger village, at some places the whole life of Rama being enacted on the stage in the form of a drama. On the day of Dushehra, big fairs are held at certain places in the big villages where big effigies of Ravana, his brother Kumbhakarana and son Meghnadh, are prepared in paper and erected at a public place. At a fixed time in the evening, these are set fire to. The festival also occasions universal excitement and enthusiasm in village life.

14. Pitra Paksha. Pitra Paksha is the occasion for a fortnight of one's worship of one's ancestors. It takes place in the first half of the month of Kwaar in which no sexual pleasure is permitted and besides, water is offered in addition to other sacrifice demanded by religion. In shradh, the priest and the barber are particularly important. In the shradh feast the relatives also take part besides the Brahmins. Presents are also given to these people. Almost all the castes among the Hindus observe this occasion.

15. Karva Chauth. The festival of Karva Chauth is observed by women as it assures longevity and over-all welfare of their husbands. On this day they maintain a total fast, abstaining even from drinking water. After sighting the moon and worshipping it, they break their fast.

16. Kartika Poornima. This festival falls on the day of the full moon in the month of Kartika. On these days, very big fairs are organised along the banks of the Ganges where people proceed in their millions by whatever means of transportation they can manage to acquire. On the particular day people bathe early in the Ganges, worship Mahadeva.

17. Diwali. The festival of Diwali is quite as important, if not more important, than the festivals of Holi and Dushehra. In most villages Diwali is celebrated with a lot of pomp and majesty, and it, too, like Holi, is spread over two days. The first day is called small Diwali and the second day the bigger Diwali. It is the festival of light, small earthen-ware pots called 'deep' being filled with oil and lighted through a wick. The day is festive in remembrance of Shri Ram Chandra's return to Ayodhya after having spent fourteen years in exile. Some of the 'deeps' are filled with ghee instead of oil and are placed at the place of worship. Fried food is prepared this day. The children buy toys made of sugar while the older people buy small busts of the various gods like Ganesh, Lakshmi, etc., for these gods are to be worshipped. Before the Diwali day dawns, the houses have gone through the ordeal of another thorough wash and brush up. The actual festival falls on the next day. Besides the lights, a good amount of firecrackers are also set off by the children, particularly. The confectioners make toys of sugar, which are eaten with *kheel*. The festival of Diwali is understood to augment prosperity. Many people gamble throughout the night on this occasion and stay awake till midnight, and even after because it is traditional belief that Lakshmi, the goddess of wealth, enters the house at this time and she is apt to turn back if she finds the door barred. Some people worship Lakshmi while others worship books and pens. In the temples ghee is burnt to give light. The entire village gets a thorough cleaning.

18. Bhaiya Dooj. The day following Diwali is meant for Govardhan pooja and the day next to it is an occasion for another festival, called Bhaiya Dooj. This is especially a sister's affair since it is meant and celebrated for the welfare and good health of the brothers. On this day, the sisters make a mark with saffron and stick some rice on their brothers' fore-heads and give some sweets to eat. The brothers also give presents to their sisters.

Story of Satya Narayan

It is traditional in the North Indian villages to hear the story of Satya Narayana on all festive occasions, over and above the special programme fixed for the occasion. It is told by priest, and neighbours and relatives, in addition to the members of the family, take part. The recitation takes a fairly long time. In this connection stories are told about importance attached to the worship of Satya Narayan, all of which convey the meaning that the worship of Satya Narayan and listening to his stories can ward off people's many catastrophes. After the recital, prayers are offered and people offer presents to each other which they put in ceremonial plate. The cash is pocketed by the priest besides which he is given food and some cash by the host after the prayers are over.

Profanation of a festival

The Hindu people look upon a day of festival as sacred. If some person dies in the family on a day of festivity, that particular festival is not celebrated any more in the family since it has been robbed of its sanctity. But if in future, a son is born in the family on the same day its profanation is wiped out and its sanctity redeemed, and it is once again celebrated.

Religious importance of festivals

Festivals have a lot of importance in Indian rural life. The greatest importance is attached from the religious point of view. As is obvious from the foregoing description of the festivals, there are as many occasions for prayer and worship as for enjoyment. Different gods and goddesses are worshipped. Benevolence and piety also come to the forefront on these festive occasions and people give alms to the poor and feed them. On the day of the festival the people bathe and keep themselves pure, even preventing bad and base thoughts from entering their minds. On occasions of festivity religious meetings are organised, devotional songs are sung collectively. The spiritual atmosphere seems to pervade everything, and there is a stream of people coming from and going to the temples.

Social importance of the festivals

But, the social importance of the festivals perhaps surpasses their religious importance. On the occasion of festivals people of different castes meet each other, and this helps to reduce the tension existing between them. People belonging to same classes visit each other's houses and on the occasion of Holi even embrace each other. This serves to strengthen the organisation of the castes. And, on many festivals, even personal grievances are forgotten. On the occasion of Holi, for example, people forget their grievances and embrace each other in a spirit of mutual wellbeing, a practical exposition of the proverb let bygones be bygones, which advocates the disregard of old misunderstandings and living a life of love and co-operation in the future. On the occasion of major festivals like Holi and Dushehra, the ceremonies of the festival are directed along communal lines. This develops the community consciousness among the people and strengthens the organisation of the village. On many occasions of festivity, girls and boys, besides other near relatives, gather in one house. It increases their regard for one another. The festivals serve as an excuse for the parents to call their wedded daughters home again, and these married women also get an excuse of meeting their relatives once a while. In this way, the festivals accord people whether they are different relatives, members of different castes or belonging to different classes in society, an opportunity for increasing mutual intercourse. On these occasions, the work of organisation and arranging for these festivals in public fails to the lot of the head of the village. It serves to maintain their leadership.

Recreation through festivals

Festivals are occasions for merry-making. A lot of excitement and enthusiasm is in the air when festivals like Holi, Diwali and Dushehra are approaching. People wear new clothes on these auspicious days, after a more than normally refreshing bath, and roam around. On the major festivals, people take the day off from their work and get a chance to have some rest and introduce a bit of much needed variety into their humdrum life, which refreshes them as water does withering plant. The festivals are very important from the recreational point of view, as every festival does include some material which has recreational value. On Dushehra the dramatic societies perform for ten days while on the occasion of Diwali the people put on many lights and explode many crackers. On Naag Panchami wrestling matches are held and the dolls are given a thorough thrashing. In the month of Saavana, people use the swings and sing to heart's content whenever there is some festival afoot. On the occasion of Holi, there could hardly be more recreation than when the colours are flying in the air. People dance with pleasure. From the psychological point of view occasions like Holi have their importance because they are an opportunity for the people to give expression to their various tendencies, all of which make it easier for them to keep their mental balance and to cooperate with each other. The different games arranged on the occasion of festivals are meant to allow boys and girls to meet and to express their mental tendencies in various ways. Besides, the people get the opportunity to dress properly because on the normal days their activities are such as to prohibit the use of any gaudy clothes and ornaments. In consequence, the people justifiably dress in their best clothes and roam about. A lot of jokes and familiarity are tolerated on these occasions. On many festivals, the men and women get an opportunity to meet each other.

Artistic importance of festivals

In addition to this, the festivals are important from the cultural viewpoint. In India, some or the other artistic figures are made on festive occasions, and figures are drawn on the floors, and the walls. Many kinds of things are made from cow dung. The house is cleaned and the things arrayed in new form. On the Janam Ashtami festival, the Ramdol is a very artistically prepared object, worthy of praise. And when the Ramlila is dramatised, the actors are the villagers themselves. Folk music is almost an inseparable part of festivity on any pretext, many instruments being employed for the music accompaniment to the devotional singing collectively. Community singing and community dancing increases the community consciousness of the villagers, in addition to maintaining a high level of cultural activity and cultural environment.

Place of festivals in rural life

From the foregoing description of festivals, it is obvious that they bear a close relation to the season and various activities characteristic of agriculture. In this way, the festivals become a normal part of the life in the village. Actually, the festivals are those occasions when the villagers having seen to their business and agricultural responsibilities, express natural joy and enthusiasm in the work they are to tackle in this season. The poor people benefit in great measure on these festive occasions. Often, they are enabled to store food grains which they can consume over a number of days. And besides, they sometimes receive gifts of money and clothes. The people who benefit most on these occasions are the Brahmins or the priests, who get work to do as well as lavish presents in food and cash. In this way, the festivals are instrumental in reducing the economic inequality and satisfying many of the needs of the poor.

It is obvious from the preceding delineation of the importance of festivals in rural life that they are valuable not merely from the religious viewpoint, but also from other viewpoints like social, recreational, health, sanitary', cultural development etc. The festivals manifest the inner core of villagers and enhance their life force.

RURAL RECREATION

Lack of Healthy Recreation in Villages

Recreation is essential for the physical and mental health of an individual as well as a social group. If healthy recreation is not available in a community, a number of mental and physical faults overtake the personality of man. In the absence of salutary recreation men take to intoxicants, prostitution and many such evils. Therefore, for the health and mental sanity of man, wholesome and healthy recreation is indispensable. The need for and importance of recreation is recognised by all thinkers. Unfortunately in India, whose 75% population lives in villages, hardly any attention is paid to providing good recreation in rural India. The chief profession in villages is agriculture. Farming is seasonal and, therefore, there is plenty of spare time for villagers. Even persons engaged in other professions find plenty of spare time. It is necessary to provide sufficient amenities for salutary recreation to fill the spare time. If there are no good recreations people take to such bad habits as drinking and gambling.

Games in Villages

In different parts of world different types of games are played. In rural India we find children busy in various types of games and plays. The most outstanding game of rural India is *Kabaddi*. Besides *Kabaddi*, some play marbles and *gilli danda* and young men *kabaddi*, the elders are busy playing cards in corners. But these games are not sufficiently varied and diversionary to provide adequate recreation. It is not possible to spend hours together in *kabaddi* etc. and playing cards cannot be considered a healthy recreation. In the absence of good entertainment people in villages take to gambling and smoking hashish. Prostitution is not common though sex scandals are by no means uncommon. Indeed we find a raw display of emotions in rural life. Following are the chief sources of entertainment and relaxation in rural India.

(i) *Gossip*. In villages gossip is a common means of whiling away time. In evenings people assemble together at various chopals and are busy chattering. In these assemblies news from various centres, stories and local talk form the subject-matter of gossip. In these assemblies hookah smoking is very common. The nicotinic smoke relaxes the mind and helps whiling away time.

(ii) *Alha*. Another means of amusement and relaxation in villages is the singing of Alha, the story of heroism in love and war. There is much singing of Alha during rainy days. Some professional singers are very competent in rendering Alha. The enthusiasm released by their singing is very effective upon listeners. There have been instances when people have drawn up their swords listening to Alha. Alha is in three languages or dialects: (1) Bundelkhandi, (2) Avadhi, and (3) Rajasthani. In Uttar Pradesh Avadhi rendering of Alha is common. Sometimes competitions in Alha singing are arranged, in which professional and amateur singers from far and near come accompanied by drumming.

Unhealthy Means of Recreation

As discussed earlier, in the absence of sufficient amenities for recreation, people in villages tend to take to injurious types of amusements. The most important of these is intoxication. There are many varieties of intoxication. Among these are drinking liquor or tadi, smoking hashish or charas and, of course, smoking and chewing tobacco. *Bhang* is quite common and is regarded as a gift of Shiva. On account of poverty villagers do not generally drink high quality liquor, they drink *Tharra* (a country-made liquor). *Tadi* is also popular. Though some persons are regular in using intoxicants, mostly orgy of drinking and intoxication is indulged on festivals, especially *Holi* inasmuch as villagers have so much spare time that they require lot of fun but owing to inadequate facilities take to unhealthy means of recreation. It is well said that an empty mind is devil's workshop. Without providing them adequate means of recreation it is futile to expect major change in their style of life.

Suggestions

It is an absolute must that there should be adequate and healthy means of recreation, the lack of which is telling upon the health of villagers. The government, social reformers and Panchayati leaders should pay attention to this aspect. Radio, television etc., are good means of entertainment. There should also be reading rooms and libraries in the villages. These days, radio, transistors and televisions provide a lot of recreation to the rural people.

QUESTIONS FOR EXERCISE

1. Describe the festivals of Rural India.
2. Write short note on Rural Sanskaras.
3. Write short note on Rural Recreation.

12

The Rural Religion

Nature of Rural Religion

In all parts of the world, the rural population compares favourably with the people who inhabit the cities in matters of religion, being more inclined in this direction. This disparity arises from a number of factors of which the most prominent is the pre-occupation with agriculture, which depends very much upon Nature despite stupendous progress that science may have made in any country. This dependence upon Nature gives an added importance to the natural forces in the life of man, who consequently indulges in a variety of religious activities, offerings and prayers designed either to pacify or to please the deified powers which play such an important role in his life. In the village, life is spent in the lap of Nature, in sharp contrast with the life in the cities, where the invention of modern scientific implements has reduced materially the influence of the seasons and Nature upon the lives of the inhabitants. The life of the people in the villages is almost completely exposed to the vagaries of Nature, but at the same time the rustic derives satisfaction from the opportunity of observing, at first hand, Nature at its most beautiful and red in tooth and claw as well. Thus, rural religion originates in the worship of Nature. The same holds true in the context of Indian society also, where the rural population comprises some 80% of the entire population of the country. Besides, 60% of the villagers are farmers. Science has not made much progress in India, the preponderance of Nature being evident in every aspect of life. All these various causes, taken collectively, have the effect of giving great importance to religion in the life of the rural people in India, thereby making a study of rural religion necessary for rural sociology.

The influence of education may diminish the influence of religious consideration, although education does not necessarily make a man irreligious. Most rural people are uneducated, in consequence of which they nurse all kinds of superstitions and dogmas, religious in nature. In the social life of the village, many beliefs — in ghosts, witches, good and bad omens — are operative, for the understanding of which a study of rural religion is necessary.

Religious-mindedness in India

Thinkers in all times and at all places have agreed in regarding Indians as religious-minded people. In the words of Sir Harcourt Butler, "The Indians are essentially religious as Europeans are essentially secular. Religion is still the alpha and the omega of Indians' life." Besides being religious, Indians are also professed to be of a philosophical propensity. Many people have looked upon Samkara's Mayavada as representative of Indian thought. Most thinkers conceive of Indians as a people who contemplate interminably upon religion and philosophy, the afterworld, heaven, hell and salvation. Morris Opler has written, "The fact that the highest goal of Hindu is to eliminate earthly concerns, desires and personal existence itself, introduces a large element of asceticism, intellectualism, detachment and withdrawal into Hindu philosophy. In no other country have so many men renounced the world, and in no other place is there so much fasting and mortification of the flesh. The world is considered transitory. In reality it is an escape from the world and from the forms which make existence in the world necessary." Thus, Opler conceived Indian religion as practical and escapist in the extreme. But, on the other hand, Oscar Lewis found Indian religion essentially practical and realistic, in the course of his study of Rampur village.

Distinguishing between Indian classical religion and Indian rural religion, S.C. Dube has written, "Clearly, Hinduism, as it is practised in the village is not the Hinduism of the classical-philosophical systems of India for it possesses neither the metaphysical height nor the abstract content of the latter. It is a religion of fasts and festivals, in which prescribed rituals cover all the major crises of the life... Analysis of life histories reveals that spiritualism cannot be said to be keynote in the life of the community, far from it the religion appears to be a practical one." In substantiating the opinion of Dube, Lewis adduced evidence which was the result of a scientific study of religion carried out in Rampur village. These proofs make it obvious that religion in the village of India has been practical. Although, it would not be very advisable to apply the conclusion derived from the study of one particular village to the rural population of country as a whole, it can nevertheless be confidently asserted that rural religion which does not bear the mark of Sanskritisation, is realistic and practical. There are numerous causes which have precipitated this state of affairs, among them is the tremendous effort every villager has to exert in ensuring the livelihood of his family besides himself, which has the effect of limiting his viewpoint to the practical aspects of life. For another, the villagers of India are not properly acquainted with the traditional Indian philosophy and in the absence of this, they do not evince any vivid evidence of philosophical thought. Yet another reason is the poverty and lack of education existing among the villagers. They harbour many superstitious beliefs, and they have to labour hard in life. In these circumstances, it is almost conceivable that there should be an element of intellectuality and spirituality in their religion. In the absence of scientific data, it cannot be said inconclusively that Indian rural religion is realistic and practical but this contention is borne out in a general way by a view of the life of the villages of India. It is a different matter that it may appear more spiritual and escapist or fatalist in comparison with the rural religious characteristics of other countries.

ASPECTS OF INDIAN RURAL RELIGION

The main aspects of Indian rural religion are the worship of gods and goddesses, sacrifices for them, belief in ghosts, various kinds of sanskaras or rituals and religious festivals. To religion are attached many moral beliefs. At present, a discussion on the gods and goddesses will precede anything else, for the simple reason that rural religion develops around them.

1. Gods and goddesses. In general, the following classes of gods and goddesses are worshipped in Indian villages:

(i) *Gods and goddesses of Hindus.* The rural Hindus everywhere worship the gods and goddesses of the Hindu religion. The most important among them is Shiva, who is worshipped in different forms, and under different names. Besides Shiva, the names of Sanskara and Bohlabela are also famous for this deity. Hanumanna is also worshipped in the villages. He is also called by other names and his worship is believed to be instrumental in preventing many kinds of catastrophes. People of all castes in India worship Shiva and Hanumana. Besides these two, the other deities worshipped in the villages of India are Vishnu, Rama, Krishna, Agni, Valmiki, Jagannath and Sun god etc. After bathing themselves in the morning, the people offer water to the Sun god, who is believed to ensure a good day ahead for the worshipper. Besides the gods, numerous goddesses are worshipped, among them are Durga, Kali, Lakshmi, Sarasvati, etc. On the festival of Diwali, Ganesha is worshipped along with Lakshmi. The worship of Ganesha is considered essential on all auspicious occasions. Kali is believed to be capable of getting rid of different diseases. Durga wards off any impending disaster, while Lakshmi is the goddess of wealth, Sarasvati is the goddess of knowledge.

(ii) *Non-Hindu gods and goddesses.* The credulous Indian villager does not rest satisfied with worshipping this formidable repertoire of Hindu gods and goddesses, but extends his respect and reverence to many other deities which cannot be called Hindu by tradition, among them being Shitala Maharani who protects people from smallpox epidemic and who sends troubles in the form of smallpox when displeased, Bhuiyaan Devi who is considered very powerful and Sati Maharani, etc. In any village where any Sati has become famous, the place in the village is worshipped and sometimes even fairs are organised. Besides them, many saints are also worshipped In some villages. To these acts of worship are attached many stories of local interest.

(iii) *Rural gods and goddesses.* Besides the above-mentioned gods and goddesses, every village has its own rural gods and goddesses which are essentially local. Often the place of worship of such a deity is outside the village, and it is worshipped from time of time. To it, too, are attached many interesting and common tales.

2. Worship of plants, trees and animals. In the villages of India, many trees, plants and animals are considered divine. The banyan, neem and pipal are treated as divine and are worshipped. The worship of Tulsi, in particular, is considered important everywhere in India. The cow is called Gaumata and is considered to be divine. Cow dung is used to cover any place which is to be purified. At some places even the ox and the snake are objects of worship. In the villages where a tribe lives the animals and plants of totem are considered divine.

3. Beliefs in ghosts and witches. Besides the numerous gods and goddesses worshipped in the Indian villages, the rural populace credit the existence of ghosts, instituting different kinds of activities designed to appease them, please them or get rid of them. Whenever a man or a woman in the village comes to an untimely demise, or dies in an accident, or is murdered, or commits suicide, it is believed that his or her soul is dissatisfied and roams the village in some or the other form. The souls of men become ghosts while the souls of the women witches, both of which are believed inhabit trees, graveyards, the banks of rivers or ponds and sometimes even in the houses. The two kinds show an affinity for their own types and harass the living members of their corresponding sexes. When any man or woman comes under the influence of these ghosts and witches, his or her behaviour becomes manifestly abnormal, and unconventional, and all the efforts made by the affected person take on a peculiar hue. The many kinds of mental derangements are not recognised as mental diseases afflicting persons but are considered to be the effects of ghosts and witches and are treated accordingly. In order to get rid of the shadows of ghosts which hover over the demented persons, peculiar kinds of treatments are applied. The specialist in these matters is called an Ojha or witch doctor, who may belong to any tribe. He is supposed to do away with the ghosts and witches by the force of his magic. He sometimes makes use of food and sweetmeats in getting rid of the ghosts. In this way, every effort, in the form of violence, threat, entreaty and skill, is made to appease these cruel souls and to get rid of them. In the process, the diseased person suffers extreme persecution which often takes form of extreme physical torture which may sometimes lead even to the death of the person. But sometimes the person is cured and the witch doctor retains his popular appeal. As a protective measure the witch doctor dispenses some charms also, which are tied round the arm or the neck of the person in the belief that it will cope with, and negativite the effects of the wicked souls.

4. Belief in good souls. The inhabitants of the villages do not confine their credulity to a belief only in wicked souls but they extend to it belief in some good souls as well. These souls do not suffer from any discrimination on account of sex, being either feminine or masculine. They are benevolent and assist people in different ways. If after the passing away of a saint or a great personage, the people believe his soul to be dwelling within the village. They take it for granted that it is protecting the entire village. All kinds of gifts are deposited at the supposed dwelling place of this magnanimous being.

5. Faith in dreams. Besides a belief in these invisible souls, rural religion also includes faith in dreams. The faith in the importance of dreams is almost universal but their explanations in different places do not correspond. Generally, when a person dreams after four o'clock in the morning it is believed to be prophetic, either for good or bad. Actually, even though the villagers themselves do not perceive any visible and special relation between what they see in dreams and the real world, yet they persist in their beliefs about the dreams. The main cause of this notion is their lack of education, due to which many facts are unthinkingly associated with dreams.

6. Ideas of auspicious and inauspicious. Many kinds of superstitions concerning good and evil, are to be found in rural people. For a particular activity some particular days and months are considered auspicious and as having a good portent. In the case of important works and rituals the local pundits make calculations and advise the interested parties in respect of the auspicious day and hour. In this way, every particular work and ritual necessitates the determination of a particularly auspicious moment. But in a general sort of way, Friday and the month of Chaita are considered auspicious. Besides these, particular attention is directed towards this aspect by the villagers in respect of travel. For example, it is considered a bad omen, even, down-right ominous, to travel towards the north on Thursdays and Fridays. Travel in an easterly direction is not advised on Mondays and Saturdays. Sundays and Fridays are not to be utilised for travelling to West while Thursdays are not to be considered fit if one contemplates travelling towards the South. But to acquiesce to this consideration of the auspiciousness of particular days may become a hindrance in the performance of important activities. It is saying something in favour of human inventive genius when we say that the pundits have overcome this difficulty by suggesting that if one leaves the village before the break of day, he leaves the direction of travel unmolested or uninfluenced by its auspiciousness or maliciousness.

7. Religious consideration in dietary habits. Besides travel, another aspect of human life to be influenced by the auspiciousness of the various days in a week is the food taking. The morning meal, to be taken after a bath, consists of different ingredients on different days, so is ordained. For example, it is good to eat betel on Sunday and curd on Tuesday.

8. Considerations of good and bad omens. Along with the thought of the auspicious, rural religion devotes attention to considerations of good and bad omens. Especially, it is considered very detrimental if some bad omen bodes ill when some new activity is being initiated. These bad omens take a variety of forms. It is considered to be a bad omen if one comes across a person blind in one eye during travel. It is not considered good form to sneeze at the outset of a journey and if one dose sneeze, one can wait for a few moments. Similarly, it is a bad omen if a cat crosses one's path while one is proceeding somewhere. If a wolf accompanies a cat on such an occasion, it does not do anything to improve matters and the bad omen stay bad. If one looks into an empty pot, the success of a venture is jeopardised it being safer look into it when full, whence it constitutes a good omen. Similarly washerman or a dead body are good omens towards the successful completion of work.

9. Superstitions in natural phenomenon. The villagers attach all kinds of superstitions to natural phenomenon. For example, the solar and the lunar eclipses are believed to be the causes of the catastrophes of Rahu and Ketu. An earth tremor is attributed to the undulations of the snake which bears the earth on its fangs, a hard job by any standards. Absence of rain or drought, too much rain, untimely rain, etc., are attributed to the displeasure on the part of the god Indra. Superstitions are even more numerous in tribal villages where there is even greater ignorance and lack of education, the fundamental causes of superstitions.

10. Assumptions concerning the supernatural. In rural religion where there is superstition, ignorance, unnecessary ritualism, etc., on the one hand there are also a considerable number of assumptions pertaining to the supernatural on the other. For example, heaven, hell, rebirth, salvation, virtue, sin, etc. are everywhere believed to be real though people differ from village to village in their explanations and understanding of them. Most of the people believe that heaven and hell are two good and bad places where the souls of good and bad people respectively enjoy in pleasure or suffer pain after death. On the other hand, some people believe that heaven and hell are attained not after death but in this very life. In the same way, people believe that man has to pass through eighty-four lakh forms of life (*yonian*), although some, and probably a large majority of people do not corroborate or agree with this. Good action is known as virtue and bad as vice but there is no agreement of opinion with regard to what constitutes good or bad activities.

11. Moral beliefs. In this way, many moral beliefs are also conjoined to rural religion. A good person is a soul superior to all and sundry, and yet all people do not agree to the elements which are characteristic of those who are superior. Nevertheless, a benevolent person of high character is one who worships God with fervour. He is commonly recognised as a religious person or superior soul. And yet there is a fair amount of polemic on what exactly benevolence is. Some people look at public service in the concrete — constructing wells and tanks — as benevolent while others would append benevolence to lending money without charging interest. In spite of a lack of agreement, people generally look upon acts of kindness and assistance, both moral and concrete to the poor and the helpless, as benevolent. In quite the same way, people have not any one recognised opinion regarding sin. Theft is considered sinful in all civilised villages but tribal villages are more tolerant in this respect because they do not call this human shortcoming of making unpermitted use of another's property, as sin. In the same way the rural population of India does not tolerate extramarital sexual relations and does everything to prevent their inception, and yet the same strictness of spirit on this subject is not universal. Prevarication, chicanery, etc., are everywhere considered sinful. Homicide or murder is almost universally considered justified by a group of persons under certain conditions which are unusual. Most of the people in the village consider every act of violence or killing as sin, while others differ in their opinions.

VARIOUS INFLUENCES ON RURAL RELIGION

As a matter of fact, people belonging to a variety of religious beliefs and cultures are found co-existing in the villages of India. The difference in culture is very well marked and evident in a comparison between civilised village society and tribal village society. And there is an adequate difference between Hindu religion and tribal religion. In the same way, some particular religions characterise certain villages when there is preponderance of people of one sect over people of another, while in most villages one comes across the most divergent religions. One comes across people belonging to both Hindu and Sikh religions in the villages of India, and Muslims are scattered over the entire country. Besides the influence of the variety of religions, rural religion is influenced also by the distance which separates the village and the town. The village further away from the town will generally have a religion which is more dogmatic, superstitious, ignorant and credulous in matters pertaining to the supernatural, in comparison with the religion existing in a village which is more accessible to urban influence. There the influence of the town has the effect of moderating these factors. Another influential factor is the effect of education upon the institution of rural religion because in village where educated people abound, the religion will not include much faith in superstitions, ghosts and the like. Thinking about such matters becomes common in the absence of education. In much the same way, transformation in rural religion as a result of modern scientific tendency is fairly evident because in areas which have progressed scientifically the introduction of the modern means of communication has led to a closer touch with science, the cumulative effect of which has been to dispel the clouds of ignorance and superstition. Again, rural religion is not immune from the effect of economic conditions since, generally speaking, the poor people as a class are more superstitious.

DYNAMIC ASPECT OF RURAL RELIGION

In this way, it is necessary to keep an eye on the dynamic aspect of rural religion, as it is to be understood in India. In the present age, efforts are being made to achieve progress in every sphere. In the villages of India, the efforts at progress are all-embracing, encompassing the political, social and economic aspects. Education is spreading in the villages. With the increase in urbanisation of the country, the villages are also being continuously transformed. Besides, the increase in railways, buses and other travel facilities has led to an increase in the mobility of the villagers, and the rural population is adopting the habit of travelling far and wide. The adventurous and ambitious young men of the villages travel to big cities to try their luck and, upon returning, tell their comparatively immobile and senile kins-folk about what they have seen. The radio serves to keep the village-folk generally in touch with the major happenings of the world. In the exhibitions which are organised from time to time they see novel things. All these things have their effect upon rural religion. One of the first effects of these influences is that they put an end to the beliefs in ghosts, witches, etc., and thoughts of superstitions and omens. Religion is sanskritised and modernised. Secondly, the religiousness itself looses its grip upon the individual, and faith is transferred to science from religion. But this does not lead to the utter annihilation of rural religion. Religiousness is a fundamental element of Indian culture. The villager of today still clings to tradition and is in no way less religious than his ancestor, despite the many and varied changes that may have intruded into his religious notions and beliefs.

THE VILLAGE TEMPLE

The village temple holds a very important place in the life of the village. It, of course, has its religious importance but in the village it also exerts ostensible influence upon the social sphere as well. As a matter of fact, the temple in a village becomes the centre to public programmes. And even otherwise, the inseparability of rural relation from the villager lends to the village temple an importance in rural life.

Sometimes some property in one form or another is attached to the village temple, the income from which serves to meet the expenses of decoration, communal feeling and the livelihood of the priest or pundit. Some villages have more than one temple. In the villages in India, different temples are constructed for different deities, these temples differing somewhat in structure. Among the Indian gods the more popular, in the sense of the number of temples dedicated to them, are Mahadeva or Hanumana and Mahadeva or Shankara. In a village where people have faith in different groups or schools of thought, the temples are dedicated to them so that in a village where people belong to the group of the disciples of Shakti the temple is also dedicated to Shakti while the same temple would have been dedicated to Shiva had the villagers belonged to his disciples. Besides these, one can see temples dedicated to many other female deities like Kali Devi, Saraswati Devi, Durga Devi, Sati Devi etc. in a number of places. Wherever a woman sacrifices herself on the burning pier of her husband and some supernatural element is seen in her, a temple is erected in her honour and the other women in the village visit it from time to time to offer prayer. As a general rule, the local god also finds some place in the village but this place is more in the form of a sacred place than a temple.

The rural temples are looked upon as community property and a particular family traditionally looks after it and performs the part of the priest. But some temples are also private, as are the ones constructed by the rich landlords within the precincts of their own gardens. Commonly, the public temples are in no worse condition than those privately maintained, the former being visited by all the villagers. Formerly, members of the lower or untouchable castes were not permitted to enter them but since the anti-untouchability campaign and the declaration of the practice of untouchability as illegal, the temples in most villages are open to all and sundry. But even then the people who perform menial tasks are generally prohibited from entering the temples. On the other hand, the private temples are utilised by members of only one family though, as a general rule, no one is barred from worshipping in the temples.

Importance of the Temple in Village Life

The temple is not merely a place of worship. If the priest of the temple is an intelligent and learned person he has an important status and role in the village life. He becomes a respected leader of the village, to whom much importance is attached by the villagers who look upon him as a representative of God. Often his premonition and forecasts have profound influence upon the thinking and conduct of the villagers. In this way the temple priest is an astrologer, prophet and doctor, conductor of the prayers and story-teller all the same at one time. In these circumstances, the temple in the village, has a comprehensive influence upon the life of the village, and instead of remaining merely a place of worship the temple becomes an institution.

1. Religious importance. First and foremost, the temple has a religious importance. At almost all the major occasions of religious importance festivals are held and the entire population of the village congregates to the temple to worship. In the temple an idol of God is placed. A Brahmin priest makes arrangements for the maintenance of the temple. He bathes the idol of God and worships it daily and at these occasions many villagers are present. After the prayers the priest distributes sweets among the predominantly adolescent audience. In addition to this daily routine, special congregations are invited and organised for praying, at more or less regular intervals. Group discussions are also held. At the major festivals the idol is decorated, the attendance being more numerous and the distributed sweets being in greater quantity.

2. Social importance. As has been mentioned on a number of previous occasions the temple has importance in the life of the village from the social viewpoint also. The temple becomes a place for congregating when people from all the castes get together to take part in the occasion being celebrated at the temple. Through the medium of the temple people of different castes get an opportunity to meet each other. In this way the temple becomes a centre of social meeting. And at times, other than when the prayers are being conducted, old men and women can be seen gossiping, thus transforming the temple into a place for mutual relief of overwhelming thoughts and desires or some such thing. Sometimes even the most important meetings of the village are held in the temple, for it is a sacred and important place besides which it is spacious enough to accommodate many people. Many programmes for social welfare are conducted in the temples. Sometimes the temple is used as a medium for collecting funds in order to finance different kinds of public works in the village.

3. Moral importance. Besides its social and religious importance, the village temple is important from the moral viewpoint as well, because it is a symbol of the village morality and its religious fervour. Often the priest in the temple is called upon to make judgment of good and bad in the moral problems which beset the villagers. The sort of thing has been carried very far because incidents are not completely lacking where a person considered guilty and worthy of punishment is released on the mere word of the pundit on the ground that the priest is a religious and benevolent person whose words are invaluable.

4. Cultural importance. The cultural life of the village is also enriched by the temple. In the temple devotional songs and congregations for this purpose, are held. On such occasions all sorts of musical instruments are used. Dances are also arranged in temple and performed in front of the idol of God. This kind of practice is particularly in vogue in temples of South India. The temples which possess a fair amount of property are generally well and lavishly decorated. In this way, the temple has both artistic and cultural value.

There is yet another point of cultural importance of the temple. In the life of the rural people many kinds of rituals are related to the temple. The marriage performed in temple, be it publicly performed or secretly, is held to be sacred and inviolable. In many villages the marital rituals are performed in the village itself. On some sacred occasions the husband and wife go together to visit the deity and to receive his blessing. In the temples, the wives and mothers propitiate respectively for their husbands and their children and make presents when their desires are fulfilled.

5. Educational importance. In ancient India the temples were educational centres as well and even today schools are held in many temples. Mostly, the priest is the teacher. And this leads the people to believe that the education imparted by the priest to them will make them religious and moral. Besides the children, the priest educates adult men and women also in various things. If the personality of the priest is magnetic and inspiring the villagers take their problems to him and accept the solutions which he suggests.

6. Recreational importance. The temples do not also fall short of material for the recreation of the village people. Often gymnasia are attached to the village temple, because, for one, the temple is generally situated outside the village in a clean and open place and, for another, it is considered more beneficial to take exercise under the protection and the benevolence of gods like Hanumana than otherwise. Every now and then, competitions in wrestling are organised, the whole affair being characterised by a lot of fanfare and public acclaim. The arrangement for new programmes at regular intervals in the temple serves to relieve monotony and create variety, all of which serve to entertain the people.

The population of the Indian villages looks upon a person invested with the powers of meeting out justice as a representative of a messenger from God. And for this reason, the village priest, in this part, of a representative or messenger of God, is sometimes called upon to intervene in complicated cases and to do justice. In addition to doing justice the priest also prescribes the kind penance which a person should do in order to remove the stains of sin done to him.

Festivals of the Temple

The festivals of temple often take place at times when they can influence quite considerably the activity of agriculture. And because the festivals of the village generally coincide with these, the whole process attaches even more importance for the villager to the temple and makes it the actual symbol of the religious aspects of rural life. The result is that the temple thus becomes related to the general life of the village.

From the preceding description of the importance of the temple in rural life, it is evident that the temple contributes in an important way to each and every aspect of life which the villager leads. By the advent of new thought and the influence of the town, which is making rural life secular, the temple is losing its importance. Since the institution of zamindari has been abolished, the landlords can no longer afford the lavish expenditure they were accustomed to and the temples consequently suffer because of the discontinuation of grants and aid given by the landlords. But nevertheless the villages that retain their faith in religion still attach the old traditional importance to the village temple. Now India is a secular state but it would not be advisable to abolish or be careless towards the temple because it is not merely a place for religious practices but a centre of die various activities of village life. The need is for a slight transformation in the programmes organised in the temple.

Table 1: *Population According to Religion*

	1961		1971		1981	
Religions Group	Population in Millions	Percentage	Population in Millions	Percentage	Population in Millions	Percentage
1	2	3	4	5	6	7
Hindu	366.5	83.5	453.4	82.7	547.8	82.6
Muslim	46.9	10.7	61.4	11.2	75.6	11.4
Christians	10.7	2.4	14.2	2.6	16.2	2.4
Sikh	7.8	1.8	10.4	1.9	13.1	2.0
Buddhist	3.2	0.7	3.9	0.7	4.7	0.7
Jain	2.0	0.5	2.6	0.5	3.2	0.5
Others	1.6	0.4	2.2	0.4	2.8	0.4
Total	439.2	100.0	548.2	100.0	665.3	100.0

QUESTIONS FOR EXERCISE

1. Discuss the importance of village temple.
2. Explain the rural religious system and its tearing on social life.

13

THE JAJMANI SYSTEM

Importance of Jajmani System

Jajmani system is the backbone of rural economy and social order. Oscar Lewis has defined it thus: "Under this system each caste group within a village is expected to give certain standardised services to the families of other castes."[1] Thus, the barber dresses the hair of villagers; carpenter meets the wood-work requirements and ironsmith makes agricultural implements and other household effects, tongs, hammer, buckets etc., which are made of iron. The class of shopkeepers, Banias make the provision for numerous articles of daily use available by collecting them from a wide variety of sources and the Brahmins help in carrying on various religious rites and ceremonies. Everyone works for a certain family or a group of families, with whom he is linked hereditarily, that is, his forefathers and father were rendering same type of services to same group of families for whom he is working presently. Even his sons will perform same kind of duties for the specified families in future as well. Thus, professions and services in villages are determined by the caste and have become fixed by long traditions. Under Jajmani system the family or families entitled to certain services from certain persons are called Jajman and the persons rendering those services are called Kameen of the Jajman. The term Kameen means one who works for somebody or serves him. The terms Jajman and Kameen, patron and auxiliary are popular in North Indian villages. Though Jajmani system is found all over India, the terms used for Jajman and Kameen are different. The first detailed study of Jajmani tradition in India was made by William H. Wiser in his book The Indian Jajmani System, He, for the first, drew attention to Jajmani as a tradition and system. However, Wiser did not know that Jajmani system is nearly universal in Indian villages. In fact, Wiser had no idea about the extent to which Jajmani system was prevalent in India. Oscar Lewis had made more elaborate study of this system. The sociological studies of Eastern Uttar Pradesh, Malabar, Cochin, Mysore district, Tanjore, Hyderabad, Gujarat and Punjab regions have revealed that Jajmani system prevails in all regions though there are minor local differences. Therefore, we all are fully

---

1. Oscar Lewis: *Village Life in Northern India*, University of Illinois Press (Illinois, 1958), p. 56.

justified in saying that Jajmani system is universal in rural India, some minor regional variations notwithstanding.

Indian Society is structured on caste patterns and the economic and professional relationship between various castes in this set-up is called jajmani system. It is a pre-established division of labour among the castes sanctioned by religious and social traditions.

Jajmani is a peculiarity of Indian villages. In India, professions are generally hereditary and there is a long tradition of families carrying on self-same professions over generations. Normally, there is no deviation from the hereditary professions. Thus, the son of carpenter will become carpenter and the son of an ironsmith will become an ironsmith. Every Indian villager considers it natural and right to engage in professions peculiar to his caste and, on account of long tradition, feels at home in it and easily acquires proficiency.

DEFINITION OF JAJMAN AND KAMEEN

According to Webster's Dictionary jajman is "a person by whom a Brahmin is hired to perform religious services, hence a patron, a client."

Etymologically, the word jajman is derived from the Sanskrit word Yajman which means a person who performs a Yajna and for the purpose of performance of Yajna one has to hire the services of a Brahmin. Gradually, this word came to be applied to everyone who hired services or to whom some service was given. As N. S. Reddy observes, the farmer who engages carpenter or iron-smith for manufacture or repair of his tools is Jajman and the carpenter and the ironsmith are kameen or parjan.[2] Between Jajman and Parjan the relationship is hereditary and is based on tradition. Jajmans get a variety of jobs done by parjans, as for example, the barber dresses the hair and shaves the beard: Kahar brings water from the well or river as the case may be, sweeper does sanitary jobs. For these services parjans are paid something. In a majority of cases farmers in Indian villages give grains for the services of the parjans. In modern times currency notes are fast replacing all other media of exchange even in villages. In Jajmani system, Jajman enjoys so much respect that he is often referred to as Rajah (King) and parjans as subjects.

STUDIES OF JAJMANI SYSTEM

Various studies of Jajmani system in India have been made. As referred to earlier, Oscar Lewis studied Jajmani in North Indian villages. Jajmani in Eastern U.P. was studied in 1948 by Opler and Singh in 1955. N.S. Reddy studied this system in North India. Miller studied Jajmani system in Cochin in 1952, and in 1955, Sri Niwas and Bir Singh studied the same system in Mysore District. S.C. Dube's Indian Village is based on his classic study of Jajmani in Hyderabad. Jajmani in Tanjore was studied by Gouth in 1955. In Gujarat Jajmani was studied by Steel in 1953. An early study, in 1934, of Jajmani in Punjab was made by Darling. All these studies revealed and

2. Reddy, N.S., Functional Relations of Lohars in a North Indian Village, in *Eastern Anthropologist*, No. 18, March to August, 1955, pp. 129-40.

4. Peace and contentment. According to W. H. Wiser, a significant feature of jajmani system is the peace and contentment which is provided to villagers.[7] The kameens of a jajman feel a sense of security. They are free from the worry of finding employment to make both ends meet. As the nature of the tasks they have to perform is well-known to them in advance, they feel great mental peace and are well prepared for these tasks; and this saves them the botheration of adjustment. However, the picture is not altogether rosy. There are quite a few instances in which kameens are exploited and given too little for their services.

5. Difference in the scope of work. Under jajmani system the range of activity of different kameens is not uniform. It is not necessary that a certain kameen should work only for a single family or even a single village. If the nature of his work or activity is such that he can effectively cater to the needs of two or three villages, there is no provision in jajmani system against such an arrangement. For example, a family needs the services of a barber once or twice a week and these, too, for an hour or so. Naturally, therefore a barber can easily cater to the needs of a dozen or so families. He can even work in more than one village. In certain instances, a shopkeeper is able to carry on his activities of making general provisions available in a range of 10 to 20 miles from a village. Thus, in many villages we do not find one shopkeeper carrying on his duties exclusively in one village, in which he has his headquarters. The range, scope or spread of activities of any kameen is determined by the nature of his activity. For example, while it is not possible for a sweeper to cater to the needs of more than a handful of families, a barber or a shopkeeper may be able to operate in more than one village. Another factor which restricts or widens the spread of one's activity is the nature of demand and supply. If a village is prosperous, it may have one or more shopkeepers but if the village is small and demand of goods is low, there may not be one exclusive shopkeeper in that village. We do not find shoemakers in every village. S. S. Nehru studied 54 North Indian villages and found that only in 18 out of these there were shoemakers. Potters were in 30% of the villages and shopkeepers only in 16%. Ahirs were found in 60% and Brahmin, barber and ironsmith and Teli were found each in 40% of the villages.[8] From the above survey it is plain that not every type of kameen is to be found in every village. In the absence of a particular kameen people perform that task by themselves or go to another village for it. For example, residents of a village may get hair dressed from a neighbouring village.

Advantages of Jajmani System

The foregoing account brings into dear relief the advantages and disadvantages of jajmani system. Its chief advantages are as follows:

1. Security of service. As has been mentioned earlier, the professions in jajmani system are hereditary; and are, therefore, fixed and permanent. The sons of a kameen do not have to look for jobs; they get jobs as a matter of birthright.

2. Economic security. In jajmani system jajmans look after each and every need of their kameens. Thus, a kameen enjoys economic security.

---

7. Wiser, W.H., *The Hindu Jajmani System*, Lucknow Publishing House (Lucknow, 1951), p. 187.
8. Nehru, S.S., *Caste and Credit in the Rural Area*.

3. Close personal relations. In as much as jajmans and kameens are related to each other by heredity and long tradition, their relationship is intimate and personal. They know each other very well and are, therefore, sympathetic to the needs of each other. Their relationship is not purely economic or professional. As a matter of fact, their lives are interlinked.

Disadvantages of Jajmani System

However, jajmani system is not free from faults. Like caste system it was of great value in the past but has now degenerated into an instrument of exploitation and discrimination. As Oscar Lewis has pointed out in his study of jajmani system in Rampur village, whereas in past it was based on personal relationship, it has now become an instrument of exploitation of kameen by jajman. In jajmani system, the kameens are treated as inferior and lowbred. In fact, the word kameen itself means lowly or inferior. Thus, the upper castes exploit and abuse the low castes. D.N. Majumdar and colleagues found in their survey of the villages that the conditions of kameens are miserable and the upper castes subject them to great harassment and trouble.[9]

Change in Jajmani System

These days there is a gradual change in the jajmani system. This system is disappearing because old caste system is giving way to groupism and class struggle. Another important factor contributing to the disintegration of jajmani system is the gradual weakening of faith in religion and performance of rituals. This has resulted in decline of Brahmins' prestige. They are no longer in much demand. The rapid expansion of the fast means of communication and transport has made it easy for workers to seek work outside their town and for jajman to receive improved services somewhere else. However, professions are no longer heredity based. It is possible, indeed is quite the case, for a village Brahmin to take to shopkeeping. The agricultural profession is no longer an exclusive profession of any particular caste. People of different castes are engaged these days in agriculture. Finally, the greatest set-back to jajmani system has come from reform movements like Arya Samaj. In brief, it can be said that all the factors which are responsible for decline and disintegration of the caste system are also responsible for the decline and disintegration of the jajmani system.

QUESTIONS FOR EXERCISE

1. Discuss the organisation of Jajmani system in Indian villages. What are the recent changes in the system?
2. Write short note on Jajmani system.
3. Write a short essay on "Inter-caste relationship in Indian villages."

---

9. Majumdar, Pradhan, Sen and Misra, Inter-caste Relations in Kohana Kalian, a village near Lucknow, in *Eastern Anthropologist*, March-Aug. 1955, pp. 191-214.

14

THE RURAL CASTE SYSTEM

The word 'caste' is used in everyday life and we use it to distinguish one person from another. We say that such and such person belongs to a particular caste. In saying it we generally mean to convey that he is born of parents or is a member of the family said to belong to a particular caste. In this way caste is a hereditary group. In biology this word is used only for descent or heredity. But this definition is inadequate for the purpose of sociology since it requires a more comprehensive and clear definition. Caste may be defined as a hereditary, endogamous group which decides the individual's status in the social stratification and his profession, etc.

DEFINITION OF CASTE

Of the many definitions of caste offered by different scholars some are reproduced below:

1. *Sir Herbert Risley.* "A caste may be defined as a collection of families, or groups of families, bearing a common name, which usually denotes or is associated with specific occupation claiming common descent from a mythical ancestor, human or divine, professing to follow the same professional calling and are regarded by those who are competent to give an opinion as forming a single and homogeneous community." Criticising this definition of caste Hutton has said that it is the people of class who claim descent from a mythical ancestor and not members of caste.

2. *Martindale and Monachesi.* "A caste is an aggregate of persons whose share of obligations and privileges is fixed by birth sanctioned or supported by religion and magic." This definition of the caste is not complete since it does not include several main characteristics of the caste.

3. *A.W. Green.* "Caste is a system of stratification in which mobility, movement up and down the status ladder, at least ideally may not occur. A person's ascribed status is his life-time status. Birth determines occupation, place of residence, style of life, personal associates and the group from among whom one must find a mate. A caste system always includes the notion that physical or even some forms of social contact with the lower caste people is degrading to higher caste

persons. The caste system is also protected by law and sanctified by religion." This definition of caste is more satisfactory and all-round.

Characteristics of Caste

Modern thinkers consider it best to enumerate the features of caste in defining it. This is what Hutton, Ghurye, N. K. Dutta[1] and many others have done. Of the predominating characteristics of caste, the following are the most important:

1. Determination by birth. The membership of caste is determined by birth. A person remains the member of the caste into which he is born and his membership does not undergo any change even if change takes place in his status, occupation, education, wealth, etc.

2. Rules and regulations concerning food. Each individual caste has its own laws which govern the good habits of its members. Generally, there are no restrictions against fruit, milk, butter, dry fruits, etc., but kachcha food (bread, etc.) can be accepted only from a member of one's own or of a higher caste.

3. Definite occupations. In the Hindu scriptures there is a mention of the occupation of all varnas. According to Manu the functions of the Brahmin, Kshatriya, Vaishya and the Shudra were definite. The functions of the Brahmin were to study, teach, guide and perform religious rituals, and to give and receive alms; that of the Kashatriya to study, perform religious rituals, give alms, punish the evil and go to war; that of the Vaishya to study, perform religious rituals, give alms, work in agriculture, trade and animal husbandry; that of the Shudra to do menial work for all the other varnas. Having developed from varna system the occupations in caste system are definite. In Hindu society even today in most cases the son of a blacksmith pursues the occupation of his father, the son of a carpenter becomes a carpenter while the son of a shoemaker becomes a shoemaker.

4. Endogamous group. The majority of persons marry only within their own caste. Brahmin, Kashatriya, Vaishya and Shudra all marry within their respective castes. Westermarck has considered this to be a chief characteristic of the caste system. Hindu community does not sanctify inter-caste marriage even now.

5. Rules concerning status and touchability. The various castes in Hindu social organisation are divided into a hierarchy of ascent and descent one above the other. In this hierarchy the Brahmins have the highest and the untouchables the lowest position. To the sense of superiority among the Brahmins is also conjoined the law of untouchability. This sense of superiority is much exaggerated and manifest in the South. The very touch and sometimes even the shadow of a member of the lower caste is enough to defile an individual of high caste. In Kerala a Namboodiri Brahmin is defiled by the touch of a Nayyar, but in the case of a member of Tiya caste a distance of 86 feet must be kept avoiding being defiled and in the case of a member of the Pulayana caste the distance must be ninety-six feet. The stringent observation of the system of untouchability has resulted in some low castes of the Hindu society being called untouchables who were consequently forbidden

1. Dutta. N.K., *Origin and Growth of Castes in India* (1931).

to make use of places of worship, cremation grounds, educational institutions, public roads and hotels, etc., and were disallowed from living in the cities.

The above mentioned characteristics of the caste system do not take into account all the numerous variations presently taking place in the caste system. Actually, it is difficult to formulate a definite and permanent definition of caste. The most that can be done is to describe the features of the caste system in a particular context, since the caste system is undergoing considerable modification and transformation. It would not be surprising if castes were eventually reduced to a word signifying merely a group, since inter-caste marriages are increasing and the restrictions on mutual behaviour, exchange of goodwill and conduct are breaking. Some people are changing their caste on the strength of their monetary wealth, the occupations for the various castes are no longer fixed, a member of any caste takes to any profession that he desires, the Brahmins have been deprived of much of their past glory and respect, very few caste panchayats are to be seen and even they have no control whatsoever over the members. Many people have even started excluding their caste name from the name they use. In this way, caste is continually taking on the shape of class and casteism is growing in the form of classism. On the one hand, some conditions are favouring its existence while on the other they are unfavourable.

THEORIES OF THE ORIGIN OF THE CASTE SYSTEM

Theories about the origin of caste in sociology may be classified as — Political theory, Traditional theory, Economic or Occupational theory, Ethical theory, Ethnic theory, Theory of Mana, Theory of occupational classes and religious theory. The explanation concerning these theories is as follows.

1. Political Theory. According to Political Theory of caste the caste system is the Brahmin progeny of Indo-Aryan culture which developed in Gangetic plain and spread from there throughout the country. According to prof. G. S. Ghurye, this theory was invented due to the political interest of the Brahmins. In his own words, "I may conclude that caste in India is a Brahminic child of the Indo-Aryan culture, cradled in the land of the Ganga and the Yamuna and thence transferred to other parts of the country." Political theory was propounded first of all by the French priest Abbe Dubois in twelfth century A.D. In his work Hindu Manners and Customs, Abbe Dubois called caste the scheming of the Brahmins. Denzil Ibbetson has supported Abbe Dubois in pointing out that in caste system the occupations held by the Brahmins and Kshatriyas have been considered as the best and the highest. Thus, according to political theory, caste system was invented in order to dominate the entire Hindu society by the higher castes. Against the political theory as an explanation of the origin of caste system in India, Dr. D. N. Majumdar has given the following arguments in his famous work *Races and Culture of India:*

1. This theory has neglected the racial distinctions found among various social classes in India.

2. Looking at the complex Hindu social structure based upon caste, it appears impossible that the aim of caste system would have been to maintain the dominance of the Brahmin priests over Hindu Society.

2. Traditional Theory. According to traditional theory the caste system was created by the Creator Brahma himself. According to Rigveda, Brahmins are like the mouth, Kshatriyas like the arms, Vaishyas like the stomach, and the Shudras like the feet of the social body. This explanation of the origin of caste may be suitable as an explanation of the origin of Varna system. It cannot explain the origin of thousands of castes in Hindu society.

3. Economic or Occupational Theory. Explaining the origin of caste system in India, Nesfield has said "Function and function alone is responsible for the origin of caste system." The ancient traditions of the Hindus support this theory. In Bhagwadgita, Sri Krishna has pointed out that the fourfold varna system has been created by God himself. In Buddhist literature, there is a mention of so many castes according to occupational distinction, busy in various crafts and industries. It is a fact that the occupation of most of the castes in Hindu society were fixed. The words Lohar, Sunar, Chamar, Julaha etc. signify the economic occupations of these castes. However, the economic or occupational theory about the origin of caste systems in India suffers from the following defects:

(i) *It does not explain the hierarchy in caste system.* Occupational theory does not explain why some castes are considered higher than other castes. The function of a Lohar or a Chamar is as vital for the society as that of any other caste and yet why these castes are considered as lower castes. In south India even the cultivators are held to belong to lower castes, while their function is definitely most important for the society. Thus, no one can deny the political intrigue of the higher castes to maintain their hold on Hindu society through the caste system.

(ii) *Why all the farmers do not belong to one caste.* About 67% Hindus are busy in agriculture. These farmers, however, come from all the castes. If occupational theory were true then they should belong to one caste on the basis of economic occupation. This, however, is not so. In India there are not as many occupations as there are castes which number up to thousands. Thus, Prof. D.N. Majumdar has rightly pointed out that though function has been the basis of social stratification in ancient India, but it cannot properly and completely explain the Hindu social structure based upon the caste system.

(iii) *It neglects racial elements.* The occupational theory does not accept any distinctions between castes on the basis of race. This, however, has been proved wrong by modern discoveries.

4. Ethical Theory. S.C. Roy has propounded ethical theory about the origin of caste system in India. According to this theory caste system originated in the class system of Indo-Aryans, the tribal system of pre-Dravidians and conflicts among various occupations. This theory, while emphasising the philosophical aspect of the caste system, does not explain the contradictory and complex circumstances leading to the evolution of caste system in India.

5. Ethnic Theory. Some scholars have propounded ethnic theory about the origin of caste system. According to this theory castes are ethnic groups. Risley pointed out that the Aryans gave a lower place in society to the Dravidians. This was because the nasal structure of the Dravidians was different from that of the Aryans. The groups resembling the nasal structure of the former were, therefore, labelled as lower castes. According to Prof. G. S. Ghurye, the caste system was a clever scheme of the Brahmins to maintain their hold on Hindu Society. According to D. N. Majumdar the aim of caste system was to maintain the purity of blood. To quote his words, "Nesfield said that superiority or inferiority of occupation is represented in the hierarchy of the castes. We should think that the status of the caste depends upon the degree of purity of blood and the extent of isolation maintained by the social groups." N. K. Dutta also agrees with Risley on this point. However, J. H. Hutton has criticised the ethnic theory about the origin of caste system on the following points:

(i) Why did Ethnic distinctions not create caste system among Muslims and Christians?

(ii) Though Ethnic distinctions are found in most of the countries of the world, the caste system is peculiar in India — Why?

(iii) This principle does not explain untouchability.

(iv) This theory does not explain how various castes originated from races?

(v) This theory is disproved by facts. In the census report of 1931 by Dr. Guha in India, the Nayyars of Malabar, the Pathans of North-West Frontier province and the Brahmins of Bengal have same caste. Such examples can be multiplied.

6. Theory of Mana. According to J.H. Hutton, the caste system originated in the religious customs and rituals of the non-Aryan groups particularly the theory of Mana. Mana is a mystic power. According to Hutton the traditions of endogamy, untouchability etc. have their roots in defence against the influence of Mana. Criticising this theory of the origin of caste system, D.N. Majumdar has pointed out that it is absolutely controversial as to what role may be assigned to Mana in the origin of caste system. This theory does not explain that whereas belief in Mana is found among most of the primitive tribes all over the world, why did it create caste system in India?

7. Theory of Occupational Classes. In his book *Punjab Castes*, Denzil lbbetson has maintained that occupational classification is the root of caste system. Thus, caste system originated due to distinctions of tribes, occupational guilds and religion. The tribes following different occupations created different castes.

In ancient India the priests were given the highest status in the hierarchy of occupational system. Gradually, occupations became hereditary and led to the customs of endogamy. These ultimately led to the formation of hundreds of castes in India. The occupational theory of the origin of caste system in India does not explain the fact that while occupational classification is found everywhere in the world, why did it lead to caste system only in India? The development of caste system in India, therefore, must be due to some other causes besides occupational differences.

8. Religious Theory. Hocart and Senart, the two scholars, have advanced what is known as religious theory of the origin of caste system. According to Hocart the division of labour in Indian society has been based upon the religious principles and customs since in ancient India *Dharma* occupied the most important place. The king was considered as the representative of God. The administrative system, therefore, drew its authority from divine power. Therefore, the religious priests were given the highest status in caste system. Gradually, different social groups hardened in propounding this religious theory of the origin of caste system. Hocart has, however, forgotten that the caste system in India is primarily social institution and not a religious system. Therefore in spite of religious element in it, it cannot be termed as a religious institution. It will, however, be admitted that religious element had been an important element in the origin of the caste system in India. Hocart's theory does not explain the prevalence of taboos concerning food and marriage etc., among different castes.

Senart has explained the origin of caste system on the basis of taboos concerning food. He points out that there were restrictions upon taking food with members of other castes as their systems of worship and their family deities were different. Persons worshipping one deity were considered to be descendants of the same ancestors.

They used to offer different types of food to their various gods. These practices gradually led to distinctions among various religious groups which ultimately led to the caste system in which Brahmins were given the highest status. Against this theory of the origin of caste system in India it has been pointed out by Dahlmann that it suffers from oversimplification and is, therefore, not scientific. It is difficult to understand as to how a complex institution like the caste system could develop purely on the basis of religious distinctions. This theory also confuses between the castes.

Besides the above-mentioned important theories concerning the origin of caste system in India some other scholars have also advanced significant views. According to D.N. Majumdar, caste system was developed to save Aryan race and culture from intermixing with other races. According to Slater, caste system originated in order to safeguard the professional and occupational secrets. According to Gilbert, the geographical distinctions led to the development of the caste system. Jackson points out that Hindu kings made it obligatory for everyone to follow his caste occupation. All these various views about the origin of caste system are one-sided explanations. They are true so far as they go but they do not extend all the explanations of this complex social institution. Caste system, complex as it is, could not originate in someone circumstance or due to someone factor. The different factors pointed out by the theories mentioned above may be taken together to arrive at a multisided explanation of caste system. In the words of J.H. Hutton, "It is urged emphatically that the Indian caste system is the natural result of the interaction of a number of geographical, social, religious and economic factors not elsewhere found in conjunction."

CONDITIONS FAVOURABLE TO THE CASTE SYSTEM

Since hundreds of years caste system is prevalent in India. And even now it is firmly rooted in Indian social structure. The following conditions have continued the existence of caste system in India:

1. Geographical isolation. Geographical isolation has a large part to play in rendering a society static and powerless. The absence of adequate means of transport leads to the geographical isolation, from others, of people who inhabit distantly situated areas and this fosters old customs, mores traditions and superstitions, all of which encourage caste system.

2. Static society. Hindu society has never been very dynamic. There has never been any stupendous variation in its political circumstances and economic conditions. Its social mores, customs and traditions have failed to change over the ages as times have marched along. But this does not mean that Hindu society has not changed at all. To say that it is not dynamic is only to indicate the extremely slow rate at which variations and modifications are instituted in it. In this way, the comparatively static nature of society is a condition favourable to the continued existence of the caste system.

3. Foreign aggression. A further contribution to the desirability and utility of the caste system was made by foreign aggression. Many scholars hold that the caste system started in India when the Aryans invaded the country. The Aryan victors were fair skinned and the natives of India were black. Thus, two castes were formed in India. The victorious race considered itself superior to the victimised one and considered it below its dignity to associate itself and to marry into latter. In this way, strict laws regarding conduct, diet, marriage, etc., were formulated. These were the fundamental constituents of the caste system.

4. Rural social structure. The rural social structure is usually unchanging and static. Ancient traditions are better respected in it. As the rural structure weakens and urbanisation increases, the caste also becomes progressively weaker.

5. Influence of religion. The influence of religion is the most important factor contributing to the continuation of the caste system. The Hindu caste system is looked upon as a divine institution. People who violate it are considered sinners and it is believed that God will punish them. Due to this reason people do not have the courage to violate the laws of the caste system.

6. Variety of racial strains. The existence of many races in the country led to the formulation of many strict laws concerning discrimination since each race endeavoured to maintain its purity. In the medieval period of Indian History strict laws concerning caste were laid down to protect Hindu society from the Muslims.

7. Lack of education. Lack of education occupies an important position among the factors which have encouraged the existence of caste system in Hindu society. Superstitions, traditions and mores breed freely among uneducated people. Thus, lack of education favours caste system.

CONDITIONS UNFAVOURABLE TO CASTE

And yet the bonds of caste have gradually weakened. The following elements have tended to weaken the caste system in the present century:

1. Modern education. A major part in weakening the caste system is played by the modern education. It emphasises democratic values such as liberty, equality and fraternity. It bears the stamp of the scientific and free thinking in the West. It has laid great stress upon human dignity. Thus, the expansion of education, communication and association is proportionately weakening the ties of caste. It has encouraged inter-caste marriages. The feelings of superiority and untouchability are being gradually eliminated from the minds of school going children of all castes.

2. Industrialisation. Industrialisation has led to a decrease in the intensity of caste fervour because persons from all castes have sought and obtained employment in factories. According to A.W. Green, although the Brahmin has to take prolonged religious bath in order to purify himself against the defilement caused by the mere shadow of a Shudra, yet it is not possible to avoid the shadow of Shudras in the crowded lanes of city and the busy offices. As a result of industrialisation individuals of all castes came into mutual contact in the factories, hotels, markets, trains, trams and buses etc., and the observance of laws concerning touchability became impossible.

3. Increase in thc value of money. It the modern age wealth is replacing caste as the basis of social prestige. A person adopts the occupation which appears to him to be the most profitable. The consideration in the choice of profession is no longer caste but individual capability and the facility in earning wealth. A wealthy Shudra is more respected than a poor Brahmin. For this reason the ties of the caste are being loosened in the frantic race after wealth.

4. Social reform movement. As a result of the influence of modern education there has been a flood of movements for social emancipation.

5. Means of transport and communication. Means of transport and communication developed in India. This put an end to geographical isolation and the thoughts, customs, etc., of various places influenced each other. It became difficult to maintain the rigidity of caste in the whirlwind of communication set into motion by industrialization through such means as buses, trains, trams, etc. In this connection Risley has written in *People of India* that on a platform where the train halts momentarily one does not inquire the caste of the seller while purchasing something from him.

6. Political movement. To end the discriminatory practices on the basis of the caste system, was a part of the aims of the national agitation for a political awakening of the people in India. The objective of this national movement was the establishment of a democratic pattern of society in India. For this reason it made efforts to weaken the caste consciousness in the people.

7. New legislation. In the legal machinery of the British Government all castes were similarly punished for the same offences. The establishment of judicial courts deprived the caste panchayats of their power and they no longer retained the authority to punish a criminal. In this way, the restrictions upon the opponents of the caste system were removed and gradually its laws also lost their meaning and significance.

8. Rise of new social classes. New classes are appearing in Hindu society based on economic status. These social classes are replacing the caste. The organisation of castes was vertical and that of economic classes is horizontal. As the class consciousness is increasing, caste consciousness is decreasing.

9. Country's freedom. The most severe shock to the caste system was the country's gaining freedom from British rule. Para 15(2) of the Constitution of Independent India declared all citizens equal. Thus, the fortress of the caste system collapsed. According to the Untouchability Crime Act of 1955, it is a crime to prevent any one from using a public place. The respect once accorded to the caste system dwindled through the influence of the rapid growth of the means of transport, educational facilities, industrialisation, the democratic method of government, etc.

In spite of the presence of so many unfavourable circumstances the caste system continues to exist in an aggravated condition in the country and at some places it has become even stronger through being identified with political interests.

NEW TRENDS IN CASTE

The disorganisation of the caste system has led some to infer that in the future caste system will cease to exist. But some scholars have refuted this doubt. According to G.S. Ghurye, there is no fear of the extinction of the caste system in the near future due to the following two conditions:

1. Elections based on casteism. On the establishment of a democracy in India the government machinery is operated by representatives elected by the people.

The method of election has done much to encourage the caste system because the candidates want to achieve their end by drumming the cause of casteism among the voters. In this way, people are asked to vote for their caste candidate and this casteism is maintained by the elected leaders after the elections are over. Some political parties sponsor only that candidate for election in a particular area whose caste is the most numerous among the voters.

2. Special constitutional provisions for backward classes. The Indian Constitution has provided for the protection of the backward and scheduled castes. Some posts have been reserved for them in government services. They are given all types of facilities and special scholarships for education. All this is most welcome and even necessary and yet more special rights have encouraged casteism in the backward classes since the caste is proving beneficial to them because of these prerogatives.

In India, on the one hand, the caste is becoming weaker due to the influence of such factors as industrialisation, urbanisation, increase in the means of transportation, popularity of English education, political and social awakening, democratic government and laws abolishing untouchability, etc., and on the other hand such new organisations as labour unions, etc., on the basis of occupation, post, capacity etc., are being established. Due to an increase in the desire for money caused by the influence of Western education, the sense of superiority or inferiority is now based on wealth and social power rather than on caste. The class consciousness, based on occupations, etc., is replacing the caste consciousness.

All these changes led people to believe that the caste system will generally take on the form of a class system. But while, on the one hand, class consciousness seems to be progressing, on the other one can see progress in casteism as well. For people who are especially gifted in a particular occupation, other occupations are very limited in India and the paths to those that are available are difficult. Children of those parents who have a small income or who have no wealth look out only for service. In some big business institutions and sometimes even in educational institutions what happens is that the people who are employed in various posts belong to the castes of the proprietors, organizers and senior officials. Casteism of a similar type prevails also in government services and political elections. Hence, it cannot be asserted that at the present time the caste is disappearing and classism is increasing. Actually, in India casteism is being transformed into classism.

FUTURE OF THE CASTE SYSTEM

It is difficult to make an unqualified statement concerning the future of the caste system in India. It is certainly true that the restrictions of marriage, diet, mode of life, behaviour, etc., based on the caste system are breaking down. But, as has been described previously, casteism is increasing and caste system is being encouraged by caste practices in election. Actually, it seems more or less definite that there is no possibility of the caste system being eliminated from the Indian society in the near future. The root of the caste system goes deep in Hindu society and at its base are the important and beneficial principles of division of labour, specialisation, etc. Foreign invaders made their best efforts to wipe out the Hindu caste. But in spite of all efforts of the Muslims and Christians not much change was wrought in caste system. It has definitely been affected somewhat by the influence of Western education and Western culture and its form has undergone a vast change. There is no room for doubting that this form of the caste system will change further in fixture, it may even change, beyond recognition. It will also be influenced by the development of the sense of democracy and nationalism, industrial progress and by new political and economic movement.

CASTES AMONG MUSLIMS

Though, Islam does not admit any type of distinction among its followers, the Indian Muslims have adopted caste system due to the influence of the Hindu social organisation and because most of the Indian Muslims are converts from Hindu religion. It is, hence, that one finds caste system and even casteism prevailing among Indian Muslims. Those Muslims who, before conversion, belonged to higher castes in Hindus consider other Muslims lower in social status. Among the more important castes found in Indian Muslims are the following:

1. Ashraf castes. The word *sharif* in Arabic language means a gentleman. Ashraf is the plural of this word. Thus, Ashraf are those castes which are respectable and gentle. They are considered Ashraf since their forefathers came from Arabia, Persia. Turkey and Afghanistan. These ashraf castes are four in number — Sayyad, Sheikh, Mughal and Pathan. The ancestors of Sayyad and Sheikh are considered to have come from Mecca and Madina and since these two places are important in Islam, these castes are considered as highest among Muslims. Mughals were the inhabitants of Mongolia in Central Asia and they ruled over India for a long time. Thus, the present Mughals consider themselves to be higher than other Muslims. The Pathans are considered to be the original inhabitants of Afghanistan. Now, we will discuss these four Ashraf castes in more details.

(i) *Sayyad.* Just as Brahmins are on the apex in Hindu social organisation, similarly, Sayyad's are considered to be the highest among Muslims in India. Literally speaking, the word Sayyad means a prince. Persons belonging to this caste use the word Mir and Sayyad before their names. Among Sayyads again, there are many sub-castes such as Askari, Bakri, Hasani, Hussani, Kazmi, Naqvi, Rizvi, Zaidi, Alvi, Abbasi, Zafari and Hashimi etc.

(ii) *Sheikh.* Literally Sheikh means the chief or the head. Among Muslims Sheikhs are counted after Sayyads. Generally, the religious teachers are known as Sheikhs. Among Sheikhs there are several sub-castes such as Usmani, Siddiqi, Ansari, Farookhi, Khorasani, Milki, Qureshi and Kidwai, etc.

(iii) *Mughal.* Mughals are so-called after the country of their origin, Mongolia. They use the surname Mirza after their name. Among Mughals there are several sub-castes such as Uzbeg, Turkman, Tazik, Taimuri, Chugtai and Zilbash, etc.

(iv) *Pathan.* Ancestors of Pathans came to India from Afghanistan. They use Khan surname after their proper names. Among Pathans also there are several sub-castes such as Afridi, Bangash, Barak, Durrani, Khalil, Lodhi, Rohilla and Yusufzai etc.

2. Muslim Rajput Castes. In India, In Rajasthan the Muslims converted many Rajputs to Islam with the force of sword. Some Rajputs embraced Islam due to greed of money or prestige. Therefore, in Muslim society there is a class of Muslim Rajput caste. Since among these the idea of higher and lower castes was already deeply imbedded, they maintained the same attitude even after embracing Islam. It is due to this attitude that they do not mix up with lower caste Muslims and do not entertain marriage relations with them. They keep their relations confined to equal or higher caste Muslims. Notable among the Rajput Muslim castes are Tomar, Chandel, Bhatti, Gautam, Chauhan, Panwar, Rathaur and Somavanshi etc.

3. Professional Castes. In this class of Muslim castes, as is clear by their name, castes have been distinguished on the basis of professions such as Barhai, Dhobi, Lohar, Hajjam, Kumhar, Teli, and Sunar, etc. These are the professional castes which were formerly Hindu and were later on converted into Muslims. Besides, these, there are some professional castes which are no more found among Hindus but only among Muslims. Notable among these are Atisbazz, Bavarchi, Bhaliara, Bhand, Gaddi, Faqir, Momin, Julaha, Mirasi, Naubat, Kunjara, Dhunia, Kabaria, Chikwa, and Manihar etc.

4. Untouchable Castes. Though the Muslim saints considered all human beings to be equal, but one may find untouchability prevalent among Muslims. For example, the Muslim Bhangi or Chamar may enter a mosque for Namaz and not for any other purpose. This proves that untouchability among Muslims is not religious but social. Thus, it is less rigorous than that found among Hindus. Even the untouchable castes among Muslims have several sub-castes such as Ghazipuri, Rawat, Lal Begi, Patthar Phora, Sheikh, Mehtar, Bansphora, Balmiki, etc. .

Casteism in Muslim Marriage

Just as Hindus have caste considerations in matrimonial relationships and do not like inter-caste marriages, similarly, among Muslims also one finds caste considerations in marriage. Just as among Hindus only Anuloma marriages are permitted and Pratiloma marriages are rather exceptions, similarly, among Muslims also Anuloma marriages are generally prevalent and the cases of Pratiloma marriages are rather few. In Anuloma marriage a higher caste male marries a female of lower caste. Referring to this custom among Muslims, it has been pointed out by some authors that the males of Ashraf castes first of all try to get a girl in their own caste, if this is not available, they want to marry a girl of equal caste. If even in these one does not get a suitable match, one marries with a girl of lower caste. A Sayyad may marry a Sheikh girl but cannot many a Sayyad girl to Sheikh boy. Similarly, Sheikhs marry among Sayyad but do not give their daughters in marriage to Pathans. Among Rajput Muslims almost the same rules are observed as among Hindu Rajputs. They prefer to marry their daughters among Ashraf Muslims though the latter do not like to do so.

An extreme example of casteism among Muslims may be observed in the case of occasional conflict between Shia and Sunni Muslims. These two groups often indulge in violent riots. They do not like inter-marriage. Like Hindus, Muslims also like endogamy though their rules concerning exogamy are not as strict as in the case of Hindus. The Muslim social rules prohibit marriage only among very close relatives. Thus, among them marriages between maternal and paternal cousins and other relatives are permitted. Just as one has to face social boycott for violating caste rules among Hindus, similarly among Muslims also social control is exercised on marriage relationships.

Caste Panchayats among Muslims

Like the Hindu castes one may find caste panchayats among Muslim castes as well. Just as among the higher caste Hindus the caste panchayats do not yield much authority, similarly among high caste Muslims also caste panchayats do hot have wide rights. Thus, among high caste Hindus and Muslims social control is mostly exercised through the joint families. But among professional castes and untouchable castes one finds organised caste panchayats. For example, among Muslim's castes like Manihar, Teli, Dhobi, Bhangi, etc., have organised caste panchayats which apply their rules upon members. Offenders are boycotted from society and so long as they do not make up for the social loss and repent for it, they are kept out of the caste.

Changes in Muslim Castes

Like Hindu castes, Muslim castes are also constantly changing. Urbanization, industrialization, Westernization and secularisation are constantly undermining the influence of caste among Hindus and Muslims. Incidence of inter-caste marriages is increasing among educated persons. Untouchability is gradually decreasing. Social intercourse is more influenced by economic status than by the castes. Like Hindus one finds taboos about social intercourse among Muslims. But caste rules among Muslims are not as strict as among Hindus. On festivals and religious occasions one finds fraternal behaviour among members of different castes. This is due to the reason that caste system among Muslims is more social than religious. Among Hindus it is based upon religious conceptions. It is hence that as compared to the Muslim community casteism has deeper roots among Hindus.

Castes among Christians

The Western Christians are broadly Catholic and Protestants with so many sub-classes. Though caste distinctions as noticed in Hindu society are absent in the Christian society, but the evil of casteism has superstitiously infiltrated into the 'Indian Christian Community'. In his Myth of Caste System, Dr. N. Prasad has distinguished following groups in Kerala Christians. Kerala, incidentally, is the Indian state which has highest concentration of the Christians. In Kerala the Christians control and dominate the state politics. Following are the groups of Christians in Kerala — (I) Chaldean Syrians; (2) Jacobite Syrians; (3) Latin Catholics; (4) Marthomite Syrians; (5) Syrians Catholics and (6) Protestants.

In these groups of Christians we find same type of differences, tensions and competition as in the castes among Hindus. Each group considers itself to be more near the original Gospel. Thus, though Christianity is strenuously opposed to casteism and, therefore, higher than others in order and hierarchy, many Christians look down upon backward Hindu castes and observe a system of untouchability. They do not employ them as domestic servants. Christians are against caste and classes among men in theory, in actual practice they observe casteism and practise untouchability. As India's most enlightened and Westernised Statesman Jawahar Lal Nehru observes in his book, *Discovery of India*, "Christianity comes here 1800 years ago and settles down and gradually develops its own castes."

QUESTIONS FOR EXERCISE

1. What do you understand by caste? Discuss its vertical and horizontal dimensions.
2. What are the chief characteristics of caste system in India? Explain
3. Examine the structural and functional features of Caste in India.
4. Enumerate and explain the outstanding features of caste system in India
5. 'Caste System' is weakening in some respects and strengthening in others. Elucidate.
6. Examine the functions and disfunctions of caste today.
7. Discuss the effects of caste on Hindu society.
8. How did the British rule effect the caste system in India?
9. Discuss the recent trends in the caste system.

Table 1: *Scheduled Castes and Scheduled Tribes in India*

State/ Union Territory	Scheduled Castes Population ('000)	Scheduled Castes Percentage	Scheduled Tribes Population ('000)	Scheduled Tribes Percentage
1	2	3	4	5
India	1,04,755	15.8	51,629	7.8
A.P.	7,962	14.9	3,176	5.9
Assam	NA		NA	—
Bihar	10,142	14.5	5,811	8.3
Gujarat	2,438	7.2	4,849	14.2
Haryana	2,464	19.1	—	—
Himachal Pradesh	1,054	24.6	197	4.6
J & K	497	8.3	—	
Karnataka	5,595	15.1	1,825	4.9
Kerala	2,549	10.0	261	1.0
M.P.	7,359	14.1	11,987	23.0
Maharashtra	4,480	7.1	5,772	9.2
Manipur	18	1.3	.388	27.3
Meghalaya	5	0.4	1,076	80.6
Nagaland		—	651	84.0
Orissa	3,866	14.7	1,915	22.4
Punjab	4,512	26.9	—	—
Rajasthan	5,839	17.0	4,183	12.2
Sikkim	18	5.8	74	23.3
Tamil Nadu	8,881	18.4	520	1.1
Tripura	310	15.1	584	28.4
U.P.	23,453	21.2	233	0.2
W. Bengal	12,001	22.0	3,071	5.6
Andaman and Nicobar	—	—	22	11.9
Arunachal Pradesh	3	0.5	441	69.8
Chandigarh	64	14.1	—	—
Dadra & Nagar Haveli	2	2.0	82	78.8
Delhi	1,122	18.0	—	—
Goa, Daman & Diu	23	2.2	11	1.0
Lakshadweep	—	—	38	93.8
Mizoram	—	—	462	93.6
Pondicherry	97	16.0	—	—

15

RURAL UNTOUCHABILITY

In 1935, the Government of India prepared a list of castes for providing special facilities to the untouchable castes. This list included castes whose total population today numbers over eight crores. These castes were called scheduled castes by virtue of their inclusion in the list. These are called untouchables. The problem of untouchability is a serious social problem in the Indian villages.

DEFINITION OF UNTOUCHABILITY

It is extremely difficult to define untouchability. Actually, untouchability implies those disabilities which were imposed upon the Harijan castes by the superior castes. In the Untouchability (Offences) Act, 1955 the word untouchability was given this connotation. In this way according to the above law, "It is an offence to prevent any person on the ground of untouchability (a) from entering any place of public worship which is open to other persons, professing the same religion; (b) from worshipping or offering prayers or performing any religious service in any place of public worship or bathing in or using the waters of any sacred tank, well, spring or water course in the same manner as is permissible to other persons professing the same religion; and (c) from access to or use of a shop, hotel, public restaurant or place of public entertainment or public conveyance or hospital dispensary or educational institution or charitable trust." Dr. Bhim Rao Ambedkar and Mahatma Gandhi have also defined untouchability on the basis of some disabilities. In this way, disabilities are a sign of untouchability. Dr. D. N. Majumdar has written, "The untouchable castes are those who suffer from various social and political disabilities, many of which are traditionally prescribed and socially enforced by higher castes."[1] in brief, Untouchable are those castes which are subject to same disabilities in every walk of life, social, religious, economic and political. This definition will be further clarified by a detailed description of these disabilities.

DISABILITIES OF HARIJANS

Untouchables suffer from the following disabilities:

A. Religious disabilities. In India the Harijans were subjected to various religious disabilities in the society. They were prevented from entering temples, monasteries

1. Majumdar, D.N., *Races and Cultures of India*, Asia Publishing House, Bombay (1958), p. 326.

and cremation grounds and were not permitted to make use of them because it was believed that these places would become impure by their touching them. In this way, the Harijans could not worship in the temple. Their presence was considered sufficient to defile the gods, let alone their worshippers.

But the disabilities imposed upon the Harijans in India are pre-eminently social and economic, the removal of which will, in itself, eliminate their backward condition in respect of political status. Actually, the religious disabilities of the Harijans are also their social disabilities.

B. Social disabilities. In the social sphere, the disabilities of the Harijans are the following:

1. Prevention from the use of public roads. Hudson has recorded that the presence of a particular untouchable caste in Tamil Nadu was considered so derogatory that their members were prevented from using the public roads in the daytime and consequently they were obliged to do their work at night. Their shadow was enough to defile the members of the higher castes. Thus, upon seeing the members of the higher castes the Harijans would adopt prostrate posture upon the ground so that their shadow may not fall on the members of higher castes.

2. Prevention from the use of public wells. In almost, all Indian villages the Harijans were forbidden the use of the well for drawing water, and this convention was enforced with a greater or less degree of strictness. In Bengal they were permitted to go near the well but not allowed to draw water from it. Only a higher caste Hindu could draw water for them. In some other states, the untouchables were not permitted even to approach the well.

3. Prevention from entering schools. The Harijan children did not have the right to enter the schools because had they sat down to study beside other children it would have defiled the children of the higher castes. On the other hand, there were no separate schools for the Harijans. Actually, education was not even considered necessary for them. If they insisted upon being taught then they had to sit out in the open-sun in order to study. In many religious texts study has been forbidden for the Shudras.

4. Other social restrictions. Besides the following disabilities the Harijans were subjected to many other social restrictions. In marriage, the Harijan bride and bridegroom were not allowed to sit in the palanquin. Among the Chamars the bridegroom was harassed by the Rajputs if he rode on a horse. The Harijans were not allowed the freedom of adopting a respectable outfit. The hairdresser would not tend their hair. "The washerman would not wash their clothes and the shopkeeper would not supply them with food.

C. Economic disabilities. The disabilities of the Harijans were not restricted only to the social sphere but these extended into the economic sphere too. Due to their social disabilities they could not retain any interest in or enthusiasm for their occupation. They did not have the permission to engage in the professions of the higher castes. And even as it is their conventional occupations were dirty and soiled and their means for earning their bread and butter were limited. Even now there is next to no education among the Harijans. They are burdened with debt while poverty and famine conditions prevail among them. They live in dirty slums in which new diseases are always making their life miserable. There is no medical provision for them, since the high caste doctor becomes defiled merely by touching them.

CAUSES OF UNTOUCHABILITY

There are many racial, religious and social causes of untouchability in rural India. The major cause is the caste system. The untouchable castes are the most inferior among the numerous castes in Hindu community. To the caste system is attached the sense of high and low, which is the fundamental cause of untouchability. Another cause of untouchability is the prevalence of many taboos in the caste system. Just as there are taboos for the higher castes intermarrying, eating and mixing with the lower caste, in the same way taboos were created, for preventing touching and even seeing of the lower castes which did the dirty work, as a consequence of the feeling of superiority and inferiority. These castes came to be called the untouchables. In this way untouchability in India is based upon the caste system. Untouchability is the result of the sense of superiority and inferiority and social taboos. In *Caste and Class in India*, Ghurye has written that in Poona, during the reign of the Marathas the untouchable castes Mahar and Mang were not allowed to enter the gates of towns between three o'clock in the afternoon and nine in the morning because the shadows were at their longest at this time and there was the fear of the higher Brahmins being defiled. In Maharashtra the members of Mahar caste could spit only in small containers tied around their necks because were they to spit upon the road it might defile some superior Hindu by touching his foot. Often if some Brahmin passed their way, the Mahars had to destroy the imprints of their feet with brambles and lie down at a distance in order to protect the Brahmin from their shadow. In Malabar, the Shanar had to keep a distance of twenty-four feet from the Brahmin, the Tiya a distance of thirtysix feet and the Pulayan a distance of more than ninety-six feet. It is obvious that the biggest cause of untouchability is the segregation of relations within the castes.

ORIGIN OF UNTOUCHABILITY

But all this does not mean that untouchability is caused solely by the caste system and the elimination of the latter would mean the automatic eradication of the former. Actually, there are other causes of untouchability beside the caste system. In *Castes in India*, J. H. Hutton writes, "The origin of the position of exterior caste is partly racial, partly religious and partly a matter of social custom."

1. Racial factors. The fundamental causes of untouchability are racial factors. The victor always considers himself superior to the vanquished and wants to be spared the latter's influence. This is no less true in the case of races. In the opinion of some scholars the Aryans designated to some derogatory names the non-Aryan races settled in India and considered them untouchable. In Assam the Ao branch of the Naga tribe is not allowed to wear ivory ornaments on both arms. According to Hutton this restriction has been imposed upon the Ao people because they are different from the other Naga clans from the racial viewpoint. In Garhwal the bride and bridegroom belonging to the artisan and Harijan races, which had low social status, were not allowed the use of the palanquin or the horse. The cause of this has been explained by some sociologists to be the advent of the higher castes from the plains into the native homeland of the artisans and Harijans. These examples prove that racial distinctions have some hand in the origin of the custom of untouchability. Dr. D. N. Majumdar has written correctly, "The disabilities of the so-called 'depressed' castes are not ceremonial but probably founded on racial and cultural differences."[2]

2. Religious factors. Religious beliefs and conventions are also causes of untouchability. In religion much importance is attributed to purity and divinity. As a result of the religious importance of this purity it was considered essential to remain aloof from the people who engage in impure occupations. In this way untouchability originated in the religious factor. In the words of Dr. Ghuyre, "Idea of purity, whether occupational or ceremonial, is found to have been a factor in the genesis of caste or the very soul of the idea and practice of untouchability."[3] It was the sense of purity which led to the sweepers and cobblers being designated as untouchables in Hindu society. Besides purity another cause of the origin of untouchability is the social taboo. Inter-marriage among castes, consumption of the object of totem, or its disrespect in any way are forbidden. Besides these, there are a number of other taboos prevalent in the castes like avoiding washerman because he washes clothes seeped in the secretions of the women's menstrual cycle. Thus, in the vol. I of Census of India, Hutton has written. "There can be little doubt that the idea of untouchability originates in taboo."

3. Social factors. The practice of untouchability has its origin in some social factors as well. Social customs and conventions shared the burden of maintaining the untouchability of the untouchables recognised by the religious and racial causes. Social conventions are so influential that even the members of the untouchable caste, dare not violate the customs of untouchability. In The Hindu of 24th Dec. 1932, it was written about the Puraadavannon caste established in the Tirunelveli district of Madras that they are not only considered untouchable but even unpresentable, and, they cannot leave their dwelling places in the daytime because there is a fear of their defiling the other castes. They wash their clothes at night. When Thakkar Bapa went to meet them they came out only upon extreme entreaty and when they came their entire body was trembling because they were burdened by the social stigma of untouchability.

In this way the racial, religious and social factors are the major ones among many causes of the origin of untouchability. All of these have had a hand in the custom of untouchability and it would be difficult to remove untouchability as long as ignorance in these spheres continues to exist.

---

2. *Ibid.*, p. 32.
3. Ghurye, *Caste and Class in India*, Popular Book Depot (Bombay, 1957), p. 24.

EFFORTS TO ERADICATE UNTOUCHABILITY

There have been numerous governmental and non-governmental efforts towards the eradication of untouchability in India and the improvement in condition of the prevention of untouchability on the one hand and improvement in the condition of the untouchables on the other. In the paragraph 46 of the Indian Constitution much emphasis has been laid upon the spread of education among the backward castes and the protection of their economic interest.

In the Indian Constitution the equality of all citizens of India was announced. The following paragraphs in the Constitution provide for the eradication of untouchability.

Paragraph 15. (1) The state shall not discriminate against any citizen on grounds only of religion, race, caste, sex, place of birth or any of them.

(2) No citizen shall, on grounds only of religion, race, caste, sex, place of birth or any of them, be subject to any disability, liability, restriction or condition with regard to:

(a) access to shops, public restaurants, hotels and places of public entertainment, or

(b) the use of wells, tanks, bathing ghats, roads and places of public resort maintained wholly or partly out of state funds or dedicated to the use of the general public.

Para 16. (1) There shall be equality of opportunity for all citizens in matters relating to employment or appointment to any office under the state.

(2) No citizen shall, on grounds only of religion, race, caste, sex, descent, place of birth, residence or any of them, be ineligible for, or discriminated against in respect of any employment or office under the state.

(3) Nothing in this article shall prevent Parliament from making any law prescribing, in regard to a class or classes of employment or appointment to an office under the Government any local or other authority within a State or Union Territory, any requirement as to residence within that State or Union Territory prior to such employment or appointment.

Para 17. 'Untouchability' is abolished and its practice in any form is forbidden. The enforcement of any disability arising out of 'Untouchability' shall be an offence punishable in accordance with law.

2. Arrangements under the Directives of Government Policy. The following arrangement has been made for the eradication of untouchability in the Directive Principles of State Policy in the Indian Constitution:

Chapter 46 —

Article 46. The state shall promote with special care the educational and economic interests of the weaker sections of the people and in particular of the Scheduled Castes and the Scheduled Tribes and shall protect them from social injustice and all forms of exploitation.

Article 164. Provided that in the State of Bihar, Madhya Pradesh and Orissa, there shall be a Minister incharge of tribal welfare who may in addition be incharge of the welfare of the Scheduled Castes and backward classes or any other work.

Article 330. (i) Seats shall be reserved in the House of the People for:

(a) The Scheduled Castes;

(b) The Scheduled Tribes except the Scheduled Tribes in the tribal areas of Assam; and

(c) The Scheduled Tribes in the autonomous districts of Assam.

(2) The number of seats reserved in any State or Union Territory for the Scheduled Castes or the Scheduled Tribes under clause (1) shall bear, as nearly as may be, the same proportion to the total number of seats allowed to that State or Union Territory in the House of the People as the population of the Scheduled Castes in the State (or Union Territory) or of the Scheduled Tribes in the State or Union Territory or part of the State or Union Territory, as the case may be, in respect of which seats are so reserved, bears to the total population of the State or Union Territory.

Article 332. (1) Seats shall be reserved for the Scheduled Castes and the Scheduled Tribes, except the Scheduled Tribes in the tribal areas of Assam in the Legislative Assembly of every State.

Seats shall be reserved also for the autonomous districts in the Legislative Assembly of the State of Assam.

Article 335. The claims of the members of the Scheduled Castes and the Scheduled Tribes shall be taken into consideration consistently with the maintenance of administration, in the making of appointments to services and posts in connection with the affairs of the Union or of a State.

Article 338. (1) There shall be a Special Officer for the Scheduled Castes and Scheduled Tribes to be appointed by the President.

It shall be the duty of the Special Officer to investigate all matters, relating to the safeguards provided for the Scheduled Castes and Scheduled Tribes under this Constitution and report to the President upon the working of these safeguards at such intervals as the President may direct, and the President shall cause all such reports to be laid before each House of Parliament.

Article 340 (1). The President may, by order, appoint a Commission, consisting of such persons as he thinks fit, to investigate the conditions of socially and educationally backward classes within the territory of India and the difficulties under which they labour and to make recommendations as to the steps that should be taken by the Union or any State to remove such difficulties and to improve their condition and as to the steps that should be made for the purpose by the Union or any State and the conditions subject to which such grants should be made, and the order appointing such Commission shall define the procedure to be followed by the Commission.

According to the 17th paragraph of the Indian Constitution, untouchability is a punishable crime. In 1955, the Indian Government passed the Untouchability

(Offences) Act in which any person forcing the disabilities of untouchability can be sentenced to six months imprisonment or a fine of Rs. 500 or both for his first crime. For every subsequent crime the sentence will include both a term in jail as well as a fine. If considered necessary, the punishment may also be increased. According to this Act the following activities were declared criminal — preventing entrance into public temples or places of worship, preventing the drawing of water from sacred lakes, wells, falls or springs, preventing people from the use of Dharmshala, inn, hotel, river bank, cremation ground, water tank, water tap, educational institution, public hospital, public restaurant, preventing the Harijans from pursuing any general occupation, doing a barber's job or any general activities and harassing them or discriminating them on the basis of untouchability at such times as religious festivals, residential houses, business or profession.

Besides enacting laws against untouchability the government of India also instigated propaganda against untouchability throughout the country. All the states observe 'Harijan Weeks' and 'Harijan Day'. In States and districts, advisory committees have been made which increase contact between untouchables and high caste Hindus. Books, handbills, posters and pamphlets are printed in Hindi, English and regional languages and distributed among the public in large number. Films and radio are also used as means of propaganda against untouchability.

Economic improvement

Realising the financial problems of the Harijans, the Government have taken the following steps in the direction of their financial improvement:

(i) Laws for escaping debt. In nearly all the States of India laws have been enacted for defending the untouchables from the Mahajans.

(ii) Laws for defence against the tradition of slavery. In Bihar and Orissa the Harijans had to become slaves of the Mahajans in the event of their inability to repay debt. Now this tradition has come to an end due to laws.

(iii) Distribution of land to Harijans. In Andhra, Bihar, Orissa, Maharashtra, Madras, Uttar Pradesh, Saurashtra and many other states the Government have turned useless and unoccupied land into cultivable land and distributed it among the Harijans.

(iv) Laws making the farmer the owner of the land. The Governments of Andhra, Bihar, Orissa, Assam, Madhya Pradesh, West Bengal and many other States have enacted laws by virtue of which the Harijan cultivating the land is to be considered the landowner and cannot be deprived of it.

(v) Financial assistance to agriculture. The government is rendering financial assistance to the Harijans in order that they may be able to buy agricultural implements, animals, manures, superior seeds, modern tools erf agriculture etc.

(vi) Assistance in Agriculture, Cottage industries and Animal husbandry. In Assam, Bihar, Maharashtra, Uttar Pradesh, A.P. and West Bengal the Harijans are being assisted financially as well as otherwise for the development of their cottage industries. Training centres are also being opened for teaching people and making them skilled in cottage industries. Animal husbandly and poultry farming are also being encouraged among the Harijans.

(vii) Financial assistance to non-governmental efforts. The Government of India is also providing to all non-governmental institutions which are exerting effort for the eradication of untouchability. In 1954 the Indian Government aided the state governments, Harijan Sevak Sangh, Indian Depressed Classes League and the Harijan Ashram of Prayag to the extent of four crores of rupees.

(viii) Educational facilities. The educational facilities provided by the government to the Harijans take the form of free education, scholarships, books, stationery and other educational needs, mid-day meals, grants for construction of schools etc. All eligible students of Scheduled Tribes are given scholarships without merit list.

(ix) Other government facilities. According to the Indian Constitution candidature has been reserved in government services for untouchables for a period of ten years. This concession was later on extended up to 25 Jan. 1980 and further. Not only in Central Government services but also in state government services seats are reserved. The condition of the untouchables improved due to the 'Admission to Malabar Mandir Act' and 'Prohibition of Public Disability Act' of the Madras government. In order to arrange for the progress of the Harijans the Tamil Nadu government appointed a Labour Commissioner and enacted many laws for defending the Harijans from the landlords and also in order to provide them with land. The governments of other states also followed the lead. In Uttar Pradesh two Parliamentary Secretaries were appointed for improving the condition of the Harijans. Many co-operative societies were also opened for the Harijans. Many Harijan students were given scholarships.

Non-Governmental Efforts

Besides the programme for political awakening, the Indian National Congress made efforts for the eradication of untouchability. The attempts made by Gandhiji in this direction are well-known. As a result of his efforts the untouchables slowly got rid of their social disabilities. The doors of the universities, temples, public places etc. were opened to them. In the beginning the caste Hindus opposed these improvements but they later agreed to them. Besides the Congress, many other political parties took part in the emancipation of the Harijans. Among them the work done by the Depressed Class Union, The Social Service League, Depressed Classes League, Andhra Been Seva Sangh, Depressed Classes Conference and Scheduled Class Federations deserve mention. But the Maryan Sevak. Sangh had made the maximum efforts in this direction, In 1932 this Sangh was started under the leadership of Thakkar Bapa. There are many branches of this Sangh in Andhra, Tamil Nadu, Mysore, Hyderabad, Gujrat, Maharashtra, Karnataka, Uttar Pradesh, Bihar and Delhi, 120 Boarding Houses are being managed by the Harijan Sevak Sangh. As a result of the efforts made by the Tamil Nadu Sangh, 100 big temples were opened for the Harijans. The Sangh achieved much success in opening the public places to the Sangh for their scholarships which they got mainly due to the efforts of the Sangh. Technological schools have also been opened for imparting skill in cottage industries and this too has come about mainly through the efforts of the Sangh. Among these institutions the Harijan Audyogik Grab, Delhi, Harijan Audyogik school and Hostel Kadambokam, Harijan Ashram, Prayag, Harijan Audyogik School, Kanjivaram, deserve to be mentioned. Institutions for women include Harijan Balika Vidyalaya, Sabarmati, Harijan Balika Sadan, Hugh, Anjani Harijan Girls Hostel, Bezwada, Kastoorba Balika Ashram, Okha etc.

Suggestions for the eradication of untouchability

The methods of eradication of untouchability are now known to all educated people. The following suggestions can be made in this direction:

1. Increasing education among the Harijans. Education should be spread among the Harijans and this should include both general education as well as technical education. Education should be free, coupled with facilities of scholarship, books, stationery, hostel, etc.

2. Laws for economic improvement. Laws should be formulated for legal protection from interest upon loans and deprivation of land in order to improve the financial condition of the Harijans.

3. Removal of economic disabilities. The Harijans should be helped in every conceivable way so as to end their economic disabilities.

4. Assistance in agriculture and cottage industries. The Harijans should be provided with land, animals, ploughs, seeds, manure and agricultural tools for agriculture. Financial assistance for cottage industries should be supplemented by technical training.

5. Laws against social disabilities. Laws should be formulated for preventing the Harijans from being subjected to social disabilities.

6. Laws against religious disabilities. Laws removing the religious disabilities which burden the Harijans should also be enforced.

7. Propaganda against untouchability. Platform speeches, radio, newspapers, the press and other means of communication should assist in the propaganda against untouchability.

8. Reserved seats in services. Despite the enforcement of all the above mentioned measures, it will take the Harijans a long time to achieve equality with the caste Hindus. Until they do so, some seats should be reserved for them in all services.

9. Reserved seats in the legislatures. It is necessary that seats should be reserved for the Harijans in the legislatures for some time to come. Some people contend that this violates the democratic principle of equality, but the people who have been deprived of equality for hundreds of years need some privileges in order to restore them to the general level. Once they have become equal to the higher caste people, these privileges will no longer be necessary.

10. Eradication of the caste system. The eradication of the caste system is very essential for the removal of untouchability. Actually, the caste system is the biggest single cause of untouchability even though it is not the sole cause. Thus, the eradication of the caste system will also remove the tradition of untouchability.

11. Contact between caste and scheduled caste Hindus. It is necessary that there should be an ever-increasing contact between the Harijans and the caste Hindus at the same time that all the above measures are being put into practice, so that the tradition of untouchability should be destroyed and the feeling of disgust which the superior Hindus harbour for the untouchables as well as the sense of inferiority of the Harijans should be eliminated. This contact will reduce mutual discrimination and culminate in the untouchables becoming like the other Hindus.

It is a matter of no small pleasure that the Union and State governments, along with many other political and religious associations of the country, are making tremendous efforts in achieving these improvements. Awakening is also spreading among the Harijans. It is hoped that, with the effort of the Harijans themselves, Government and other social associations, Harijans will become equal to the caste Hindus and untouchability will be wiped off from the villages.

QUESTIONS FOR EXERCISE

1. What are the disabilities of untouchables? Discuss the efforts made by the Government to remove them.
2. Explain the role and status of untouchable groups in Indian rural life.
3. Review briefly the anti-untouchability movement in post-independent India estimating its success and failure.
4. Review briefly the milestones in the anti-untouchability movement in India.
5. How does the Constitution of India envisage the uplift of Harijans?
6. Critically evaluate the efforts made in India to eradicate untouchability.

16

CASTEISM

In India, on the one hand, the caste is becoming weaker due to the influence of such factors as industrialisation, urbanisation, increase in the means of transportation, popularity of English education, political and social awakening, democratic Government and laws abolishing untouchability, etc., and, on the other hand, new organisations as labour unions, etc., on the basis of occupation, post, capacity etc. are being established. Due to an increase in the desire for money caused by the influence of Western education, the sense of superiority or inferiority is now based on wealth and social power rather than on caste. The class consciousness, based on occupations, etc., is replacing the caste consciousness.

All these changes led people to believe that the caste system will generally take on the form of a class system. But while, on the one hand, class consciousness seems to be progressing, on the other hand, one can see progress in casteism as well. For people who are specially gifted in a particular occupation, other occupations are very limited in India and the paths to those that are available are closed. Children of those parents who have a small income or who have no wealth look out only for service. Most commonly, in the biggest business institutions and sometimes even in educational institutions what happens is that the people who are employed in various posts belong to the castes of the proprietors, organisers and senior officials. Casteism of a similar type prevails also in Government services and political elections. Hence, it cannot be asserted that at the present time the caste is being destroyed and classism is increasing. Actually, in India casteism is being transformed into classism.

It is difficult to make an unqualified statement concerning the future of the caste system. It is certainly true that the restrictions of marriage, diet, mode of life, behaviour, etc., based on the caste system are breaking down. But, as has been described previously, casteism is increasing and caste system is being encouraged by some political and social factors. Actually, it seems more or less definite that there is no possibility of the caste system being eliminated from the Indian society in the near feature. The root of the caste system goes deep in Hindu society and at its base are the important and beneficial principles of division of labour, specialisation, etc. Foreign invaders made their best efforts to wipe out the

Hindu caste. But in spite of all efforts of the Muslims and Christians, not much change was wrought in the caste system. It has definitely been affected somewhat by the influence of Western education and culture. And its form has undergone a vast change. There is no room for doubting that this form of the caste system will change further in future, it may even change beyond recognition. It will also be influenced by the development of the sense of democracy and nationalism, industrial progress and by new political and economic movement.

WHAT IS CASTEISM?

Casteism is partial or one-sided loyalty in favour of a particular caste. When any mode of thinking assumes the form of an ism, it becomes rigid and partial. The sense of caste when it implies a specific status in society does not pertain to casteism. The sense of caste is converted into casteism only when consideration of superiority between castes and the tendency to consider the interest of one's own caste as opposed to the other castes are attached to it. In this manner the members of one caste do not hesitate to give fatal blows to the interests of the other castes, if the interests of their own caste are furthered in so doing.

DEFINITION OF CASTEISM

It is necessary to define casteism if its form and nature are to be clearly and precisely understood. According to one view casteism is loyalty to the subcaste. In this way it is only because of casteism that the Smiths want to benefit only the Smiths while the Joneses want to come to the aid of the other caste Joneses. It matters little if the members of the other caste are irreparably harmed, if it does not cause any concern to the Smiths and Joneses. But casteism is apparent also in the form of loyalty to the caste. In the words of D. N. Prasad, "Casteism is loyalty to the caste translated into politics,"[1] In this way, caste has been dragged into the political arena in the form of casteism such as 'Brahminvada and Kaysthavada'. Thus, it has been called blind group loyalty. In this opinion casteism is the blind and consequently irrational loyalty to the community. In this all considerations of proper or improper, justice or injustice, etc., are thrown to winds in the face of the interest of one's own caste, and these must be achieved. Casteism, therefore, is an overriding, blind and supreme group loyalty that ignores the healthy social standards of justice, fair play, equity and universal brotherhood. In this way, putting it briefly, casteism is a blind group loyalty towards one's caste or sub-caste which does not care for the interests of other castes and seeks to realise the social, economic, political and other interests of its own group. This definition of casteism includes all the preceding definitions of the concept and tends to clarify further the political aspect of casteism.

CAUSES OF CASTEISM

Now-a-days casteism is at its height in India, the culmination of many causes. Some of the many causes are as follows:

---

1. Prasad, D. N., *The Myth of Caste System*, p. 124.

1. Sense of caste prestige. The most important cause of casteism is the desire of people belonging to a particular caste to enhance the prestige of their caste and in so doing they see no wrong in adopting even the most downgraded and deleterious methods. But the prestige of the caste can be maintained only on the ground that every opportunity be availed of in order to improve the social status of members. In order to achieve this objective every caste provides its members with all possible privileges in order to raise their social status. This tends to increase casteism.

2. Marriage restrictions. The second causes that encouraged the development of casteism is the restriction on marriage that prevails in Hindu society. Under the caste system the restrictions that apply to marriage turn every caste into a monogamous group in which each individual looks upon himself as related in some way to all the others and for this reason everyone pays proper attention to the interests of others. Such action encourages casteism.

3. Urbanisation. With the advent of the tendency of urbanisation, it became possible for all castes to collect in large numbers in towns.

At the same time the lives of members of various castes became beset with problems as a result of which it became necessary to provide security for them on a communal basis. Casteism is spreading because of the necessity to fulfil this need of security.

4. Increase in the means of transport and propaganda. One factor that has assisted the development of casteism is the increase in the means of both transport and propaganda because this improvement has led to the establishment of relation between members of a caste who were previously separated because of distance. And the feeling of casteism is being rapidly propagated through the medium of newspapers and communal magazines.

CONSEQUENCES OF CASTEISM

On the one hand, casteism serves to further the interests of a small number of individuals but, on the other hand, it is proving harmful to the nation as a whole. Some of the major consequences of casteism are the following:

1. Hindrance in the development of nationalism. Casteism hinders the growth and development of nationalism. On the one hand, casteism has divided Indian society into many parts while on the other hand, much tension and conflicts between these various parts have been created on the basis of casteism.

2. Hindrance to democracy. Many of the professional leaders in the political field exploit casteism and at election time ask the people to vote for them on communal considerations and they also succeed in their evil designs. This, sometimes, results in the election of unscrupulous individuals who do not hesitate in crushing common interests in the consideration and promotion of caste interests. In practice, the glories of casteism are sung even behind the scenes where there is professedly equality. In this way, casteism is fatal to democracy. According to

K. M. Pannikar, "In fact, no organisation of society on the basis of equality is possible so long as the sub-caste and the joint family exist."[2]

3. Corruption. People inspired by the sense of casteism try to provide all kinds of facilities to people who belong to their own castes and in doing so they resort to all kinds of immoral and improper activities. In this way, extreme corruption in the society is increasing.

4. Hindrance in technological efficiency. Because the appointment to Government and private services is done on the basis of caste, there seems to be a continuing increase in the number of inefficient and worthless people. On the other hand, the efficient and able individuals do not get the opportunity to find employment. Thus, a great obstacle is placed in the path of the nation's industrial and technological advance.

REMEDIES TO CASTEISM

The following are some suggestions concerning the solution of the problems arising out of casteism:

1. Proper education. The greatest need for a solution of the problem of casteism is proper education. The educational institutions should be able to provide an atmosphere in which caste distinctions are not encouraged while at the same time the children are allowed to develop a distaste for this kind of discrimination. A healthy point of view in the public for casteism can thus be generated. Casteism can be destroyed only by the development of new psychological tendencies and behavioural patterns.

2. Inter-caste marriage. Another way of combating the continuing increase in casteism is the encouragement to inter-caste marriages. Inter-caste marriage provides an opportunity for two families belonging to different castes to come together not only for two individuals, one male and the other female, to do so. In this way, the seed of casteism shall be unable to take root and even if it does, the resulting sapling will be so weak that it will subsequently be wiped out.

3. Lesser use of the word 'caste'. One way of solving the problem of casteism is to make less frequent use of the word 'caste' so that there may be no traces of it left in the minds of the impressionable children and they should not be imbued with the idea of caste distinction. In this way, at least it will become possible to destroy the notion of casteism in the coming generations.

4. Cultural and economic equality. Another way of facing the problem of casteism is to introduce cultural and economic equality in the minds and the lives of the various castes. Inequality in the sphere of cultural and economic welfare between the races promotes jealousy and competition among them which, later, assumes the form of casteism. Hence, the restoration of cultural and economic equality among various castes is an important step towards the abolition of casteism from the society.

---

2. Pannikar, K.M., *Hindu Society at Crossroad* (Bombay 1956), p. 24.

SUGGESTIONS FOR THE ABOLITION OF CASTEISM

Mahatma Gandhi had compared caste to the appendix in the human body. As long as it continues to enjoy health it serves its purpose but when it becomes diseased the only course is to eliminate it because if it is not removed it poses a threat to the existence of the entire organism. In this way, it is opined by some people that this conflict can be eliminated from democracy only when the caste system is completely removed from it. But in the present context, in which the castes have taken on the form of classes and casteism is on increase, it seems impractical to harbour any hopes for the complete removal of casteism from society. Castes cannot be legalised and then infringed. It is the foundation of Hindu society. A strong and tremendous revolution is needed to get rid of it. But the artificial simulation of a revolution proves harmful in the long run of time. Hence, as long as the society is not prepared to change the system and to adopt some other social order in its place, it is best to confine oneself to corrections and improvements. In this connection different scholars have expressed different views and have made various suggestions. In Dr. M.N. Shrinivas's opinion, most of the shortcomings of the caste system can be removed and the door opened to democratic equality through adult franchise, five year plans, the provision of education, constant progress of the backward classes and the influence of the culture of higher castes on the living standards for the lower castes. According to Dr. Ghurye, the conflict originating in casteism can be removed by encouraging inter-caste marriages. Co-education should be introduced at the primary level and boys and girls should be given the opportunity to come together. This will lead to improvement of behaviour between different sexes simultaneously with which casteism will be actively refuted. Inter-caste marriage will be encouraged and the individuals marrying out of their own castes will be instrumental in creating an atmosphere that will be fundamentally opposed to casteism. According to the suggestion put forward by Dr. Rao, in order to put an end to casteism and to deprive it of its very basis, the creation of some optional groups should be encouraged in which the communal tendencies of the individual can be manifested and organised. Casteism will decrease as the number of these groups increases because the individuals will have the opportunity to express their instincts and mores outside the castes. It is suggested by Mrs. Iravati Karve that in order to put an end to the conflicts arising out of casteism, it is necessary to create economic and cultural equality between the castes. According to Prabhu, the conflicts created by casteism can be ended only when the internal aspects of conduct are influenced. For this, it is necessary to try and develop new attitudes in the people. The cinema can do much towards the creation of these attitudes.

The notion of caste has been existent in Indian society for almost thousands of years. Today it has become an impediment for the progress of the country. It is necessary to change its form in order to ensure the development of national sentiment and the progress and success of democracy in the country. But this cannot be achieved in a matter of few years. For this, it is necessary to determine the extent to which caste system should be developed and then all governmental and non-governmental sources in the country should be employed for the achievement of that level of development. The first step would be to remove the idea of caste discrimination from the minds of the future generations. Co-education will encourage inter-caste marriages. Further, the idea of eliminating words that indicate caste from names should also be propagated and made popular. Caste committees and associations should be prevented legally and the Government should prevent appointments being made to posts on the basis of caste, whether in government or non-government organisations. In this way, it is necessary to make efforts in every direction for improvement of this horizon.

QUESTIONS FOR EXERCISE

1. Bring out clearly the implications of caste for the economic organisation of rural community in India.
2. Write short note on Casteism in Indian villages.
3. Analyse the evils of casteism.
4. Discuss the various ways in which caste sentiments get strengthened in modern India.

17

RURAL FAMILY

Characteristics of Rural Family

The important characteristics of rural family are as follows:

1. Joint family. The most important feature of the rural family in India is the practice of joint family system. In a joint family are included husband, wife, uncles, aunts, sons and nephews etc. In a joint family, the authority rests in the oldest male member in the family. The property is deemed to be the common possession of all the members of the family. The head of the family uses it for the good of all members of the family. A joint family runs a common kitchen and every member share common board and lodging.

2. High status of women. In Indian villages women get a place of pride. She is highly regarded. According to the lawgiver Manu, gods reside where women are worshipped and where women are not worshipped, failure haunts all activity. In rural society, women work along with men in fields. Excepting the women of high castes who do not step out of the four wails of the house, women share with men all work.

3. Religion and spirituality. The third main characteristic of rural family is its religious and spiritual basis. The rural family is bound by religious principles and its aim is spiritual instead of being materialistic. On account of the religion-spiritual orientation of rural family in villages more emphasis is laid on duties than rights. This is why the relations between family members are very cordial and respectful. In a rural family everyone performs jobs dutifully and there is disciplinc, harmony and pcacc among family members.

4. Hospitality. Another important feature of the rural family is its attitude towards the guests. A guest is always welcome. In particular, Hindus regard the guest as a divine visitor. A Hindu family will go without meals but would not permit a guest to go unentertained. The high ideal of hospitality found in rural India is unique and unparalleled anywhere in the world.

5. Homogeneity. The relationship among the family members is far more cordial and harmonious in villages than in towns. We find rural family a homogeneous unit.

6. Economic co-operation. Compared with the urban families we find far greater economic cooperation in the rural families. In peasant families each member participates in the production of wealth and every member is suitably looked after. The children look after the cattle; women harvest crops and menfolk do hard agricultural labour. They do the job of tilling the fields and protecting them from wild animals.

7. Discipline and mutual dependence. In comparison to urban families we find much discipline and spirit of mutual give and take in the rural families. All members of the family, generally, obey dutifully the orders of the headman. The marriages are, as a rule, settled by the parents.

8. Family honour. Compared with urban families, rural families are very begrudging of their honour. In them, group feeling is more dominant than the personal feeling. A hurt to family is considered personal hurt by each member and the honour of family is considered to be the personal honour. Therefore, no family member is allowed to do anything which may be disgraceful and thus compromise the honour of the family.

9. Influence of tradition. In villages, traditions are given a place of pride and are zealously guarded. No one can ordinarily think of breaking a tradition. The more ancient a tradition, greater is its hold on the rural mind. Compared to urban populace, the rural people are much less affected by technological development and the social change. The relationship within the family is determined by tradition.

10. Family, an economic unit. The rural family can be treated as a unit in respect of production, distribution and exchange, that is from the economic viewpoint. In economic relationship, the family and not individual plays the central role. The barter system, under which things are exchanged, is still prevalent in villages to a certain extent.

11. Authority of father. The system of family in rural India is patriarchal. In a patriarchal family the seat of authority and honour rests in the patriarch, the father. Accordingly, the families in rural India are dominated by fathers. No matter how old children are they usually respect the father and dare not defy command. Compared to cities, young person's pay much more respect to their elders in villages.

12. Familial social control. In rural society, control of the society on its members is exercised through the medium of the family. Family is the social unit in the rural society. It is the family which puts social responsibility on the members and sees to it that it is fully discharged by its members. It is the status of the family, which in turn, determines the status of the individual. It is the family which gets social laws respected and obeyed by the members.

13. Ancestor worship. In rural India the ancestor worship is very common. The deities worshipped are usually such as to form family constellation. For example, Shiva or Shankar is the husband of Parvati and the father of Ganesh.

14. Family, a social unit. The rural family is a religious, economic and political unit of the rural society. No moral, social or political rules are workable if these attach to the basis of family structure. All rules and laws workable in the rural society strengthen the roots of family structure. For example, in order to maintain the sexual morality in the villages, the villagers regard the women of the village as daughters and sisters. Thus, the moral rules in the rural society are based on the family system.

The salient features of rural society outlined above are to be found more or less in all parts of rural India, though there may be some regional differences which are quite natural in a vast country like India. The features given above are, however, not stable or static. They are liable to undergo change due to factors like urbanization, industrialization, spread of education and technological changes, particularly the development of fast means of communication. Nonetheless, the above features are very much in evidence particularly if we take a comparative view of rural and urban societies.

Relationships in Rural Family

The central patterns of relationship in rural family are as follows:

1. Head of rural family. In rural society, the eldest member of the family is, as a rule, the head of the family. In family matters he is absolute authority. The family bears his name. The agricultural plots, farms and other properties are held in his name. But in certain families in the event of the death of the head of the family, the family property does not stand in the name of eldest brother only but is in the joint ownership of all the brothers. In certain families the status of women is higher than that of men. However, such families are looked down upon in the village.

2. Husband-wife relations. Generally man enjoys superiority over the woman. Accordingly, husband is superior to his wife and commands her. But this does not mean that the wife is treated cruelly. In Hindu families the wife is considered as embodiment of the goddess of wealth, Lakshmi. She has full say in family affairs. In the middle class families usually men and women enjoy equal rights. In poor families both men and women work at home and outside. The system of purdah is to be found in high caste homes. However, in all rural families some women observe purdah in the presence of some persons. For example, wife of a person would observe purdah in the presence of his father, grandfather, uncles and elder brothers, etc., but would not do so in the presence of his younger brother. In low castes purdah is, more or less, not observed. In rural homes husbands and wives do not call the names of each other. Whenever there is a necessity of beckoning each other by speaking names the husband would call his wife by innuendoes like are! or mother of my son etc. The wife would say 'father of B' etc. Wherever women earn some money this is not necessarily turned over to their husbands; sometimes they hand over the money and sometimes they keep whole or part of the money with themselves. In villages women usually eat after whole family has eaten.

3. The relationship between mother-in-law and daughter-in-law. In old times the authority of mother-in-law over the daughter-in-law was absolute and unquestioned; but now this has become more formal than real. Though even today daughter-in-law regularly touches the feet of her mother-in-law every morning as a symbol of the formal acceptance of the authority of the mother-in-law, in reality daughters-in-law no longer tremble in fear in the presence of the mother-in-law. Soon after coming to her husband's home, daughter-in-law tries to present herself as an equal and demands her share in the family affairs. This inevitably leads to tension and ill-will in the family. As a matter of fact smooth, cordial and harmonious relations between mother-in-law and daughter- in-law are things of the past. Though, there are still stray instances of cruelty by the mother-in-law, the daughter-in-law has on the whole, emancipated herself from the authoritarian clutches of the mother-in-law.

4. Relations between father-in-law and daughter-in-law. In rural families, daughter-in-law observes purdah in the presence of her father-in-law and regularly touches his feet as a sign of respect. Usually, a daughter-in-law avoids the presence of her father-in-law but there are stray instances of illicit sex relation between father-in-law and daughter-in-law.

5. Relations between parents and children. In rural families, the relations between parents and children are, on the whole, cordial. The parents spare no effort in bringing up their children. The sons are given a place of pride and family control over them is loose. They are allowed full freedom of development. As a result of this freedom sometimes children tend to develop bad habits of smoking and loafing about. However, as a matter of fact, smoking by young persons is not taken seriously in villages. The conduct of girls, on the other hand, is very strictly controlled. The girls help their mothers in household chores and also take cooked food for brothers and fathers to the fields. They are married young. The sons help fathers in fields. Thus, the relations between parents and children in villages are, on the whole, quite cordial. However, there are some instances of family feuds and litigation. Once in a while there are murders even.

The Indian village still remains a group of joint families in which everything is more or less, peaceable. But due to a number of social, economic and historical causes the joint family is showing slow but sure disintegration. However, as yet the importance of family in rural society is unique.

6. Relations between husband's younger brother and his wife. The relationship between a wife and her younger brother-in-law is very intimate and informal. The younger brother of man has easy access to his wife and the wife does not observe purdah in his presence. Though sex relations, as a rule, are confined to man and his wife, it is not altogether uncommon to find the women having sex relation with her younger brother-in-law. Many rural sociologists have observed that in the majority of extra-marital relations, the man in question is the younger brother of the husband. Though, precise statistics are not available, there are cases where after the demise of the husband the woman marries the younger brother of her deceased husband. The relations between the elder brother-in-law and the woman are on the other hand, very much like the relations between her and the father-in-law.

7. The condition of widows. In Indian society husband is regarded very highly. By religion and tradition he is held in very high esteem. On the contrary, the widows have a miserable status and their general condition is pitiable. She is not allowed to decorate herself or participate in any auspicious activity. She is considered to have been accused by God. People wish to avoid infection of her curse by avoiding her.

8. Illicit marital relations. In rural India the vow of marriage is taken seriously and marriage is a religious sacrament instead of being a contract. The Indian society is non-permissive insofar as sex morality is concerned. Nonetheless the instances of irregular and illicit marital relations do occur in villages. After the demise of the wife and at times even when she is alive, some men keep another woman. Even without ceremony of marriage the kept woman is considered to be his wife. Sometimes the kept woman belongs to another caste. For example, a Brahmin keeps Thakur woman and a Thakur keeps a Brahmin woman. In villages keeping a woman as a wife without actually marrying her is not considered immoral or wrong. In some villages the custom of marriage by purchasing the wife exists.

As has been already pointed out, rural family is joint family. It would be, therefore, relevant to discuss the institution of joint family in more details.

JOINT FAMILY

Definition of joint family

Joint family is a group of kins of several generations, ruled by a head, in which there is joint residence, hearth and property and whose members are bound with each other by mutual obligations. The chief characteristics of the joint family are common residence, common kitchen, joint property, common worship, rule of the pater familiar and consciousness of mutual obligation among family members. This will be clear from the following definitions of the joint family:

1. *Karve.* "A joint family is a group of people who generally live under one roof, who eat food cooked at one hearth, who hold property in common and who participate in common worship and are related to each other as some particular type of kindred."[1]

2. *Jolly.* "Not only parents and children, brothers and step-brothers live on the common property, but it may sometimes include ascendents, descendents and collaterals up to many generations."[2]

3. *Desai.* "We call that household a joint family which has greater generation depth, (*i.e.*, three or more) than the nuclear family and the members of which are related to one another by property, income and mutual rights and obligations."[3]

1. Karve, *Kinship Organisation in India.*, p. 10.
2. Jolly, *Hindu Law and Custom,* p. 168.
3. Desai, I.P., *The Joint Family in India,* an article in Sociological Bulletin.

Advantages of Joint Family

The chief advantages of joint family are as follows:

1. Economic advantages. The joint family system has proved to be a very advantageous institution from the economic viewpoint. It prevents property from being divided. Land is protected from extreme sub-division and fragmentation. When divided into many small pieces land becomes an uneconomic holding. Besides keeping the land intact, the joint family also assists in economic production. In a joint agriculturist family the male members do such work as furrowing, sowing and irrigation. Women assist at the harvest. Children graze the cattle and collect fuel and manure. In this way, the cooperation of all the members helps to save money which would otherwise be paid to labourers. In the rural areas, the joint families are such in which men, women and children collaborate. Even among the middle and upper classes the family can obtain capital and reliable assistants from the joint family for establishing and expanding a business.

2. Protection of members. Praising the joint family system Jawahar Lal Nehru had said that the system of joint family is an insurance for the family members which has carried a guarantee for those who are mentally and physically weak. In times of crises the joint family can provide assistance to the children, the women, the old, the insane, the widows and the helpless. The joint family is capable of providing much assistance at such emergencies as pregnancy, sickness, etc. If a person dies, his wife and children are looked after properly in the joint family. In the joint family a place is provided for all members to which they can retreat at all times and their honour, wealth and prosperity are protected collectively.

3. Means of recreation. The joint family is one of the best means of recreation. A stimulating atmosphere is created by the cumulative effect of the stammered talking of the children, love between brother and sister, mother's love, the reproach of the elder and the fun frolic of the other family members. In this way, the joint family also naturally takes over the role of a club.

4. Development of good qualities. In this way, the joint family system makes possible the ideal development of the good qualities of man. In the care of elders the undesirable and anti-social tendencies of the young are checked, they are prevented from straying from their path and they learn to exercise self- control. In the joint family, young men and women learn the lesson of generosity, patience, service, co-operation and obedience. A sense of sacrifice replaces selfishness in the bosom of each member of the family. All members learn to obey family control and to respect those older than themselves.

5. Co-operation and economy. The joint family fosters co-operation and economy to an extent achieved by few, if any other institution. A sense of cultural unity and an associational feeling exists among the members. There can be much economy in expenditure. The joint family can be rightly called an ideal centre of co-operation and mutual aid.

6. Socialism in Wealth. According to Sir Henry Maine, the joint family is like a corporation, the trustee of which is the father. He is known as Karla. About him

D. N. Majumdar has written, "The Karta. of the joint or extended family has the right to make the decisions for his family, he is the working head, the judge and the jury, he decides family quarrels, he is the political head as every family has a place and is represented by the head of the family in the social, ceremonial and community activities, and in the local Gram Panchayat."[4] According to Jather and Beiy, everyone in a joint family earns according to his capabilities but obtains according to his needs and in this way to a large extent achieves the socialistic ideal: from each according to his ability, to each according to his needs.

Disadvantages of Joint Family

The following are the main disadvantages of the joint family system:

1. Hindrance in the development of personality. The most glaring defect of the joint family system is the hindrance in the development of the personalities of its members. In the joint family the head is the absolute ruler. He is usually the oldest member of the family who looks upon and treats men and women as children even when they attain adulthood. In this way there is very little opportunity for the fostering of individual autonomy or self-dependence.

2. Bad condition of women. The bad condition of women is also a major defect in its disintegration. In the joint family, the daughter-in-law does not get an opportunity to develop her personality. She looks after her children. She hardly ever meets her husband during the day and even when he returns late at night he gratifies his sexual desire with her and falls asleep. The invariable presence of other family members ashamed the brides, they do not receive love from any source. There is no limit to the injustice done by mother-in-law and the other relatives do everything to add to that suffering. In some cases this oppression is so inhuman and unbearable that the women become fed up and commit suicide. Any natural love between the husband and wife or between the mother and children is prevented from blossoming by these artificial circumstances.

3. Strife. If the daughters-in-law contradict this oppression or if their husbands choose to speak in their favour, the house becomes strife-born and centre of conflict. When the daughters-in-law talk back to their mother-in-law they are abused and even beaten by their husbands who are provoked by their mothers. Hatred and jealousy between the wives of brothers can lead to a conflict between brothers which can assume dangerous proportions.

There is continuous strife and fighting over the doings of children. Much of the time of the adult members is consumed in the solution of petty problems.

4. Laziness. Due to common responsibility many people take their minds off their work and become completely lazy. In this state, the condition of those who literally break their backs and those who are very lazy is, more or less, the same. Hence, laziness is encouraged. When a person can eat comfortably without exerting himself he is unlikely to indulge in any strenuous activity. And the wives of the hard working people tell them to desist from such toil as they do not benefit

4. Majumdar, D.N., *Races and Culture of India* (Bombay), 1958, p. 250.

from it. Mostly, in the joint family it happens that some people have to exhaust themselves while others lead a life of utter lethargy. There is no dearth of such people in big and rich joint families whose entire routine in life consists of eating, sleeping and begetting children.

5. Uncontrolled reproduction. In a joint family the responsibility for the upbringing and education, etc., of children is shared. Thus, no individual considers it necessary to lay stress on controlling procreation. In the family, no distinction in the status of the family members is made on the basis of their respective earnings and the corresponding number of children. The offspring of one member will be treated on the same footing as of others irrespective of the high level of his earning and the fewer children. In this way, in a joint family, no direct benefit accrues to any individual by family planning or by earning more. Consequently, the enthusiasm of the people in this direction loses much of its fervour and intensity, and they become lazy and procreate more.

6. Poverty. As a consequence of almost daily strife, the bad condition of women, absolute rule, lack of responsibility and blind procreation, the economic condition of the joint family becomes very unenviable. If the conflict is strong enough to bring about division of land and property, the condition becomes even worse. The property of the family, being jointly owned, is sometimes allowed to go waste and it is gradually lost through constant neglect.

7. Other defects. In addition to the afore-mentioned major shortcomings the joint family system is further blemished by many other minor defects. Family strife leads to litigation. Customs and traditions are strictly adhered to in the joint family and superstition reigns supreme because the guiding hand is that of the oldest member. Due to the strict administration of the old men the younger people do not gain self-confidence and self-dependence, and they fail to adopt new currents of thought. Thus, the disadvantages of the joint family far outweigh the advantages which accrue from it and have negatived them. Consequently, the joint family is, in fact, becoming disorganised. It is impossible to save the institution of joint family from disorganisation, though its advantages can, with effort, be reinstituted in novel form in the small families.

Role of New Social Legislation

In India joint family has been very much influenced by certain new social legislation. These have some direct bearing on the characteristic features of joint family, viz., joint habitation, joint kitchen, joint property and the authority of the head. The following are the major ones among these social legislations:

1. Hindu married women's right to separate residence and maintenance Act. This legislation was enacted in 1946. According to it, under specific conditions a wife can demand alimony while living separately from her husband.

2. Hindu Marriage Act. According to para 13 of this Act, any husband and wife, who have been married either before or after the enactment of this legislation can, under specific conditions, apply to the court for divorce. This law was enacted in 1955.

3. Hindu Succession Act. This Act became law in 1956. According to it the daughter was given equal rights to the property of the father and the women also got the right to dispose of mortgage and use their property in any manner they pleased.

The foregoing Acts of legislation have influenced the solidarity of the joint family. As a consequence of the Hindu Marriage Act the number of divorces is increasing. Previously, the women silently suffered many injustices and outrages. In joint families the status of women was extremely low. Sometimes the mother-in-law behaved inhumanly towards them. Their husbands also treated them as they wished and yet the joint family did not disintegrate. Now having got the support of the law, women have initiated a strong revolt against this oppression which is leading to a disorganisation of the joint family. With the enactment of laws providing for their separate maintenance and residence, the women no longer need to submit to oppression in the joint family due to financial considerations. Upon being maltreated they can now leave their husbands, live separately and demand money from them in order to meet their expenditure. This provision has dealt a severe blow to the joint families. One feature of the joint family is that of joint property. The Hindu Succession Act has influenced it adversely. Now that women have the right to sell their property and the girls too share equally in the property of their father, it is almost impossible to maintain the family property conjointly. Hence, the result is that the joint families are disintegrating at a rapid rate. Modern legislation has put an end to male ascendency. This too has profoundly influenced the organisation of the joint family. The daughters-in-law in the joint family come from other families. Thus, it is only natural that they should resent having to sacrifice their own pleasure for the well-being of the family. Previously, they had to suffer silently the doings of their husbands. Having got equal rights in almost all respects as a result of modern legislation, the women whose husbands earn more can now force their husbands to break off from the joint family and set up an independent establishment. The parents-in-law also realise their power. The husbands too cannot behave indiscriminately with them. They also have the same rights over the children as their husbands. Due to all these causes even the slightest misunderstanding results in a situation where separation from the families is the only course open to the couple as they cannot coexist with their relatives. Actually, the causes of the disorganisation of the joint family are not constitutional but mainly social. But there is no doubting the fact that the present legislation has also played a part in its disorganisation.

Future of Joint Family

The future of joint family, according to some thinkers, is not absolutely dark. According to K. M. Kapadia, "Hindu sentiments are even today in favour of joint family. The destruction of joint family by legislation is, therefore, rightly considered to be non-Hindu because it ignores Hindu family history and sentiments.' This view, however, does not hold water about joint family system, its disadvantages are amply clear and its continuance is neither feasible nor desirable.

The rural people should, however, save the nuclear family from disorganisation. This will involve maintaining most of the advantages of joint family in nuclear family.

QUESTIONS FOR EXERCISE

1. Write short note on Rural Family.
2. Discuss relationships in rural family.
3. Discuss the characteristic features of the Joint Family. In what has the present legislation affected the solidarity of the Joint Family?
4. Is Joint Family disorganising? Write about disorganisation of Indian Joint Family.
5. Describe the functions of family.
6. Discuss with causes the disintegration of Rural Joint Family in India.

18

Rural Marriage

Patterns and Restrictions

In the villages of India two kinds of marriages are generally in vogue. The first kind is village exogamy and the second is Gotra exogamy. In village exogamy the boy and the girl who are to be married must not be from the same village; and in the Gotra exogamy, the boy and the girl marrying must not be from a single clan but belong to different clans. Though most of the marriages in rural India are between different clans or different villages, they are nonetheless between the same caste. The number of inter-caste marriages in the Indian villages is insignificant and negligible. As a matter of fact intercaste marriages are very uncommon in the Indian society, though now-a-days the number of such marriages is growing in Indian metropolises. In villages there is as yet not much change in this respect.

In Indian villages marriages between cousins are taboo. As regards hypergamy (Anuloma marriage) and hypogamy (Pratiloma marriage), the cases of hypergamy are more frequent than those of hypogamy. This is because according to *Dharmashastras* of Hindus, a marriage between a high caste boy and a low caste girl is permissible but the marriage between a high caste girl and a low caste boy is not permitted.

Generally, the villagers are reluctant to marry a girl from a village to which a girl from their village has been given in marriage. Thus, if A and B are the two villages and a girl of the village A is married in the village B, then the boys of A would not like to marry a girl from the village B. This is due to the belief of the villagers that the status of a village which has accepted a girl from their village is lower than theirs. In rural India, the status and reputation of family is of paramount importance in matters of match-making; but of late there is some change in thinking and attitudes in this regard. These days intelligent and progressive villagers have started giving due weightage to ability and competence of the boy in selection of a match for their girl. In different villages there is considerable variation in the scope of marriage. In some villages, marriage may be contracted between villages five to ten miles apart, whereas in some other villages this distance must not be less than forty miles. The distance from the village considered necessary for the purposes of marriages varies not only from village to village but also from caste to caste within the same village. There are certain families in the villages which do not accept a match for marriage who is living within one hundred miles distance from the village; it should be more than 100 miles for these people. Generally, marriages in villages are pre-arranged and not out of choice of the boy or the girl. Usually, the boy and the girl see each other's face only after the wedding. The marriages are arranged by the eldest member of the family who normally is either grandfather, father or uncle of the mate. Though friends may suggest suitable matches but the match is not arranged or matured until the eldest member of the family gives his consent.

DIFFERENT STAGES AND STEPS OF MARRIAGE

The consummation of marriage in rural India is not a simple affair of boy meeting the girl and going to church or court to certify the fact of becoming husband and wife in the presence of friends, family members and the certifying authority. In Indian villages marriage is an extremely elaborate and complex affair which has to pass through a number of stages and in each there are a number of steps. Though the customs and rituals connected with marriage differ in detail from region to region, it is possible to draw a broad outline of various stages and steps of marriage in a standard village. Oscar Lewis has divided the Indian village marriage into five stages. These are:

(A) Search of a suitable match

(B) Betrothal

(C) Marriage

(D) Reception of bride in bridegroom's village.

(E) Consummation of marriage.

In every stage of marriage there are a number of steps. These are —

(A) Search of suitable bridegroom

1. Consent of the eldest members of the families of bride and bridegroom to the prospective marriage.

(B) Betrothal

2. Exchange of suitable gifts as confirmation of marriage.

(C) Preparation of marriage

3. Declaration and formal announcement of the day and data of marriage.
4. Lagan.
5. Ban.
6. Gift of Bhat by maternal uncle.
7. Erection of Madha.
8. Ghurchari (procession of bridegroom seated on mare).
9. Jauhari.

(D) Marriage

10. Milani (introduction of the close relatives of bride and bridegroom and garlanding of each other).

11. Reception of Barat.
12. Barauthi.
13. Chunari.
14. Phera.
15. Kanyadan.
16. Moodh opening.
17. Vida (sendoff).

(E) Reception of bride in bridegroom's village

18. Dwar Rokana.
19. Mukh Dikhana (showing bridegroom's face).
20. Kangana play.
21. Visit to the village temple.

(F) Gauna or Consummation of Marriage

As soon as a girl in an average Indian village attains the age of puberty, the parents become concerned and initiate the moves for the search of suitable bridegroom. In most of the villages, even at present, most marriages are arranged by the village barber. The barber arranges a meeting between the parents or grandparents or uncles of the bride and bridegroom as the case may be. For his services as a go-between he gets paid from both the sides. Generally, the marriages arranged by the village barber are those of high caste Hindu families. As regards the marriages of low caste families, services of the village barber are not usually needed. Indeed the marriages of the low caste families are much simpler than those of high caste families. The chamars and other low castes arrange their own marriages and do not follow the long and elaborate stages and steps of marriage outlined above. However, whenever and wherever the marriages are arranged by the parents of bride and bridegroom, the services of the barber are invariably availed of This is because the village barber has access to all families and by convention his movements are not restricted. Therefore, he knows most of the families from inside and is privy to their secrets. In the choice of the bridegroom, the parents attach great importance to the property considerations. Everyone naturally wants that the girl should go to well-to-do family so that she may have easy and happy life. Now-a-days there is a trend to ensure that the bridegroom is a gentleman and educated. The educated bridegrooms get much more by way of dowry than the uneducated bridegrooms. In settling the marriages, the consent of grandparents, uncles, brothers of the bride or bridegroom is also sought. The consent of the bride or bridegroom is not sought and they are not supposed to see each other before actual marriage. This is a curious and interesting feature of Indian marriages. Non-a-days there is change in the attitudes and rebellion against strict orthodoxy.

As a concession to this, there is a tendency to exchange photographs of the bride and bridegroom and even a chance view of bride is allowed. In Indian marriage, it is of utmost importance to compare the horoscopes of the bride and bridegroom. When a barber succeeds in finding a suitable bridegroom, he convinces the father of the bride to pay a visit to groom's family and see the boy for himself and assess his suitability. If the father of the prospective bridegroom consents to the gift being given to the boy, the marriage is held to be confirmed. In marriage the beauty, charm and physical appeal of the girl is of utmost importance. Keeping in view the girl's accomplishments, the boy of corresponding qualities is chosen. Once the marriage is acceptable to the parents of the boy and girl, the father of the boy lays down the conditions for the proposed marriage. These are concerned mainly with the kind of reception for Barat, the number of Baratis and above all, the cash and kind in dowry. In villages the trend is to have largely attended Barats, because this is a point of prestige. The feasting in marriages is also given much importance.

1. The ceremony of betrothal. Once everything preliminary about the marriage is settled there is the ceremony of betrothal. In the elaborate series of ceremonies and rituals, the ceremony of betrothal is the first step. In olden times the time gap between betrothal and marriage used to be ten to twelve years; but now-a-days this gap is getting progressively less and less. In villages early betrothal and considerable delayed marriage are approved because the betrothal eliminates the anxiety about the marriage, however delayed it may actually take place. Generally, betrothal, the promise of marriage solemnly and ceremonially given is not broken. If the betrothal ceremony takes place immediately after the proposal of marriage is accepted by both parties the chances of marriage become very bright and the path to it is greatly facilitated. The ceremony of betrothal puts a seal of society witness to the acceptance and readiness for marriage of the two parties. In order to signify mutual assent to the marriage the father of the prospective bride gives some money which is always a rupee more than the round figure, *e.g.* 11, 101, 501, etc. The gift of money and its acceptance affirm the assent of both consenting parties. If there is considerable time lapse between the settlement of the marriage proposal and the betrothal, the situation is greatly complicated and the betrothal ceremony becomes an elaborate ritual. The parents of the bridegroom get their house white-washed and repaired. The relatives and friends get together. An arrangement for lodging the members from the bride side is made. Then in a public ceremony the father of the bride places money in the lap of the bridegroom and the Pundit chants mantras. The father of the bride puts a sacred mark on the forehead composed of a paste and rice grain and the pundit ties a thread on the wrist of the prospective bridegroom. Then the groom goes to his mother and hands over the money to her. Sometimes the relatives of the groom and the villagers accompanying him are also given suitable amounts. Sometimes there is feasting but the parents and close relatives of the bride don't partake in the feast. At the time of betrothal there is singing and merry-making.

2. Announcement of the day and date of marriage. After betrothal the second step in the preparation of marriage is the formal announcement of the day and the date of the marriage. The day is fixed primarily to suit the convenience of the parents of the bride. The other factors which influence this decision are the age of the boy and the girl and the economic condition of the families. Ultimately, the date is determined by the pundit who gives the date after taking into account various astrological considerations. When the date is settled, the pundit writes his ceremonial calculation on a paper which is besmeared with a paste made of saffron and rice grains and this paper is duly signed by the father of the bride and some responsible villagers. This paper is rolled and tied with a yellow thread. Now this paper is sent to the father of the groom by hand through the barber or some other messenger. If the parents and relatives of the groom are satisfied by the details of the paper, it is returned through the same person and he is paid some money. This settles the day and the date of the proposed marriage.

3. Lagan. The term lagan is used for the various festivities which take place in the house of the bride and the groom in connection with the marriage. In the ceremony of lagan, there are different types of festivities in the homes of the boy and girl. At the time of lagan the parents of the bride send suitable gifts for the parents of the groom. For his mother coconut etc., and for his father a pair of footwear and some clothes are sent. As these materials reach the home of the groom, the festivities of lagan begin. In lagan all members of the family are gathered and the groom is made to take his ceremonial seat and various gifts are placed in his lap. Women sing marriage songs and the groom hands over the gifts given to him to his mother. In lagan all requisite materials must be furnished, because if the gifts are short of groom's family's expectation, the anger of his parents is aroused and may lead to cancellation of the marriage. After the lagan ceremony in the groom's house is over, the parents of the groom send suitable gifts to the house of the bride.

4. Ban. In Ban, people from the side of both bride and bridegroom pour oil at their houses a number of times. The number is determined at the time of lagan. Usually, the number of Bans of the girl side are two less than those of the boy side.

5. Gift of Bhat by maternal uncle. In rural marriage uncle enjoys a place of pride. The maternal uncle gives the gift of Bhat both in the marriage of his nephew and niece. The uncle of girl gives a ring to his niece and the uncle of the boy gives new dress to his nephew. Besides this, some money is also given. After the marriage the formal send-off of the bride is done by the uncle. In the event of the death of the maternal uncle, responsibility of Bhat devolves upon his son.

6. Madha. After the arrival of the maternal uncle, women go out in procession to worship the potter's wheel. They return with some earthen pots which are pierced with holes. These earthen pots are usually saucers. With the help of saucers and a bamboo pole, Madha is stuck on the ground. Madha is stuck in both the families. The ceremony of Madha is performed both in bride's place as also in groom's place.

7. Ghurcharhi. On the eve of the departure of Barat (marriage party) the boy wears the marriage dress, puts on a ceremonial head-wear (Mohar) and rides the mare and is taken out in procession. This ceremony is called Ghurcharhi.

8. Johari. Lewis, who made a detailed study of all the customs, traditions and rituals in the village of Rampur, mentions ceremony of Johari after Ghurchari According to Lewis when the procession of Ghurchari reaches the outer limits of the village, a mat is spread and the groom is seated there. In the ritual of Johari the bridegroom symbolically sucks the breasts of his mother and aunt and a tika is put on his forehead. The ceremony of Johari is not prevalent in all the villages. Its discontinuance or non-observance may be due to the sense of modesty gradually overtaking the villagers, but there are still places where it is observed even now.

9. Milni. Milni is the preliminary ceremony of the actual process of marriage. As soon as the marriage party reaches the village of the bride, news of arrival is conveyed to bride's side by the barber. These days this is not necessary, because the day and time of arrival is prefixed and some persons from the bride side are present at the entry of the village to welcome the Barat. They lead the marriage party to the Janvasa (the lodging house) directly. At the Janvasa the father of the bride formally welcomes the Barat by paying some money to groom's father. This ceremony is known as milni.

10. Barat Lena. After milni some members from the side of the bride alongwith the barber and the pundit come to the bridegroom and give him sweetmeats and place a ceremonial Tika on his forehead. This ceremony is known as 'Barat Lena', that is, to formally accept the marriage party.

11. Barauthi. After the formal welcome of the Barat, the bridegroom wears mohar (headgear) and ceremonial dress, rides a mare and goes to bride's house along with his family members. There women welcome him with nuptial songs and he stands at the doorstep. Here the bride is in her full ceremonial regalia, and she throws two handful of rice on the bridegroom and garlands him with Jaimala indicative of the fact that he has emerged victorious and chosen by the girl to be her groom. After this the groom stands on a Chauki and his Aarti *i.e.* a prayer for his well-being is made. After Aarti the mother-in-law of the groom places tilak on his forehead and he also receives some cash.

12. Choonary. After the ceremony of Barauthi is over the father of the bridegroom presents some ornaments and cosmetics to bride's mother for the use of the bride. This ceremony is called Choonary.

13. Phere. In a Hindu marriage, the ceremony of Phere is the most important of all the ceremonies connected with marriage. Phere means going round the sacred fire amidst chanting of the sacred mantras by the bride and the bridegroom tied together, that is, coupled. The appropriate time of the phere is selected by pundit taking into consideration the various astrological considerations. In pheras the pundit, after making preliminary preparations, ties a piece of groom's turban end with the choonari of the bride and instructs the couple to go round the sacred fire seven times, each time following a rigid and well established order of taking out the first step. If the bride and the bridegroom are educated they are also made to take oaths of marital fidelity etc. However, now-a-days, pundit himself iterates the oaths of both bride and bridegroom. After taking oaths or having them iterated by the pundit, the couple goes round the fire. After going round the sacred fire seven times the pundit puts tika on the forehead of the bride and the bridegroom.

14. Kanyadan. Now comes the occasion for giving the bride formally to the bridegroom. This is known as Kanyadan (gift of girl). The father of the bride does the Kanyadan. Dowry is also given at the time of Kanyadan. In olden days Kanyadan used to be made at the time of departure of Barat. But these days this practice is rarely followed. The amount of dowry is not fixed. It can be a rupee or thousands of rupees. Dowry, besides cash, includes garments, ornaments, nuptial beds, furniture, toys etc. It may include sweetmeats.

15. Madha Dismantling. After phere, the uncle of the bride brings the bridegroom to the home of the bride. Here the groom is feted. He meets the bride and her relatives in an atmosphere of informality and good humour. Both bride and bridegroom put the impressions of their palms on the wall. On this occasion lot of jokes and light banter is made. The maximum attempts are made to tease and embarrass the bridegroom. The treatment meted out to the groom at this time is comparable to the ragging of hostlers on the first night. Many demands are made of him and he must give some token gifts to his sisters-in-law. He is also asked to recite some appropriate poetic composition called chhands. He gets suitable payments for these. After this there is a lot of feasting.

16. Bida. Same day or on the next at a time selected auspicious by the pundit, marriage party returns to the home of the groom. Women sing parting songs and the bride is sent along with the bridegroom on the vehicle arranged by the side of the groom. This parting scene is full of pathos. Whereas the family members and friends of bridegroom feel a sense of joy and triumph, the relatives of bride weep bitterly. This scene embodies the essential pathos as well as joys of human existence. In villages, the marriage is not consummated after the wedding ceremony. The bride returns to her parents after a short sojourn at the home of her in-laws and the consummation of marriage is not made till after another ceremony known as Gona.

17. Dwar Rokna. As the bridegroom arrives home with his bride, his sister stops them at the doorstep of the house. Bridegroom gives some money to his sister and then they enter the home. This ceremony is known as Dwar Rokna, that is stopping a person at the doorstep.

18. Mukh Dikhana. When the bride comes to her in-laws' place, on next day the female relatives and friends of the family visit her to see her face. For seeing the face some token money or gift is given. This ceremony is known as Mukh Dikhana.

19. Kangan Khelna. After the ceremony of face showing there is the ceremony of playing the kangan. In this ceremony besides bride and bridegroom, mostly the females of the family are present. In this ceremony, sister-in-law has the crucial role. In this ceremony, milk, water and grass are placed in a big pan and the finger ring of the groom is put in it and at the signal of go both bride and bridegroom make frantic attempts to retrieve. Whosoever succeeds is declared the winner.

After this the bride and bridegroom, turn by turn, hold the ring right in their fist and the other party is asked to force open the fist. Bride and bridegroom also unknot the Kangana tied on their wrists. On this occasion jokes are freely made. Many a time the younger brother of groom sits in the lap of his Bhabhi and demands of her a piece of sweetmeat and this in turn will give her by grace of God a son. Bride gives him *laddoo* (a sweetmeat) and gently takes him off her lap.

20. Visit to Temple and Beating. After the ceremony of playing Kangana, bride and bridegroom visit the holy places in the village. They go to the village temple and other hallowed comers in the village. In some villages, bridegroom and his sister-in-law beat each other with feather sticks. In certain villages, mutual beating is done on the occasion of *kangna* ceremony itself.

21. Gona. In the cycle of marriage Gona is the ultimate. It is only after Gona that the marriage is consummated, and bride and groom live as husband and wife and can mix together without restraint. In olden days, a long period stretching over a number of years used to lapse before Gona ceremony took place after marriage. Now-a-days, however, the time gap between marriage and Gona is becoming progressively less. This is due to the fact that while in olden days marriage used to take place at a very young age and the couple did not become mature for many years. Today, marriages are taking place at relatively mature age and it will be unnatural to prevent the married couple from consummating the marriage and enjoying marital bliss. When the date of Gona is fixed, a message to this effect is conveyed to the groom's parents by the parents of the bride. Then bridegroom and barber go to bride's place for this purpose. Many times they are made to make repeated visits for the purpose. However, when the decision to send the bride is ultimately made, the bride is washed, perfumed and ceremonially dressed in best clothes and bejeweled. Then she is allowed to accompany the bridegroom. The groom is also given many gifts which include, primarily household effects. When the parents of the bride send off their daughter at the time of Gona, they and other villagers accompany the bride, bridegroom and barber for about one mile distance. When the groom with his bride reaches home there is not much ceremony except singing of nuptial songs by women. Villager and relatives examine the gifts. The sisters of bridegroom can pick any item from the gifts. They enjoy this privilege.

QUESTION FOR EXERCISE

1. Briefly describe the rituals and ceremonies connected with Indian rural marriage.

19

RURAL POLITY

What is Rural Polity?

Rural polity refers to the power of taking decisions in different matters of social and economic matters in rural areas. It means as to who holds the power or say political power to decide the disputes in the rural community. So in this sense our query is about who holds the power in rural communities.

The caste groups

The local politics in village is dominated by caste. Each caste wants to get maximum power in the village set-up. The groupism in rural politics is centered around certain factional leaders, each being usually representative of a particular class and caste. Thus, we have in villages groups like Paridit group, Chamar group or Jat group etc.

MODES OF RURAL POLITY

Literature on rural polity shows various modes of rural polity as below:

Andre Batielle in Caste, *Class and Power* (1969), in the chapter, "The Changing Patterns of Social Stratification," studied the conflict between low and high class in 'Sripuram' village in Tanjore District. Sripuram village is an agrarian village. The whole village had been donated by the king to the Brahmins to look after the temples and other buildings of the village. Before 1920 the Brahmins were the landowners. Of these most families came from Maharashtra. Brahmins did not cultivate their land themselves but gave it to non-Brahmins on tenancy basis. Therefore, one finds three economic units in the society: Brahmin owners of the land, non-Brahmin tenants of Brahmin owner, Aadi Dravids, sub-tenants or labourers.

In the social stratification Brahmins were at the top stratum of the society. Non-Brahmins were next to them. The Aadi Dravids were at the bottom of the social stratification. They were treated as untouchables.

In the political sphere or say in the village panchayat Brahmins were occupying the power. They decided the disputes within the village. Sometimes they also interfered in caste panchayats. Before 1920 the Brahmin group was enjoying the political power. Non-Brahmins and Aadi Dravids were having no say in the village Panchayat. Again, before 1920 Brahmin group was enjoying the political power as well as economic power and social power. Andre Batielle calls it cumulative inequalities.

THE PRESENT CHANGES

In 1960 the situation was wholly changed. In the economic sphere Brahmins lost the economic power because they lost the ownership of the land. They were only having 10 to 15 acres of land. Land went to non-Brahmins. They got more economic power in the society. Aadi Dravids also got 3 to 5 acres of land but they remained low in the economic status.

In the social stratification Brahmins were having only conventional high status but they were no more the patrons of non-Brahmins and Aadi Dravids. Non-Brahmins claimed for high status in society and, therefore, developed a conflict between Brahmins and non-Brahmins. Non-Brahmins launched a self-respect movement. They developed their own priests. Aadi Dravids remained at the bottom of the stratification.

In the political sphere non-Brahmins got the political power as well as they got the economic and social power. Brahmins were mostly in Congress party. They killed some Britishers. Therefore, Britishers were against them. They were trying to crush them. Non-Brahmins supported the Britishers against the Brahmins. They demanded reservation in the government jobs. They participated in anti-Brahmin movement and also formed a Justice Party. Britishers reserved some seats in government jobs for them, because they supported them against the Brahmins. So non-Brahmins captured the political power. They became influential in the village panchayats. They were also linked with high officials. In 1950 Panchayat Raj System was introduced and through it every adult got the right to vote in Panchayat election. Therefore, this election was won by non-Brahmins from the village and the non-Brahmins' number increased in population. Aadi-Dravids also occupied a little political power.

In this way three changes occurred as follows:

1. Demographic change. A number of Brahmins migrated from the village and non-Brahmins' number increased in population.

2. Caste conflict. A conflict between Brahmins and non-Brahmins also arose.

3. Supremacy of non-Brahmins. Non-Brahmins got political power as well as economic power and social power.

4. Sources of change. Within the village, conflict between Brahmins and non-Brahmins was the cause of change. Outside the village, Panchayati Raj System 1950, non-Brahmins movement, education, governmental support, job reservations etc. were the causes of change.

Thus, political power and economic power go side-by-side.

DEMOCRACY AND RURAL POLITY

Somjee, the author of the book "*Democracy and Political Change in Village India 1971*" studied the political system before democracy and after democracy. Before democracy the situation was as follows:

In village panchayat upper caste persons played dominant role. Lower caste was having no say in village panchayat. Members were belonging to high caste, old age and high economic status. In panchayat, decisions were taken unanimously.

In caste panchayat members were caste elders. Panchayat maintained the norms of castes and penalised the guilty.

In 1947 democracy was introduced, the situation was different. The Author compared:

1. Age composition of members in village panchayat.
2. Caste of members in village panchayat.
3. Economic status of members in village panchayat.
4. How decisions took place?

1. Age of the members. Formerly, members were of old age in village panchayat, but when the members were selected by the elections, the old aged found it difficult to fight an election. Therefore, middle aged persons won the elections and became the members of the panchayat.

2. Caste of the members. Some seats are reserved for the lower castes. Mostly middle caste persons are the members of the panchayat. Formerly, high caste persons were the members.

3. Economic status of members. Formerly, economic status of the members was high but now the members are belonging to the middle class due to the links with outside politics.

4. How decisions take place. Decisions are now made after a long debate. They are not unanimously made but the members are divided in the groups having different opinions about the decision. Formerly, decisions were made unanimously.

Therefore, the persons belonging to middle class and middle age are occupying the political power. Formerly, high caste, high class and old aged persons were having political power.

Rajani Kothari in "Caste in Indian Politics" studied how far caste is influencing the rural polity. He finds that caste is becoming more and more strengthened because castes are forming caste associations. Caste association works for the caste. It provides the following:

1. Educational facilities. Caste association starts some schools and provides the facilities of hostels to the caste members and also provides them some scholarships.

2. Political Sphere. In political sphere, the caste associations ask their members to vote the persons belonging to their own caste and he may be of any political party. Caste members become more and more powerful in politics. They try to get reservations in government jobs for their caste members.

3. Associations. Caste associations try to raise the status of their caste high in social stratification.

4. Agricultural Castes. Agricultural caste associations demand for high prices of production output and lower prices of input of production.

Therefore, castes are trying to strengthen their position and get as much political power as possible.

ECONOMIC FACTOR IN RURAL POLITY

In "*Caste and the Economic Frontier*" F. G. Bailey studied the Bisipara village in Orissa state. Bisipara is located in the hill region and is isolated up to some extent. The author shows that the economic power is accompanied by the political power. In early 9th century Britishers came to the village and gave the right of private property to the landowners. Therefore, the possessors of the land became the owners of the land. Britishers also introduced the dual policy. On the one hand they had an anti-attitude towards the liquor traders and on the other hand they participated or rather allowed the liquor trade. Landowners had to sell their land due to the following causes:

1. To buy the inputs of production.
2. For legal disputes which were taken to the court.
3. For the ceremonies in the life cycle for which they needed money.
4. For daily consumption for which they needed money.
5. Through inheritance every member of the family inherits a small piece of land which, being not an economic unit, he used to sell.

Liquor traders were getting a lot of profit from the trade. They purchased all the land. So with the change in the property right over the land the following two more changes occurred:

1. Sanskritisation. Liquor traders claimed for a high status in society.

2. Political power. Liquor traders previously having no say in village panchayat or political power were now enjoying political power also.

Therefore, the author concludes that the economic power and political power go side-by-side.

NATURE OF THE CHANGES IN RURAL POLITY

In sum, the nature of the changes in rural polity is as follows:

1. Castes are playing more influential role in polity. People are forming caste associations.
2. In social stratification middle caste persons are getting power.
3. Due to the reserved seats some lower caste persons are also getting political power.
4. Middle class persons are getting political power.
5. Brahmins are losing political power.
6. Middle aged persons are getting political power.
7. Economic power and political power go side-by-side or go to the same group.

8. Panchayati Raj System 1950, effected the rural polity to a very large extent. It provided the right of vote to every adult.
9. Anti-Brahmin movement also effected the polity of rural communities.

IMPORTANCE OF RURAL POLITY IN INDEPENDENT INDIA

In Rural Sociology it is very important to study the role and importance of village in the political life of the nation. Though, as a rule, villagers are less active and interested in politics than town dwellers and the political life of a nation is controlled, more or less, by city people, the villagers do play an important role. Their political power and influences are tremendous though dormant. If and when their dormant energies come to surface, there can be little doubt that Indian politics would be completely dominated by villagers. As a matter of fact the reverberation of village power in Indian politics is being already felt. The villagers had played a significant role in the freedom struggle of the nation and it is natural that they should participate in national politics after independence. In all movements launched by Mahatma Gandhi like Civil Disobedience, Non-co-operation, Swadeshi etc. Indian villagers had participated whole-heartedly. They took active part in Quit India Movement of 1942.

After independence the importance of villages in Indian political scene has increased multifold. This is obviously due to the fact that India is a democracy and villagers far out-number townsmen. India is a democracy in which elected representatives of the people govern the country. And when 83% of Indian population lives in villages, it is but natural that the levers of political power should be in the hands of villagers. In India elections are conducted on the basis of adult franchise under which each adult, irrespective of his qualifications and status, has a single vote. The political rights of people are unaffected by their sex, creed, religion and region. Thus, each adult is to count for one vote and none less and none more. In view of these facts, it is clear that in due course Indian politics will be fully controlled by villagers. The Indian villagers are quite conscious of their political power and as can be seen from election statistics, they are regularly and consciously making use of this right. Even women, old and sick show remarkable enthusiasm during voting, some people are lifted on their beds to polling booths in order to vote. It is very obvious now that the future politics in India should be dominated by villagers. A factor that goes in their favour is that they have more spare time than their city counterparts. The study of rural political life is important in another respect too. The village happens to be a primary political unit. Therefore, the feelings and thinking of villages are bound to influence greatly the national politics.

ASPECTS OF RURAL POLITICAL LIFE

We may study rural political life under three aspects:

(1) Rural Administrative Machinery;

(2) Role of political parties in villages;

(3) Local Politics;

(4) Political Behaviour of villagers.

1. Rural Administrative Machinery. As far as official administration is concerned we find it of two types. In villages on the one hand, there are autonomous agencies and on the other hand official machinery.

(i) *Autonomous Agencies.* The autonomous agencies are Gram Sabha, Gram Panchayat and Panchayati courts. The executive branch of a gram panchayat is known as Gram Sabha. The panchayat looks after general administration. Its main functions are the maintenance of roads, water-supply, cleanliness, cottage industry development, defense, education, medical aid etc. The president and vice-president of gram panchayat are usually the president and vice-president of gram sabha as well. There is direct election for the president and vice-president. It is so provided that whosoever is elected president will preside over both gram panchayat and gram sabha and that the vice-president will assist him. This dispensation of justice is entrusted to panchayati courts. A Panchayati Adalat (court) is comprised of five representatives of gram sabha. These judges are elected by direct voting. In every court there are twenty to twentyfive panchas, of these one is elected sarpanch. The judgments of panchayats are final and normally these are non-appealable.

Official Interference in Panchayats

According to Panchayati Raj Act, state government have a right to supervise and if need be, to interfere in the functioning of panchayats. Panchayat Inspectors and other officials look after the functioning of panchayats on behalf of the government. It is necessary to seek the sanction of Panchayat inspector for the formulation of panchayat budget. The government is authorized to suspend or dissolve panchayat if its functioning is so corrupt or bad as to be unjust or if its acts are likely to injure social harmony or peace. The government also gives financial assistance.

As the government has the right to look after the panchayats which include right to interfere and enquire or investigate, it is natural that there is clear impact of official policy on panchayats. The problems of rural administration are now part of overall national administration.

(ii) *Official Administration.* Besides autonomy of administration in certain respects, the rural administration is connected and involved in general national administration. This connection is provided by the fact that a village is part of a tehsil and through tehsil of a district. Besides members of gram panchayat, gram sabha and gram panchayati adalat (court), the village administration is also connected with and is under Tehsildar, Kanoongo, police officials, Deputy Collector or District Magistrate. On behalf of police administration there is one Chowkidar in every village who is supposed to maintain peace and report criminal cases of violence and dacoity etc., to higher authorities. On the canal quarters there are Ziledar and Pataraul who collect water tax from villagers. For measurement of land-holdings and collection of maps there is one Patwari in each village. The village Chowkidar is under Sub-Inspector of Police. Tehsildar collects land revenue from all villages under his province and also keeps a watch on administration. Similarly, Sub-Inspector is responsible for the safety and security of all villagers under purview. Thus, we have a sort of administrative diarchy in villages, that is, villages are ruled by a double tier system of administration. On the one hand, we have a rule of officials and, on the other, a rule by elected representatives of people. The diarchy creates a host of problems. If there is no harmony in two tiers of administration there is likely to be harm to village interests. Occasionally, the government officials look down upon the elected rural representatives. This is unjustified and immoral. Indeed government officials should give due respect to the unpaid elected representatives of people.

According to Dr. A. R. Desai, the following criteria can help us to judge the village administration:

(i) How far the administrative machinery is according to the wishes of people?

(ii) How far people come into contact with the administration?

(iii) How far is it cheap and efficient?

2. Role of Political Parties. As we have mentioned above, the primary source of political strength in India is a village. Therefore, each political party tries to dominate the village politics and swing the villagers to its fold. The main political parties like Congress, Socialists, Communists and Bharatiya Janata Party have their ramifications in villages. The Congress party has maximum influence. Actually, every party these days is concentrating on building hold over villages. The Congress being the oldest party which is credited with having won independence for India, naturally enjoys advantage in this respect.

3. Local Politics. The local politics in villages is dominated by caste and creed considerations and each caste wants to get maximum power in the village set up. The groupism in rural politics is centred around certain factional leaders, each being usually representative of a particular class and caste. Thus, we have in villages groups like Pandit groups Chamar group, Bania group, Jat group etc. Within each political party these groups flourish and that is why there is cross voting.

4. Political Behaviour. In rural political behaviour all kinds of behavioural tendencies are to be seen. While some persons try to gain power by constitutional and valid means others try to gain it by illegal, nay, immoral means. In villages, political struggle sometimes degenerates into cut-throat competition in which people do not shirk from using violent methods to low down opponents. In south in Telangana small farmers had launched violent struggle to eliminate rich farmers. The Naxalites preached and practised violence. They launched movement in villages. With the spread of democracy and official administration rural violence is now less and people recognize the value of peaceful competition.

The propagation of democracy is the best means of introducing self-rule in villages.

QUESTIONS FOR EXERCISE

1. Critically examine the changes that are taking place in the power structure of the village community in India since independence.
2. Is there a relationship between power and caste? How?
3. Describe the role of local communities of India in national politics.
4. Write an essay on rural power structure.

20

RURAL HOOKAH GROUP, FACTIONS AND LEADERSHIP

In almost all Indian villages there are various kinds of groups. Besides groups based on caste, there are many other types of groups which are based on clan or even on a single family. In the context of Indian rural life, there is nothing like freedom of the individual. The concept of personal freedom over and against the will of the group is indeed unthinkable. An Indian villager places little value on his personal freedom, honour or prestige and identifies his interests wholly with those of his group. The unit of Indian rural society is a group and not an individual. Generally, there are joint families in villages and in joint families, the head of the family enjoys sweeping powers and privileges. However, there are groups broader and wider in scope than family and family as a group is to be absorbed in them so as to cease to have an independent existence. A group that is wider in scope than family, and in which family as a group merge and loses independent status, is clan group. The families whose ancestors are same, form a clan group. A clan may and usually does have its ramifications outside a village and it may be spread over numerous villages. Besides groups like family and clan, there are Hookah groups in Indian villages.

RURAL HOOKAH GROUP

Meaning of Hookah Group

Hookah group is extremely common in Indian villages, young and old all are used to smoking hookah. It is common sight in villages to find groups of persons taking puffs at hookah. Farmers, Ironsmiths, Goldsmiths, Potters, Barbers, in short, people from all walks of life find time between their working hours to smoke hookah. Smoking hookah apparently refreshes them and they re-engage in their respective works after short spells of hookah smoke. Though smoking hookah is intoxicating and its use as narcotic cannot be condoned, it serves an extremely useful social purpose. Hookah in villages provides an occasion for get-together and gossip. Hookah is symbolic of inter-caste and inter-group distinctions. If anyone smokes hookah in anyone's company he is considered to belong to his group. Smoking hookah in common is indicative of an expression of affirmation of friendship. This is why usually persons of high caste do not smoke hookah of low-caste persons. This is because they wish to maintain and preserve their distinction and smoking hookah with low-caste is regarded degrading. If a group of persons sitting together belong to any single caste they can be seen to smoke from the same hookah. Whenever a guest arrives in any home in a village and if he is of the same caste as the host, he is entertained with milk or beverages and then in a relaxed atmosphere is offered hookah to smoke. The guest and the host take turns at hookah and engage in slow relaxed conversation. At marriages hookah is freely used and all persons belonging to one caste or group smoke from one hookah and this is considered to be an affirmation of fraternity and friendship. However, persons from different castes do not smoke the same hookah. Among certain castes there is no barrier on smoking from a common hookah. For example, Brahmins can smoke the hookah of jats and vice-versa. However, a Brahmin would never smoke a hookah of a Chamar and would not allow a Chamar to smoke from his hookah.

Though in general, there are no restrictions on hookah smoking in villages, there are some occasions on which smoking hookah is taboo. For example, smoking hookah on Janamashtmi day is not considered proper, because on this day it is forbidden to take any food, water or anything which would involve introduction of any foreign thing into stomach. Naturally, therefore, smoking would involve breaking fast and this is considered bad.

Importance of Hookah Group

1. Source of Relaxation. On account of permissive attitude of villagers to hookah smoking, we find a number of Hookah groups in villages. A Hookah group is that congregation of individuals who collect at certain places and smoke hookah and engage in gossip in a relaxed manner to while away their time pleasantly.

2. Symbol of Acceptance. Besides being a source of relaxation, hookah in villages serves as a symbol of acceptance or non-acceptance of someone into one's fold. Thus, Hookah group serves as an indication of one's social status. If someone accepts hookah of any person he expresses thereby his fraternity with the man.

3. Modes of Social Examination. Therefore, if anyone is to be punished with excommunication from any caste or group he is disallowed to mix in that group or the Hookah groups of a particular caste. To exclude someone from Hookah smoking is a great punishment. It is a strong disapproval of the conduct of man excluded from a Hookah group. As exclusion from a Hookah group is a special disapproval and punishment, it has great value in dispensation of social justice within a caste or group in a village. Therefore, whenever any person violates the code of his caste or does anything disgraceful to his community, a council is called to discuss his guilt. If it is proved, he is declared as an unacceptable person and is not to be allowed to smoke hookah of that community and no member will touch the hookah used by him. However, this excommunication from a group is not permanent. After doing the penance prescribed by the community and making apology for his misconduct, the excommunicated person can be readmitted to the community and the ban on his hookah smoking repealed.

Even if a person unwillingly violates the restrictions placed on hookah smoking the person is punished. For example, if an upper caste person smokes the hookah served by a low caste and this fact becomes public, he is liable to be duly punished and prevented from smoking hookah of his community till the time he makes suitable amends by tendering apology and performing penance prescribed by the community. Thus, in a hookah group, hookah is an effective means of exercising social control.

4. Symbol of fraternity. Hookah is a symbol of mutual relations and fraternity in villages. It keeps a person in a fold and provides an effective means of social disapproval and punishment. In modern progressive society, it would appear that mere hookah cannot be a thing of great social significance. Nonetheless it continues to be something of great social significance in Indian villages.

RURAL FACTIONAL GROUP

Meaning of Faction

Besides the groups mentioned above there are some other groups in Indian villages. In villages we can find political' groups based on political ideologies, caste-power or simply due to clash of personalities. On these and other bases we find considerable factionalism in villages. However, by far the most important of all village factions and groups is a group known as Dhara in Rampur and other villages. The literal meaning of the word dhara is trunk, that is, main structure of the body. Actually dhara or trunk means main body of a tree or human or animal body without head and limbs. Probably a group is called dhara because of its essential physical and structural unity. J. T. Plants in his Hindustani Dictionary has translated dhara as human body and faction. The word dhara in the sense of faction is popular in Northern India. According to Lewis the meaning of dhara is faction but dhara does not connote political faction. All sociologists writing in English have used dhara and faction, synonymously, though the term faction is not wholly appropriate. The main difficulty in the use of the term faction in the sense of dhara is that the former suggests rivalry, opposition and tension whereas it is not necessary that a dhara should be rival to or opposed to some other group. As H. S. Dhillon has pointed out in his book 'Leadership and Group in a South Indian Village' while rivalry and opposition to some group is a general feature of a faction and that faction usually comes into existence on account of mutual rivalry and conflict or clash of personalities these are, by no means, the only features of factions. The factions may not be characterised by mutual opposition but may also exhibit signs of cooperation and goodwill. Thus, it is clear that though conflict and rivalry are usual features of factions, there may be limited cooperation and give and take between them in matters of economic cooperation and celebration of festivals and other social occasions.

Structure of Faction

There can be more than one faction in the self-same caste. In every faction there are numerous families. Though there are usually numerous factions in one caste, it is quite possible that one faction may be comprised of families from different castes. It is not necessary that families comprising a faction should be neighbours, these can be far removed from each other or may conversely be neighbours. There is no limit on the number of members in a faction nor on the number of families.

Essential Conditions of Faction

The factions in villages bear traditional names. Usually, the factions are comprised of members of a single caste, though the functions of the caste and the factions are quite different. A faction may consist of more than one Hookah group. According to Oscar Lewis a faction must possess the following essential features:

(1) A faction should be so strong and well-organised as to be able to function as a unit. Each member of the faction must owe a sense of allegiance and loyalty to the group, its aims and aspirations.

(2) A faction should be large enough to hold festive occasions on its own. For example, it should have enough members to take out a Barat on marriage or hold religious or social functions peculiar to it independently.

(3) It should be economically viable. That is, it should have property and wealth sufficient, to function without external financial help.

CAUSES OF FORMATION OF FACTIONS

The main reasons for the formation of factions in villages are a sense of economic, social or political insecurity. Many a villager has no or a little land, and they are, therefore, so poor that without external help they cannot maintain themselves. They need good organisation to be able to secure official or unofficial assistance. Similarly, for successful litigation and securing of justice a strong organisation is needed. By belonging to some or other faction they can face the threat to their physical or economic welfare in a better way. Without belonging to any faction it is difficult to feel secure in villages. Each member of a faction feels a sense of political, social or economic security. In an event of difficulty or trouble the other members of the faction are ready to help him. In the event of his untimely demise, the group looks after his family and children. In case of threat to his honour the members of his faction protect him and also help him in his bad times. Besides, in time of need he can use the house of others and seek financial help. For example, in time of marriage his guests can stay with his friends and his friends make their contributions towards marriage. A faction does not remove only a feeling of insecurity from the minds of its members but also fulfils many a social need of theirs. A member of a faction does not suffer from the sense of isolation and loneliness and feels a sense of gratification as the power and influence of an entire group are behind him. In his study of Rampur village Oscar Lewis has given the following causes for the formation of factions:

(1) Quarrels over succession of property.

(2) Quarrels over adoption of male child.

(3) Quarrels over property and irrigation rights.

(4) Quarrels over sexual offences.
(5) Murders.
(6) Inter-caste rivalries.

Thus, we find that as men may quarrel over land, woman and property these disputes and quarrels lead to the formation of factions.

Internal Organisation of the Faction

For the successful functioning of any faction it is necessary that there should be some prosperous and wealthy families in each faction. For collective action aimed at self-defence and aggression we need surplus funds and these will be available only if there are persons of means in a faction who can provide hinds for collective action. Besides, prosperous families in a faction lend money to the needy members and also keep them as tenants at their farms. In villages people generally like to lend and borrow money and give tenancy rights only to members of their own group and avoid transactions with outsiders. Generally, a group includes members having common ancestry. However, sometimes members of a Khandan (families having common ancestry) belong to various factions. Therefore, obviously there is difference between a faction or a group and Khandan. On festive occasions, particularly betrothal, marriage, all members of a group get together. In litigation they help each other. These days voting patterns in elections to Panchayat, District Board, State and national assemblies is determined by castes and factions. In common quarrels over land, sex offence etc. members of a faction put up a united front and pull their common weight in litigation etc. Ordinarily no one is willing to engage anyone outside his faction or group as tenant or lend money to him if there is any needy member of his own faction. Similarly, no one likes to mortgage his property with anyone outside his faction. As we here said earlier, we find a kind of organic unity in faction like of which is to be found in human body. However, every faction does not exhibit equal unity. Various factors affect the unity and cohesiveness of a faction. The more important among these are family relations of the members, the economic condition and social status of the members, the housing conditions, the age, the structure and the history of the faction. If the families constituting a faction belong to a common ancestry the organisation of such a faction is naturally cohesive and unified, whereas if there is much diversity among families, the organisation is loose and disjoined. Similarly, if a faction is economically strong and self-sufficient, it can maintain its own independence against rival factions, whereas if the economic conditions of a faction are bad, it will fritter away and become non-existent. Sometimes people in villages do not like to borrow money from moneylender of their own village but prefer to borrow money from the moneylenders of other villages. Some factions are more than hundred years old whereas others are only five to ten years old. Generally, there is more cohesion in older factions though some factions which are relatively new may also possess great cohesion. A faction having a multiplicity of Hookah groups is apt to have loose organisation and unstable structure. This is quite easy to understand. The members of a Hookah group have great cohesion and owe deep and strong loyalty to their respective groups. This naturally comes in conflict with their loyalty to a faction whose constituent their Hookah group is. Again, if the members of a faction are close neighbours and reside in same mohalla or adjoining mohallas they can form a Hookah group and thus the faction to which they belong will be closely knit and possess great cohesion. They can consult each other even in small matters and without least trouble. On the contrary, if members of a faction live at considerable distance and are scattered they can get into consultation only on special occasions. The inability to get-together easily militates against cohesion and unity of a faction. A strong sense of rivalry and the imperative need to guard one's independence and security also provide impetus to unity in a faction.

Inter-factional Relations

Though as a rule it is rivalry and contention which give birth to factions and in the absence of contrary self-interests the factions would merge, it is nonetheless true that there are moments and points when the factions come together and cooperate. In many a festival we find such coming together of factions. Holi, Diwali and bathing festivals are occasions, when members of contending factions forget altogether the differences and celebrate them cooperatively. However, the difference between infrafactional and interfactional relations is made evident by the modes of invitation for festive occasions extended to persons to one's own faction and the persons of other factions, whereas an invitation extended to persons of one's own faction is for the entire family of a man, it is enough to invite only one person from a family from outside factions. The ladies from outside factions are not invited, only a single male member is invited. Generally, ladies mix up with ladies of their own group and avoid contact with the members of external groups. The occasions for get-together of women of diverse groups are rare.

Factional Vanity

In the interfactional relations each faction does not enjoy the same status or equal privileges. Certain factions are bitter rivals and animosity and acrimony among them is persistent, there are others which are neutral and have neither friendly nor inimical relations with other factions. Obviously, the groups which are neutral enjoy good relations with other factions, whereas rival groups are perennially at loggerheads. The occasions for quarrels, acrimony, bitterness and mudslinging present themselves at every turn. The factions which are neutral naturally enjoy better prestige and more respect in society. The festivals of Holi and Diwali offer splendid opportunities for get-together of persons from diverse factions. In comparison to persons of other villages people attach much more importance to persons of their own village. A villager normally considers every girl of his village as his daughter and if any girl of his village is married in another village which he happens to visit he makes it a point to visit her. Thus, in spite of much factionalism in villages there is an element of basic unity and this is not affected by factionalism.

The relations between various factions are determined by a number of factors. For example, if the persons of one faction offer economic aid to the persons of other group or are engaged as tenants on their land or are related by jajmani system the relations between two factions become strong and cordial. Similarly, if a leader of one faction helps another faction in matters of litigation or some rivalry and quarrel, the ties between two factions get cemented. Of course, if two factions hail from the common ancestry their relations are bound to be cordial. As per contra, if there are persistent quarrels, litigation etc., the relations between factions are bound to be bitter and inimical.

Besides friendly and inimical factions there are factions which are neutral. For a faction to be neutral and maintain its neutrality, a faction must be economically self-sufficient, A faction's ability to maintain its neutrality is directly dependent upon its capacity for economic self-sufficiency, the greater the economic self-sufficiency, the greater is a faction's capacity for maintaining its neutrality. Besides economic self-sufficiency, another essential factor needed for neutrality is the neutral attitude of the members of a faction. Thus, three types of relations can be seen among factions: (1) Cordial, (2) Inimical, and (3) Neutral.

If we are able to understand the nature of various factions and the quality and standard of their leadership we can have some insight into the development potential of the village. Though multiplicity of factions proves to be obstructive in the development in the village but if we are able to appreciate the inter-factional ties and see them in proper perspective, the multiplicity of factions may not be obstructive but, on the contrary, helpful in the village development. The rivalry of factions can be so moulded as to become a healthy competition for fast achievement of goals. By understanding the structure of factions and by seeking the co-operation of the leaders of various factions we can launch progressive schemes in villages. By seeking co-operation from few individuals who are the leaders of various factions we need not appeal to each individual in the village. By accentuating rivalry into competitive spirit it is possible to achieve progress.

RURAL LEADERSHIP

Kinds of Rural Leader

In every group there are several leaders. Leader is a person who, by virtue of magnetism of his personality, social status or economic affluence, is able to command respect from or dominate the wills of a group of persons so as to be able to mould and direct their energies into channels of his choice. A leader is a person who is both respected and obeyed by his followers. Unless respect and obedience are both simultaneously present there can be no effective leadership. More obedience can be due to brute force or some other compelling factors but such relationship is not durable. In Indian villages people are modest and therefore hardly anyone claims himself to be a leader, though leaders are easily spotted by their peculiarities, the forcefulness of their personalities. There are several grades among leaders. There is also a hierarchy among leaders in the same community, group or faction. The superior leaders may be called primary leaders; generally they are the senior-most members of their communities. Their number is not more than a few and usually they are of ripe age. Junior to these primary leaders there are other leaders who may be called secondary leaders and they are also inferior in status. In actual practice all practical and field work is entrusted to the secondary leader and primary leaders function as advisers.

Fundamentals of Rural Leadership

There are certain pre-requisites of leadership. Everyone is not capable of being a leader. In villages the first and foremost requirement of a leader is that he must be of ripe age and must belong to a family which has large number of members. Another qualification of a village leader is his economic status. A person, in order to become a leader in a village, must enjoy economic freedom and relative prosperity. A person who can spend lavishly and can hold large feasts to which very large number of persons are invited becomes a leader. In order to buy such leadership people are known to hold feasts to which people from as many as twentyfive villages are invited. These feasts create name and fame for the host and he is held in high esteem. Such feasts are usually given at the time of marriage. Charity also earns name for the man. A person, who can run educational institution, hospital or serai and dharamshala on charity, easily earns name and fame and becomes a leader. Besides the number of family members, economic status, lavish spending and charity, other factors which help a man to become a leader are his political and official contacts. A person having contacts with political leadership and high ups in government service can naturally help villagers in having their problems resolved and also can obtain economic aid for his village These things naturally can earn him name and respect.

Characteristics of Village Leader

Moneylenders are also respected in villages and they also easily turn into leaders. Similarly, an elder member of a family which has one of its members at high government office, particularly an official in the Revenue Board also starts getting respect and becomes a leader. The leaders in villages are also subject to being dethroned and cease to be leaders. This happens if the family of a leader mortgages land or one of its members is guilty of moral turpitude. Of course, there are some persons who become leader by use of brute force and maintain their leadership by striking terror in the hearts of villagers. But as observed earlier, such tactics cannot earn anyone respect and whatever following such leaders have is temporary and when declines in ability to terrorize, it sounds death knell to their leadership. Following are the chief characteristics of a village leader:

1. Age and education. As observed earlier, in rural leadership age plays a very significant role; only adults can be leaders. Generally, rural leaders are men of ripe age though these days some young rebels can be seen playing the role of leadership in villages. Besides age, education is also an important determinant of leadership. It is not necessary that a leader should be educated but nonetheless education is highly desirable inasmuch as leaders are required to look after management of educational institutions and panchayats.

2. Personal character. The character of a man plays a crucial role in rural leadership. The character traits highly valued in a leader are civility, politeness, spirit of sacrifice, generosity etc. The rural leaders are extremely polite. They are so polite in conversation that they refer to even their personal property as "Yours". A leader must be a man of word. He should be willing to make sacrifices to keep his word. He must never forget his promises and break them. In villages a man, who does not live according to the standard of his caste and lack firm conviction, is universally looked down upon. In the event of rivalry and strife between factions the leader must be bold and blunt in the handling of situation. Honour rather than security should be his motive. However, violence and volatility of temperament are demerits rather than merits in a leader. Generally, leaders are peace-loving, non-violent and civil. Last but not the least, a leader must be an impressive speaker. Unless a leader can express his views in general public effectively and make a convincing speech he cannot become a first-rate and widely followed leader.

3. Time for public service. An important quantification of a leader is that he must have enough spare time from his routine work in which he can devote himself to public service. In order to redress or get redressed the grievances of his followers he may have to spend days with them and this is possible only if he does not have many personal preoccupations. This is the main reason that leaders are mostly from rich landlord class or are retired civil servants. However, these days many an unemployed young man is trying to fill his role.

4. Influence potential of a leader. One more essential qualification of a leader is his ability to influence. He should possess a dynamic and impressive personality. Generally, the capacity to influence others is not an innate trait in village leaders but is an indirect result of their contacts with high-ups in officialdom by virtue of which they can help their followers. Thus, it is not any genuine character trait of theirs which impresses, but their resourcefulness. For example, a leader by virtue of his contacts can get employment; can help win a legal case; can help obtain freedom from jail etc. Thus, capacity to deliver practical good is generally responsible for the scope and influence of leaders.

Nature of Rural Leadership

It is evident from the foregoing discussion that the nature of family, the economic and social status of the person, personal character, age, education and devotion to public work are some of the factors which determine rural leadership. In rural life, its development, progress and advancement depend largely on the calibre of its leadership. If leaders are true and enjoy genuine respect from villagers, they can easily implement most ambitious projects, but on the other hand, if they are inept and self-seeking village life may deteriorate. Leaders are constantly in touch with the members of their group and try to enjoy their confidence. Should a village have a dynamic leadership, it is easy to make plans successful by enlisting their help. Rich leaders are a boon. They can extend economic help to the needy. There are examples where such leaders have lent money without charging interest.

As yet women are not playing much role in rural leadership. This is, of course, due to generally conservative outlook of villagers. In recent panchayati elections, however, several women were chosen panchas, and some of them even became sarpanch. This illustrates gradual changes taking place in villages. Slowly but surely women are beginning to play some independent role in villages. Similarly, now rural leadership is gradually passing into the hands of educated young men. The citadel of orthodoxy has already cracked.

From the foregoing discussion, it is plain that in villages there are hardly any leaders who command the following of the entire village. An important reason for such a state of affairs is the deep-rooted caste stratification of rural India. Every leader represents his own faction and there are no villages which do not have multiplicity of these. However, factionalism in villages may not necessarily come in the way of village development because these leaders are eager to cooperate inasmuch as it improves the image of leaders as well as raises the prestige of their faction.

QUESTIONS FOR EXERCISE

1. Write short not on faction in rural social organisation.
2. Discuss the nature of group conflict in the context of rural India.
3. The pattern of leadership in countryside is qualitatively changing in free India. Discuss.
4. Describe the main traits of rural leadership in India.
5. Discuss the concept of leadership. What problems and patterns of leadership are emerging in the present rural society in India?
6. What are the factors weakening the power of traditional leadership in rural India? Answer with causes.
7. Describe the changing patterns of rural leadership in Indian rural communities.

21

RURAL EDUCATION

Problem of Illiteracy

If an analysis of the different problems of Indian rural society be made, it may become evident that the biggest fundamental cause of these problems is illiteracy. Being illiterate, the villagers cannot become acquainted with the latest developments in modern science and consequently agriculture and cottage industries are deprived of necessary degree of progress. It is due to illiteracy that the rural people are ignorant of the basic principles of health which makes them an easy prey to sickness. Illiteracy also causes them to dwell in dirt and filth and does not give them an opportunity to become cultured. Illiteracy is the base upon which ignorance and superstitions are built. Moneylenders and lawyers make full use of the ignorance of their rural clients who are incapable of discerning their shrewd practices. The narrow and the limited viewpoint of the villagers, which bars them from understanding each other and leads them into conflict, can also be attributed to illiteracy. Their capacity for earning money is further diminished by the absence of any educational qualification, the latter being a further cause of their persistent poverty. It is not at all possible that the children of the uneducated rural women may be properly brought up, and in its absence if their personality were to remain extremely underdeveloped, should it occasion any surprise? As long as they lack education the Indian rural people cannot acquire the essential traits, characteristics of a democracy. In Principles of Social Reconstruction, Bertrand Russell has written quite correctly, "In its modern form, democracy is completely impossible in a country where many people are unlettered." It was for this reason the Mahatma Gandhi stressed the need for primary education in the plan for rural development. But the lack of education, which is the basis of rural problems is not information but rather education in its comprehensive sense, meaning adequate encouragement to the physical, mental and spiritual development of man. Such an education can undoubtedly remove most of the problems which exist in the Indian villages but it cannot be concluded from this statement that education is the complete solution of the problems of rural India. Besides education such other factors also have their place in the solving of these problems as will help to emancipate their way of life, *e.g.*, social awakening, economic improvement, constructions of roads, encouragement to cottage industries, adequate arrangement of agricultural implements, seeds and financial assistance, provision of manures, development of the means of irrigation, popularising co-operative societies, Zamindari abolition, reorganisation of panchayats etc. Nevertheless it can be sagaciously remarked that in order to benefit from these moves, the villagers need to be educated. Even if education is not the comprehensive solution of every rural problem, it is certainly an indispensable condition.

Need of Education

Thus, in order to solve the rural problems, basic education and social education should be disseminated in the villages. The basic education will serve to develop the children into useful members of society while social education can be relied upon to improve the adults in every way possible. Social education should not be exclusively confined to the teaching of the language but should also include and impart education relating to agriculture and industries, health recreation, domestic and economic life as well as good citizenship. In this education, other means besides the classroom such as radio, dancing and singing, puppet shows, religious singing and chanting of hymns, should also be utilised. Social education and basic education should be made to conform to the local conditions and should be imparted through medium of daily activities. Besides this general curriculum, special training should be imparted by the trained personnel from the universities. The Planning Commission has made some very practicable suggestions on this subject. The basic education should be able to give comprehensive education to the children. The education should be both free as well as compulsory.

Two types of education stand out in the educational aspect of rural India — 1. Basic education, 2. Social education. A brief description of the two follows.

BASIC EDUCATION

Meaning of basic education

Basic education is based upon the fundamental needs of human life. Man is dynamic by his very nature and wants to manifest himself through his actions. Different people are interested in different activities. Thus, only that education can be interesting and beneficial which gives the child the opportunity of becoming active, facilitates his unhindered development and approximates to the curriculum to life. Basic education is blessed with all these characteristics. It educates the personality of the child comprehensively. It educates the child in self-dependence and makes him capable of standing on his own feet. In it the different tendencies of the child are developed by means of many programmes and those qualities which make a man a citizen is cultivated in him, Basic education, as a method, is unlike ancient education. Mahatma Gandhi has said, that, due to the peculiar education adopted today, life has been divided into two parts. In the first fifteen years of his life a person should acquire education without involving himself in living and afterwards should wrap the education in a bag and live successfully till death. This kind of education is most undesirable for an underdeveloped and poverty-stricken country like India. Basic education claims that it can do away with the defects of the traditional system of education. Defining the object of basic education, the Central Advisory Board pointed out in 1955, that no system of education can properly be called basic until it can provide for:

1. An integrated course for both junior and senior stages.
2. Adequate emphasis on the system of education from the viewpoints of both education and production. Basic education is that system of education which possesses both the above characteristics.

Revolution by basic education

Basic education seeks to free the Indian villages from exploitation, social as well as class distinctions, and establish a self-dependent, non-violent and democratic society in them. In the Harijan of 9th October 1937, Mahatma Gandhi wrote that it (Basic education) will form a healthy and moral basis for the relation between town and village and in this way eliminate, to a large extent, the defects of today's social insecurity and poisonous class relation. It will prevent the increasing loss of our villages and lay the foundations of a just social order in which there will be no artificial distinction between the rich and the poor and being secure in the knowledge of his economic prosperity he will be in a position to engage in creative activity, and all this can be achieved or will come about without the frightening incidents of war, the expenditure of money on a large scale in the mechanization of such a sub-continent as India. And neither will it be necessary, in that stage, to be dependent upon machines imported from some other countries nor upon the skill of mechanism. Finally, reducing the need of the skill of specialist, it will make the public the architect of its own destiny. Basic education, as is evident by its name, lays stress upon the development of basic traits in the child.

Aim of basic education

The founder of basic education was Mahatma Gandhi. With regard to its aims, Mahatma Gandhi wrote in the Harijan of July 1937, "By education I mean all round drawing out of the best in child and, man, body, mind and spirit... literacy itself is no education. I would therefore, begin the child's education by teaching it a useful handicraft and enabling it to produce from the moment it begins it training. Thus, every school can be made self-supporting, the condition being that the state takes over the manufactures of these schools." In this way, with ideas of a new education on the horizon, a meeting of famous educationists was called in Wardha on 22nd October, 1937 in which Mahatma Gandhi presented his plan of a new education. He said that it was his belief that if we want to make improvement in the country we should attach intermediate education to primary education. Thus, the plan of education which we are about to present should be primarily rural. The aim of this plan was not to teach some handicrafts along with the above mentioned lavish education. He wanted that the entire education should be imparted through the medium of some handicraft or industry. Improvement can be affected only by teaching some art of labour or science practically and imparting the entire education through it. For example, while teaching the method of spinning cotton on the spindle, things like the kinds of cotton, proper land for them in Indian provinces, the history of the decline of this industry, their political causes, and mathematics etc., ought to be taught. It was Gandhiji's opinion that the centre of basic education should be the spindle. Spindle will make possible production also, because there will be demand for cloth manufactured by children. Gandhi formulated seven years course whose aim will be the teaching of the practical knowledge of spinning, weaving, colouring and making designs. He was conscious of arranging for the salary of the teacher. The means to this could be had by selling the objects made by the children. Otherwise there is no other means for the education of crores of children. In this education, besides the knowledge of the general laws of cleanliness, health, defence, food etc., the principle of self-dependence and assistance of parents is also inherent. The criterion of the success of this education is making it self-dependent. At the end of seven years the children should pay for their own education and become earning members. After the necessary discussion upon Mahatma Gandhi's plan the Wardha Committee accepted the following proposals:

1. Arrangement should be made for seven years of free and compulsory education for the nation.
2. The medium of instruction should be the mother tongue.
3. The entire activity of education should be carried out through the medium of productive work of some or the other form of handicraft.
4. The system of education should become self-dependent.

Commission for basic education

In order to form a syllabus on the basis of the suggestions of the Wardha Committee a commission was appointed under the leadership of Dr. Zakir Hussain. In March 1938, the commission published its, "Wardha Education Plan Report". In order to implement the plan presented in this report Hindustani Talimi Sangh was established. The Central Government appointed two committees in 1938 and 1940 under the leadership of B.G. Kher in order to study the Wardha Plan. These committees made the following recommendations about basic education:

1. The basis of education should be some handicraft.
2. The handicraft predominant system of education should be activated first of all in the villages.
3. The time period of basic education should be of eight years extending from the age of six to fourteen.
4. The entire course should be divided into two levels — Junior level from 6 to 11 and senior level from 11 to 14.
5. After the fifth class, *i.e.,* at eleven years of age children should be able to go to other kinds of schools.

6. The medium of education should be the mother tongue. In 1944 the Sargent scheme tried to give practical form to these recommendations of the Kher Committee. After independence the comprehensive syllabus laid down by the Hindustani Talimi Sangh was adopted in almost all the states of the country. The National Planning Commission accepted the Basic Education Plan.

Characteristics of Basic Education

Basic education is the education of an integral life. Vinoba has pointed out that basic education lays foundation for the recognition of the fact that every person in the society must do some work and should treat it as his social and moral duty. If he makes hill contribution towards making the society ideal it would be the best education. Speaking in the 1955 Shimla Conference, Mr. Jawahar Lal Nehru said that "Basic education means a social revolution in our ways of life which is creeping gradually but surely over the vast border of India." The chief characteristics of basic education are briefly the following:

1. Based on basic handicraft. Basic education is so called because it is based on some basic handcraft. Thus, the education is imparted in this method, through activity. In this way basic education is nearer to life. In basic education handicraft is no separate subject but it is the medium through which all the subjects are taught. For example, if spinning is regarded as the basic handicraft then through it the knowledge of farming of cotton, methods of weaving cloth, areas growing cotton, the history of the development of the industry, can be given in agriculture, geography, history, gardening etc. According to the report of the Zakir Hussain Committee, the main object of this new educational system is not to create mechanics who will work automatically, its aim is to use the means inherent in handicraft for the purpose of education. This does not mean that general subjects which are not in any way connected with handicraft are to be ignored. Man naturally takes more interest in things connected with the daily life, and this is the psychological basis of basic education. Thus, the subjects which cannot be taught through their relations with handicrafts will be taught by being related to the other fundamental needs of life. According to the Zakir Hussain Committee, a subject which cannot be related to handicrafts will be conjoined with the child's natural or social circumstances in which the child has much interest as he has in handicraft.

2. Feeling of self-dependence. Thus, basic education wants to make the citizens of India, or in other words, the village in India, self-dependent, and to fill in the gulf between the village and town. It will minimize the difference between mental and physical labour. The children will meet the expenses of their education from their own earnings. In this way, the children will learn the doctrine of self-dependence. Gandhiji has written, that he had the courage to say that education should make us self-dependent. The degree of the child's self-dependence he could treat as the criterion of its success. In this way, Gandhiji wanted to realise the dream of a society in which every person is self-dependent. Whatever the children will produce in the basic schools will be acquired by the government. From the sale of these things the government will be able to pay the teachers. In this way, a poor country like India, will be able to arrange for free and compulsory education.

3. Stress on the character and personality of teachers. It is obvious from the description of basic education that it needs teachers of a sterling character and an impressive and magnetic personality. These teachers should be trained in special training institutes.

4. Emphasis on free development. Basic education stresses the free development of the children. In it all the tendencies of the children are given the opportunity of developing unhindered. In it the child is not tied down but he is given the opportunity of expressing himself. In 'Towards the Basic Pattern' Ramachandran insists that it must be remembered that the children should be encouraged to carry out various useful activities which will afford them the pleasure of discovery and the delight of learning.

5. Mother tongue as the medium of education. One special feature of basic education is that the mother tongue is used as the medium of instruction. This move is justified by the fact that the child experiences some facility and expediency in acquiring knowledge and manifesting his emotion and reaction.

6. Rejection of the examination method. Basic education rejects the existing examination method. In it the children are promoted on the basis of their progress and ability.

7. Stress on the ideal of citizenship. The main purpose of basic education is to achieve an integral development of the children, making them useful citizens of the country. In it national occasions and festivals, Sharamdan, exhibitions, tours etc. are given special importance in order that the children may develop the sense of patriotism. Through the practice of handicrafts the children are taught the lesson of self-sufficiency. By basic education the children realise their economic, social, political and cultural responsibilities and become capable of shouldering them.

8. Based on non-violence. Non-violence is the fundamental formula in all of Gandhi's teachings. Basic education too is based on non-violence. Its aim is to establish a non-violent society in which there is no exploitation. Basic education wants to root out class distinctions, party-politics, casteism, etc.

9. Democratic foundation. The basis of basic education is democratic. Children organisations have been arranged for in basic education in order to develop democratic qualities. In these organisations children learn and acquire such qualities as will make them good citizens, for-example, morality, secularism, world brotherhood etc.

10. Free and compulsory. Finally, one main characteristic of basic education is that it is free and compulsory. In a poor country like India, it is essential that the education be free. There is very little education in the country at present. Thus, it should be compulsory for everyone. Basic education is indispensable for children and its expenditure is borne by the school or the State. According to Mahatma

Gandhi the new education should not depend upon money. Education is not real as long as it is not self-dependent.

Basic Syllabus

The syllabus for basic education has been constituted keeping in view the above mentioned characteristics of basic education. As has been mentioned earlier, it lays utmost stress upon the education of handicrafts which include spinning, weaving, carpentry, agriculture, gardening, leather work, pottery and allied industries of toy-making, fisheries etc. The female children are made proficient in home science. Besides handicrafts, the curriculum of basic education includes the education of mother tongue, mathematics, social science, history, geography and civics, general knowledge, Hindi and music and drawing and other arts. Besides the training in these spheres, basic education accords adequate importance to games and exercise. Religious education has no scope in basic education. Education up to the fifth class continues without any segregation of the sexes. After this the girls are to study home science in place of general science. English, too, has no place in basic education. In basic education the children learn by doing something and this activity is productive and not purposeless. In this system of education it is the child who is given more importance than are the books or the examination. In this way, in basic education all the major characteristics of the different theories propounded by famous Western educationists have been synthesized.

Objections to the Basic Method

As a general rule the basic education system has been praised by all thinkers, but some thinkers have also raised some objections against it. The major objections are as follows:

1. More stress has been laid on handicrafts in basic education than is strictly necessary. Although it cannot be denied that handicraft may, to a major extent, help to alleviate the misery of poverty in the country, one would do well to remember that heavy industries are also needed for the attainment of this end and these will need engineers and scientists. This is what the basic education has ignored.

2. All children do not equally take to handicrafts. It is certainly very important to make education interesting and to approximate it to life but all children cannot possibly have the same amount of interest in handicrafts. This being true it would be extremely differential to their freedom to press any handicraft on them.

3. The economic aspect has incessantly been stressed in basic education. India is a poor country and it is essential that primary education here should be free. But it does not seem to be correct to make the children produce compulsorily for this reason. A member of the Basic Education Committee, Mr. K. T. Shah, pointed out that making education self-dependent one would fill the children with a mercenary motive from the start which will not be creditable in any way. If at the age of seven years one is going to involve the students in financial problems, then a kind of slavery will necessarily be induced in them. The truth is that it is for the government to supply the financial resources for providing free education. When the public pays taxes to the government then why should it not provide free education?

4. The problem of the sale of produced goods. What arrangement will be made for the sale of the products of children in basic schools? In answer to this question Mahatma Gandhi pointed out that the government should buy all these products and it would be able to dispose them off easily because there would be a great demand for things produced by children. This hope seems extremely impractical. The articles produced by the children would be inferior in every respect and very few people would be prepared to buy them merely on the ground that they were made by children.

5. Wastage of raw material. Children cannot become skillful at any handicraft expeditiously. Hence, there would be much wastage of raw material in the basic schools. As a consequence, will not economic problem become even more complicated instead of being solved? Gandhiji believed that the teachers would be able to prevent this loss, but this belief certainly does not seem practicable.

6. Defects of syllabus. The syllabus constructed for the basic education is defective. Of the five and a half hours of school time, almost three and a half have been allocated to handicraft. It is not at all difficult to realise that no child would voluntarily work on some handicraft for such a long time. In this way the schools will become factories in which the mental development of children would not be adequately achieved.

7. Disregard of the interests of teachers. The method of basic education is characterized by an utter lack of consideration for the interests of teachers. It has been tried to make them work more with lesser remuneration. Under these conditions it is very impractical to expect high ideals from the teachers. The result of such conditions will be that good people would not venture into this occupation. The truth is that Mahatma Gandhi based the plan for basic education upon his personal experience and thoughts and ignored the fact that other people may differ in their experience and ways of thinking. As a matter of fact, being a religious person, Gandhiji was apt to acquire some beliefs, completely forgetting psychological and economic facts. Sir P. C. Ramaswami Aiyar has written correctly that. "The biggest defect in Gandhi's education is that he assumes that everyone is like him."

Gandhiji has given answers to these objections raised against his plan for basic education. The same impractical idealism may be glimpsed in these answers. It is possible that upon being applied, it may have achieved some success but with regard to the present conditions the above criticisms of the basic education plan seem quite relevant. Many people may still be in agreement with Mahatma Gandhi's opinion in their theoretical aspect, but if one were to cast a glare at the existing schools, the picture would be very different. Undoubtedly, handicraft has an important place in education but it cannot be correct to burden everybody compulsorily.

Progress of Basic Education

The present Indian government has accepted the pattern of basic education and is trying to mould primary education according to it. The government is expending much energy in this direction and is adopting numerous measures for achieving this end. The old primary schools are being converted into new basic schools. New basic schools are being opened and even in non-basic school's handicrafts are being made popular. New literature is being produced and adequate arrangements are being made for training teachers for basic schools. The government is making constant efforts in this direction along the lines suggested and recommended by the Assessment Committee on Basic Education established in 1955. In the Indian Constitution it was laid down that education would be free and compulsory within a period of ten years although the present rate of its progress does not suggest that anything of this magnitude will be achieved by the stated time period.

According to INDIA 1993, the literacy rate in India has gone up from 16.6 per cent in 1951 to 36.23 per cent in 1981 and 52.11 in 1991. Primary education is now free in all states and compulsory in most of the states.

The difficulties of the basic schools have been increased by problems relating to land. They neither have any arrangement for land or the necessary apparatus nor the money to construct buildings. In schools which propose to undertake the teaching of agriculture there is no land to have a farm. According to the report of a committee of the Education Ministry appointed to carry out research upon the productive aspects of basic education, some 31,46,460 acres of land is necessary for basic schools and the training of their teachers. But the land requisitioned for this purpose is not even a considerable fraction of this estimate.

Suggestions of the Planning Commission

The Planning Commission has made the following suggestions with respect to the land problems of basic schools:

1. Gift of land. The Planning Commission has suggested that new basic schools should be opened or the old schools converted into basic schools only where the people are prepared to donate five acres of land to the school and the local society is prepared to meet the expenses of the building. The state government can induce the people to donate land in this way through programmes of social education.

2. The right of schools over unused land. Another, suggestion which the Planning Commission has made with a view to relieving the schools of their need about land is that the land which the government has acquired through zamindari abolition or in any other way and which is lying unused, should be considered the rightful property of the basic schools.

3. Use of the demonstration farms of the government. It has been suggested that the demonstration farms maintained by the government should be used for the training of teachers for the basic schools.

4. Provision for the school when consolidation is being done. The Planning Commission has made another suggestion in this respect. According to it the land needed for the school should be left aside while the land holdings are being consolidated.

5. Making fertile the land adjoining the schools. It has generally been seen that the land donated to schools is not fertile. The agriculture department of the government should take steps to make the land adjoining the schools fertile.
6. Land on rent. Where every other method has failed to produce the desired result, the land should be rented for the schools.
7. Acquisition of land through communal labour. Land should be acquired through communal labour under the guidance of teachers. This suggestion is based upon the experience of the village Bechari in the Surat district of Gujarat.

Although, many years have passed since the inception of the basic education plan, the problem of land for the schools has not yet been solved. The suggestions put forward by the Planning Commission are both practical and proper. Gifts in the form of land as well as labour can certainly bring success to the movement as is evident from the success of the Bhoodan movement of Vinoba Bhave. But where land cannot be obtained from the public, the government should arrange for the land by renting it or by any other method because without its basic education cannot achieve its objective. Thus, it is necessary for the government as it is for the public to pay special attention to this problem.

SOCIAL EDUCATION

What is Social Education?

Inaugurating the Village Adult Education Seminar of UNESCO in 1949 Maulana Abul Kalam Azad, erstwhile Education Minister defined social education by pointing out that it means education for the entire man. It will make him literate so that the knowledge of the world may become available to him. It will tell him exactly how he has to adapt himself to his environment and how he has to derive the maximum benefit from his physical conditions. It will teach him the modern methods of handicrafts and production, so that he may be able to realise his financial needs. It will teach him about the science of immunity from disease, of individual and community so that his domestic life may be prosperous and happy. Finally, this education will impart to him the education of citizenship so that he may be, able to assist his government in the decision for making the country strong and establishing peace after he has acquired some knowledge of the corporal things. Originally the meaning attached to social education was merely literacy of adults. But now it has come to include all kinds of education for the adults. In the words of Biharee, "Social education is the stimulation in each citizen of a greater awareness of the advantage of the pattern of society as conceived in the Constitution and a persistent desire for progress towards such a pattern socially, economically and culturally."

Aims of Social Education

In the words of Pt. Jawahar Lal Nehru, "To educate the adult in the three R's and the affairs of the world, a network of social education organisation has been set up."[1] In this way, while social education aims at removing illiteracy it also endeavours to acquaint the adults with the problems of this world. In the words

1. Nehru J. L., *Our Planning* (1954), p. 54.

of K. G. Saiyeden, "The aim of the movement is to create a spirit of friendship between people by bringing together men and women of different nationalities." In this way, the aim of social education is both individual as well as social. It seeks to elevate all the various kinds of standards of life, be they physical, mental or intellectual, in order that people may be in a position to make active contributions in all spheres of national progress. It teaches them about the reconstruction of the village.

Programme for Social Education

The programme for social education has been divided into the following five phases:

(1) Spread of literacy, (2) Acquainting people with the laws of health and sanitation, (3) Improvement in economic level, (4) Encouraging the sense of citizenship and imparting awareness of rights and duties, (5) Healthy recreation concurring to the needs of society and individual.

Characteristics of Social Education

The main characteristics of the above mentioned programme of social education are the following:

1. Spread of literacy. Social education spreads literacy among the adults.

2. Advancement of handicrafts and cottage industries. Besides spreading literacy, social education makes handicrafts and cottage industries popular.

3. Training in self-administration. Social education trains the adults in self-administration.

4. Training for ideal citizenship. Social education tries to make the adults ideal citizens.

5. Education in health and cleanliness. Social education informs the villagers about the laws of health and cleanliness.

6. Knowledge of the problems of the world. Social education imparts the knowledge of the problems of the world to the adults.

7. Integral development. Social education directs its efforts at achieving the integral development of the adults.

8. Organisation of healthy recreation. Social education, besides formal education, organises healthy recreation through the medium of radio and cultural programmes.

9. Contribution in rejuvenation. One of the major characteristics of social education is that, besides education, it contributes to every programme for rejuvenation.

Method of Social Education

It is on the basis of these characteristics that the method of social education has been developed. Hence, night schools have been arranged in the village centres for teaching the adults. Social education is not limited only to adult males. This education is imparted even to adult women as well as to young men and adolescents, boys and girls and the syllabus laid down for them concurs harmoniously with their peculiar psychology. In order to increase the attraction of the programmes such means as the movies, exhibition vans, posters and charts are employed. A characteristic of this method is the broadcasting of programmes over the radio. Community consciousness and nationality are popularized and communicated to the people through social acting, folk dances and folk songs. The people are also informed about the scientific means of agriculture and handicraft and attempts to develop the qualities of leadership are made. At regular intervals sports competitions and development fairs are organised. Educational excursions are also arranged periodically. Programmes for composing adult literature are made and mobile and permanent reading rooms are also arranged for.

Progress of Adult Education

To further the National Policy on Education, the Ministry of Education operates a scheme to eradicate illiteracy among the adult population. The central idea behind the programme is to enable them to improve their lot and create in them an urge for change from traditional to progressive society. The field programme of adult education with adult literacy as the core activity is the responsibility of state governments and union territory administrations. The Union Ministry of Education co-ordinates programmes, provides supporting services or conducts pilot projects which are of importance to the programme of social education in the country.

A pilot project called the Farmer's Functional Literacy Programme was launched in 1967-68 in three selected districts as a Joint integrated programme of three central ministries, namely Education, Agriculture and Information and Broadcasting, to help the illiterate farmers to acquire not only literacy skills but also agricultural know-how which could be used by them. So far, 2,00,000 adult farmers have been made functionally literate. Another 1,00,000 are undergoing functional literacy courses.

Facilities for adult education for industrial workers and their families are also provided by the Ministry of Education through institutes in selected areas where there is a concentration of industrial population. Two such institutes, one at Indore and the other at Nagpur, are functioning.

The National Board of Adult Education promotes and evaluates the programme of adult education in the country. It also provides financial assistance to voluntary organisations for adult literacy work.

Women's Education

The Central and State Governments have taken a number of steps to stimulate the education of girls and women. These include creation of separate cells in the state Directorates of Education to look after programmes for girls' education, establishment of polytechnics for girls, construction of staff quarters for women teachers in rural areas and girls' hostels, introduction of condensed educational courses, assistance to voluntary educational organisations working in the field of women's education and holding of seminars in different states to discuss problems and programmes of girls' education.

The National Council for Women's Education advises the Central and State Governments in framing programmes and policies for education of women.

Literacy

In 1951, only 16.6 per cent of the people in India could read and write. The percentage went up to 24.0 in 1961 and to 29.45 in 1971, 36.23 in 1981 and 52.11 in 1991. According to the 1991 census Kerala had the highest literacy rate, 90.59 per cent and Tamil Nadu and Maharashtra came next with 63.72 and 63.05 per cent respectively. Despite the rise in the literacy rate and the total number of literates, the number of illiterates has increased from 33.4 crores in 1961 to 38.6 crores in 1971 and 64 per cent in 1981, due to fast growing population. Rural folk and women form the bulk of illiterates. Kerala topped the states in women's literacy also, the percentage being 86.93. Tamil Nadu with 52.29 and Maharashtra with 50.51 came second and third respectively.

Rural Higher Education

The scheme of Rural Higher Education was launched in 1956 with the object of providing higher education, after the secondary stage, to the rural youth and inculcating in them a spirit of service to the community and sympathy for the rural way of life, besides training them for careers in the rural development programmes of the central and the State governments. The National Council for Rural Higher Education advises the Central government on the development of rural higher education. At present 12 rural institutes are functioning at Coimbatore and Gandhigram (Tamil Nadu), Udaipur (Rajasthan), Birouli (Bihar), Bichpuri (Uttar Pradesh), Amravati, Gargoti, and Wardha (Maharashtra), Rajpura (Punjab), Hanuman Matti (Karnataka), Tavanur (Kerala) and Indore (Madhya Pradesh).

Problems of Social Education

In India, there are many problems which plague social education. The major ones are the following:

1. The rural people are not very spirited in their approach to social education.
2. Often the adults do not show much of an inclination towards social education.
3. The night schools are terminated during the peak season in agriculture.
4. There is a serious absence of proper literature for social education.
5. Being brought up in an urban atmosphere, most of the workers are unable to take proper interest in social education.
6. Other programmes, beside literacy, are not emphasised properly.
7. Proper and adequate means for social education are not available.

Table 1: *Literacy Rate among Persons, Males and Females, 1991*

Rank	Persons		Males		Females	
	State/ Union Territory	Literacy rate (Per cent)	State/ Union Territory	Literacy rate (Per cent)	State/ Union Territory	Literacy rate (Per cent)
1	2	3	4	5	6	7
1.	Kerala	90.59	Kerala	94.45	Kerala	86.93
2.	Mizoram	81.23	Mizoram	87.06	Mizoram	78.09
3.	Lakshadweep	79.23	Lakshadweep	85.67	Lakshadweep	73.61
4.	Chandigarh	78.73	Chandigarh	85.48	Chandigarh	70.88
5.	Goa	76.96	Goa	84.06	Goa	68.20
6.	Delhi	76.09	Delhi	83.91	Delhi	68.01
7.	Pondicherry	74.91	Pondicherry	82.67	Pondicherry	66.22
8.	A & N Islands	73.74	A & N Islands	82.63	A & N Islands	65.79
9.	Daman & Diu	73.68	Daman & Diu	79.68	Daman & Diu	61.38
10.	Tamil Nadu	63.72	Tamil Nadu	74.88	Tamil Nadu	55.72
11.	Maharashtra	63.54	Maharashtra	74.84	Maharashtra	52.46
12.	H.P.	63.05	H.P.	74.57	H.P.	52.29
13.	Nagaland	61.30	Nagaland	72.98	Nagaland	50.51
14.	Manipur	60:69	Manipur	72.98	Manipur	50.01
15.	Gujarat	60.91	Gujarat	70.08	Gujarat	49.72
16.	Tripura	60.39	Tripura	67.85	Tripura	48.64
17.	W. Bengal	57.72	W. Bengal	67.24	W. Bengal	47.23
18.	Punjab	57.14	Punjab	67.24	Punjab	47.23
19.	Sikkim	56.53	Sikkim	65.09	Sikkim	47.15
20.	Karnataka	55.98	Karnataka	64.34	Karnataka	44.78
21.	Haryana	55.98	Haryana	60.68	Haryana	44.34
22.	Assam	53.42	Assam	62.37	Assam	43.70
23.	Orissa	48.55	Orissa	62.4	Orissa	40.94
24.	Meghalaya	48.26	Meghalaya	57.43	Meghalaya	34.40
25.	Andhra	45.11	Andhra	56.24	Andhra	33.71
26.	M.P.	43.45	M.P.	55.35	M.P.	29.37
27.	U.P.	42.71	U.P.	55.07	U.P.	28.39
28.	Arunachal Pradesh	41.22	Arunachal Pradesh	52.63	Arunachal Pradesh	26.10
29.	D & N Haveli	39.45	D & N Haveli	52.07	D & N Haveli	26.02
30.	Rajasthan	38.81	Rajasthan	51.57	Rajasthan	23.10
31.	Bihar	38.54	Bihar	51.10	Bihar	20.84

Suggestions Advanced by the Planning Commission

The Planning Commission had made some very important suggestions, for the solution of the problems which infest social education, the more important of which are given below:

1. In social education, education of health, recreation, domestic and economic education should also be given the necessary attention.
2. After imparting the knowledge of language, efforts should be made to strengthen this knowledge through films, radios, libraries, reading rooms etc.
3. The programmes for social education should be adopted and modified according to the local needs.
4. Much care should be exercised in the selection and training of the personnel for social education.
5. The Teachers Training Colleges should carry out research about the ways of making people literate.
6. There should be a suitable administrative machinery for maintaining a certain standard in the work of social education.

It must have become quite obvious from this brief description of the different aspects of social education that this plan has some predetermined objectives which are immensely beneficial to the country. There can be no two opinions on the subject that the Indian villages are in great need of social education and it is the only means to their redemption. As it is made obvious by the survey of the progress of social education in India, there is need for much work in this direction. But there is no doubt that the present progress of social education is not entirely dissatisfactory. The suggestions made by the Planning Commission for the solution of the problems of social education are very useful. Indian social education is still in its infancy. But nevertheless, "If today the villages of India are humming with greater activities than ever before some credit for this must go to the social education movement."

QUESTIONS FOR EXERCISE

1. Analyse the problem of rural education in rural India.
2. Bring out the nature and aims of social education.
3. Write short note on Rural Education.

22

THE VILLAGE PANCHAYAT

The organisation, administration and all kinds of progress of the rural communities in India is based on village panchayats. The village panchayats are the pillars which support the Indian rural social system. The present chapter is devoted to the study of these village panchayats.

Village Panchayats of Ancient India

In India, in the Vedic age there were panchayats in every village. According to K. M. Panikkar, this is the sole permanent basis of ancient history on which each dynasty of India has prospered. On this subject, Dr. Altekar bas pointed out that these gram panchayats worked for the defence of the village and collected the revenue of the State. They imposed new taxes, arbitrated in the disputes of the villagers and implemented the projects for public welfare. Through public loans these panchayats made arrangements for alleviating the distress caused by famines and other calamities. They also organised and established schools, orphanages and colleges and did much cultural and religious work through the temples. With the exception of declaring war and entering into treaty, these panchayats were vested with all the rights and authorities of the State.

According to a 10th century text, *Shukra Neeti Sar,* the ancient Indian village panchayat had the following characteristics:

1. The members of village panchayats were elected. 2. The members had the rights of the Executive as well as the Judiciary. 3. The members were held in due respect. 4. The panchayats collected the tax on the land and controlled its distribution. 5. The pasture of the village and other forested land were treated as the property of the panchayat. 6. The panchayats also undertook such activities like maintenance of peace, security, health, education and public constructions. 7. The panchayats also negotiated between warring factions of the villages.

Electoral Procedure of the Panchayats

In the village in ancient India the entire population elected the members of the panchayat. Certain manuscripts discovered in South India provide some knowledge of the electoral procedure and functions. The manuscripts found in the village of Maroor North of Chingleput district in South India show that the members of the village executive were elected by casting votes. In the Maroor village there were thirty wards. In these wards the names of many people were proposed for the membership of the executive. Then the name of each candidate was written upon a piece of paper and the names of all the candidates in any ward were put in some vessel. Then some innocent child was asked to pick up any one piece of paper. The piece of paper which the child selected carried the name of the representative of that ward. This kind of election did not give any opportunity for propaganda, party politics or bias.

Village Republics

The name village republics was given by the English to these ancient panchayats of India. These panchayats had the right to nullify any excessive, improper or new taxes imposed by the king. They collected the revenue from the public and thus the king too did not interfere in their working but rather listened to them. Sir Charles Metcalf has written that these panchayats had all the characteristics of a republic. Every village was a small independent country. It was completely free from external control. Those things which have not been defended anywhere else have been protected in the village. The organisation of the panchayats of the village was such that every village was like a small independent nation. Considering the high standard of their independence, self-dependence and prosperity, we can well understand the importance of the panchayats.

Panchayats under British Rule

Although the Englishmen had great praise for the panchayats, in the British government the rural panchayats of India started vanishing for a number of reasons. In the British states, the state revenue was collected from the individual and not from the village as a whole. The work of collecting revenue was also taken away from the panchayats and handed over to government officials. The disturbances of the village came under the authority of the police. This served to reduce further the responsibility and the rights of the panchayats. Civil and Criminal cases were now dealt within the official courts. As a result, the panchayats were deprived of their judicial rights. As a result of industrialisation and urbanisation the rural community disintegrated; the consequence of this was the disintegration of the panchayat organisation. The influence of Western civilisation resulted in the strengthening of the individualistic tendency and the weakening of communal feeling. The panchayats were no longer respected.

Along this before India became independent, some attention was given to the reconstruction of rural communities. The Royal Commission for Decentralisation of 1909, placed particular emphasis upon the fact that the panchayats should be organised and developed in order to establish local self-government in the villages. In 1915 a Bill was passed and the instructions were issued to the provincial governments that full efforts should be made to initiate panchayats in the villages through cooperatives. In the Act of 1919, special emphasis was laid on the same policy. Following this, Village Panchayat Acts were passed in different provinces, in 1919 in West Bengal, in 1920 in Bombay, Central Provinces and U.P. After this the governments of Assam, Orissa, Bihar, Travancore, Cochin, Punjab, Mysore, Baroda and Indore followed suit and passed village panchayat Acts.

Panchayats in Free India

But while the British rule lasted, these Acts did not succeed in reorganising village communities. When India became independent the national Government paid special attention to this aspect. Mahatma Gandhi used to say that freedom should start from the grassroot. Every village should be a small republic in which should be vested every right. Provision has been made in the Indian Constitution that the government will organise the village panchayats and give them all the rights so that they may be in a position to function as units of Swarajya. After the independence of the country the state governments have made efforts and established gram sabhas, independent village panchayats and Panchayati Adalats (Courts) in the villages of India.

STRUCTURE OF PANCHAYAT RAJ

Gram Sabha

The U.P. Panchayat Raj Act presents a general pattern of the structure of panchayat Raj in the country. According to this Act the structure of Panchayat Raj is as follows:

A Gram Sabha has been established in those villages whose population exceeds 1000. Where the population of the village falls short of this number several neighbouring villages have been combined to constitute gram sabhas. In case of villages more than three miles apart, they have the right to form individual sabhas even though their population may be less than 1000. All individuals who have the capability of being members and who are also the permanent residents of the area of the gram sabha will be its members. In order to be eligible for membership both males and females should have attained the age of 18 years. But lepers, insane people, bankrupts, those who have served a sentence and those who are government officials cannot be members of the gram sabha. If a person does not suffer from any of these disabilities and continues to reside within the area of the sabha, he can be its member as long as he lives. The gram sabha meets twice in a year, once at the Rabi crop and again at the Kharif crop. From among the members of the sabha one chairman and one vice-chairman are elected. Their term of office is three years. The gram sabha plans all the programmes for development. Members of the gram sabha can oust the chairman and the vice-chairman by a two-thirds majority. The gram panchayat actively wields the power of the gram sabha. It imposes taxes and incurs expenditure only if approved by the gram sabha.

Village Panchayats

The executive constituted by the Gram Sabha for the management of the village is called the Gram Panchayat. The chairman and vice-chairman of the Gram Sabha are also the chairman and vice-chairman of the village panchayat. The election of the members of the village panchayat and the chairman and vice-chairman of the Gram Sabha is carried out by the direct vote system on the basis of the cumulative vote system. The polling officer appointed by the District Magistrate counts the votes through the hands raised by the voters.

It will be the duty of every Gram Panchayat to arrange for the following things within the area of its authority as far as its funds allow:

1. Public roads. Constructing public roads, repairing them, maintaining them in good condition and arranging for their lighting and cleaning.

2. Arrangement for water. To contract public wells, tanks and wells for providing water for drinking, bathing and washing clothes; to improve and to maintain them in good condition and to keep control over the means of obtaining drinking water. To maintain the water drains and places for drinking water in good condition and to look after them.

3. Medical treatment and health. To arrange for the care of pregnant women and their delivery, to provide medical aid and to enforce medical measures to prevent infectious diseases and maintain sanitary conditions.

4. Education. To open schools for the primary education of boys and girls and to maintain them.

5. Statistics. To maintain a register of vital statistics and marriages and to acquire detailed information about such other items as animal census, population census, as are required by law.

6. Progress of agriculture and cottage industries. To assist in the progress of agriculture, business and cottage industries and to determine the place for collecting manure. To look after the Kaiser Hind forests and class two of the mountain ranges of Kumaun division, to provide public pastures, to maintain them and look after and arrange for them. Without infringing the 1938 U.P. Act for exhibitions to control those exhibitions, markets and fairs which are in their areas and which do not include those exhibitions, markets and fairs, organised by the government.

7. Control of buildings. To protect, to maintain in good condition and to look after those buildings placed under the protection of the gram panchayat and other such property and the building of the gram sabha. To lay down rules for the construction of new buildings and transformation or extension of the existing buildings.

8. Sanitation and security. To maintain security in the village. To make proper arrangement for the dead bodies of human beings and animals as well as other foul smelling things. In the event of fire, to help in putting out the fire and saving the lives and property of the people.

9. Administration. To prevent the placing, constructing or throwing of any improper object on public roads, public places and the property of the gram sabha. Arrangement for criminal and civil judicial procedure. To elect the panchas for the Panchayati Court.

10. Other activities. Besides these activities, the panchayat can carry out following activities for the benefit of the village — planting trees, improving the breed of animals, cleaning dirty ditches, organising volunteer groups, establishing cooperative societies, arranging for public radios, lectures and exhibitions etc.

Panchayati Adalat (Rural Court)

Generally, there is one Panchayati Adalat for four or five gram sabhas. In every panchayati adalat there are five representatives from each gram sabha. These representatives are elected by direct vote system. In this way there are twenty or twenty-five panchas. One Sarpanch is selected from among these panchas. His period of office lasts for three years. For every case, a committee of five is selected, of which the Sarpanch is the chairman. Of these five panchas one pancha necessarily belongs to that place from which the case comes. The judgment on the case is decided by the majority. The decisions of the panchayat court are final and no appeal can usually be made against them but in special cases one can appeal to the Munsif or Hakim Pargana.

Control of the Government

According to the U.P. Panchayati Raj Act the State government has the right to intervene in and control the activities of the panchayat through Panchayat Inspector, Panchayat Officer and Panchayats on behalf of the state. The compliance of the Panchayat Inspector with regard to the budgets of the gram sabha, panchayat and court is essential. The government can dissolve them, check their activities and stop any activity harmful to the public interest or likely to disturb peace.

Ideal Panchayat

In every tehsil of the state the U.P. government has established an ideal panchayat. The members of this ideal panchayat are members of the District Board, District Development Board and District Congress, Health Officer and Engineer, Commander of the P.R.D., Inspector of Schools and officials of the Information and Cooperative Department. The district panchayat officer is its secretary. These panchayats make much arrangement for health, education, progress of agriculture etc. as may be imitated by other panchayats of the tehsil and from which these latter ones may draw inspiration and guidance.

Similarities in Ancient and Modern Panchayats

The following similarities between ancient and modern panchayats become evident from a comparative study of them:

1. Election of members. Both in ancient and modern panchayats the members are elected.

2. Many similar duties. The duties for making arrangements for education, security, health, public construction, peace, protection of pastures, public roads and water etc., are found equally in ancient and modern panchayats.

3. Many similar rights. In the same way the ancient and modern panchayats also have parallel rights, *e.g.* right over the pastures of the village and other public lands, the right to decide cases of civil and criminal conflict, the right to spend money in the activities of public welfare etc.

4. Similar objectives. The objectives of both the modern and the ancient panchayats are similar. Both have been desirous of achieving peace, security, prosperity, happiness and self-dependence in the village.

5. Similar basis. The basis of the modern panchayats is community feeling, which was also the basis of the ancient panchayats. Both depend upon the co-operation of the villagers.

Difference between Ancient and Modern Panchayats

The following differences become evident in a comparative study of ancient and modern panchayats:

1. Intervention of the government. The major difference between the ancient and modern panchayats is in regard to the extent of government intervention. In ancient India the activity of the village panchayats was free of any government intervention and instead, it was the panchayats which sometimes contradicted the orders of the government. At their request the king would make a reduction in the tax and would even completely forego it. In the modern village panchayat the government officials do interfere. The panchayat inspector, panchayat officer and panchayat director are authorised to check the activities of the panchayats. Unless the panchayat inspector gives his consent, the budget for the gram sabha, Panchayati Adalat or gram panchayat cannot be passed or finalised. The government reserves the right of not only looking into the affairs of the panchayat but also the right to disband them altogether. The panchayat officer can prevent any action which is liable to disrupt peace or to injure the interests of the public. In this way the village panchayats of ancient India were completely independent whereas the modern panchayats are controlled by the government.

2. Right to collect state revenue. The second difference between the ancient and the modern panchayat is with regard to the collection of state revenue. Whereas the village panchayat of ancient India collected the state revenue and passed it on to the king, the modern panchayat performs no such function.

3. New duties. With the progress of time the modern village panchayats of modern India have been entrusted with some new duties like making arrangements for public radios, meetings, speeches, exhibitions, cooperative societies, self-dependent groups etc.

Panchayati Raj

Panchayati Raj, which was introduced in 1959, is a three-tier structure of local self-government at the village, block and district levels. However, the states are free to make changes in the structure to suit local conditions. All Panchayati Raj bodies are organically linked up. Special representation on these bodies is given to interests like backward classes, women and co-operative societies. Elected directly by and from among villagers, the Panchayats are responsible for agricultural production, rural industries, medical relief, maternity and child welfare, common grazing grounds, village roads, tanks and wells and maintenance of sanitation. In some places they also look after primary education, maintenance of village records and collection of land revenue.

Coverage

Panchayati Raj now covers all the states excepting Meghalaya, Nagaland and 24 out of 29 districts in Bihar. The institution of Village Panchayats exists in all the Union Territories except Lakshadweep, Mizoram and Pondicherry. Arunachal Pradesh has a three-tier system of Panchayati Raj.

There are, at present 2,17,319 Village Panchayats. In addition, there are 4,526 Panchayat Samitis and 297 Zila Parishads.

Activities

The panchayat, the co-operative and the school are the basic institutions at the village level for carrying out the programme of democratic decentralisation. The elected Panchayat is incharge of all development programmes in the area. The co-operative functions in the economic sphere. The village school, which is also a community centre, looks after educational, cultural, recreational and allied fields. Associate organisations, such as women and youth organisations, farmers' and artisans' associations functioning in their respective spheres are linked up with the panchayat in its development activities and are supported in turn by the Panchayat in their work.

With most of the country covered by Panchayati Raj, the emphasis now is on consolidation of these institutions and bringing into sharper focus their role in the rural development effort.

Finance

Panchayati Raj institutions have their own powers of taxation. They levy taxes on houses and some types of lands, fairs and festivals and sale of goods and impose octroi duties. They also build up remunerative community assets.

The powers and responsibilities of Panchayati Raj institutions are derived not only from the respective state legislations, but also from the procedures — administrative and financial — laid down by state governments to give effect in practice to the statutory provisions. Gujarat, Maharashtra and Tamil Nadu have invested their institutions with programme responsibilities over a wide and growing range of activities. Some other state governments, namely, Andhra Pradesh, Gujarat, Maharashtra and Rajasthan are trying to effect improvements in the system through high power committees.

Nyaya Panchyayats

For providing speedy and inexpensive system of justice to the villagers, Nyaya (Judicial) panchayats or village courts are functioning in some of the states.

Role of Panchayats in Rural Reconstruction

The reconstruction of rural life in India depends upon the village panchayats. The economic, social and political reconstruction of the village can be brought about only through the panchayat. Pt. Jawahar Lal Nehru rightly said that three factors are necessary for the solidarity of India: community development projects, superior village panchayats and good village cooperative societies. If these three are properly developed, the foundation of our country will be so strong and solid that it will face all kinds of political and economic catastrophes, fearless even of the atom bomb. The role of panchayats in rural reconstruction is as follows:

1. Decentralisation of administrative authority. The administrative power has been decentralised in India by the village panchayats and the village people obtained the right of self-government. These panchayats have been given the right to all kinds of reconstruction in the village. The government officials are anxious to give them assistance and suggestions.

2. Social reconstruction. The gram panchayat cultivates in the village people the habit of working together, owning responsibility for the various activities of the village, understanding things of public interest and living in co-operation and chastity. The Panchayati court teaches them to resolve misunderstanding through mutual negotiation. The panchayats did much towards increasing the communal feeling by decreasing the effects of urbanisation which had been manifested in the village youths in the form of a lack of responsibility, selfishness and impetuosity. The tendency to look upon the entire village as a family was born in the village people as a result of the communal contribution of labour in the construction of roads, lanes, drains, tanks, schools and panchayat houses. In this way, the panchayat has a major role in removing the irresponsibility which had been the outcome of the disintegration of the joint family and the removal of caste panchayats. By arranging for radio sets and lectures etc. the panchayats created awakening in the villages. Thousands of primary schools were opened in the villages to spread education among the village children. In order to educate the older members of the community, adult education centres and night schools were opened. Literacy weeks were celebrated, and resolute efforts were made to remove illiteracy from the country.

3. Economic reconstruction. The economic condition of the villages of India is far from satisfactory. The responsibility for this reconstruction rests with the panchayats. Before the panchayat courts were instituted much of the hard earned income of the villagers was unnecessarily spent on litigation. Even the most trifling quarrels were taken to the courts and it sometimes took months and even years before any decision was arrived at. The cases were always postponed while a major part of the villagers' earnings found its way into the pockets of the advocates, peons, and agents. In spite of all this, justice was at a premium because it was not particularly difficult to get false witnesses. Some villagers had even adopted art of giving false witnesses as a lucrative profession. During the British rule the rural cottage industries of India suffered a devastating blow.

Some cottage industries breathed their last because they could not compete with the cheaper foreign goods on the one hand while on the other did not get any assistance from the government. The industries of the village came to grief also as a result of urbanisation which resulted in the transportation of most rural commodities into the town and also a lack of demand for rural products. On account of this condition of the rural industries, the artisans came to work in the urban factories. The village panchayats provided a cheaper means of getting justice and also encouraged the rural industries. Thirty-three per cent of the cases are now settled by mutual negotiation and understanding. Bearing false witness has become impossible because the matter is now solved within the precincts of the village. Justice has been rendered free and expeditious. The village panchayat assists the cottage industries. It arranges for the sale of the produce by organising exhibitions, markets and fairs. It introduces new methods into the villages through radio and other modern innovations. As a result of the spread of education the people have come to know many new facts regarding production, sales etc. in cottage industries. Besides the cottage industries, the village panchayat Raj has also encouraged agriculture. India is predominantly an agricultural country. The reconstruction of the villages of the country is dependent upon agriculture. As a result of illiteracy the methods of farming, tools etc. have remained antique and the yield per acre is very low. The Panchayats have arranged for modern agricultural implements and cooperative societies for superior seeds, superior manure and lucrative sales etc. They have increased the knowledge of specific aspects of agriculture in the people through radio, exhibitions and speeches and got financial assistance from the government. Besides these activities towards economic reconstruction, the village panchayats have participated in the work of economic upliftment through many other activities like arranging for pastures for animals, plantation of forests for firewood and carving wood for architectural purposes and improving the breed of the cattle etc.

4. Political reconstruction. The panchayats created a social and national consciousness among the people of the villages in the modern individualistic and egoistic age. In the villages there are panchayat houses in which the people can congregate and discuss over the progress of the village. In thousands of villages Gandhi squares have been constructed so that the ideal of Gandhiji is always present and the patriotic feeling is awakened. At the same time the sense of self-dependence and co-operation is being developed in the villagers through the influence of the cooperative movement. A considerable number of roads, wells, schools etc. have been constructed with the help of voluntary labour. The elections of the panchayats and the panchayat courts educate the villagers in the democratic method. As a member of the panchayat, their ability of administration increased in arranging for the village. In spreading the democratic qualities of liberty, equality and fraternity the gram panchayats have played a major role.

Actually the Indian village panchayats are the centres of all kinds of reconstruction in the village. They provide the villagers with opportunity of meeting at one place, sitting together and thinking as well as working cooperatively, solving their quarrels mutually, arranging for their own village and making efforts for their mutual progress. The responsibility of making the villages ideal rests almost entirely with the panchayats. It is through their efforts that poverty, illiteracy, narrow-mindedness, disunity, frivolity and disorganisation can be removed from the village. Only these can make the villagers the ideal citizens of free India. Only these can give material shape to the dreams of Swarajya and Ram Rajya of Mahatma Gandhi, the Father of the Nation.

Suggestions for Improvement

The panchayats are making considerable progress in the direction of rural development but this progress cannot be said to be entirely satisfactory. It is true that the villages of India are in such a backward state that much time must lapse before they can be developed democratically, but nevertheless some suggestions may be given in this respect. The gram panchayat can mould the life of the rural community into the right channels by removing its defects and fulfilling the needs of the modern changing life. For this there is need for some change in the management and rights etc. of the panchayats, In this regard some suggestions follow.

1. Education of panchayat in administrative function. In the villages education is not very widespread. Many of the panchas elected by the villagers are only nominally literate. Most of them are completely ignorant of administration and justice. Most often the revered elders are elected who have not the least idea of modern changes, democratic thinking and scientific research. It is true that the officials of the government can assist them in this respect but then it no longer remains the administration of the panchas but rather becomes the administration of government employees, annihilating in the process the very ideal of panchayat. Thus, there is every need for educating the panchas in respect of administration, of doing justice, modern scientific research and democratic ways of thinking, etc. After being elected they should be educated in the training centres and their knowledge increased through the media of national and international exhibitions. They should be brought into contact with the leaders of the nation in order to remove and dispel their dogmatism. It is a matter of satisfaction to know that the state governments are working in this direction. Some time back many panchas came from Rajasthan to see the international agriculture fair in Delhi and gained inspiration by meeting the Prime Minister. Prior to this a trainload of villagers had travelled around the country. Much work is still needed in this direction.

2. Decrease in the intervention of the government. Beside educating the panchas the interference of government officials in the activities of the panchayats should be given full rights in matters of the village. The government officials sometimes intervene unnecessarily in the activities of the panchayat. This not only hinders the work of the panchayat but also detracts from the respect of the panchas and deprives them of their enthusiasm for the work. It is usually seen that the panchayat officer and panchayat inspector is given the most respected place when he adorns the meeting, while even the sarpanch occupies a position of comparatively lower status. This is very improper. The government official, no matter what his rank, is always a paid and hired servant of the public. He has the freedom of making use of all rights in serving the public but he will always be given a position lower than the representatives of the people in the government of the people and even more so when this representative is an honorary leader. The government officials should try to increase the respect of the panchas in the eyes of the villagers but this can happen only when there is adequate education among them and they understand their rights.

3. Control over formation of political parties. Democracy is the government of the people but there is just that much more opportunity for party politics. As in the state and central elections, the elections of the panchayats are also infested with the formation of parties on the basis of caste, class and other mean interests, and even after the election the activities of the panchayats are interrupted by this party politics. This defect is found not only in respect of panchayats but in all kinds of elections in the country. There is need for a strong revolution to root out this evil. Without this revolution the foundations of democracy can never be strengthened in India.

4. Increase in the rights of the panchayats. The rights of the panchayats should be increased for rural reconstruction. The panchayats should be given the right to demand exemption from payment of taxes in the event of any famine or disaster in agriculture.

QUESTIONS FOR EXERCISE

1. Write note on Village Panchayats.
2. Point out briefly the nature and function of Village Panchayats in ancient India.
3. Discuss the composition and function of Village Panchayats in modern India. Will they succeed in playing successfully the role assigned to them under Panchayati Raj?
4. Discuss the composition and functions of Village Panchayats in modern India. How far would they succeed in promoting community development programme?
5. Discuss the constitution and functions of the modern Village Panchayats in India and underline the social significance of the change.

23

RURAL ECONOMY

The rural life is generally, more or less, self-sufficient. The ordinary needs of villagers are met by resources available within the village. Not only are goods of daily need available in the village, but the villages have also enough and can easily spare, particularly, the farmer. A farmer is very resourceful and is able to manufacture minor items of daily use by himself; he prepares the rope strings for his bed and also strings it himself. A farmer is resourceful enough to do minor repairs; he can repair his agricultural implements. Thus, a farmer is able to deputise for ironsmith, potter, carpenter etc., as far as minor repairs are concerned.

Different Occupations in Rural Economy

However, not every farmer is so versatile as to do the jobs of carpenter, potter etc., himself nor are all jobs of the nature that they can be performed by the farmer. Therefore, we find professionals other than farmers in villages. Thus, we can see an example of division of labour at the village level. Broadly, following are the occupations generally found in villages:

(1) Priest, (2) Carpenter, (3) Ironsmith, (4) Potter, (5) Washerman (6) Barber, (7) Cobbler, (8) Shepherd, and (9) Milkman.

In the following paragraphs we shall discuss each of these professions in detail:

1. Priest. In village priests play an important role. In religious matters, their authority is undisputed. Marriages and naming ceremonies cannot be finalised without the presence of a priest. Priests belong to Brahmin caste. Some of them are doing the business of worship and performance of religious and secular ceremonies, they look after temples and live on charities; they also help performance of marriages, Mundan and Namakaran ceremonies. However, not all Brahmins In villages are engaged in priestly work; many of them are farmers. As regards livelihood of priests they are entitled to certain portion of charities received by the temple. Besides, on occasions of marriages and deaths, priests are fed by their jajmans (clients) and also given handsome presents in the form of cash, clothes and goods. Some educated priests do astrological work; they prepare horoscopes, declare auspicious moment for the performance of various ceremonies by the house-holder. It is they who determine the time and date of marriage, Mundan and Namakaran etc. The astrological business pays rich dividends. Though with the spread of modern education and its impact on villages, there is some decline in the value of priests yet their functions and importance are, by no means, finished; they continue to play an important role and enjoy respect in villages. The religious traditions are far too deep rooted in Indian life to give way to current waves of modernization.

2. Carpenter. In villages carpenters manufacture and repair the materials made of wood. They prepare beds, tables, chairs, ploughs etc. Many carpenters receive sometimes cash and sometimes grain from farmers. In this matter the practice is not uniform in all villages. The farmers are required to make available the wood required for the manufacture of agricultural implements. A carpenter is able to earn fifty rupees or more per day on an average. A skilled carpenter is quite well off.

3. Potter. In villages people are in the habit of using utensils made of clay. The cooking pots are usually made of clay. On festive occasions earthen glasses are used for drinking water and earthen saucers for curries etc. Halwais use earthen vessels for curd and milk. On the festival of Deepawali, earthen lamps are very much in vogue. Thus, potter is necessary for a village. In every village one or two potters can make easy living. Potters manufacture not only earthen vessels but toys also. These toys are decorated, polished and painted. Such attractive toys fetch good prices. The clay from which various utensils and toys are made is usually available from the village tank. The dry earth is mixed with water and made into dough by mixing with foot work. When dough is formed and appropriate consistency achieved, the dough is kept on the potter wheel. Now the potter revolves the wheel very fast with the help of a round stick and by manual manipulation produces fine utensils. Generally, people go to the house of the potter to buy utensils. However, some potters go to market particularly, on fair or festival to sell their wares. Normally, potters are paid in cash for their utensils and toys though sometimes they exchange their goods for food grains. Though making utensils is the normal job of potters, some of them do farming over and above their business of pottery.

4. Ironsmith. As the very name indicates, an ironsmith manufactures goods made of iron. In agriculture, there are quite a few implements which are made of Iron. It is the job of the village ironsmith to manufacture and repair these things. Ironsmiths also work as cycle repairmen and these days the use of bicycles in villages is growing very fast. Besides agricultural implements, ironsmiths make a number of things of daily household use. For example, ironsmith manufactures spoons, tongs, saucepans, knives, hammer, fork etc., which are required for common use in every household, and sells them in the marketplace or in fairs. For repair of agricultural implements, farmers give food grains to the ironsmith. A few ironsmiths used to farming along with their own job. This is so because the occupation of an ironsmith requires a small factory with all its paraphernalia. Therefore, it is not possible to cany on the job of an ironsmith as part time or side business. An average village usually has work enough for one or two ironsmiths.

5. Barber. In rural India, the barber occupies a place of pride. More important of his functions are outside of his normal routine of dressing hair and cutting beards. As major ceremonies in India in villages are not complete without the presence of the priest, so is the case of the barber. In his absence marriage etc., cannot be finalised. In majority of villages, the barber settles marriages even today. On Janmashtami he acts as an assistant to the priest. On funerals, too, he has some functions to perform. In Mundans (shaving head hair ceremonially) barber's role is primary. These are, of course, his social functions. His primary job is to dress hair, cut beards and act as a masseur. For his services barber is paid either in cash or in kind. The wife of the barber also performs successful functions on festive occasions.

6. Washerman. In village some families work as washermen (Dhobi). Their job is to wash and iron the soiled clothes against payment. It is not necessary that a washerman would wash clothes of his own village, he may bring these from other villages.

Many washermen live in villages on account of easy availability of water; but they collect clothes from towns. In past every washerman used to keep a donkey for the purpose of carrying clothes. These days, however, cycle is fast replacing the function of donkey.

7. Shepherd. As is clear from the name, shepherd is a person who looks after sheep. Shepherds keep cattle and live on the various products available from their animals. For example, by shearing the sheep they get wool and from goats they get milk. Shepherds are found generally in hill villages. Some shepherds weave blankets and sell them in markets or at fairs.

8. Cobbler. In villages scheduled castes or untouchable castes are known as Chamar. These persons manufacture and repair footwear. They buy leather from weekly market and as per order make shoes, sandals and chappals. Their products though unsophisticated, are durable. They sell their products against cash. Some Chamars also unskin the dead animals and prepare raw hides from it, some Chamars work as farm labour. Some of them work as sweepers. In Chamar families each and every member does work. Chamar children start working young. Usually they find work as farm labourers.

9. Milkmen. Ahirs keep and breed cattle. However, all those who keep milk animals are not Ahirs. In Northern India Ahirs are engaged in animal husbandry. They keep cows and buffaloes.

PROPERTY IN RURAL ECONOMY

In any economic structure property plays a pivotal role. This is so because property constitutes capital and the capital is the root of all business and profession. Without capital no business, occupation can be run or maintained. The tradition of keeping, maintaining and building of property is a long one.

Sacrosanct Character of Personal Property in India

In India the tradition of property is long and hoary. In the villages property has existed always in some form or the other. The property of the other person is considered sacrosanct and is protected by religious and cultural traditions. The usurper of property is regarded to be an offender and there is provision for punishment for offences against property. The state punishes anybody who takes away the property of others by force or mischief. Neither State nor society however try to take away the personal property. The fundamental principle generating respect for private property is the law of Karma. According to the law of Karma, the present economic stature, fortune or misfortune, is due to our past actions; and therefore to attempt to deprive one of one's property is tantamount to an interference with the law established by God. An Indian, being innately religious person, would not dare to do anything against the will of God. It is due to religious disposition of Indians that there is nothing like class struggle or civil war in India. At least it has not assumed an intensity witnessed in other countries.

However, along with an emphasis on the sanctity of private and personal property, Indian thinkers have also laid stress on the value of charity and almsgiving. It has been made a religious duty and moral obligation to give away a certain portion of one's wealth as charity permanently. Thus, in India people offer in charity cash, land, cattle, goods and other valuable things. A thing once offered as charity is not to be taken back. The goods offered in charity immediately become the property of a person or an institution to whom the donation is made and the donor ceases to have any proprietary rights over them. Thus, side by side with the institution of private property and an emphasis on its sanctity, the idea of compulsory charity has been a safety valve, on account of which, equitable distribution of wealth has been taking place and hoarding of wealth has not occurred in India. However, in due course of time the emphasis on charity has gradually reduced but the emphasis on the sanctity of personal property remains as before. This naturally leads to inequities of wealth distribution and the wealth gets hoarded in a few hands and in a particular class of persons. Generally, the economic condition of upper caste is good whereas that of lower castes poor and unsatisfactory. The condition of landless labour is miserable in particular. The wide economic disparities existing in Indian society make it vulnerable to totalitarianism. Therefore, Indian social thinkers are busy finding out ways and means to remove wide economic disparities and bring about better and equitable distribution of national wealth. The abolition of landlordism, that is, absentee ownership of land is a positive step in this direction. Almost all states have already abolished landlordism and taken away the surplus land and distributed it among landless labourers. The reformers like Vinoba Bhave tried to bring about better distribution of wealth by their movements like Bhoodan, Gramdan etc.

Mobile and Immobile Property

In Indian villages we find two kinds of property: mobile and immobile. In mobile property we include all kinds of goods which can be moved or taken to other places, that is which can be transported. This includes cash, cattle, weapons, ornaments, vehicles, bullock carts, furniture, tractors etc. In immobile properly are included items like land, houses etc., which are incapable of being transported.

In rural India almost every farmer keeps bullocks for ploughing etc. In the wealth of farmer, the value of bullocks is next only to land. If a farmer loses his bullocks he loses means of livelihood. Thus, the life of a farmer is unthinkable without a pair of bullocks. Of course, now-a-days with mechanization of farming the importance of bulls has lost its old value and importance. Besides bullocks, we find in houses of farmers at least one milch cattle. This usually is either a cow or a buffalo. Majority of farmers keep bullock carts. They use these as means of transportation or for carting agricultural produce to the market. Rural women of India are very fond of ornaments. Whether rich or poor they must adorn themselves with ornaments. Rich adorns themselves with ornaments made of gold or silver whereas poor use silver or alloy made ornaments. Among ornaments, necklace, pendants, bangles, rings, waist belts and various other adornments for thighs, ankles, hair are employed. Besides ornaments for adornment villagers like to collect silver coins etc. Owing to the non-availability of banks in villages some time back people liked to keep their wealth and gold coins buried underground. But. now the facility in the form of banks is gradually being available in villages. Besides cattle, land and ornaments, every home in the village has some furniture, agricultural implements, and some weapon. Among weapons, Lathi (a long, thick and round stick of bamboo or other wood) is most common. In order to make lathi more potent as a weapon, it is studded with a cap of brass or iron. A lathi with metallic top is a very effective weapon of attack; it is cheap as well as useful. In villages inhabited by tribals, bow and arrow is used as substitute for lathi. In villages of Punjab swords are common. Besides these *ballam* (stick with sharp pointed iron piece) and *pharsa* are also used. These days people in villages keep pistols, revolvers and guns. Because of the widespread availability of weapons, dacoities have increased. As mentioned earlier, village womenfolk are very fond of ornaments. Some women have their bodies tatooed. As regards clothing, various types of dresses are in vogue in different parts of India. In Punjab, Salwar, Kurta and Dupatta are used commonly by women. In villages of Uttar Pradesh women use lahanga (multifold petticoat) and blouse. In many parts of India ladies wear few clothings, bodice and petticoats are used. The use of undergarments is not common. Even bodices are sufficient to cover a small portion of breasts. The light and loose clothings are common because of warm climate and the need to breastfeed babies and also due to the fact that villagers usually answer calls of nature in open. There is difference in men-wear and women clothing. Men wear dhoti and kurta, women blouse and petticoat or salwar and kameez. Different castes use distinctive clothings.

The chief item of immobile property in villages is land. Besides land, most villagers possess their own houses. In villages the rental housing system is virtually non-existent. The upper castes possess fruit orchards besides land and houses. The various types of trees in orchards constitute the immobile properly. In the past most farmers were tenants of landlords and did not possess ownership of land tilled by them. But, however, with the abolition of zamindari most of the tenants have become owners of plots of land tilled by them. The housing in villages is according to one's status and ability, but everyone is an exclusive owner of his house and can make any alterations he likes in his house.

Means of Acquiring Property

In Indian villages there are many improper or unlawful ways of acquiring property. While studying the question of property in Indian rural economy it is imperative to study the ways of acquiring property. The chief means of acquiring property are the following:

1. By inheritance. The most important means of acquiring property is inheritance. After the death of the father, sons and daughters inherit his property. Both mobile and immobile property is inherited by children unless a man has left a testament regarding disposal of his property. If the succession takes place within a joint family the property remains as it is and is not divided or split. If the successors to property put up their separate family units, then naturally the property is split up. Both mobile and immobile property is divided among successors. In the past only sons were legal heirs to father's property, but now-a-days the widow of dead man and his daughters are also among the heirs. If a man dies and he had no child, the entire property goes to his widowed wife and in case of her death, to the next kin. Thus, generally, land, houses and orchards are acquired by inheritance.

2. By marriage. Another main means of acquiring property is marriage. In India the bridegroom gets plenty of cash, furniture etc. in dowry. The dowry is usually in the form of mobile property though the cases of gift of immobile property are there. This is, of courses, quite uncommon. If, per chance, the bride happens to be the only daughter of her parents and they have no son, in the event of their death both mobile and immobile property comes to the daughter.

3. Through interest. In rural India usury is still quite common. Usually the moneylenders charge exorbitant rate of interest from illiterate farmers and mortgage their land against the money paid. The rate of interest is so exorbitant that what to say of the principal, the poor farmer fails to pay off even the interest and, as a consequence, loses his land which he had mortgaged. Thus through interest money-lenders in villages acquire huge wealth. Now, with the enactment of new legislation the rate of interest is well under control.

4. By labour or work. The most important means of acquiring wealth, of course, is labour and work. Against labour and work people get paid and by saving part of their wages, gradually acquire wealth. Thus, farm labour and artisans in villages earn their livelihood by hard work or labour.

5. By selling goods. Another means of acquiring wealth is the sale of commodities and goods. The farmers earn wealth by the sale of their agricultural produce, dairy products and fruits if they have orchards. The ironsmith sells iron wares the carpenter sells furniture and potter sells clay pots. Thus, all of them earn wealth by the sale of goods. Ahir earns wealth by the sale of milk. The shepherds, besides selling milk, sell wool and blankets woven of wool. The weaver weaves cloth and sells it. Thus, the producers of various types of commodities and goods earn cash by selling them.

6. By purchase. The purchase of land, orchards or other goods is also a means of acquiring wealth. When someone has plenty of cash, he buys land etc. The cattle, the bullock carts, the tractors, furniture, agricultural implements, weaponry etc., are bought from the market against cash and thus these become the property of the purchaser. Thus, most of goods found in the homes of farmers are acquired by purhase. The same is the case with persons of other professions.

7. By donation or charity. Some persons, Brahmins, barbers etc., acquire property by acceptance of donation or charity. After the death of an elderly person Brahmins in villages are given cash, clothes, beddings, utensils etc. It is believed that the charity given in this world is indirectly received by the soul of the dead person. In this charity a certain proportion is reserved for the barber. Sometimes Brahmins are given land and trees in charity. Not only on the occasion of death but on birth and marriages etc. Brahmins are given cash and goods as donation. On particular occasions of marriage not only Brahmin but barber also gains economically. Besides Brahmins and barbers, beggars etc. are also given charity.

8. By reclaiming wasteland. The wasteland is no man's property and nobody likes to buy it. But if someone, by hard work and labour, clears the wasteland and reclaims it for agriculture, he automatically becomes its owner. Even government has encouraged this tendency. In this way, many persons have acquired ownership of land.

The above means of acquiring wealth and property are valid and lawful. Besides these, there are many unlawful and invalid means of acquiring wealth and property. The rich and powerful persons in villages usurp the property of others by illegal and deceitful means. They do it by means of deception, force, mischief, seduction etc. Many a villager is a professional dacoit and naturally his acquisitions are unlawful. The persons who acquire wealth by deceit and force not only commit illegal acts, but they are looked down upon by society as well.

INDIAN RURAL AGRICULTURAL SYSTEM

India is a predominantly agricultural country, the majority of Indians are engaged in agriculture and 83% of Indian population lives in villages. In rural economy agriculture occupies a place of pride. Though not all villagers are engaged in agriculture, yet almost all the persons living in the village are, in one way or the other, connected with agriculture. Thus, agriculture can be considered to be the pivot or focus of rural economy. Apart from persons exclusively engaged is agriculture there are many others who are, somehow, connected with agriculture as a side-business. Thus, dhobi, barber, potter, shepherd etc. do some agriculture apart from their main professions. Besides farmers, there is farm labour who work on the land under other's ownership and who get paid in cash or kind for their services. Before abolition of Zamindari system a sizable number of farmers did not own their land but used to work on the land of Zamindars who were entitled to a major share of crop. After the abolition of Zamindari, the tillers became owners of their land which was being tilled by them. However, the system of farm labourers still exists in Indian villages.

India is a vast country. We find various types of soils, irrigation systems, vegetation and rainfall patterns. On account of this variety, there is no uniform agriculture system or pattern. On the contrary, a wide variety of agriculture systems or patterns are to be found here. 'The sowing and harvesting times are not uniform in India; there are many regional differences. Moreover, in different parts of India, different crops are mainly grown. For example, in Bengal, rice is the main crop but in Punjab, wheat is the main crop and rice is subsidiary. In Uttar Pradesh wheat and sugarcane are the chief crops. In villages all over India vegetables are grown along with main crops. Among vegetables, potatoes, tomatoes, onions, carrots, radishes, peas, beans, mustard, spinach, grams, are the important vegetables grown. In order to study the rural agriculture system we must study it region-wise. However, we do find certain uniformities or general features in all regions. The bases of all-India agricultural patterns are as follows:

(1) Kind and Fertility of land,
(2) Irrigation,
(3) Manures,
(4) Instruments of Agriculture,
(5) Main crops,
(6) Sale of products,
(7) Others.

1. Kind and fertility of land. In different regions of India we find considerable difference and variations in regard to soils, their kinds and fertility very considerably. In the plains of Ganga-Yamuna the soil is alluvial, transported and deposited by rivers and floods. Such soil is extremely fertile. In the plateau of Madhya Pradesh and Maharashtra black soil is amply found. The villages are full of greenery and vegetation. In north, villages are closely situated because most of the land in north India is under cultivation. Owing to paucity of water, large tracts of land in Rajasthan are desert and intractable to agricultural operations. Wherever there is cultivation in Rajasthan, conditions are not as favourable as in north India. The black soil is eminently suitable for growing cotton. There are also large tracts of barren land in India. The barren land is used as pasture for grazing cattle.

2. Irrigation. The chief source of irrigation in India is tube wells or wells operated by bullocks. This is so because the network of canals is not sufficiently widespread and vast areas have no canals. Besides, even where the canal water is available there are seasons when enough water is either not released or becomes so turbid and muddy as to be unusable. Therefore, tube wells remain as the only source of irrigation in most parts of India. The government is trying to help digging of tube wells. Irrigation with tube wells is easy and good. The only thing one is required to do is to make proper lanes and by-lanes so that water can be carried to fields and when a field is sufficiently irrigated the flow of water can be stopped by mudding the mouth and cutting a fresh channel for a different field. The irrigation by canals is also done in the above manner but where there is difference in the level of canal and the level of fields, special means are to be employed. The watering device used for water is known as *Dhenkali* or *Pur*. This consists of bamboo, the sides of which are tied to a large iron bucket and big load. One side is fitted with load while the other is fitted with special type of bucket. The bamboo is not adjusted on a wooden anvil in such a way that it can be moved on either side. By pressing down the bucket side the water gets filled in the bucket. The moment it is left free the bucket water is lifted under pressure of the other side and the water is thrown to fields. For operating this water device (*dhenkali*) two or three hands are needed. In irrigation through wells *dhenkali*-like mechanism is used. This is known as *Pur*. *Pur* is big leather bag tied to a rope. The other side of the rope is tied to one or two bullocks. The rope is needed through a *Ghirre* (wheel) fitted on the well. As the bullock goes near the well the rope is drawn in the well and the bucket falls into the well and water is filled in it. It contains 20 to 30 kilograms of water. As the bullocks go away from the well the water bucket is lifted and its water is released. As soon as bucket reaches the top of the well the bucket is tilted and all water runs out of it. For irrigation from wells, a mechanical device known as Rahat is employed. By this large quantity of water is drawn from well within a short time. However, inasmuch as Rahat is costly, it can be used only by rich farmers. The poor farmers are unable to use any costly devices for irrigation and have to content themselves to drawing water from the well by their own hands. Though government has done a lot to improve irrigation facilities by laying of canals and digging of tube wells, the overall position with regard to irrigation is far from satisfactory. All said and done, the Indian farmer is fully dependent on rain and weather gods. The artificial means of irrigation are not sufficient. Therefore, whenever there is failure of rains, the corps wither. The government is doing its utmost to improve the irrigation facilities; but dependency on weather is an inescapable fact of rural Indian life.

3. Manure. As yet Indian agriculture is, by and large, unmechanized, employing traditional means of ploughing, harvesting etc. The Indian farmer has not much benefitted by science and technology. This sad state of affairs is due to illiteracy and poverty of the Indian farmer. Most of the farmers use traditional pits and deposit in it all refuse. In villages of Northern India manures and chemical fertilizers are either not known to them or are beyond their reach, The villagers dig manure pits and compost manure is used. However, in most villages sufficient manure is not available and therefore these are not well-nourished with manure. The lack of good and adequate manuring is due to a number of reasons. Firstly, formers are not well informed about chemicals fertilizer and secondly, cow dung is used as fuel. Now-a-days, however, the use of chemical fertilizers, insecticides, pesticides and the use of cow dung for manuring purposes is being stressed on government publicity and propaganda and through television and radio. Some progress has already been made in this direction. This is evident from the increasing demand for chemical fertilizers, insecticides and pesticides these days. This shows that the Indian farmer is quite open to new ideas and can be easily taught modern science and technology of agriculture. The government has set up a number of agricultural universities and it has been found that the farmers living in the vicinity of the universities and visiting consultancy and training centres operated by the universities are greatly benefited, they achieve best results.

4. Agricultural implements. The villages which are in the vicinity of the towns are well supplied with modern tools of agriculture. This is because the villagers frequently visit towns where they learn about latest additions to the repertoire of agricultural implements. Moreover, due to proximity of towns it is possible to get these implements repaired if these go out of order or break down. However, even today most of the villages are far removed from towns and during rains they become virtually inaccessible. In these villages even now traditional agricultural implements are used. The plough is the mainstay of traditional agriculture. The ploughs in India are driven by bullocks. The use of horses for ploughing is very uncommon in India. There are two types of ploughs — Nagara and Lotana ploughs. These ploughs can dig up land three to four inches only. This is not conducive to good yield. After digging up land, a flat plank of wood driven by bullocks is used for levelling up the earth. Two persons stand on this plank so that the load crushes big clods. The sowing is usually done with hand. For proper interculture hose etc. are used. The harvesting is done by cutter, usually sharp sickle. Now-a-days, however, agricultural technology has advanced so much that there are harvesting combines which mechanically do all the work connected with harvest, the cutting, thrashing and sifting.

5. Main crops. In India, due to the vastness and variety of land the main crops are not same for every region. In northern India, Rabi and Kharif are two main crops. In Kharif season, the crops grown are paddy, jawar, pulses, maize, etc. In Rabi season, the crops grown are wheat, peas, gram, mustard and flex. The Rabi crop is harvested in April, therefore, it is also called April crop. Besides Rabi and Kharif some other crops are also grown. In Uttar Pradesh sugarcane is an important crop.

6. Sale of products. Mere good yield is no guarantee that the farmer would make good money. It is not necessary that the farmer will get sufficient payment for his produce, particularly, the fanners of villages which are far off from towns, usually do not get enough for their produce. The farmers living in villages which are in the vicinity of towns are much better off. These farmers cart their produce to town markets and sell them for good amount whereas the farmers of remote villages have to spend money and time to bring produce to market. Therefore, they are in poor condition. The agents of Banias who go to remote villages buy the produce at throw away prices. In order to cater to the needs of small and remote villages, weekly markets are held in nearly all bigger villages in which iron-smiths, carpenters, potters and farmers bring their goods for sale. Sometimes big markets are held, where large scale sales and purchases are made. In these markets traders and buyers assemble from far and near. In these markets, various cattle are also brought for sale. From these trade fairs, farmers buy goods after selling their produce.

7. Measurements. Though the government has long since introduced metric weights and measurements, in villages old weights still continue to be used. The government is trying hard to propagate the use of metric measurements. In villages there are two kinds of measurements — Kuchcha and Pucca measurements. However, now only scientific metric measurements are used.

INDEBTEDNESS

The moneylender holds an important place in the rural economic system. In most areas the term sahukar is used for a person who loans money although other words, peculiar to their place of origin are also used to designate the same person. In ancient India, the system of lending money and taking loans was not based on laws. This was based on the personal and conventional relationships between the two parties. However, both debtor and the creditor had good mutual relations. With the advent of English people when new laws were made for agreements the creditors got the opportunity of getting rich quickly. Now the relations between the debtor and the creditor were no longer personal. Their basis now became law and money.

Although the condition of the cultivators in ancient India was quite good, their financial condition became deplorable in the English period and has continued to be such to the present day. The cultivator in India is generally poor. But, at the same time he wants to maintain his dignity in the social and communal circles, for which purpose he often does not hesitate in spending far beyond his means on such occasions like marriage. Thus, indebtedness is omnipresent in India. In all the states of the country there are large number of people who have been under the burden of debt for many generations. Further, the modes of expenditure are also increasing. With every increase in the population the pressure on the land is proportionately increasing. Usually, the village people take loans when they marry off their daughters and not many of them are able to repay this loan. The condition of the cultivator of India has further deteriorated under the impact of some very serious famines in the country not so very long ago. These famines had the effect of placing the unfortunate agriculturist in an even more unfortunate plight as far as his debt was concerned.

Problem of indebtedness

Loans used to be forwarded on the basis of individual relationships. Now the loans have come to be given or taken against secured land. Both the Indian Agreement Act as swell the Civil Procedure Code worked towards the detriment of the debtor and the enhancement of the creditor. These give the creditor not only the right of taking possession of the secured land in the event of the debtor's failing to repay the loan but also the authority to take possession of the domestic articles and animals of the debtor. He could prosecute them and get them imprisoned. The Registration of Documents Act of 1864 and the Transfer of Property Act of 1882 both helped to increase the number of secured immovables in the form of land. The creditors grew continuously richer while lands of the debtors passed into their hands. The number of creditors grew and so did the quantity of loan. According to Sir Edward Maclagan, the total rural debt in British India in 1911 was of the order of rupees 300 crores. In 1924 Sir M.L. Derling estimated it at rupees 600 crores. In 1930 this debt was of the order of rupees 900 crores according to the estimates of the I.C.B.I. Committee. In 1938, total debt in British India was 1800 crores of rupees according to S.E.V.S. Manium. It is evident from these statistics that the extent of loan increased sixfold between 1911 and 1938 in British India. Since the latter date this indebtedness has continued to increase.

Causes of Indebtedness

This increase in the indebtedness has been attributed to a multitude of causes, the major of which are the following:

1. Absence of necessary laws. The greatest cause of indebtedness was the absence of laws for protecting the debtor. Due to his special superior status the moneylender would not let the poor man slip out of his clutches once he had got hold of him. The cultivator in the village became so involved in it, once he had taken a loan, that the burden of debt increased continuously.

2. Neglect by the government. The British government did not make much efforts to protect the ingenuous farmer from the evil designs of the moneylender, although many people drew the attention of the government towards this problem.

3. Economic upheaval. As a result of the economic disturbance of 1929 the condition of the farmers deteriorated further and they could not prevent themselves from sinking further into debt.

4. Extravagance. Although most of the people are poor in the rural area, they do not hesitate in availing themselves of the facilities and taking loans to spend upon such occasions as marriage or the observance of the death anniversaries, this, obviously, tends to increase the burden of loan.

5. Facility in taking loans. The facility with which loans could be taken also helped to increase the tendency of taking a loan. Often the moneylender of the village would encourage the villager to take loans by talking suave.

6. Tricks of the moneylender. The tricks of the moneylender had also much to do with the indebtedness in India. Often the moneylender would charge such a high rate of interest that the debtor could not easily pay it. While providing the loaned money, moneylender would take away the amount of interest at the start. Consequently, the farmer receives a very small amount of money. In a few years the loan would be doubled and trebled, with the result that, principal aside, it became difficult to pay even the interest. As a result of the religious tendency most of the rural people felt it necessary to pay even the loans incurred by their predecessors. Consequently, the loan continued through generations. The illiteracy of the village farmer is also a major cause of his indebtedness. Taking unfair advantage of his ignorance, the unscrupulous moneylenders would give one amount to the farmer while he wrote a different one upon the paper. This malpractice has been known to go to the extent of the former being compelled to put his thumb impression upon a blank paper which would later be used for divesting the poor creature of his entire stock of belongings. In the Indian village, the moneylender usually belonged to the higher caste. Thus, the debtors did not have the strength to oppose him to his high social status, which was used to keep the poor in their places.

Result of Indebtedness

Many results of increasing indebtedness are manifest in the villages of India. Some of the major consequences are the following:

1. Slavery. The worst result of indebtedness was seen in an increase in the number of landless labourers. As has been mentioned earlier, the moneylenders took advantage of the ignorance and helplessness of the farmers to dispossess them of their land. Consequently, the former became a labourer and started ploughing his own land for the moneylender. Sometimes the debtor had to serve the moneylender in return for his loan, in which situation his condition was no better than that of a servant. In some villages, it has been a custom that the parents take a loan from the moneylender and send their children to work for the moneylender as unpaid employees. The condition of these children was worse than slaves even. In this way the system of debt has indirectly compelled thousands of people in the villages to spend the life of slaves.

2. Increase in poverty. The most explicit result of indebtedness is the increase in the poverty of the people because once he becomes entangled in debt he remains poor no matter how much he may exert himself. It was no easy matter for them to repay their loans, so that, in some families, the lives of generations were spoiled in repaying the debts incurred by their ancestors.

3. Deterioration of agriculture. As a result of indebtedness the condition of agriculture also deteriorated because most of the farmers had to work on their moneylenders' land as servants. Obviously, they could not take that interest in their work which they would have taken had they owned the land.

4. Low standard of health. The farmer, burdened with a heavy debt, was continuously growing weaker because he was beset with the problem of repaying it. Many people tried to repay the loan by working extremely hard but when they foiled to do so even after the maximum of efforts they sank into a premature decrepitude. In this way, indebtedness is one cause of the foil in the level of health in the Indian villagers.

Suggestions for Removing Indebtedness

Many suggestions have been put forward for eradicating indebtedness from the village. Of them the major ones are the following:

1. Government loan at low interest. The government should make arrangements for giving loans to the farmers at low rate of interest.

2. Communal societies and banks. In order to arrange for loans in the villages, communal societies and banks should be created.

3. Arrangement for declaration of bankruptcy. There should be some arrangement by which the farmer can be declared bankrupt when the loan increases beyond his capacity to repay it.

4. Laws for preventing dispossession of land. Laws should be laid down which may prevent the moneylenders from taking possession of the farmer's land.

5. Control over the rate of interest. The maximum rate of interest in the village should be determined and punishment should be meted out to anyone charging a higher rate of interest.

6. Checking the accounts of the moneylenders. The government should carry out a check of the registers and accounts of the moneylenders from time to time and punish the moneylender if any discrepancy is found.

7. Registration and licensing of moneylenders. Only the registered and licenced moneylenders should have the right to provide loans.

Efforts for the Prevention of Indebtedness

In 1875 very large number of people forced individuals of the moneylender class in 45 villages of Poona district and 22 villages of Ahmednagar district, to hand over the papers of the cultivators which were then publicly put to fire in the villages. The Commission which was appointed to look into these disturbances recommended that laws should be made to prevent the farmers from being dispossessed of their land. On the basis of the recommendation of this Commission the Deccan Agriculturist Act was passed in 1889, which was the first government step towards improving the condition of the debtors. Following this, Acts were then passed at intervals for improvement in this direction besides a number of commissions which were appointed. As we have had the occasion to mention earlier, both the Registration of Documents Act of 1864 and the Transfer of Property Act of 1882 worked in favour of the moneylenders who embarked on large-scale exploitation of the poor debtors. In 1874 in Punjab alone ten lakh acres of land was secured and by 1891 this had risen to forty lakh acres. Between 1875 and 1893 moneylenders in the different parts of Punjab Province took possession of II lakh 89 thousand acres of land. In order to put a stop to this exploitation, the Punjab Land Alienation Act was passed in 1900. Similar steps were taken in 1903 in U.P., in 1904 in the Northwest Frontier Province and in 1916 in the Central Provinces. According to these Acts the secured land could remain with the moneylender only for a short period after which it was to be necessarily returned to the farmer. These Acts gave the Collector and the Deputy Commissioner the right to negotiate a settlement between the moneylender and the debtors. But these provisions did not go a long way in achieving any material success because the moneylender had the right to dispossess the cultivator of his land. Thus, these laws did not solve the problem of indebtedness' in any of the provinces.

Besides these Acts, the government also made certain laws for checking the business of the moneylenders. The Accounts Regulation Act was passed in 1930 in Punjab. Following this, rules were made in every province by which the moneylender was obliged to keep an account of his business. It was provided that these accounts could be checked at any time and the moneylender was to be held responsible, if no such accounts were kept and any unwritten business was not to be considered official and was to be disregarded. According to these Acts the moneylenders had to keep the debtor informed about the state of his debt and also to issue a receipt for every amount received. But even these Acts did not prove particularly beneficial since the illiterate farmer could not make use of them and the moneylender was apt to solve his problems without having recourse to judicial procedure.

Many laws were also enacted for the purpose of limiting the rate of interest. But the moneylenders used to find out some loophole in these laws to crawl through in order to continue their nefarious activities. The notable feature of efforts in this direction is the Agricultural Reliefs Act of 1934. In many provinces the respective governments tried to finalize the rate of interest but it did not bring any positive results.

The government also took steps to see that the moneylenders in Punjab were registered. In the laws which provided for this registration the term moneylender was not clearly defined. This too served to obstruct the improvement in the existing situation. Debt Conciliation Acts were passed in many provinces for the mutual resolution of loans. Such Acts were passed in 1933 in the Central Provinces, in 1934 in Punjab and in 1936 in Assam, Bengal and Madras as well as in some other Indian states. These Acts provided for the appointment of Conciliation Boards for achieving settlement between the moneylenders and the debtors. Upon disregarding the decisions of the said boards the moneylenders had to suffer numerous disabilities. This system proved beneficial to the farmers. In 1940, in Punjab alone 26 thousand applications for the settlement of loans were disposed of. Of the amount, rupees 91.45 lakh represented the actual debt, of which the debtors were prepared to pay rupees 35.85 lakhs. In the same way these Acts also had good results in other provinces as well. But, this system of settlement did not include all kinds of loans so that in many cases advantage could not be derived from it. Besides, some cases of corruption in the Boards also came to light. In some Boards completely unlettered people had been included, who were absolutely incapable of discharging their duties.

Defects in the Preventive Measures

Besides the above Acts, the provincial governments passed many laws for the essential reduction in the debt as well as for a moratorium. These Acts were called the Debt Relief Acts. By means of these statutory measures the government sought to control the rate of interest and improve the conditions of the debtors in a number of ways. There is no need for a defiled description of all these Acts. It can briefly be said that due to a number of causes all these Acts did not prove as beneficial as they should have been. The major causes among them are the poverty, ignorance and illiteracy of the farmer which prevented him from taking full advantage of these Acts. Secondly, even the government did not help and protect the debtor adequately enough. Thirdly, these Acts contained such defects that the moneylenders managed to carry on their activities without being endangered. Finally, it may be said that the laws made for solving the problem of indebtedness have proved completely inadequate. They undoubtedly did achieve a certain degree of improvement but they could not put an end to the immoral and corrupt practices of the moneylender. Even though they have helped the cultivator at some places, the moneylender has again managed to get into control of the situation because the cultivator is compelled to come back to the moneylender and the government has not provided arrangements by which the farmer can avail himself of loan.

Since the country attained independence, the solution of the problem of indebtedness has been receiving the special attention of the Indian government. For this Co-operative Credit Societies Act has been passed. According to this Act co-operative credit societies were established in the villages of India. Besides these societies, State and Central Co-operative Banks have been established. In order to supply grains to the cultivator grain banks have been established. Land mortgage banks have been established in order to provide the farmer with long term loans.

QUESTIONS FOR EXERCISE

1. Describe important occupations in rural economy.
2. Write short note on Property in rural economy.
3. What are the means of acquiring property in rural society?
4. Write short note on Indian Rural Agricultural System.
5. Discuss the problem of Indebtedness in Indian villages.

24

RURAL HOUSING

Some people are under the impression that the problem of housing is peculiar to big cities and towns and that it is non-existent in villages. However, this is not true. As a matter of fact if we undertake a survey of housing conditions in village we shall find that the facilities of housing and accommodation are much worse in villages than in towns. In small towns the problem of housing has the form of less space and accommodation, that is, the number of houses is disproportionately low in relation to needs. But whatever houses are available they are of good quality. In industrial towns the problem of housing is in the form of growing slums and the need is of the removal of slums and building good houses. But in villages the problem of housing is not that no houses are available or that the pressure on space is undue but that whatever houses are available are unhygienic and their construction is haphazard and unsatisfactory. The Indian farmer is extremely poor. He does not work round the year. Consequently the daily income of an average farmer is extremely poor. Therefore, it is natural that they have no reserves or spare funds to build good houses. Whatever housing they have is a makeshift; most of the houses are Kacha and the facility of good drainage system is undreamt of in the context of rural housing and planning. Besides poverty, another reason for inadequate and bad housing in villages is illiteracy and superstitious outlook of the villagers. In view of the easy availability of land and cheap housing raw material, it is more near the truth to say that the chief cause of bad rural housing is illiteracy and not poverty. For example, it is not very costly to have windows and ventilators in a room but most of rural houses are ill-ventilated, the reason for this is not lack of funds but lack of knowledge that such a thing is necessary or worthwhile. It has been observed that even when owing to official pressure or persuasion windows are dug out, they are thickly covered at the first available opportunity. Having become used to living in dark dingy houses, they find bright and ventilated houses unnatural. Many superstitions are responsible for bad housing in villages. It is believed for example, that if a householder lives in the vicinity of cattles they are better looked after and are more productive. As a consequence of this we find cattles and human beings coexisting in same rooms.

According to 1971 census there is a shortage of 1.16 crores house units in rural India. A recent study by the National Buildings Organisation showed that on the eve of the Fifth Plan there was a shortage of 1.18 housing units in rural areas.

Kinds of Houses in Villages

The houses available in the villages can be divided into the following classes:

1. High quality houses. In villages, we find three types of houses which may be called high, medium and low quality houses. The high quality houses are made generally of kiln bricks. These contain separate provision for animal and human quarters though these may be under the same roof. Even where there is separate quarters we find that some persons prefer to sleep with animals under the belief that this way cattles yield more. The high quality houses have three or more rooms and a courtyard. However, the rooms are not well ventilated. Though, these houses are better than other houses they are not properly built and are unhygienic; the drainage is non-existent or poor and this breeds disease. In some big villages, however, we do find some Havelies (big houses belonging to very rich) which are ventilated and correspond to modern scientific standards.

2. Medium quality houses. The medium quality houses are mud houses. Their walls are of mud and roofs of tiles and thatch. Usually, these have one or two rooms and a small courtyard. These houses are usually dingy and unventilated; they have neither windows nor ventilators. The drainage is poor. Their surroundings are full of dirt, filth and slush. These houses have no latrines. This is due to the villager's habit of going to fields for evacuation. As children and the sick cannot go to fields they defile the lanes. There is no proper scavenging system. Particularly in rainy season most of the villages reek with filthy bad odours. As an average villager is illiterate and ill-educated he does not comprehend the need and importance of cleanliness and hygiene. Besides lack of latrines most of the houses do not have outlets for smoke to go out. This results in pollution and bad environment. As a consequence disease is rampant in villages.

3. Low quality houses. The labourers and other indigent persons in villages live in poor low quality houses. As a matter of fact, these houses are so inferior that it is paradoxical to call them houses. These consist merely of muddy walls covered with thatched roof; these are devoid of any drainage facility. These have no separate quarters for bathroom, latrine etc. During rainy season these houses are virtually unusable. They leak and walls cave in. After heavy rains and storm these are liable to be reduced to shambles. There is merely one room which serves purposes of store, bedroom, kitchen etc. Actually, these houses are slums of villages. The poets who sing of rural charms have probably not spent much time in Indian villages.

Housing in Villages

According to 1951 census, there were 5,40,56,388 residential houses in villages. Of these about 5 crores needed radical alterations or even to be pulled down. After the commencement of planning, government has paid some attention towards the problem of rural housing. In October, 1957 a Rural Housing Board was created whose business was to look after the housing schemes launched in about 5,000 selected villages. These villages were selected under Community Development Scheme. The schemes were based on self-reliance and self-sufficiency. For rural housing two-thirds of actual amount spent or 2000 rupees whichever may be less were to be given as loan for building modern houses. The same government decided to give free consultancy service in this regard. Excepting Gujarat, J & K all other states set-up Rural Housing cells. About 3700 villages were chosen for this purpose. In December 1960 up to 1600 villages had been surveyed. With the growing political influence of villages on Indian politics, it is natural that the development of villager should receive active and serious attention of the Government. Till 1961 State Government had constructed 15000 rural houses at the expense of more than 218 crores. According to India 1975, "The Village Housing Projects scheme provides for the grant of loan for construction of houses by villagers to the credit of 80 per cent of the cost of construction subject to a maximum of Rs. 4000.00 and also for providing streets and drains to improve the environmental hygiene of the village. Upto 30 April, 1974, 53697 houses, about 118 km of streets and 138 km of drains had been completed."

Besides the above mentioned efforts, the Government of India has prepared a Draft Manual which contains maps for suitable houses in villages. This manual contains valuable practical advice on all building matters. Besides, advice is given regarding ovens. After a review of the state housing policy by the State Ministers of Housing at two conferences held in 1973 and 1974, it was recommended that rural development should be considered as a compact whole, including housing, water supply, link roads, education, health, sanitation, employment and recreation and all-round development of the rural areas should be taken up. A separate Rural Finance Corporation may be established to enable taking up of construction of rural housing and to attend to other rural development programmes.

At present five rural housing wings are functioning under National Buildings Organisation (NBO) for research at Anand, Bangalore, Calcutta, Chandigarh and New Delhi. Ten states namely, Bihar; Gujarat, Karnataka, Kerala, Maharashtra, Orissa, Punjab, Tamil Nadu, Uttar Pradesh and West Bengal have adopted legislative measures to confer homestead rights on landless workers who are in occupation of such sites in rural areas. From the commencement of the Fifth Plan, the above scheme has been transferred to the state sector. State governments can now scrutinize and sanction the projects, in accordance with the provisions of the scheme, in the respective jurisdiction as one of the minimum needs programme. In the Fifth Plan, Rs. 108.16 crores have been set aside, under the Minimum Needs Programmes for annual plan allocation to the states, for provision of house sites to landless workers in rural areas. It is expected that about 40 lakh landless workers will be provided with free house sites during the Fifth Plan period.

Conclusion

The above efforts of various governmental agencies are quite laudable. In this connection, a full scale briefing of Panchayats has helped somewhat. Whenever Panchayats have taken interest in the matter there has been some improvement. The villagers are quite enthused in these programmes and have co-operated whole-heartedly. But, however, even Panchayats cannot accomplish much. The best means of rural reform and development is indirect, that is by spreading education. The primary need is to do a good deal of educational propaganda for the necessity of having good and clean houses. Without removing poverty and imparting education the problem of rural housing is not likely to be solved. Unless villagers realize the need of good houses and have the wherewithal to realize their needs and wants, a permanent solution of rural housing is not possible. However, whatever little effort is being made in this direction is welcome and the primary need is to intensify it.

QUESTION FOR EXERCISE

1. Discuss the problem of Housing in Rural India.

25

RURAL WELFARE AND SARVODAYA

The terms Rural Welfare, Community Development and Extension Service are often used interchangeably. There are, however some important differences.

1. Community Development. Community Development Programme emphasises the building up of a sense of community and making the community a dynamic force in solving its own problems. People's participation and the development of local leadership are important aspects in developing the facilities in the community. This approach assumes a democratic form of government. The provision of amenities or services is incidental to it.

2. Extension Services. In 'extension services' the emphasis is on helping the individual to meet his needs particularly in the field of agriculture or home management. Developing the community and providing may be a by-product of this approach, but they are not its primary objects.

3. Welfare Programme. In a welfare programme the primary emphasis is on the provision of amenities, so as to help the individual, the family and the community attain a state of well-being.

4. Rural Welfare. Rural welfare is a broader concept and takes into account all the tangible and intangible factors in its attempt to create a state of well-being in rural areas. While self-help and people's participation are encouraged, they are not necessary pre-conditions for the provision of amenities and services (*e.g.*, malaria eradication programme, or mid-day meals for school children).

Need for Revitalising Village

If the level of living of the people of the country has to be raised, adequate attention has to be paid to the appalling conditions prevailing in the five and a half lakh of villages. Tagore said a long while ago: "Man has been digging holes into the very foundations, not only of his livelihood, but also of his life, he is feeding upon his own body. The reckless wastage is best seen in the village, where the light of life is being dimmed, the joy of existence dulled, and the threads of social communion snapped. It should he our mission to restore the circulation of life's blood, in these maltreated limbs of society; to the villager's health and knowledge, wealth of space in which to live; wealth of time in which to work, rest and joy, respect which will give them dignity, sympathy which will make them realise their kinship with the subservient position."

The graphic and tragic description of the conditions of the villages makes it unnecessary to further elaborate on the same.

Rural Welfare

There is a need to infuse vitality and vigour and thus energise the rural society. The purpose of organising welfare programmes for the rural people is to better their living conditions. Welfare is said to be the organised system of social services, social welfare services and institutions designed to aid individuals and groups to attain satisfying standards of life and health and personal social relations which permit them to develop their full capacities and promote their well-being in harmony with the needs of their families and community The objectives of welfare programmes whether in urban or rural areas, would be the same as Friedlander says: "To secure for each human being the economic necessities a decent standard of health and living conditions, equal opportunities with fellow citizens and the highest possible degree of self-respect and freedom of thought and action without interfering with the same rights of others."

In the early times, when the villages were isolated and to some extent self-sufficient, the social and community structure had built-in provisions for meeting various social needs of the individuals as they arose. The orphans, the widows and the aged were taken care of within the family. There are indications of provisions being made against the eventualities of floods and drought. With an increasing population, the centralisation of administration and the loosening of the social structure, these provisions have become less and less operative.

HISTORY OF RURAL DEVELOPMENT IN INDIA

1. The Beginnings. There is a general feeling that during British regime, no attempt was made at providing welfare services to the rural areas. In one sense this is true, in another it is not. There was no concerted and direct effort by the government at alleviating the difficult rural conditions. The establishment of co-operative societies and agricultural departments laws with regard to agricultural improvement, the appointment of the Royal Commission on Agriculture, were aimed at improving the living conditions of the rural people. In the early thirties a large number of provinces and native States had departments concerned with rural development, *e.g.* Bombay, Central Provinces, Mysore, United Provinces, Bengal and Baroda. In general, the programme in all these areas was to improve agricultural techniques, provide better sanitation, education and medical facilities. There was some attempt to involve the people. The efforts were probably greater in the Punjab and Madras.

2. The Punjab Experiment. The Punjab experiment generally known as the Gurgaon Project, was initiated by F. L. Brayne. He said that the purpose was to "jerk the villager out of his old groove, convince him that improvement is possible and kill his fatalism by demonstrating that climate, disease and poverty can be successfully fought; further to laugh him out of his unhealthy and uneconomic customs". His programme was concerned with (1) increase in agricultural production, (2) stoppage of waste, (3) improvement in standard of health, and (4) improvement of home and raising the status of women. The programme functioned well as long as Brayne was in the district (1925-1933) but after his departure there was at decline.

3. The Firka Programme. The Firka development programme was launched in Madras in 1946. The object of the scheme was to attack the rural problems as a whole as well as in its several aspects. The short-term plan was for the development of rural communication and rural water supply, formation of Panchayats, organisation of co-operatives covering every village, implementing a programme of sanitation, etc. The long-term plan was designed for the attainment of self-sufficiency through agricultural, irrigational and livestock improvements and the development of khadi and cotton industries. The scheme was merged with the national extension scheme in 1953-54.

There were other attempts which need to be mentioned as they have had some influence on the planning of the development of a programme for rural welfare. The phrase "Rural Welfare" is not specifically used in all the programmes described, but the overall aim was rural welfare whatever the nomenclature.

4. Gandhiji's Contribution: (i) *AVIA*. Gandhiji evinced keen interest in rural development programmes. Though one identifies "Sevagram", where work began in 1933, as a sort of beginning of his interest in rural development, actually even as early as 1920, he had encouraged the organisation of the All-India Spinners Association and later in 1925, the All-India Village Industries Association (AVIA). The purpose of the A.V.I.A. was described thus:

(1) It tries to stop wastage and to convert waste materials to good purpose.

(2) It attempts to conserve the resources at present available to villagers.

(3) It attempts to utilise profitably the hours of leisure and introduces such work as will increase the wealth of the people.

(ii) *Gram Swaraj*. Gandhiji's plea was to develop a "Gram Swaraj" (a village self-rule). The major planks of his approach to rural development were: (1) village autonomy, (2) identification with villagers, (3) self-purification, self-example and self-reliance, (4) development of cottage industries, (5) basic education and (6) production for village consumption. His purpose was to build a society in which there would be equal opportunities for individuals for educational, economic and social development.

(iii) *Sarvodaya*. Another programme with which the name of Mahatma Gandhi is associated is Sarvodaya. It stands for the all-round well-being of all. It believes that love and cooperation are the only enduring forces that bind the society together. It believes in a decentralised, democratic and equalitarian society. Specifically the objectives of Sarvodaya are as follows:

(1) To provide full and integral employment to every member of the society;

(2) To ensure that every member of the society gets the material requisites for the essential well-being and the development of his personality and is enabled to contribute to the welfare of society,

(3) To encourage and foster self-sufficiency in the elementary requisites; and

(4) To ensure that techniques of production adopted are in keeping with the idea of reverence for life.

The work is carried out by trained workers called 'Sanchalaks' at the village level. The programme activities are related to education, agriculture, village industries, health, social amenities and welfare. It emphasises cooperatives principles in organising the activities and inculcating of habits of self-help, mutual aid, tolerance and thrift. The approach can be said to be comprehensive. The Bhoodan (gift of land) and Gramdan (gift of a village) movements are in a sense off-shoot of the Sarvodaya programme.

5. Contribution by Tagore. The Sriniketan programme was started by Rabindranath Tagore in 1922. He was drawn to village uplift work because he was distressed at the cultural degeneration of the country. He felt that the village was the base of the indigenous culture. He, therefore, worked for a cultural regeneration by a process of "bringing back life", to the village. The programme included agricultural improvement, raising of the health standards, having demonstration centres, youth activities and literacy classes.

6. Contribution by YMCA. A rural development programme was launched under the auspices of the YMCA at Martandam (Madras) in 1920. Spencer Hatch was incharge of it. The purpose of the programme was to bring about a "complete upward development, towards a more abundant life for rural people, spiritually, mentally, physically, socially and economically." The programme was based on the idea that felt needs must be met and the benefits must reach the poorest. The activities were comprehensive and broad-based including a demonstration centre and the training of workers. The India Village Service of which Dr. W. H. Wiser was incharge, started to operate in 1946 in U.P. They believed that given some guidance, the villagers had the capacity to solve their problems and act on them to realise a more abundant life. They believed in doing intensive work with well-qualified people and in dealing with the various needs of the rural people.

The Forerunners

There were major limitations in all of these projects. Most of them were extremely limited area-wise. Further, not all the aspects of the rural problems were dealt with by these projects, *e.g.*, the problems of the handicapped and the distressed were not and could not be dealt with by such small project programmes. Nor did these projects have the competence to deal with large issues like land reforms, provision of irrigation facilities and the passing of comprehensive social legislation which was necessary to deal effectively with the problems in the rural areas. Nevertheless it must be admitted that these experiments in rural welfare were the forerunners of the community development programme of India which was launched on the 2nd October, 1952.

SARVODAYA

Meaning and Objectives

The term Sarvodaya literally means "the rise or welfare of all". It consists of two Sanskrit component words, sarva and udaya, which mean "all" and "rise" respectively. It was first used by Mahatma Gandhi as the title of a booklet in which he gave a gist, in Gujarati, of John Ruskin's famous book "Unto This Last". The word later came to denote a way of life or an ideology based on truth and non-violence as propounded and exemplified by Gandhiji in his life. After his death, Acharya Vinoba Bhave has made significant contributions both to the theory and practice of Sarvodaya, particularly through his Bhoodan Movement. Today Sarvodaya stands for a philosophy of life and a programme of action which embraces many aspects of life including the social, the economic and the political. It aims at a complete transformation of the present social structure through quiet, constructive, social work carried on primarily at the village level, with a view to initiating a non-violent revolution and establishing a more just social order.

Historical Aspect

1. Hindu Tradition. Sarvodaya has its roots deep in the ancient Indian spiritual tradition. Hindu mythology is full of heroes who are depicted as paragons of some particular virtue or other. A host of names such as those of King Harischandra, King Rama, Sage Vasishtha, King Yudhishthira etc., come to mind. Their exemplary lives have moulded the character of many great men. Gandhiji has narrated in his autobiography how in his childhood a play about the truthful King Harishchandra captivated his heart. "To follow truth", says he, "and to go through all the ordeals Harishchandra went through was the one ideal it inspired in me," Truth and non-violence, as values to be cherished in life, are as old as India herself. Sage Vasishtha stood for non-violence as illustrated by his behaviour towards his self-proclaimed rival and detractor Vishwamitra. The Upanishads emphasise the unity.

2. Jain and Buddhist Gospel. Sri Mahavira and Gautama Buddha preached non-violence as a regulatory principle in daily life and compassion as a social virtue respectively

3. Islamic Ideal. Islam which came to India much later stands for peace and brotherhood. The word "Islam" itself is derived from salaam which means peace. A number of Hindu and Muslim saints belonging to the medieval period of Indian history glorified piety, gentleness, charity and spiritual brotherhood of man.

4. Christian Virtues. Christianity in its purest form is ail for non-violence, love and service to the poor and down-trodden. Indian culture has on the whole tended to be receptive, tolerant, accommodative and assimilative.

Sarvodaya draws its inspiration as much from this ancient religious tradition as from the modern national, secular, humanitarianism or even revolutionary idealism. It looks upon service to society as the *raison d'etre* of man's life on earth. In this sense, Sarvodaya is all social work and nothing else.

Contribution of M.K. Gandhi

The word Sarvodaya was no coinage of Gandhiji. He had borrowed it from the writtings of Acharya Samantabhadra, a Jain religious preacher of the second century A.D. The concept of the welfare of all, though not the word Sarvodaya, was not new even then. We find it in the *Ishavasyopanishad* which speaks of a perfect man who "sees the self in all beings and all beings in the self". The *Bhagavadgita* also describes devotees as "persons who rejoice in the welfare of all beings". A traditional invocatory verse which was included by Gandhi in his daily prayers embodied the same idea:

"May all be happy. May all be free from diseases. May all meet good fortune. May none have sorrow or misery of his lot."

No Intellectual Theory

The ideology of Sarvodaya is not a product of intellectual theorisation. It grew out of the activities, experiences and inner convictions of a great soul who wanted to do away with all kinds of social disabilities, injustices and inequalities. In South Africa, Gandhiji was engaged in resisting racial discrimination. While there, he happened to read in 1904 John Ruskin's *Unto This Last*. The book made a deep impression on him. He "determined to change his life in accordance with the ideals of the book". The teachings of "*Unto This Last*" as understood by Gandhiji were, firstly, that the good of the individual is contained in the good of all. That is why Gandhiji named his Gujarati adaptation of the book as "*Sarvodaya*". Secondly, a lawyer's work has the same value as the barber's inasmuch as all have the same right of earning their livelihood from their work. Thirdly, the life of labour *i.e.*, the life of the tiller of the soil and the handicraftsman is the life worth living.

Sarvodaya as a Movement

Gandhiji realised that it was not enough just to pray to God that all should be happy. It was every man's duty, more so of a social worker, to strive to establish a society which would be based on justice and equality. This was a stupendous task, undoubtedly. But Gandhiji decided to begin with himself. If educated persons also worked with their hands and lived simply, he thought they would not be guilty of exploiting others. At the Phoenix Settlement in South Africa, therefore, Gandhiji decided to put the ideas of *Unto This Last* into practice. Thus, with the use of his weapon of passive resistance against racialism and a deliberate attempt to live a life of simplicity and labour, the ideology of Sarvodaya began to take shape at Gandhiji's hands, while he was still In South Africa.

Sarvodaya Efforts of M.K. Gandhi

On arrival in India in 1915 it seemed that Gandhiji at first wanted to devote himself to social work alone. He had sent an application for membership of the Servants of India Society in Poona. But on learning that opinion amongst members of the

Society was divided on the advisability of admitting a passive resister like Gandhiji into the Society, he himself withdrew his application. Later, during 1920 and 1921, he became the unquestioned leader of the nonviolence struggle for India's independence. At the base of all his political activities, however, was his fourteen point Constructive Programme. "Fulfilment of Constructive Programme is Swaraj", he once declared. The Constructive Programme placed before the nation by Gandhiji was so wide in its ideational sweep that it covered almost all kinds of social work in its compass and much more. Never has social work in its history had such a deep connotation, nor has it ever been conceived on a more comprehensive or grand scale. Communal unity came first and foremost. Then there was removal of untouchability, prohibition, *khadi*, other village industries, village sanitation, *nai talim* or basic education, organisation of women, students, peasants and lastly, service to the tribal people. Though work on all these aspects of Constructive Programme was not of the same quality or intensity, there were hundreds of ardent workers in distant villages in the country under the guidance of institutions established by Gandhiji, All India Harijan Sewak Sangh, Hindustani Talimi Sangh and Akhil Bharat Go-sewa Sangh. "If we wish to achieve *Swaraj* through Truth and Nonviolence", wrote Gandhiji "gradual but steady building up from the bottom upwards, by constructive effort, is the only way ... Progress towards *Swaraj* will be in exact proportion to the increase in the number of workers who will dare to sacrifice their all for the cause of the poor."

Sarvodaya Efforts of Acharya Vinoba

(i) Bhoodan. Immediately after Gandhiji's death in 1948, Sarvodaya Samaj, a loose non-political organisation of the nature of a federation, was formed by those who believed in the Gandhian ideas. Akhil Bharat Sarva Sewa Sangh is another smaller oganisation that came into existence. With the inauguration, however, of the *Bhoodan* Movement by Vinobaji in 1951, Sarvodaya not only consolidated for itself the gains of the Gandhian era but ventured forth into a new and more extensive field of social work, which had deep economic and political significance also.

(ii) Gramadan. By its own dynamics, the *Bhoodan* Movement, between 1952 and 1958, flowered into a *gramadan* movement. Vinobaji's appeal for voluntary renunciation of individual ownership of land and for vesting it in the village community was a radical extension of Gandhiji's Theory of Trusteeship to landed property. More than four million acres of land was donated in *Bhoodan*, out of which over a million acres have been distributed amongst landless labourers all over the country. Similarly, about 8,000 *gramadans* had been declared up to March 1965. The work of distributing Bhoodan land and of getting *gramadan* land transferred from individual holders to the *gramasabha* of each village is, however, proceeding rather slowly. Legal difficulties of various kinds have mainly caused the delay. Land in gramadan villages is not necessarily cultivated collectively. Nor is there, these days, an insistence on equal redistribution of land among landowners and landless labourers according to the number of persons in each family. And yet declaration of *gramadan* is still rightly considered to be a radical step. For, in a *gramadan*, individual ownership of land comes to an end. Besides, at least one-twentieth of the total land is made available for cultivation to landless labourers in the village.

(iii) Gram Swaraj. The next step in the *gramadan* movement is the establishment of *grama-swaraj*, that is, complete self-government. Under this the villagers are expected to learn to shoulder the responsibility of village administration and village development in every sphere, This, in fact, would be democracy at the grassroots. The villagers would try to be self-reliant and make their own arrangements, as far as possible, in regard to promotion of education, provision of work to the unemployed or underemployed through a policy of encouragement of *khadi* and other village industries, village sanitation, medical aid, preservation of law and order and administration of simple justice.

(iv) Shanti Sena. The crowning achievement denoting the completion of the construction of the edifice of *grama-swaraj* would be the raising of a *shanti-sena* in each village. The members of this peace brigade would normally function as *loka-sewaks*, servants of the people of their respective localities in various capacities. In times of communal or other tensions and riots the *shanti-sainiks* would assume the role of non-violent police. It is thus obvious that the whole programme of *bhoodan* and *gramadan* is an attempt to devise ways and means to establish an ideal non-violent social order.

(v) Reconstruction work. The *gramadan* movement has, in spite of many difficulties, made considerable headway both in the tribal and non-tribal areas in some parts of the country. The first *gramadan* that was declared on May 23, 1962, is situated in 'Hamirpur district of Uttar Pradesh, which is a non-Adivasi area. It has made steady progress over years in the direction of self-sufficiency in food and, what is more remarkable, in clothing also. Loni, another non-Adivasi village with a population of 5,000, in the Vidarbha region of Maharashtra, was declared *gramadan* during Vinobaji's *padayatra* in that area early in 1964. It deserves special mention, because some of the landowners who took initiative in the matter are not only well educated but a few of them are even practising lawyers and doctors. The Batlagundu area in Madurai district of Madras State, which again is non-tribal, has some of the most active *gramadans* in the country. Similarly, there are also large tribal tracts such as Koraput district of Orissa or small compact areas such as the Rangpur group of villages near Baroda in Gujarat, where a number of *gramadans,* declared over a decade ago, have been registered under the law either as *gramadans* or *grama-swaraj* societies and are making good progress in reconstruction work.

The attitude of the Central and State governments and some of the major political parties in the country towards the *Bhoodan* and *Gramadan* Movement has from the very beginning been sympathetic. The contribution to the solution of the land problem, said the First Five Year Plan Report, which Bhoodan was then making "has a special value; for it gives to the landless worker an opportunity not otherwise easily available to him".

The Yelwal Conference on *gramadan* held in September 1957 near Mysore was attended by Dr. Rajendra Prasad, Shri Jawaharlal Nehru, some other Congress leaders and leaders of two or three opposition parties including the Communist Party. At the end of the Conference, they issued a joint appeal, which among other things said: "The participants in the Conference welcomed this gramadan movement and expressed their high appreciation of the objectives underlying it. It appealed to all sections of the Indian people to give this mission their enthusiastic support." A paragraph that followed went further and declared that "closest cooperation was desirable between the community development moment and the *gramadan* movement". But nothing much came out of this public declaration of collective support and appeal by so many prominent leaders. Many State Governments, however, set up *Bhoodan* Boards to keep proper records of land donated in *Bhoodan* and to transfer legally all land distributed among landless labourers. Similarly, some State governments such as those of Assam, Bengal, Orissa, Rajasthan, Maharashtra and Madras passed legislation with a view to facilitating the smooth transfer of ownership of land to the *gramasabha* in *gramadan* villages. It has also been the policy of the Central, as well as the State governments, to help reconstruction work in *gramadan* villages by making suitable grants and loans.

(vi) Allied programmes and activities. Apart from securing declarations of *gramadans* and initiating *gramanirman* work in those villages, there are many other allied activities which form part of the comprehensive Sarvodaya movement. In fact, *gramadan*, "village-oriented" *khadi* and *shanti-sena* together constitute a unified three-point programme, as adopted at the last annual Sarvodaya Conference held at Raipur in Madhya Pradesh in December 1964. Accordingly, enrolment and training of new *shanti-sainiks* and opening of new *shanti-kendras* are going on apace all over the country. Many experienced and trained shanti-sainiks rendered much quiet, but valuable service at the time of the communal disturbances in Calcutta and Rourkela early in 1964 and at the time of the rioting in Madras State over the language issue in February 1965. In the wake of the Chinese thrust in 1962, the *shanti-sena mandal* sent a few volunteers to the northern border areas including NEFA, where they have commenced Sarvodaya type of social work among the tribals. Apart from efforts to promote *khadi* in co-operation with the All India Khadi and Village Industries Commission and the State Khadi Boards, Sarvodaya workers organise Sarvodaya melas or fairs at various places in the country on the 12th of February every year. Believers in Sarvodaya offer one hank each of self-spun yam to local Sarvodaya *mandals* in memory of Gandhiji. The Punjab Sarvodaya mandals established an all time record by collecting 1,10,000 hanks in a single day.

(vii) Sarvodaya Patra. A novel idea for impressing upon citizens the need for some constant sacrifice for the welfare of the less privileged members of the community was invented by Vinobaji in 1958. It was the *Sarvodaya Patra.* This is a small receptacle to be kept in each house. Before lunch every day, the youngest member in the family, who would usually be a child, is to make an offering of a handful of grain into it. Offering a *paisa* is also permissible. Monthly collections from such *Sarvodaya Patras* are to be handed over to the local *shanti-sainik* for promotion of Sarvodaya work. Keeping a *patra* like this amounts to an active, daily vote for Sarvodaya programme and ideology. Though it cannot be said that this novel idea of securing mass support for a programme has caught the imagination of the people, a little headway has already been made in small towns and even big cities like Indore, Baroda, Calcutta, Bombay and Madras. But some remarkable success has attended the efforts of *Bhoodan* workers of Andhra in Tenally and other towns in that area. About 35,000 *Sarvodaya Patras* are being maintained there fairly regularly since 1958. It is quite evident that this praiseworthy measure for making social work decentralised, and what is more, financially self-supporting, has tremendous revolutionary potentialities. It need hardly be emphasised that it has also deeper cultural significance than a similar activity in the U.S.A. known as the Community Chest Movement.

(viii) Moral hygiene movement. Vinobaji's prolonged stay in the city of Indore during 1960 resulted in an addition to the already varied programme of the Sarvodaya movement. It was *satyagraha* against indecent cinema posters. While proceeding to award in the city for participating in demonstrational scavenging as part of a campaign for "cleaner Indore", Vinobaji happened to notice some unseemly cinema posters at many prominent places on public streets. It was a painful discovery for him that the residents of Indore, or for that matter any other big town or city in India, tolerated such vulgar display of erotic pictures in public places. He raised his voice against this practice in his public speeches daily for about a month. There was a good response to appeal for removing such pictures voluntarily. But in the case of recalcitrant advertisers or owners of cinema houses, he even advised direct *satyagraha* by *Bhoodan* workers and public volunteers. Within a few weeks, the campaign spread to many other cities in the country. Public conscience was roused. Women in Delhi, for example, made a demand for governmental action and check on the exhibition of unbecoming posters. Questions were asked in the Parliament. The Government gave assurances that it would look into the existing law and make suitable amendments or additions to rules and regulations if found necessary. The *satyagraha* did not last longer than a year. But as a phase of the *Bhoodan* Movement, it certainly brought to the forefront the social aspects of Sarvodaya philosophy. It emphasised that both environmental and inner moral hygiene was as important as, or more important than, outward physical hygiene.

(ix) Reform of criminals. Around 1960 there was another activity, incidental to *Bhoodan*, which Vinobaji and his followers had to undertake during his *padayatra* in Madhya Pradesh. It carried great significance for all social workers, for it was a piece of social work of a very unusual nature. People in Bhind and Morena districts had for long been harassed by dacoits who had made the inaccessible forests and ravines of the Chambal Valley their home. No previous governments before Independence had been able to completely bring to an end their unlawful activities. The State Government of Madhya Pradesh had posted, as before, armed police in the area. But the police had not succeeded in putting an end to the menace and removing from the minds of the law-abiding citizens, the sense of insecurity and danger to life and property. Vinobaji's approach to the problem was quite novel and completely non-violent. In all humility and with cautiousness, he and his followers first won the confidence of the "rebels against society" as the dacoits choose to describe themselves. The dacoits realised that not only Vinobaji, but his followers also were quite fearless though unarmed, that they believed in non-violence not as a policy but as a creed of life, and further that these well-meaning friends had nothing but love and compassion for them though society in general had branded them as "wicked devils". Vinobaji's behaviour towards dacoits was a marvel of a lesson for students of applied psychology and the change of heart of the "criminals", a fit subject for social case-work. About twenty dacoits surrendered their arms at Vinobaji's feet and expressed readiness to undergo any punishment meted out to them by law courts for their past crimes. Vinobaji's sympathetic identification with the dacoits on a spiritual level achieved in an instant what could not be achieved by bayonets and bullets over years! Dr. Rajendra Prasad, the then President of India, sent a telegram of congratulations to Vinobaji on his remarkable achievement. Unfortunately, however, there was irrational opposition from some unexpected quarters and the experiment had to be cut short. Even then limited, yet successful, the experiment based on principles of Sarvodaya indeed pointed to the direction of future reform in criminology and penology as well.

Contribution of Jayaprakash Narayan. Shri Jayaprakash Narayan, whose position in the *Bhoodan* Movement is next only to Vinobaji, has been mainly instrumental in bringing leaders of peace movements in other countries in close contact with the Sarvodaya movement in India. This process has brought benefits to both. A fairly regular periodical exchange of views and occasional reciprocal visits by prominent workers from India and from abroad have also been taking place in recent years.

QUESTIONS FOR EXERCISE

1. Write short note on Rural Development.
2. What is Sarvodaya? Trace the contribution of Gandhi, Vinobha and J.P. to Sarvodaya movement.

26

COMMUNITY DEVELOPMENT

The Planning Commission had defined the community development project in these words: "Community development is an attempt to bring about a social and economic transformation of village life through the efforts of the people themselves." In this way, the community development projects indicate those projects for social and economic reconstruction in the villages which are implemented with the co-operation of the public itself. In the words of Sri A.R. Desai, "The community development project is the method through which Five Year Plans seek to initiate a process of transformation of the social and economic life of the villages." In this way, community development project is a process controlled by the community itself. Here community implies rural community. Elucidating the aims of community development project it has been laid down in *India 1975*, published by the Government of India, "The community development programme launched on 2nd Oct. 1952, aims at bringing about an integrated development of rural India covering the social, cultural and economic aspects of community life." Prof. S.C. Dube, writing in his book *India's Changing Villages* has recognised the following two aims of community development projects.[1]

Aims of Community Development

1. To manage or achieve an increase in the country's agricultural produce and a progress in the means of communication, rural health and cleanliness, and rural education.

2. To initiate and to direct a process of synthetical cultural change aimed at transforming the social and economic life of the village.

The following major aims have been recognised in the Ministry of Community Development of the Government of India publication, *A Guide to Community Development:*

1. To create a change in the mental outlook of the masses.
2. To develop responsible and active leadership in the village.
3. To make the villagers self-dependent and progressive.
4. To modernize agriculture on the one hand and to develop cottage industries on the other, in order to raise the economic status of the villagers.

---

1. *India 1975*, p. 184.

5. To improve the condition of the women and families of villagers in order to make the suggested improvements practicable.
6. To develop properly the future citizens of the nation.
7. To protect the interests of the rural educators.
8. To raise the standard of health among the rural populace and to protect them against disease.

A. Short-term objectives. The aims of the community development project have been divided into two parts — short-term objectives and long-term objectives. The short-term objectives are the following:

1. The maximum possible increase in agriculture production.
2. To solve the problem of unemployment in the villages.
3. To develop the means of communication in the villages.
4. To improve the centres of primary education, public health and recreation in the villages.
5. To improve the conditions of the houses.
6. To encourage cottage industries and indigenous handicrafts.

B. Long-term objectives. The long-term objective of community development projects is the complete planned development of all physical and human resources. In it, arrangements will be made to provide all villages with full employment. The goal of community development project is the development of villages in such a way that the citizens of the country may not lack anything, which is the ideal of a welfare state and that everyone should get adequate food and that everyone should progress socially, morally and financially. In this way, in brief, community development projects aim at the integral development of the village through the efforts of villagers and the assistance of the government.

Importance of Community Projects

Describing the importance which the community projects have for rural life, The Planning Commission had written in the Second Five Year Plan, "It is a problem, briefly, of changing outlook of 70 million families living in the countryside, arousing in them enthusiasm for new knowledge and new ways of the life and filling them with ambition and the will to live and work for a better life. Extension services and community organisations are among the principal sources of vitality in democratic planning and rural development projects are the means by which, through co-operative self-help and local effort, villages and groups of villages can achieve in increasing measure both social change and economic progress and become partners in the national plan."

Social development projects will involve improvement in all the aspects, social, economic and others, of rural life. The main effects which development projects have upon rural life are the following:

1. Agricultural development. Agriculture is the foundation of rural economic life. The happiness and the prosperity of the village depend upon the progress of agriculture. The main cause of the poverty in the Indian villages is the backward condition of agriculture. The main problems of Indian agriculture are old techniques of agriculture, dearth of new tools, want of manures and fertilizers, excessive sub-division of land, dearth of the means of irrigation, shortage of good seeds, etc. The community development projects have made efforts to solve all these problems which beset Indian agriculture. New techniques of farming are exhibited in the villages and manures, seeds, tools and fertilizers distributed. The community projects also undertake the repairing of old wells, supplementing them by sinking new wells in order that the farmers may have available the necessary facilities for irrigation. Efforts are made to protect the land from soil erosion and other maladies.

2. Economic progress. The greatest problem of rural life in India is its poverty. The community development projects have encouraged cottage industries and handicrafts. Unemployed people are provided with work through auxiliary and useful services. Although these efforts are as yet quite inadequate, it is hoped that a continuous increase in them will lead to rural life in India becoming more prosperous in the future.

3. Development in respect of animals. Another major problem and obstacle to progress in the Indian villages is the deplorable condition of the animals which are even today employed in ploughing the fields. The ox is used for this purpose. In order to improve the strain of the species the community development projects have made use of good oxen. Improved poultry have also been arranged for the development of poultry farming.

4. Development of education. Most of the people residing in the villages of India are uneducated and illiterate. At the same time they lack modern knowledge. Without the spread of education in the rural areas of India no progress of any kind whatsoever can possibly be expected. The community development projects have paid the desired and necessary attention to the education of children and adults, men and women. Schools for primary and adult education have been opened. Arrangements have been made for social education.

5. Training for development. In the villages of India social and economic development cannot take place in the existing circumstances. It is necessary to have people trained and skilled in rural development. Under the community projects arrangements have been made to train village workers, both male and female, block development officers and other people concerned with the programme of rural development.

6. Development of the means of transport. In the villages of India there is a dearth of the means of transport, serious enough to prove a great obstacle to industry and business. The community development projects have repaired the old roads and also managed to construct new roads. At various points small culverts have also been provided. These measures will not only improve business but will also serve to maintain the contact of the villagers with the world at large.

7. Cleanliness. Dirtiness reigns supreme in the Indian villages. It is the cause of the spread of many kinds of diseases, and it lowers the general standard of health.

The community development projects have not forgotten to arrange proper drainage for the villages. A considerable length of drains has been constructed and steps have been taken to purify and keep pure the drinking water of the wells.

8. Protection of health and the maintenance of certain standard. In the villages of India epidemics and many less widespread diseases carry off many men, women and children every year due to the almost utter absence of medication and facilities for delivery. The condition of the health of women and children is extremely dissatisfactory. Arrangements have been made for one health centre in each development block. Mobile dispensaries have also been arranged for. Midwives and nurses are also being trained to staff all the new dispensaries.

9. Arrangement for residences. Most of the houses in the villages are old-fashioned and small. The community development projects have decided to assist the villagers in building houses and also arranged for providing them with modern plans and the building methods of good and cheap houses.

10. Social welfare. The community development projects have also given due attention to social welfare in the villages, making arrangements for games, variety shows etc., for the entertainment of the public. Gramophone, radio and cinema provide the villager with entertainment and also serve to enhance his stock of knowledge.

PROGRESS OF COMMUNITY DEVELOPMENT

The community development programme, which has now become a part of the rural development programme, was launched on 2nd October 1952. There are 5,004 development blocks in the country. The aim of the programme is to bring about an overall development of rural India covering resources and cultural and economic aspects of the community life. This is sought to be achieved through the fullest development of available human and material resources on an area basis, and thereby raising the rural community to higher levels of living with the active participation of the people themselves. The highest priority is accorded to agriculture. Other important sectors include improvement of communications, health, sanitation, housing, education, rural employment, welfare of rural women and children and cottage and small scale industries.

Programme Pattern

At present a community development block covers an area of about 620 sq. km with around 100 villages and a population of about 1,00,000. Supply of funds for the blocks remained mainly the responsibility of the Central Government till the end of the Third Plan (1966). But from the beginning of the Fourth Plan (April 1969), the financial arrangement became the responsibility of the states as the scheme was transferred to the state sector.

Policy

The Ministry of Rural Reconstruction lays down the broad policy relating to the community development programme. Though the main responsibility for the execution of the programme is that of state governments, the Central Government helps in developing special programmes with central assistance and guidance.

Organisation

Although a standard staffing pattern has been envisaged for the development blocks, it remains flexible from state to state for operational purposes according to the programme requirements and the size of the blocks. Generally, the cadre authority for the block development officers is the department dealing with community development/rural development/Panchayati raj in the concerned states which the cadre authority for extension officers is their respective parental department in the states. The block development officer/chairman, Panchayat Samiti exercises administrative control over block extension staff in most of the states, although there are deviations in some states from the. General pattern.

Pattern of Investment

For the Mid-term Plan (1979-83) some modifications had been made insofar as the funding of the programme is concerned. Major emphasis was now laid on block level planning. An amount of Rs. 2.50 lakh had been allocated per block per annum for taking up normal SFDA programme. 1,093 blocks out of 1,818 covered under SFDA programme had been selected for taking up integrated rural development programme (IRDP). Of the 1,093 blocks selected for IRDP 546 blocks had been selected for intensive employment programme for achieving the goal of full employment by 31 March, 1981. They had been given an allocation of Rs. 10 lakhs per annum per block. The remaining 547 blocks had been selected for normal integrated rural development programme with an outlay of Rs. 5 lakh per block per annum. From 1 April, 1979, the cost of the projects under SFDA as well as IRDP was being shared between the Government of India and the concerned state governments on 50: 50 bases.

Of the 2,000 IRD blocks selected from the special programme areas, 1,000 blocks were allocated Rs. 5 lakhs per block and the other 1,000 blocks Rs. 10 lakhs per block. The 300 blocks selected from the non-special programme areas were allocated Rs. 2 lakhs per block in the initial year and the allocation was to be enhanced at the rate of Rs. 1 lakh per block in the subsequent years. Thus, the 300 blocks selected during 1978-79 could get an allocation of Rs. 6 lakhs per block in the terminal year of the Sixth Plan. In addition, a provision of Rs. 60,000 per block had been made for conducting the base line survey of the households in the blocks selected from the non-special programme areas. The financial allocations indicated above are in addition to normal level of funding they receive under the special programmes by which they are covered. In view of the changed financing pattern, the financial allocations are shared between the Government of India and the state governments on a 50: 50 bases.

Under the integrated rural development programme', an attempt has been made to integrate the 'area' and the 'beneficiary' development approaches. Initially, it was thought that the funds provided under the programme should be entirely utilised for financing the subsidy component of the scheme eligible for assistance under the programme. But it was soon realised that investment on infrastructure will be necessary if the identified beneficiaries are to derive maximum benefit from the assistance provided to them under this programme. It was, therefore, decided to utilise 10 per cent of the outlay provided under the programme for the development of infrastructure.

It had been estimated that on an average, an investment of Rs. 5,000 would enable a rural family to get fully employed. As a major part of the funds provided under IRD programme are to be used for financing subsidy component of the schemes, on the basis of the existing pattern of subsidy under the programme, a direct investment of Rs. 1,500 from IRD funds should enable a family to go above the property line. This, however, assumes that necessary loan support of twice or thrice this amount is provided by the institutional sector. On the basis of these estimates, the number of families that can be raised above the poverty line for one year will be about 300 in blocks for which the outlay was Rs. 5 lakh and 600 in blocks where the outlay was Rs. 10 lakhs per block. The programme was intrinsically linked with the availability of bank credit and the banks will have to assume a major responsibility if the programme is to make a real success.

Applied Nutrition Programme

The Applied Nutrition Programme, a centrally sponsored scheme in collaboration with UNICEF, is intended to educate the rural people on improved nutrition. The programme specially aims at securing the needed nutritional supplements for children below five years and expectant and nursing mothers. The Gram Panchayats, Yuvak and Mahila Mandals are associated with the production of nutritional foods.

The Programme had covered 1,766 blocks up to 1978-79. Of this, 23 blocks were chosen for more intensive work. During the Fifth Plan, 585 new blocks were covered with a revised outlay of Rs. 12.99 crores.

Critical Evaluation

Looking at the above statistical details of the progress, both social and economic, achieved by the community development projects in villages, it becomes apparent that these projects have ignored many social and economic problems like the problem of the condition of the landless labourers, the problem of the backward condition of village and cottages industries etc. Secondly, even those social and economic problems which have received attention in these projects, are not being solved in an appropriate manner. For example, the provision of free and compulsory education is, as yet a thing of the future. The Programme Evaluation Organisation established by the Planning Commission put forward numerous criticisms of the community development programmes in its reports, of which the major ones are given below:

1. Lack of the solution of local problems. There is a lack of the solution of local rural problems in the community development projects. This not only hinders the progress of development programme, but it also decreases the faith of the public in these projects.

2. Dearth of harmony within the government department. The community development organisation is not in proper harmony with the other government development departments.

3. Shortage of necessary implements. There is an acute shortage of required necessary implements in the development programmes and as a result even the work which is started cannot be completed.

4. Shortage of trained personnel. Much effort has been made for training the officials in community development projects but even then, trained people are not available in required numbers.

5. Absence of proper public co-operation. The community development programmes could not become public movements. At present they are not getting the proper active co-operation of the public.

6. Shortage of female village workers. There is a great need for trained female workers for the emancipation of the rural women but, at present, they exist in very small number.

Suggestions

Actually there is an urgent need for increasing the awareness of the people towards the plans for the success of the community development projects. Some suggestions of which a few are given below, have been made in this connection.

1. Greater emphasis upon local problems. The pattern of the community development projects should not be the same everywhere. These projects should lay more stress upon the solution of problems as peculiar to the locality.

2. Appointment of officials acquainted with rural conditions. Another way of arousing the interest of the public towards the community development project is to appoint officials who are acquainted with the rural culture and its ways and are also sympathetic and respectful towards them, in order that they may be able to mix up with the villagers and to make these plans the projects and aspirations of people.

3. Appointment of workers, both male and female, selected from the village as far as possible. Another way of awakening the sense of ownership in villagers towards the projects is to appoint or select the male or female village workers from among the villagers themselves.

4. Organisation of the maximum possible training camps in the villages. If a maximum possible number of training camps are held in the villages, the villagers will undoubtedly reciprocate heartily and will take a greater interest in the projects.

5. More work and less propaganda. The officials detailed for the implementation of the development projects should adopt the principle of "More Work and Less Propaganda". It will result in public showing greater faith in the projects.

6. Establishing youth organisations and eliciting their co-operation. Before starting the programmes of development in the village's youth organisations should be established and the programmes of development should be started with their co-operation when such organisations are well under way. The result of this move will be that the whole village will soon start taking interest in these programmes.

QUESTIONS FOR EXERCISE

1. What do you understand by community development projects? Are they successful in Indian villages?

2. Examine with special reference to India, the place of community development in the field of national development.

3. Assess the contribution of Community Development Programme in rural reconstruction.

4. Evaluate the role of Community Development Programme of the Government of India in the promotion of social welfare.

27

RURAL CO-OPERATION

The co-operative idea took a concrete shape in India for the first time in 1904, when the Co-operative Credit Societies Act — a measure designed to combat rural indebtedness and to provide for registration of credit societies was passed. Later in 1912, the Co-operative Societies Act also provided for registration of non-credit societies as well as federation of co-operatives. Since then, the co-operative movement has made progress, especially in the field of agricultural credit, marketing and processing of agricultural produce, supply of farm inputs and distribution of consumer goods. By the end of June 1983, there were 2.91 lakh co-operatives in the country, of which about 65 per cent were operating in the rural areas; largely engaged in serving the farmers, landless labourers and other sections of the rural population.

The salient features and operational dimensions of the co-operative movement in India for selected years between 1960-61 and 1982-83 are given in the following table:

Table 1: *Growth of Co-operatives*

	1960-61	1970-71	1980-81	1981-82	1982-93
Number of Societies (lakh)	3.3	3.2	2.99	2.88	2.91
Members of Societies (lakh)	352	644	1,162	1,149	1,208
Share Capital (Rs. crores)	222	851	2,088	2,100	2,305
Working Capital (Rs. crores)	1,312	6,810	20,021	21,000	21,857

A study of the data in the above table shows that between 1960-61 and 1982-83, a period of 22 years, the membership of co-operative societies increased by more than three times, the share capital of all types of co-operatives increased by more than ten times and the working capital by more than sixteen times.

Primary Agricultural Credit Societies

By far the largest number of societies were in the agricultural credit sector. At the end of June 1983, there were 94,089 primary agricultural credit societies covering more than 96 per cent of the rural areas. The membership of these societies was

6.33 crores as on 30 June 1983. Universal membership has now been accepted as the policy so far as the primary agricultural societies are concerned, so that the people belonging to the weaker sections could become members of the co-operatives and avail of their services. The societies had a share capital amounting to Rs. 661.56 crores in June 1983 and short-term agricultural lending amounting to Rs. 1,908 crores during 1982-83.

Marketing and Processing Co-operatives

The co-operative marketing structure consists of about 4,000 co-operative marketing societies covering all important agricultural markets in the country with 3,632 primary marketing societies, 29 state level co-operative marketing federations and one National Agricultural Co-operative Marketing Federation. The total value of agricultural produce marketed by co-operatives amounted to about Rs. 2,566 crores in 1983-84. The value of food grains handled by marketing co-operatives increased from about Rs. 220 crores in 1968-69 to about Rs. 700 crores in 1983-84. During 1983-84, the National Agricultural Co-operative Marketing Federation's turnover stood at over Rs. 113 crores, as against Rs. 30.53 crores in 1976-77.

The structure of processing units established in the co-operative sector conforms to two distinct patterns, namely, (a) units established by independent processing societies, and (b) units established as adjuncts to co-operative marketing societies. Under the first category fall the larger units, such as, co-operative sugar factories, spinning mills and solvent extraction plants. Medium and small units, such as rice mills, oil mills, cotton ginning and processing units, jute baling units, mostly fall under the second category. During 1983-84, 2,458 units were organised in the co-operative sector. During 1983-84 sugar season, 165 co-operative sugar factories were in production. They produced 3188 lakh tonnes of sugar accounting for 53.9 per cent of the country's total production of sugar. At the national level, the National Federation of Cooperative Sugar Factories renders advice and maintains a technical cell.

Storage

The National Co-operative Development Corporation is responsible for planning, promoting and financing the programme of augmenting storage capacity of co-operatives at various levels. Storage capacity of 72.07 lakh tonnes had already been constructed in the co-operative sector by the end of June 1984 as against a capacity of 8 lakh tonnes in 1960-61. During 1983-84, 143 co-operative cold storage units with a total capacity of 2.86 lakh tonnes were installed. The Corporation has launched a large programme for construction of over 20,000 go downs with a capacity of nearly 37 lakh tonnes in 10 states and also 127 cold storages in five potato growing states with assistance from the European Economic Community and International Development Association.

Industrial Co-operatives

Co-operatives occupy an important place in the field of village and small industries and handloom weaving. As of June 1980, there were 45,154 industrial co-operatives with a membership of 33.81 lakh.

The National Federation of Industrial Co-operatives, which was set-up in 1966 with a view to assist in the marketing of products of member societies, make efforts to strengthen its position.

Co-operative Spinning Mills

The total number of spinning mills in the co-operative sector was 73 by 1983-84, 32 are growers' mills and 41 weavers' mills. During 1983-84, the number of installed spindles in the co-operative sector was 17.82 lakh.

The spinning mills have organised at the national level, the All India Federation of Co-operative Spinning Mills Ltd. The Federation is a promotional and developmental organisation.

Supply of Agricultural Inputs

To help farmers, co-operatives in India play a significant role in the production and distribution of agricultural inputs. Nearly 47 per cent of the total fertilisers distributed in the country are sold through the co-operative distribution system. The co-operatives have also diversified their activities in recent years to cover new lines of business.

IFFCO

The Indian Farmers Fertilizer Co-operative Ltd. (IFFCO), is a unique cooperative venture in the field of large scale fertiliser manufacture. It is one of the leading producers of fertilisers in the country, its share in the national production being 12.4 per cent in terms of nitrogen and 25.5 per cent in terms of phosphates. Registered in 1967, with the support of co-operatives in the country and the Government with the objective of manufacturing and marketing fertilizers for the benefit of farmer members of affiliated co-operatives, the membership of IFFCO covers about 26,000 cooperative institutions ranging from the national level federations to the village level co-operatives in 16 states and 3 union territories. It has ammonia and urea plants at Kalol (Gujarat) and a NPK complex fertiliser plant at Kandla.

IFFCO has set-up a naptha based ammonia and urea plant at Phulpur near Allahabad designed to produce 900 tonnes per day of ammonia and 1,500 tonnes per day of urea, respectively. The plant went into production in March 1981.

IFFCO's marketing strategy revolves around selling the concept of modern farming technology instead of just the fertiliser alone. For this purpose, it operates through field force of more than 300 trained agricultural technologists who function at the grassroot level in the villages and lay down practical demonstrations in the use of balanced fertilisers, improved seeds and other inputs as also in the soil testing and in obtaining credit from the co-operative societies.

Functional Co-operatives

Functional co-operatives for programmes like dairy, fishery and poultry mainly relate to the service of weaker sections. Such co-operatives provide increased employment and income opportunities to different sections of the community like small and marginal farmers and fishermen. The National Cooperative Development Corporation (NCDC) gives financial assistance to various types of co-operatives.

Dairy Co-operatives

On 31 December, 1978, out of a total of 190 dairy plants in operation in India, 80 were in the co-operative sector. On 30 June 1983, there were 36,566 primary milk supply co-operatives with a membership of 32.21 lakh. During 1982-83, the co-operatives handled milk and milk products valued at Rs. 382.8 crores. The primary milk co-operatives are federated into 203 unions. A National Federation of Dairy Co-operatives was set-up in 1970.

Fishery Co-operatives

The organisational structure of fishery co-operatives normally consists of primary fishery co-operatives at the base. A super structure of federations of primary fishery co-operative has been built-up. This consists of districts and central federations and state level federations. An All India Federation of Fishermen's Co-operative was set-up during 1979-80. On 30 June 1983, there were 7,036 primary fishermen's cooperatives with a membership of 7.59 lakh.

Poultry Co-operatives

By the end of June 1983, there were over 1,436 primary poultry cooperatives with a membership of 0.79 lakh.

Multi-purpose Co-operatives

As part of the programme of economic development of tribals, primary cooperatives in tribal areas are being reorganised to enable them to function as multi-purpose societies. State level cooperative tribal development corporations/ federations have been established in Andhra Pradesh, Bihar, Madhya Pradesh, Maharashtra, Rajasthan, West Bengal and Orissa to serve as apex organisations for marketing of minor forest produce and consumer goods.

Labour contract and construction co-operatives have been organised with a view to providing employment at reasonable wages to their members and preventing their exploitation by the contractors. During 1982-83, there were 16,467 labour cooperatives and forest labour co-operatives with a membership of 10.86 lakh.

The number, membership and working capital of selected primary non-credit societies during 1982-83 are shown in Table 2.

Table 2: *Primary Co-operative Societies*

Type of Societies	Number	Membership in '000	Working Capital (Rs. in lakh)
Milk Supply Societies	36,565	3,222	12,396
Poultry Co-operative Societies	1,436	79	1,812
Fishery Societies	7,036	759	2,924
Forest Labour Societies	1,488	245	8,728
Labour Contract and Construction Societies	14,979	841	6,084

Training and Research

A three-tier well-organised structure of co-operative training is available in India. It consists of a national institute of cooperative management known as Vaikunth Mehta National Institute of Co-operative Management (VMNICM), Pune, for catering to the training requirements of senior personnel, a network of 17 co-operative training colleges for training of intermediate personnel and 86 co-operative training centres for training of junior personnel. The VMNICM and 17 co-operative training colleges situated at state headquarters are functioning under the administrative and financial control of the National Council for Co-operative Training of the National Co-operative Union of India, which is financed entirely by the Government Co-operative centres for training of junior category personnel are functioning, under the control of state cooperative unions and state governments.

National Level Co-operative Federation

A major development over the past one decade has been the emergence of national co-operative federations, which have added a new dimension to the cooperative infrastructure. With National Co-operative Union of India at the apex, the other national level co-operative organisations include the National Co-operative Marketing Federation, the All India State Co-operative Banks Federation, the National Federation of Co-operative Sugar Factories, the National Co-operative Consumers' Federation, the National Federation of Industrial Cooperatives, the All India Federation of Co-operative Spinning Mills, the National Co-operative Housing Federation, the National Co-operative Dairy Federation of India, the National Federation of Co-operative Urban Banks and Credit Societies and the All India Federation of Co-operative Refinery Societies.

VILLAGE AND SMALL-SCALE INDUSTRIES

The development of small-scale industries has been given high priority in successive five year plans in view of its advantages in terms of low investment, high potential for employment generation and semi-urban areas. The importance of this sector has been further highlighted by its inclusion in the 20-Point Programme which lays emphasis on giving handicrafts, handlooms, small and village industries all facilities to grow and to up-date their technology.

Modern small-scale industries and unorganised traditional industries are known as Village and Small Industries (VSI). VSI sector is divided into eight sub-sectors. Small scale industries and power looms represent modern small-scale industries and khadi, village industries, handlooms, sericulture handicrafts and coir represent the traditional industries.

Policy Measures

For the first time on 6 August 1991 government had come out with a separate policy, enunciating measures for promoting and strengthening small, tiny and village enterprises.

As per this policy statement, the primary objective of the small scale industrial policy during the nineties would be to impart more vitality and growth impetus to the sector to enable it to contribute its mite fully to the economy particularly in terms of growth of output, employment and exports, promotion of entrepreneurship particularly among woman, enactment of a suitable legislation to ensure prompt payment of small industries bills, introduction of Limited Partnership Act to enhance supply of risk capital to small-scale section, implementation of special schemes for modernisation, technology upgradation and quality control, integrated infrastructural development and further promotion of internal marketing and exports are some of the measures outlined in this regard. To provide access to the capital market and encourage modernisation and technological upgradation, equity participation by other industrial undertakings in small-scale industries not exceeding 24 per cent of the total shareholding is proposed to be allowed.

As a follow-up action on policy measures, action has already been taken in respect of the following: (i) Tiny' enterprises and small-scale service establishments have been re-defined, thereby raising their investment (upper limit) from Rs. two lakhs to Rs. five lakhs, without any population/locational restrictions, (ii) Definition of women enterprise has been amended, thereby dispensing with stipulation of at least 50 per cent employment to women with effect from 16 August, 1991. (iii) All items placed under Restricted List were withdrawn with effect from 16 August 1991.

Credit Facilities

Credit provided by banks to small-scale industries is treated as credit to 'priority sector'. Commercial banks are required to lend 40 per cent of their total loans to priority sector of which 18 per is in the form of direct Agricultural advances and the rest to small scale industry, small business, small transport operators, indirect agricultural loans, etc. As at the end of March 1991 public sector bank credits to small-scale industrial sector formed 15.7 per cent of net bank credit amounting to Rs. 17,151 crores.

Share of the small-scale sector in the total outstanding loans of the priority sector at the end of March 1991, was 40 per cent, The number of small-scale units/ borrowers assisted by public sector banks at the end of March 1991 was 31.04 lakhs and the amount of outstanding loans to small scale sector Rs. 16.783 crores. Amount of financial assistance sanctioned by the State Financial Corporations to small-scale industries was Rs 1,301.9 crores and amount disbursed was Rs. 923.6 crores during 1990-91.

District Industries Centres

Centrally Sponsored District Industries Centres (DICs), Programme (launched in 1978) provides a focal point at district level for promotion of small, tiny, village and cottage industries, widely dispersed in rural and semi-urban areas and aims at providing all essential services and support as far as practicable and pre-investment, and post-investment stages at district level. Main thrust of this programme is on development of such industrial units in rural areas and small towns to create larger employment opportunities in those areas.

DIC programme has been listed as one of the Centrally-sponsored schemes by the Planning Commission to be transferred to the state sector. The programme has continued as Centrally-sponsored scheme during 1991-92 and also provision has been made in the Central Budget for 1992-93. The Central Government continues to provide Central assistance to the extent of Rs. four lakhs per year DIC as their recurring establishment expenditure. The total number of approved DICs now stands at 422. Four metropolitan cities are outside the purview of this programme.

Self-employment to Educated Unemployed Youth

The scheme for providing self-employment to educated unemployed youth remained in operation during 1991-92. Under this scheme, district industries centres (DICs), assist educated unemployed youth within the age group of 18 — 35 years and having passed matriculation and above including ITI to get self-employment through industry, services and business routes. Thirty per cent of the sanctions are reserved for SC/CS. The task force under the chairman of GM, DIC is in existence under the scheme. This task force identifies the beneficiaries and they are granted loans to the extent of Rs. 35,000 for industrial ventures, Rs. 25,000 for services ventures and Rs. 15,000 for business ventures. Rate of interest on Loan is ten per cent per annum in backward areas and 12 per cent per annum in other areas. Assistance from Government is in the shape of an outright capital subsidy to the extent of 25 per cent of the loan contracted by the entrepreneur from the bank. Subsidy is released to banks after disbursement of the loan which is to be kept as fixed deposit in the name of the borrower. After recovery of 75 per cent of the loan, balance of 25 per cent is to be adjusted by banks against deposits name of the borrower. During 1990-91, 1.01 lakh persons were sanctioned loan of Rs. 222.36 lakhs by the banks.

Second All India Census of Registered Small-Scale Industrial Units

Development Commissioner Small-Scale Industries DC (SSI) had conducted during 1989-91 the second All India census of small-scale industrial units registered with states/UTs directorates of industries up to 31 March, 1988 and falling under the purview of Small Industries Development Organisation (SEDO). A total number of about ten lakh such units producing a wide range of consumer goods, producers goods, ancillaries and components were covered during the census. Primary objective of the census was to collect from the unit's basic information in investment, employment, capacity, production, export etc., which would help in building up a data base relating to industries in the sector. The field work of the census has been completed and different statistical tables required for drafting of report have been generated by the National Information Centre under the Planning Commission. Summary results of the census were released in February, 1992.

NIESBUD

A National Board for Entrepreneurial Development and National Institute for Entrepreneurship and Small Business Development (NIESBUD) were established in 1983 for laying down policies, reviewing programmes and coordinating activities and programmes of various agencies in the field of entrepreneurship development of different target groups. The Institute has been organising and conducting training programmes for motivators, trainers and entrepreneurs preparing model syllabus of training of various groups of entrepreneurs, holding examinations and tests, undertaking documentations and research and conducting seminars, workshops and conferences, etc., for officers/motivators in the field of entrepreneurial and business development.

National Awards

Government has induced a scheme since 1983 for giving awards annually for reorganising and promoting entrepreneurship in small scale sector. The first three all-India awards carry a cash prize of Rs. 25,000, Rs. 20,000 and Rs. 15,000 respectively. A special recognition award of Rs. 10,000 is being conferred on the entrepreneur in small-scale industries in each state/UT in recognition of outstanding performance in this sector. A new scheme has been introduced from 1986-87 for small-scale units for quality production of goods from out of selected industry products groups. The awards carry cash prizes of Rs. 15,000 and Rs. 10,000 (for first and second), a trophy and a citation.

QUESTIONS FOR EXERCISE

1. Write an essay on Rural Co-operation.
2. Give a summary of development of village and small-scale industries in India.

28

RURAL RECONSTRUCTION AND DEVELOPMENT

In the words of the Planning Commission "Planning is essentially a way of organising and utilising resources to maximum advantages in terms of defined social ends." In this way the plans of rural reconstruction will try to take maximum advantage from the available resources, keeping in view the objectives mentioned above. It is obvious that planned reconstruction is the most superior method. Thus, in order to make the best use of rural reconstruction it is necessary to avail of planning. Actually, the importance which has been attributed to rural reconstruction is also the importance of rural planning because these objectives cannot be obtained in the absence of planning. In this way rural reconstruction and rural planning are of the utmost importance in a predominantly agricultural country like India.

Governmental Efforts for Rural Reconstruction

At present the government of India is making strenuous efforts to remove the defects in the rural structure and is attempting rural reconstruction by solving social, economic and agricultural problems of the villages. The specific efforts in this direction are the following:

1. Land reforms, 2. The Five Year Plans, 3. Co-operative movement, 4. Community development projects, 5. Reorganisation of village panchayats.

RURAL DEVELOPMENT

Major objective of rural development has been the alleviation of poverty in the rural areas. Indeed, this thrust has registered a success, evidenced by the fact that the population below the poverty line has come down significantly from over 57 per cent in 1961 to about 30 per cent by 1990. The experience gained in implementing a variety of community development programmes in the first three Five Year Plans and specific employment-oriented programmes in the Fourth, Fifth, Sixth and Seventh Plans have added great strength to the national capabilities. Being on the threshold of the Eighth Five Year Plan and in midst of an economic transition due to major structural changes in the economy, the programmes for rural development have to be specific in their objective to bring about a directional change.

Integrated Rural Development Programme

Integrated Rural Development Programme (IRDP) is a major instrument of the government strategy to alleviate rural poverty. The main objectives of IRDP are to raise families of the identified target group above poverty line and create substantial additional opportunities of self-employment in the rural sector. This programme is Centrally-sponsored with funds shared on 50:50 basis between the Centre and the states. In the case of UTs, cent per cent funds are provided by the Central government. The programme is being implemented through District Rural Development Agency (DRDA) and block level functionaries at the grassroots. At the state level, a co-ordination committee headed by Chief Secretary monitors its overall implementation. In the Ministry of Rural Development, a Central Committee on IRDP and allied programmes of Training of Rural Youth for Self-Employment (TRYSEM) and Development of Women and Children in Rural Areas (DWCRA) is headed by a secretary. Its main functions include framing and revision of guidelines ensuring their effective implementation. Targets and achievements for Sixth and Seventh Plan and the two successive years of 1990-91 and 1991-92 and targets and achievements in 1992-93 and 1993-94 are indicated in table 1.

The programme has been evaluated through research conducted by independent institutions and also through Concurrent Evaluation Studies (CES). According to CES of January-December 1989 about 81 per cent of the old families crossed the poverty line of Rs. 3,500 and 28 per cent the revised poverty line of Rs. 6,400. However, about 78 per cent of the families had incremental income. Nearly 34 per cent of the assisted families belong to destitute (Rs. 1 to 2,265) and 46 per cent to very poor group (Rs. 2,266—3,500).

During Seventh Plan, 181.8 lakh families were assisted with a total investment of Rs. 8,688.35 crores as against 165.6 lakh families with an investment of Rs. 4,762.78 crores in Sixth Plan. Over 49 per cent went to SC/ST families as against the target of 50 per cent. Coverage of women had increased from 9.90 per cent in 1985-86 to more than 33 per cent under IRDP in 1992-93. Major impact of the programmes was that it benefited the poorest and the most deprived sections of society, as also women in such a large number. Subsidy available to SC families under IRDP had been raised to 50 per cent and monetary ceiling to Rs. 5,000 from 1990-91. Under IRDP the subsidy limit has been raised by Rs. 1,000 in all cases with effect from 1 April 1993. The revised rates of subsidy limits are Rs. 4,000 per family in non-DPAP/ DDP areas, Rs. 5,000 in DPAP/DDP areas and Rs. 6,000 for SC/ST/handicapped persons. There is no change in percentage limits of subsidy in any of the cases.

National Scheme of Training of Rural Youth for Self-Employment

National Scheme of Training of Rural Youth for Self-Employment (TRYSEM) was launched as a Centrally-sponsored scheme on 15 August 1979. Its main thrust is on equipping rural youth in the age group of 18-35 years with necessary skills and technology to take up vocations of self-employment in agriculture and allied activities, industry, services and business. Simultaneously, another scheme for strengthening of infrastructure of training institutions was also introduced with Central assistance.

Table 1: *Targets and Achievements*

Year	Physical target	Achievement (lakh)	Allocation (Rs. crores)	Utilisation (Rs. crores)	Credit Mobilised	Investment (Rs. crores)
Sixth Plan						
1980-81	30.07	27.27	250.55	158.64	289.05	447.69
1981-82	30.07	27.13	300.66	264.65	467.59	732.24
1982-83	30.07	34.55	400.88	359.59	713.98	1,073.57
1983-84	30.54	36.85	407.36	406.09	773.51	1,179.60
1984-85	30.27	39.82	407.36	472.20	857.48	1,329.68
Total	151.02	165.62	1,766.81	1,661.17	3,101.61	4,762.78
Seventh Plan						
1985-86	24.71	30.60	407.36	441.10	730.15	1,171.25
1986-87	35.00	37.47	543.83	613.38	1,014.88	1,628.26
1987-88	39.64	42.47	613.38	727.44	1,175.35	1,902.79
1988-89	31.94	37.72	687.95	768.47	1,231.62	2,000.09
1989-90	20.09	33.51	747.75	765.43	1,220.53	1,985.96
Total	160.38	181.77	3,000.27	3,315.82	5,372.53	8,688.35
1990-91	23.71	28.98	747.31	809.49	1,190.03	1,999.59
1991-92	22.52	25.17	703.61	800.99	1,133.27	1,934.24
1992-93	18.75	20.69	662.22	693.08	1,036.80	1,347.20
1993-94	25.73	14.52	1,089.90	539.05	808.50	1,347.20

Liberalisation of norms for expenditure under recurring assistance, greater emphasis on systematic marketing and exploring possibility of setting up groups for the manufacture/assembly of non-traditional items for which there is good market demand are some of the steps taken to improve the implementation of the Scheme. On completion of training, the TRYSEM beneficiaries are assisted under the IRDP. During Seventh Plan, about 9.99 lakh rural youth were trained as against 10.15 lakh in Sixth Plan. Of the youths trained during the Seventh Plan, 4.65 lakh were self-employed and 1.31 lakh were employed on wages. During 1991-92, 3.01 lakh rural youths were trained. During the year 1992-93, 2.52 lakh rural youth were trained (provisional figure). During 1993-94, 0.83 lakh youths were trained up to December 1993.

Development of Women and Children in Rural Areas

Main objective of the programme for the Development of Women and Children in Rural Area (DWCRA) is to improve the lot of rural women through the creation of income-generating activities in a district. Districts to be covered are selected keeping in view low literacy rate and high infant mortality rate. It envisages formation of groups of 5-10 rural women each for carrying on income generating activities, Each group is sanctioned a 'revolving fund' of Rs. 15,000. In case of states, the amount is shared equally by Centre, state government and UNICEF, while in the Union Territories, the Central government bears Rs. 10,000 per group and the balance is borne by UNICEF. UNICEF also bears the expenditure on the staff component for a period of six years which is fully reimbursed. The programme has made considerable progress since it was launched in 1982. During the Seventh Plan more than 28,000 women groups with a membership of 4.68 lakh were formed. During 1990-91, 7,139 groups with 1,07,557 members were formed. During 1991-92, 8043 groups were formed with a membership of 1,41,132 women. During 1992-93, there were 9029 groups with membership of 1,28,744 women. At the end of 1992- 93, the programme was implemented in 291 districts. During 1993-94. (up to Dec. 1993) there were 4049 groups with 1,01,003 women. The programme was being implemented in 352 Districts by the end of 1993-94.

Scheme for Rural Artisans

The scheme of supply of modern toolkits to rural artisans is a supporting component of the IRDP. It was started as a Centrally-sponsored scheme from 1992-93 in selected districts. The aim of the scheme is that rural artisans will be able to enhance the quality of the product, increase their production and income and will be in a position to lead better quality of life with the use of modern tools. All traditional moral artisans living below the poverty line except weavers, tailors, needle workers and bidi workers are covered under this programme. This programme was taken up under IRDP during 1992-93 in 62 districts covering 97,585 artisans. For 1993-94, it has been decided to cover 1.3 lakh artisans in 100 additional districts, 1,300 artisans will be covered in each district at the rate of average subsidy of Rs. 1,800 per artisan.

Council for Advancement of People's Action and Rural Technology

Council for Advancement of People's Action and Rural Technology (CAPART) was registered under the Societies Registration Act, 1860, on I September 1986, with headquarters in New Delhi with the merger of People's Action for Development, India (PADI) and Council for Advancement of Rural Technology (CART). It aims at encouraging, promoting and assisting voluntary action for enhancement of rural prosperity.

In pursuance of these objectives, CAP ART makes available financial assistance to voluntary organisations under the following schemes: (i) promotion of voluntary action in moral development; (ii) Development of Women and

Children in Rural Areas (DWCRA); (iii) Accelerated Rural Water Supply Programmes (ARWSP); (iv) Central Rural Sanitation Programme (CRSP); (v) Organisation of Beneficiaries of Anti-poverty Programme (OB); (vi) Integrated Rural Development Programme (IRDP); (vii) Jawahar Rozgar Yojna (JRY) and Advancement of Rural Technology Scheme (ARTS).

Its funds mainly comprise grants by the Ministry. The Council can, however, obtain grants from various Central and state government departments and also accept donations and contributions from other sources. CAP ART had sanctioned 7,375 projects worth Rs. 145.11 crores up to 30 June 1992. Upto 30 Nov. 1993 the programme was extended to 10,891 projects spending Rs. 219.57 crores.

Rural Employment

Rural unemployment and under-employment which particularly affect the poorest segments of rural population have been major contributory factors to high incidence of poverty in rural areas. Various pilot projects were, therefore, launched to step up rural employment. Programmes like Crash Scheme for Rural Employment (CSRE) and Pilot Intensive Rural Employment Programme (PIREP) were started during Fourth Plan. In October 1980, National Rural Employment Programme (NREP) was launched as a Centrally-sponsored scheme on 50:50 sharing basis between Centre and states with the three-fold objectives of generating additional gainful employment opportunities, creating durable community assets and improving overall quality of life in the rural areas. In 1983, it was followed by Rural Landless Employment Guarantee Programme (RLEGP) as cent per cent Centrally-sponsored scheme. The objective was to improve and expand employment opportunities particularly for rural landless labourers and provide guarantee of employment to at least one member of every rural landless labour household up to 100 days in a year.

During Sixth Plan period, Rs. 1,834 crores was spent on NREP in both Central and state sectors, creating over 17,752 lakh man-days work. In first four years of the Seventh Plan, Rs. 2,940 crores was spent on NREP creating 14,775 lakh mandays work. Under RLEGP, Rs. 385 crores and Rs. 2,412 crores were spent during Sixth and first four years of the Seventh Plans creating work of 2,628 lakh man-days and 11,544 lakh man-days respectively. Since 1 April 1989, NREP and RLEGP have been merged into one single rural employment programme to be known as Jawahar Rozgar Yojana (JRY.)

Primary objective of the programme is generation of additional gainful employment for unemployed and underemployed persons in the rural areas. Besides, secondary objectives are: (i) creation of productive community assets for direct and continuing benefits to poverty groups and strengthening rural economic and social infrastructure which will lead to rapid growth of rural economy and steady rise in income levels of rural poor; and (ii) improvement on overall quality of life.

Allocations to states under the new programme are made entirely on the basis of incidence of poverty. From the states to districts, the allocation of resources is done on the basis of agricultural labourers as percentage of the main workers in rural areas, percentage of SC/ST rural population to total rural population and inverse of agricultural productivity in the weights of 20:60:20. The allocation to village Panchayats is done by giving weights of 60 per cent to SC/ST population and 40 per cent to the total population, including SC/ST population of the village Panchayats. The population of each village Panchayat having less than 1,000 population is to be taken as 1,000 and more than 10,000 as 10,000. Village Panchayat is free to choose any item of work on the basis of felt need of the people. Preference is given to works which create economically productive assets. During the year 1992-93, an allocation of Rs. 2,046 crores as Central share and Rs. 510 crores as states matching share have been made with target of creating employment of 7,537.95 lakh man-days. During 1993-94 the Centre will spend 2546 crores rupees and the states 635.22 crores on 10,609 lakh man-days.

Panchayati Raj

Panchayati Raj institutions are in existence in almost all states and union territories with variations in structural pattern. Generally, *Panchayati Raj* system involves a three-tier arrangement — village level, block level and district level. The first tier at village or groups of villages level is commonly known as *Gram Panchayat*, the second tier at block level as *Panchayat Samiti* and the third tier at district level as *Zita Parishad*, except in some states/union territories. However, the second tier is known as *Mandala Praja Parishad* in Andhra Pradesh, *Taluka Panchayat* in *Gujarat, Taluka Panchayat Samitis* in Karnataka. *Janapad Panchayat* in Madhya Pradesh, Panchayat Union in Tamil Nadu, *Kshetra Samiti* in Uttar Pradesh and *Anchal Samiti* in Arunachal Pradesh. Similarly, the third tier is called *Mahkuma Parishad* in Assam at sub-divisional level, District Development Councils in Tamil Nadu and District Council in Kerala.

The tenure of Panchayati Raj institutions ranges from three to five years. These institutions are generally responsible for promotion of agriculture, rural industries, provision of medical relief, maternity, women and child welfare, maintaining common grazing grounds, village roads, tanks, wells, sanitation and execution of other socio-economic programmes. In some places, they also provide primary education and collect land revenue. Today, gram panchayats are involved in identification of beneficiaries in anti-poverty programmes for IRDP and execution of other rural development programmes like JRY. There are about 2.20 lakh *Gram Panchayats*, 5.5 thousand *Panchayat Samitis* and 375 *Zila Parishads* (including superseded institutions). Amendment 1992 for Panchayats has been applicable since 24 April 1993.

Drought-Prone Areas Programme

Drought-Prone Areas Programme (DPAP) was initiated in 1973 as an integrated area development programme. The Programme was conceived as a long-term measure for restoration of ecological balance by conserving, developing and harnessing land, water, livestock and human resources. The objectives of the programme are: (a) to minimise the adverse effects of drought on production of crops and livestock and productivity of land, water and human resources through integrated development of the natural resource base of the area and adoption of appropriate technologies, and (b) to conserve, develop and harness land, water and other natural resources including rainfall for restoration of ecological balance in the long run.

DPAP is under implementation in 615 blocks of 95 districts in 13 states. Present coverage of the programme is based on the recommendations of the Task Force on DPAP and DDP (1982) as modified by the Inter Department Group (1984). Total area covered under the programme is about 5.54 lakh sq. km. and the total population in the areas covered by the programme is about 707.5 lakh (1981 Census).

The funds for the programme are shared by the Government of India and the states concerned on a 50:50 basis. An outlay of Rs. 237 crores was provided for this programme in the Central Plan for Seventh Plan period. During 1992- 93 an annual allocation of Rs. 102.23 crores was made to the programme states. For 1993-94 allocations for states is Rs. 153.34 crores.

Since inception (1973-74) till March 1993 an amount of Rs. 1,423.96 crores has been spent under the programme. The following physical achievements have been made under the programme up to March 1993:

Sector	**(hectares)**
Land shaping and development and soil moisture conservation	27,13,816
Water resources development	8,93,982
Afforestation and pasture development.	16,02,955

Desert Development Programme

Desert Development Programme (DDP) was started in 1977-78 with the objectives of (i) controlling desertification of the desert areas through integrating and dovetailing other related state/Central programmes with these programmes and (ii) to conserve, develop and harness land, water and other natural resources including rainfall for restoration of ecological balance in the long run. The objectives are sought to be achieved through activities such as afforestation, with special emphasis on sand dune stabilisation and shelter belt plantation and grassland development, soil and moisture conservation and water resources development. It covers 131 blocks of 21 districts in five states. The programme also covers cold arid areas of Jammu and Kashmir and Himachal Pradesh. The area covered under this programme is about 3.62 lakh sq. km. and the population in the area covered is about 1.5 crores (1981 Census).

The programme is implemented with cent per cent Central financial assistance. Allocations up to 1992-93 were made at the rate of Rs. 24 lakhs per sq. km., the ceiling per district being Rs. 500 lakhs. For cold desert areas, a lumpsum provision is made, the rate being Rs. 100 lakhs per district per year for Himachal Pradesh and Rs. 150 lakhs per district per year for Jammu and Kashmir. During 1990-91 an annual allocation of Rs. 49.50 crores was made to the programme states. During 1991-92, 1992-93 the annual allocation remained at the same level. Rate of allocations for 1993-94 is Rs. 36 lakhs per sq. km. subject to a maximum of 750 lakhs. For cold desert in J&K allocation is Rs. 225 lakhs per district and in HP it is at Rs. 150 lakhs per district. For 1993-94 allocation for states is Rs. 74.25 crores.

Since inception (1977-78) till March 1992 an amount of Rs. 387.16 crores has been spent under the programme. During the Seventh Plan period, a sum of Rs. 194.05 crores has been spent under this programme. The following physical achievements have been made under the Programme, up to March 1993:

	Sector	**(hectares)**
1.	Land shaping and development soil moisture conservation	1,22,823
2.	Water resources development	56,202
3.	Afforestation and pasture development	2,29,457

LAND REFORMS

Land reforms have remained one of the major policies for rural and economic development ever since the inception of the planning process. Old agrarian structure was not very conducive to modernisation of agriculture and was sought to be replaced by a more egalitarian social structure. Land reforms programme has, therefore, been designed to break the old feudal socio-economic structure of rural India to provide greater fillip to modernisation of agriculture and promote agricultural productivity. It is also intended to bring in the largest possible number of poor farmers and agricultural workers in the mainstream of the process of economic development. It helps to raise the status of the weaker sections of society and gives them a sense of belonging to the mainstream of social life. The programme of land reforms has, therefore, been rightly viewed not only as an economic development measure but also as a measure of social uplift. Seventh Plan viewed land reform as an intrinsic part of the anti-poverty strategy.

Among the important achievements is the abolition of intermediary tenures as a result of which more than 200 lakh tenants have been brought into direct contact with the state. Besides, a large part of an estimated 60 lakh hectares of waste, fallow and other classes of land vested in the state have been distributed to the landless and marginal land holders.

Tenancy Reforms

Legislative provisions have been made in most states of the country providing ownership rights to tenants/security of tenure to tenants/sub-tenants/ sharecroppers. Provisions regarding fixation of rents payable by the tenant and prohibition of eviction except on specified grounds further strive to safeguard the interest of the tenants, 112.13 tenants have been conferred ownership rights in respect of 153 lakh acres of land.

Several states enacted land ceiling laws in the 50s and 60s. As a result of this, more than 9.93 lakh hectares of land were taken over by the states and out of this 7.5 lakh hectares were distributed to the landless poor. The land ceiling laws were subsequently re-enacted by the states in conformity with national guidelines issued in 1972. Till December 1992, in all 73.76 lakh acres have been declared surplus in the old and revised ceiling laws. Out of this, 64.10 lakh acres has been taken possession of and 50.31 lakh acres has been distributed to 46.10 lakh landless agricultural labourers and other eligible persons. The issues relating to the completion of distribution of surplus lands and all relevant aspects of land reforms and land records management were discussed at a conference of state revenue ministers held on 14 March 1992 at New Delhi under the chairmanship of Prime Minister. It was decided during the conference that the distribution of all available surplus land free from encumbrances may be distributed by 30 June 1992 and at least 75 per cent of the land involved in litigation in revenue courts must be freed from such litigation and distributed by 30 September 1992. In addition, certain other recommendations in regard to land records and distribution of Bhoodan land were also made. These recommendations have been sent to the states/UTs for necessary follow-up action.

Since much of the land distributed under the ceiling laws is of poor quality, the assignees are being provided financial assistance at the rate of Rs. 2,500 per hectare. So far, financial assistance by way of grant to the tune of Rs. 59.72 crores as Central share has been released to different states/union territories. The assignees are also accorded priority under other-on-going programmes, *viz.*, IRDP and Jawahar Rozgar Yojana.

Land Records

Correct and up-to-date land records are an essential pre-condition for effective implementation of land reforms measures, particularly for providing security of tenure to tenants and share-croppers and for smooth flow of credit and agricultural inputs to the landholders. In some states, land records and crop records are updated periodically. A Centrally-sponsored scheme for revitalising the revenue administration and updating the land records is being implemented to provide financial assistance to the states for strengthening the machinery for survey and settlement operations, use of modern technology such as photomapping, aerial survey, mechanisation of land records, restructuring of revenue machinery and improving training infrastructure. Simultaneously, initiative has also been taken to computerise land records. Pilot projects for computerisation of land records are being implemented in one district each of the 21 selected states/UTs.

Consolidation of Holdings

Fragmented agricultural holdings stand in the way of rationalisation of agriculture and adequate investment of capital and inputs of land. Consolidation of these fragmented holdings is thus an important measure to boost efficiency and economy in agriculture. It also provides an opportunity for planned development of villages. Legislative provisions have been made in many states for undertaking consolidation of holdings. So far 602 lakh hectares have been consolidated. Bulk of this work has been done in Maharashtra, Uttar Pradesh, Haryana, Punjab, Bihar and Orissa.

Land Acquisition

The Land Acquisition Act, 1894, which is the basic law for the acquisition of land for public purposes and for companies provides for a maximum time limit of three years for completion of land acquisition proceedings. This Act was comprehensively amended by the Land Acquisition (Amendment) Act, 1984, with a view to protect the interests of land losers.

Rural Water Supply

Provision of drinking water in the rural areas is the responsibility of the state government and funds have been provided in the state budget right from the commencement of the First Five Year Plan in 1951. Taking into account the magnitude of the problem and in order to accelerate the pace of coverage of villages without water supply, Government of India introduced the Accelerated Rural Water Supply Programme in 1972-73. The states and union territories were assisted with cent per cent grants-in-aid to implement the schemes in villages without water supply. The programme continued up to 31th March 1974. In 1974-75, with the introduction of Minimum Needs Programme, the Accelerated Rural Water Supply Programme was withdrawn. However, it was reintroduced in 1977-78 when it was found that the progress of supply of safe drinking water to the problem villages ware not as per expectations.

In August 1985, the subject of Rural Water Supply and Sanitation was transferred from the Ministry of Urban Development to the Department of Rural Development with the objective of securing quick implementation and better integration with other rural development programmes. The National Drinking Water Mission was launched as one of the five societal missions in 1986. The mission was renamed as Rajiv Gandhi National Drinking Water Mission.

A survey was conducted in 1985 to identify problem villages *(i.e.* without even one source of safe drinking water). About 1,61,722 problem villages, including spill over problem villages from Sixth Five Year Plan, remained as on 1 April 1985 to be covered in the Seventh Five Year Plan, *i.e.* up to 31st March 1990. Up to 1991-92, 1,58,754 problem villages were covered, leaving a balance of 2,968 problem villages as on 1 April 1992. Out of these villages, 2,218 'No Source' villages were covered in 1992-93, leaving 750 hard-core villages. These villages are expected to be covered with safe drinking water by March 1994 with special assistance already given by the Central Government. An amount of Rs. 2,479 crores was utilised under the State Sector MNP and a sum of Rs. 1,906.64 crores was utilised under ARWSP for providing water supply in the rural areas during the Seventh Plan. During the annual plans 1990-91 and 1991-92, an expenditure of Rs. 1,265 crores were utilised under MNP and Rs. 1,055 crores under Technology Mission including ARWSP.

The total outlay provided for Rural Water Supply during the Eighth Five Year Plan is Rs. 5,100 crores under the Central Sector and Rs. 4,954.52 crores under the states to provide potable drinking water to the entire uncovered rural population during the Eighth Plan period.

In 1992-93, an outlay of Rs. 804.83 crores was provided under the State Sector Minimum Needs Programme and Rs. 459 crores was utilised under TM/ ARWSP. An outlay of Rs. 740 crores has been provided under the Central Sector and Rs. 48.15 crores by the states in 1993-94.

A massive survey of all rural habitations in the country to identify the status of drinking water supply and quality problems has been undertaken. The survey results have started coming in. Once the complete data is available, a clear picture of status of water supply in rural habitations will emerge and an appropriate strategy will be worked out for implementation of the programme during the remaining period of the Eighth Five Year Plan.

Under the guidelines, the first source of drinking water has to be provided in SC/ST localities and at the time of formulating the scheme, coverage of SC/ ST habitations should be given first preference. From the year 1990 onwards, a minimum of 25 per cent of ARWSP funds have been earmarked for provision of water supply for SCs and 10 per cent for drinking water supply for STs. Such funds cannot be diverted for any other purpose. To give a further thrust to coverage of SC/ST habitations, the Centre released special assistance of Rs. 19.80 crores in March 1990 for coverage of 11,000 SC/ST habitations in nine states. As part of Dr. Baba Saheb Ambedkar Centenary Programme, Government of India released further special assistance of Rs. 56.74 crores in 1991-92, Rs. 2.02 crores in 1992-93 and Rs. 0.75 crores in 1993-94 to 24 states for the coverage of 30,000 SC/ST habitations with safe drinking water facilities.

CENTRALLY SPONSORED RURAL SANITATION PROGRAMME

About 0.72 per cent of the rural population had been provided with sanitation facilities till the end of the Sixth Plan. Against the target of coverage of 25 per cent of the rural population in the Seventh Plan, the actual achievement till the end of 1991-92 was only 2.73 per cent of the rural population with government programme. According to the National Sample Survey (44th round 1988-89) about 10.96 per cent of rural households had access to sanitary facilities. In addition to the achievement under governments sponsored programmes, the construction of large number of sanitation toilets has been undertaken with private initiative. Inadequate financial resources, lack of demand from the beneficiaries, lack of response from implementing agencies and number of other related factors were responsible for this slow progress.

During 1991-92 and 1992-93, 35,218 sanitary latrines were provided in rural areas in addition to 2,62,391 sanitary latrines constructed under the State Sector Minimum Needs Programme. A first ever National Seminar on Rural Sanitation was organised on 16 and 17 September 1992. The seminar emphasised the sociological aspects, adoption of appropriate technology and research and development; need for institutional sectoral linkages as well as human resource development; community participation and role of women. It was reiterated that sanitation is possible only with the people's active involvement and participation with the generation of demand as the pre-requisite.

The Government has since introduced a revised Centrally-sponsored Rural Sanitation Programme according to which the subsidy will be limited to 80 per cent of the unit cost of individual household latrines for persons below the poverty line. The subsidy will be shared equally by the Central government and the concerned state government. The contribution by the users can be provided in the form of cash or kind or labour. The programme also provides for conversion of dry latrines into sanitary latrines on priority basis in order to abolish the system of manual scavenging; exclusive complex for women; the concept of total sanitation with drains, pavement of lanes, septic tanks, garbage pits, clean surroundings around the chinking water source etc. The states have also been requested to develop one model village under the integrated sanitation programme. The total outlay of Rs. 380 crores for the Centrally-sponsored Rural Sanitation Programme and Rs. 294.23 crores under the State Sector Minimum Needs Programme have been provided during the Eighth Five Year Plan. The allocation for 1993-94 is Rs. 49.86 crores under the State MNP and Rs. 30 crores as Central assistance to states and voluntary organisations through the Council for Advancement of People's Action and Rural Technology (CAPART).

QUESTIONS FOR EXERCISE

1. Evaluate the impact of the welfare activities of the Government on village life in India.
2. Explain the importance of planned rural development in India.
3. Discuss the social implications of land reform legislation.
4. Discuss the influence of the programme of rural reconstruction upon socio-cultural life of Indian rural people.

BIBLIOGRAPHY

Apthorpe, Raymond, ed., *Social Research and Community Development*, Lusaka, Rhodes, Livingstone Institute for Social Research, 1961.

Balten, T.R., *Communities and their Development: An Introductory Study with Special Reference to the Tropics*, Oxford University Press, London, 1957.

Bertrand, A.L., *Rural Sociology: An Analysis of Contemporary Rural Life*, Mc Graw-Hill, New York, 1958.

Bhattacharjee, J.P., *Refresher Course for the Field Staff*, Delhi Municipal Corporation, 1963.

Bhattacharya, S.N., *They Showed the Way, New Stories from Old Indian Villages*, Thackers, Calcutta, 1961.

Bose, S.K., *Some Aspects of Indian Economic Development: A Study of the Leading Problems of Indian Economics*, 2 Vols. Delhi, 1962, Delhi 1963.

Carstairs, G. Morris, *The Twice-born: A Study of a Community of High Caste Hindus*, Hogarth, London, 1957.

Central Institute for Training and Research in Panchayati Raj Delhi, *Role of Voluntary Associate Organisation in Panchayati Raj and Community Development*, Delhi, 1964.

Dey, S.K., *Community Development*, 2 Vols., Kitab Mahal, Allahabad, 1960.

——, *Community Development Through Panchayati Raj*, Govt. Press, Delhi. 1961.

——, *Nilokheri*, Asia, Bombay, 1962.

Dube, D.C., et al, *Village Level Workers: Their Work and Result Demonstration*, Govt. Press, Delhi, 1962.

——, *India's Changing Villages: Human Factors in Community Development*, Roultedge & Kegan Paul, London, 1958.

——, *Perspectives on the National Emergency*, National Institute of Community Development Mussoorie, 1963.

Gangarode, K.D., *A School is Built*, Delhi School of Social Work, Delhi, 1964.

Gillette, J.M., *Rural Sociology*, Macmillan, New York, 1936.

Gordon, T., *Group Centered Leadership*, Houghton Mifflin, New York, 1955.

Gupte, Ranjit, *Community Development, Cooperation and Panchayati Raj in Alipore:* A Pilot Survey, Indian Cooperative Union, Delhi, 1964.

Inamdar, N.R., *Report of the Survey of the Administration of the Community Development Block Haveli*, Poona University, Poona, 1962.

India, Ministry of Community Development, and Co-operation, *Annual Conferences on Community Development*, Mount Abu, May, 20-24, 1958, Govt. Press, Delhi, 1958.

——, *A Chronicle*, 1954-61, Govt. Press, Delhi, 1962.

——, *Community Development at a Glance*, Govt. Press, Delhi, 1962.

——, *Evolution of Community Development Programme in India*, Govt. Press, Delhi, 1963.

——, *A Guide for Secretaries of Service Cooperatives*, Govt. Press, Delhi, 1963.

——,Community Development and Co-operation, *Guide to Community Development*, 2nd rev. ed. Govt. Press, Delhi, 1959.

——, *A Guide to Gram Sevikas and Mukhya Sevikas*, Govt. Press, Delhi, 1961.

——, *Leaders in the Making*, Govt. Press, Delhi, 1965.

——, *Manual for Village Level Workers*, Govt. Press, Delhi, 1956.

——, *Manual of Agricultural and Animal Husbandry Development Work in Community Projects*, Govt. Press, Delhi, 1962.

——, *National Conference on Community Development*, Mysore, July 23-28, 1959, Govt. Press, Delhi, 1959.

——, *People in the Plan*, Delhi, 1959.

India, *Report of the Study Team on the Position of Gram Sabha in Panchayati Raj Movement*, Govt. Press, Delhi, 1963.

——, *Report of the Working Group on the Panchayats and Cooperatives*, Govt. Press, Delhi, 1962.

——, *A Report on the Annual Conference on Community Development and Panchayati Raj*, New Delhi, Govt. Press, Delhi, 1964.

——, *Report on Trading Centres Visited by the High Level Team on Training*, Govt. Press, Delhi, 1961.

——, *The Scope of Extension in Community Development*, Govt. Press, Delhi, 1961.

——, *Study, Research and Training for the Community Development Personnel*, Govt. Press, Delhi, 1960.

——, *Village Volunteer Force*, Govt. Press, Delhi, 1961.

——, *Manual on Village Road Construction*, Govt. Press, Delhi, 1961.

——, Planning Commission, Programme Evaluation Organisation, *Draft Manual of Village Level Workers'* Records, Govt. Press, Delhi, 1956.

——, *Programme Evaluation Organisation Structure, Functions and Activities,* Govt. Press, Delhi, 1964.

Karve, Irawati and Yashwant Bhasker Damle, *Group Relation in Village,* Deccan College, Pune, 1963.

Kreitlow, B.W., *et al., Leadership for action in Rural Communities*, Danville , Inter-State Printers and Publishers, 1960.

Krishnamachari, V.T., *Community Development in India,* Govt. Press, Delhi, 1962.

Kumarappa, J.C., *Overall Plan for Rural Development*, 4th ed., Akhil Bharat Seva Sangh, Varanasi, 1960.

Lalvani, K.C., *Community Development and Extension Service*, Arth Vanjya, Calcutta, 1963.

Lewis Oscar, *Village Life in Northern India*, Urban University of Illinois, 1958.

Loomis, C.P. and Beegle, J.A., *Rural Sociology: The Strategy of Change*, Prentice Hall, New Jersey, 1963.

Marriott, McKim, *Village India: Studies in the Little Community*, Asia, Bombay, 1961.

Mezirow, Jack D., *Dynamics of Community Development,* Scarecrow, New York, 1963.

Mukerjee, B., *Community Development in India*, Orient Longmans, Bombay, 1961.

Nair, Kusum, *Blossoms in the Dust: The Human Element in Indian Development,* Gerald Duckworth, London, 1961.

Nandjundappa, D.M., *Community Development and Employment,* Karnataka University, Dharwar, 1963.

Nayyar, Sushila, *Family Planning*, Govt. Press, Delhi, 1963.

Nehru, Jawaharlal, *On Community Development and Panchayati Raj*, Govt. Press, Delhi, 1963.

Nelson, L., *Rural Sociology*, American Book Company, New York, 1948.

——, *A Case Study of Panchayati Elections*, Planning Department, Lucknow, 1963.

——, *Guide to Rural Youth Organisations Based on Pilot Project* rev. ed. Govt. Press, Lucknow, 1963.

Raman, K.S.V., *Problems of Community Development in India*, Lakshmi, Patna, 1965.

——, *What is Community Development*? Govt. Press, Delhi, 1963.

Rogers, E.M., *Social Change in Rural Society*, Appleton, New York, 1960.

——, *Community Organisation: Theory and Principles*, Harper Bros., New York, 1955.

Ruopp, Phillips, ed., *Approaches to Community Development*, Lounz, New York, 1953.

Sanders, Irwin T., *The Community: An Introduction to a Social System,* Ronald, New York, 1958.

Sarveshwara Rao, B., *The Economic and Social Effects of Zamindari Abolition in Andhra*, Govt. Press, Delhi, 1963.

Sanderson, D. and Poison, R.A., *Rural Community Organisation,* Wiley, New York, 1939.

Sehgal, A.N., *Visual Aids in Community Development,* Govt. Press, Delhi, 1960.

Shah, Vimal, *Perspectives in Village Planning*, Bombay, Khadi and Village Industries Commission, 1960.

Srinivas, M.N., ed. *India's Village*, 2nd ed., Asia, Bombay, 1960.

Sorokin, P. and C.C., Zimmerman, *Principles of Rural Urban Sociology*, Holt, New York, 1929.

Sorokin, P. Zimmerman, C.C. and J. Goplin, *Systematic Source Book of Rural Sociology*, University of Minnesota Press, Minneapolis, 1930.

Taylor, C., *et al., Rural Life in the United States*, Knopf, New York, 1949.

Taylor, L. and Jones, A., *Rural Life and Urbanized Society*, Oxford University Press, New York, 1964.

Tekumalia, V.N., *Village Plans at Work*, Khadi and Village Industries Commission, Bombay, 1968.

Tewari, Ram Chand, *Village Level Worker and the Cooperative Movement,* Govt. Press, Faridabad, 1963.

Umrao Singh, *Community Development in India*, Kitabghar, Kanpur, 1962. U.N.O., Rural Development Workers, United Nations, New York, 1962.

——, *Study Kit on Training for Community Development*, United Nations, New York, 1957.

——, Bureau of Social Affairs, *Social Progress Through Community Development*, United Nations, New York, 1955.

Vakil, C.N., *Poverty, and Planning*, Allied, Bombay, 1963.

Wilner, Dorothy, *Community Leadership*, United Nations, New York, 1960.